Fodor's

SWEDEN

14th Edition

Where to Stay and Eat for All Budgets

Must-See Sights and Local Secrets

Ratings You Can Trust

Fodor's Travel Publications   New York, Toronto, London, Sydney, Auckland
www.fodors.com

FODOR'S SWEDEN
Editor: Heidi Leigh Johansen

Editorial Production: Tom Holton
Editorial Contributors: Rob Hincks, Karin Palmquist, Norman Renouf
Maps: David Lindroth, *cartographer;* Bob Blake and Rebecca Baer, *map editors*
Design: Fabrizio La Rocca, *creative director;* Guido Caroti, *art director;* Moon Sun Kim, *cover designer;* Melanie Marin, *senior picture editor*
Production/Manufacturing: Colleen Ziemba
Cover Photo (Medieval festival, Gotland): SIME s.a.s./eStock Photo

ISBN: 1–4000–1615–0

ISBN-13: 978–1–4000–1615–0

ISSN: 1528–3070

Fourteenth Edition

SPECIAL SALES
This book is available for special discounts for bulk purchases for sales promotions or premiums. Special editions, including personalized covers, excerpts of existing books, and corporate imprints, can be created in large quantities for special needs. For more information, write to Special Markets/ Premium Sales, 1745 Broadway, MD 6-2, New York, New York 10019, or e-mail specialmarkets@ randomhouse.com.

AN IMPORTANT TIP & AN INVITATION
Although all prices, opening times, and other details in this book are based on information supplied to us at press time, changes occur all the time in the travel world, and Fodor's cannot accept responsibility for facts that become outdated or for inadvertent errors or omissions. So **always confirm information when it matters,** especially if you're making a detour to visit a specific place. Your experiences—positive and negative—matter to us. If we have missed or misstated something, **please write to us.** We follow up on all suggestions. Contact the Sweden editor at editors@fodors. com or c/o Fodor's at 1745 Broadway, New York, New York 10019.

PRINTED IN THE UNITED STATES OF AMERICA

10 9 8 7 6 5 4 3 2 1

Be a Fodor's Correspondent

Your opinion matters. It matters to us. It matters to your fellow Fodor's travelers, too. And we'd like to hear it. In fact, we *need* to hear it.

When you share your experiences and opinions, you become an active member of the Fodor's community. That means we'll not only use your feedback to make our books better, but we'll publish your names and comments whenever possible. Throughout our guides, look for "Word of Mouth," excerpts of your unvarnished feedback.

Here's how you can help improve Fodor's for all of us.

Tell us when we're right. We rely on local writers to give you an insider's perspective. But our writers and staff editors—who are the best in the business—depend on you. Your positive feedback is a vote to renew our recommendations for the next edition.

Tell us when we're wrong. We're proud that we update most of our guides every year. But we're not perfect. Things change. Hotels cut services. Museums change hours. Charming cafés lose charm. If our writer didn't quite capture the essence of a place, tell us how you'd do it differently. If any of our descriptions are inaccurate or inadequate, we'll incorporate your changes in the next edition and will correct factual errors at fodors.com *immediately.*

Tell us what to include. You probably have had fantastic travel experiences that aren't yet in Fodor's. Why not share them with a community of like-minded travelers? Maybe you chanced upon a beach or bistro or bed-and-breakfast that you don't want to keep to yourself. Tell us why we should include it. And share your discoveries and experiences with everyone directly at fodors.com. Your input may lead us to add a new listing or highlight a place we cover with a "Highly Recommended" star or with our highest rating, "Fodor's Choice."

Give us your opinion instantly at our feedback center at www.fodors.com/feedback. You may also e-mail editors@fodors.com with the subject line "Sweden Editor." Or send your nominations, comments, and complaints by mail to Sweden Editor, Fodor's, 1745 Broadway, New York, NY 10019.

You and travelers like you are the heart of the Fodor's community. Make our community richer by sharing your experiences. Be a Fodor's correspondent.

Trevlig resa!

Tim Jarrell, Publisher

CONTENTS

MAPS

ABOUT THIS BOOK

Our Ratings

Sometimes you find terrific travel experiences and sometimes they just find you. But usually the burden is on you to select the right combination of experiences. That's where our ratings come in.

As travelers we've all discovered a place so wonderful that its worthiness is obvious. And sometimes that place is so experiential that superlatives don't do it justice: you just have to be there to know. These sights, properties, and experiences get our highest rating, **Fodor's Choice,** indicated by orange stars throughout this book.

Black stars highlight sights and properties we deem **Highly Recommended,** places that our writers, editors, and readers praise again and again for consistency and excellence.

By default, there's another category: any place we include in this book is by definition worth your time, unless we say otherwise. And we will.

Disagree with any of our choices? Care to nominate a place or suggest that we rate one more highly? Visit our feedback center at www. fodors.com/feedback.

Budget Well

Hotel and restaurant price categories from ¢ to **$$$$** are defined in the opening pages of each chapter. For attractions, we always give standard adult admission fees; reductions are usually available for children, students, and senior citizens. Want to pay with plastic? **AE, D, DC, MC, V** following restaurant and hotel listings indicate that American Express, Discover, Diner's Club, MasterCard, and Visa are accepted.

Restaurants

Unless we state otherwise, restaurants are open for lunch and dinner daily. We mention dress only when there's a specific requirement and reservations only when they're essential or not accepted—it's always best to book ahead.

Hotels

Hotels have private bath, phone, and TV, and operate on the European Plan (aka EP, meaning without meals), unless we specify that they use the Continental Plan (CP, with a Continental breakfast), Breakfast Plan (BP, with a full breakfast), or Modified American Plan (MAP, with breakfast and dinner) or are all-inclusive (AI, including all meals and most activities). We always list facilities but not whether you'll be charged an extra fee to use them, so when pricing accommodations, find out what's included.

Many Listings
★ Fodor's Choice
★ Highly recommended
⊠ Physical address
✛ Directions
🕮 Mailing address
☎ Telephone
🖷 Fax
🌐 On the Web
✉ E-mail
🎟 Admission fee
🕓 Open/closed times
► Start of walk/itinerary
Ⓜ Metro stations
▭ Credit cards

Hotels & Restaurants
🏨 Hotel
🛌 Number of rooms
♨ Facilities
🍽 Meal plans
✕ Restaurant
🍷 Reservations
🏛 Dress code
↘ Smoking
🍸 BYOB
✕🏨 Hotel with restaurant that warrants a visit

Outdoors
🏌 Golf
⛺ Camping

Other
☺ Family-friendly
🛈 Contact information
⇨ See also
⊠ Branch address
☞ Take note

WHAT'S WHERE

STOCKHOLM	Stockholm, one of Europe's most beautiful capitals, is hidden away on Sweden's east coast; a less-gutsy city might have faded into obscurity. But Stockholmers have always had plenty of pride in their home, and their city has proclaimed its global credentials as loud as any other great capital. Built on 14 small islands at the place where the waters of Lake Mälaren rush into the Baltic, Stockholm is a city for all types. Historians will thrill in its narrow, history-rich medieval lanes; seafarers will gush at all things marine, which seem to crop up everywhere; urbanites will delight in the classic 20th-century functionalist architecture; while visitors who don't love fast-paced cities can escape to Stockholm's acres of green spaces.
SIDE TRIPS FROM STOCKHOLM	On weekends, Stockholmers abandon the city in droves. Their destination is one of the most beautiful archipelagos in the world, right outside their doorstep. For any visitor, spending time exploring the more than 25,000 islands that fringe the city should be a priority. Of course, to see each one would require a very long vacation. Better to focus on the handful that are crowned with glorious castles, graced with fine restaurants, or wreathed by peaceful swimming spots. Farther afield is the island of Gotland, whose Viking remains and wilderness preserves make for a holiday paradise. North of Stockholm is the pretty university town of Uppsala, home to one of Europe's oldest seats of learning.
THE BOTHNIAN COAST	The Bothnian Coast, a rugged and windswept finger of land that runs up the eastern side of Sweden, is the country's physical and symbolic link between north and south. More than that, it is also a living reflection of Sweden's social history. The grand 19th-century towns that form a chain along the coast testify to the wealth that fishing and the paper and wood industries brought to the country. The tiny fishing villages and ancient religious communities are reminders of a more isolated past. All symbolism and history aside, one of the main pleasures of this landscape is finding a deserted outcrop and losing yourself in the view of the Gulf of Bothnia.
GÖTEBORG (GOTHENBURG)	Sweden's second-largest city, Göteborg, refuses to take its status lying down. Instead, it focuses on its west-coast location, carving out its own niche as a thriving international city. Historically Göteborg has used its accessibility to the rest of the

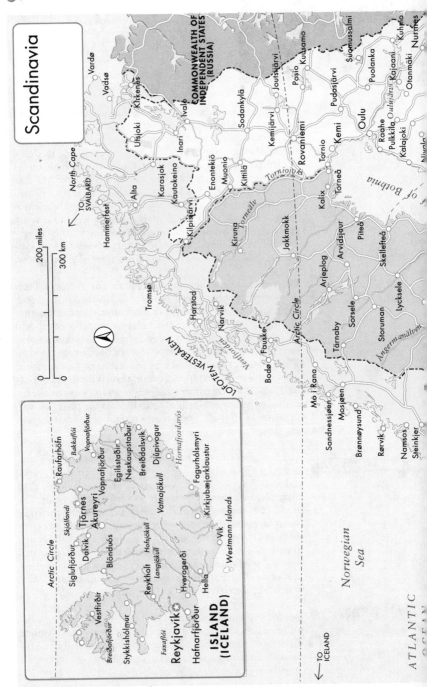

Scandinavia

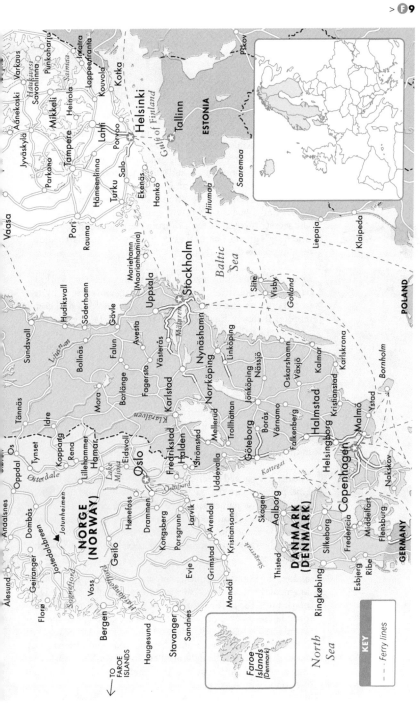

WHAT'S WHERE

world to good effect: a Viking port in the 11th century, today it is Scandinavia's busiest shipping city. Commercial success has gone to its head: among the ornate 19th-century stone edifices, tree-lined boulevards, and stunning parks are world-class galleries, museums, and cultural venues. The people, too, have embraced the city's internationalism: there is an air of vibrancy and a lust for life rarely seen in such northern climes. The secret? It could be the fish from the cold Atlantic waters, Göteborg's greatest natural asset, and a secret locals are more than happy to shout about.

SIDE TRIPS FROM GÖTEBORG

The Göta Canal long ago traded its baggage. The working barges and industrial cargo liners have been replaced by restored cruisers and deck-bound travelers; the feeling of commercial urgency has been replaced by a take-each-day-as-it-comes attitude. The canal cuts a lazy artery east to west, from Stockholm to Göteborg, through some of Sweden's most beautiful countryside. Exploring it on Göteborg's outskirts is the perfect way to spend a few days. North of Göteborg, the Bohuslän region has a rocky coastline dotted with attractive fishing villages. Among the pastel-painted wooden cottages, cruise the boardwalk and eat delicious fresh shrimp, a regional specialty. Vacationing here is as much about lazy waterside lunches as it is about lounging on sandy beaches and taking bracing dips in pure west-coast waters.

THE SOUTH & THE KINGDOM OF GLASS

The densely packed beech forests and sun-dappled lakes of Småland province are the backdrop and the lifeblood of isolated villages whose names are bywords for fine crystal glassware: Kosta, Orrefors, and Boda. The wood and water originally provided power for the early glassworks; today they provide a reassuringly traditional landscape just a few hours from Sweden's main cities.

Skåne, the country's southernmost province, along with the other southern provinces, form a different Sweden. Part of Denmark until 1658, the area has its own dialect and is fiercely proud of its independent spirit. But all are welcome to the lush farmland, coastal headlands, and miles of golden beaches. It is a place of exceptional beauty, ranging from wild cliffs to lovely nature reserves to the delightful city of Malmö. Historic castles abound, reminding you that there has always been an aristocracy in Sweden.

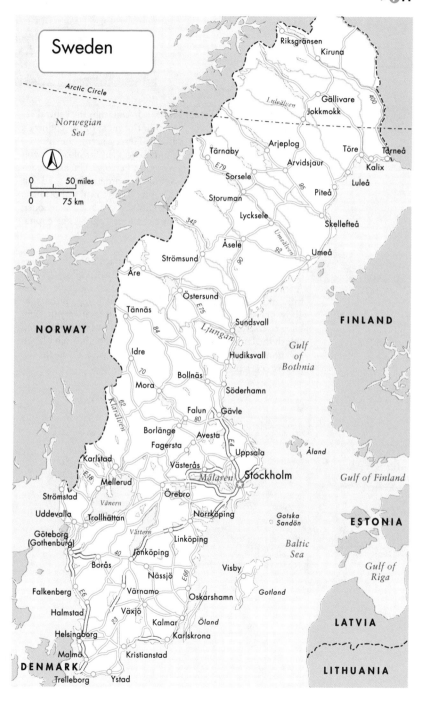

Sweden

WHAT'S WHERE

DALARNA: THE FOLKLORE DISTRICT	If Swedes have a spiritual home, it is Dalarna, the central region of Sweden, and the focal point of most of the country's myth, symbolism, and tradition. Here, among the forests, mountains, lakes, and red-painted wooden farmhouses, you can spend a midsummer feasting on herring. The area is focused around the beautiful Lake Siljan, bordered by a road that takes you to ancient villages, sights of mythical importance, and the birthplace of Sweden's national symbol, the wooden Dala horse. The ancient mining town of Falun is the capital of the region.
NORRLAND & NORRBOTTEN	In a country known for its wide open spaces, Northern Sweden, one of the least-populated places on earth, still stands out. A traveler in these parts is more likely to encounter a peacefully munching elk than a fellow human being. Birds soar above the snowy terrain while salmon fight their way up tumbling rivers; rare orchid species bloom here, and rhododendrons splash the landscape with color. This is where the nomadic indigenous peoples of Europe, the Sámi, live, and it's where you go to experience the midnight sun in Sweden.

WHEN TO GO

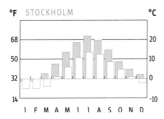

°F STOCKHOLM °C

The official tourist season—when hotel rates generally go down and museum and castle doors open—runs from mid-May through mid-September. This is Sweden's loveliest time of year; summer days are sunny and warm, nights refreshingly cool. (Summer is also mosquito season, especially in the north, but also as far south as Stockholm.) The whole country goes mad for Midsummer Day, in the middle of June. Many attractions close in late August, when the schools reopen at the end of the Swedish vacation season. The colors of autumn fade out as early as September, when the rainy season begins. The weather can be bright and fresh in spring and fall (although spring can bring lots of rain). Many visitors prefer sightseeing when there are fewer people around. Winter comes in November and stays through March, sometimes longer. In Sweden this season is an alpine affair, with subzero temperatures. The days can be magnificent when the snow and air are fresh and the sky a brilliant Nordic blue. Although many of the more traditional attractions are closed, there is skiing, skating, ice fishing, and sleigh riding on offer throughout the country.

Climate

Sweden has typically unpredictable northern European summer weather, but as a general rule it is likely to be warm but not hot from May until September. In Stockholm the weeks just before and after midsummer offer almost 24-hour light, and in the far north, above the Arctic Circle, the sun doesn't set at all between the end of May and the middle of July. To the left are average daily maximum and minimum temperatures for Stockholm.

🎦 Forecasts **Weather Channel Connection** ☎ 900/932-8437 95¢ per mi from a Touch-Tone phone ⊕ www.weather.com.

QUINTESSENTIAL SWEDEN

Smörgåsbord

There's a ritual around the Swedish *smörgåsbord* that can seem as complicated to perform as the name is to pronounce, but it's really quite simple. Literally translated, the word means sandwich table, a misnomer given the cornucopia of goodies on offer that resemble anything but a simple sandwich. Smörgåsbord is a feast table, or buffet, served on special occasions, most notably Christmas. The trick is to run from cold to hot and from sweet to spicy to vinegar-sour, all in several trips to the table. Start with herring, marinated in sweet mustard, dill, onion, or garlic, along with some crispbread and spicy cheese. Then comes other fish, such as salmon or trout, along with an array of cold cuts ranging from boiled ham to smoked reindeer. Try these with pickled cucumbers. Still have room? Hope so, because here comes the hot food: *Köttbullar* (meatballs), *prin-*

skorv (mini-sausages), and *Janssons Frestelse* (Jansson's Temptation), a dish of sliced potatoes with cream and anchovies. On the last trip, Swedish cheesecake, rice pudding, dried fruits, and candies prove the undoing of many. To drink with all of this, something simple is perfect; Swedes choose beer or spiced aquavit. As to who Jansson was, ask that and you are guaranteed hours of after-dinner opinions on the mystery potato man—the perfect pastime as your Swedish dinner settles.

Fishing & Boating

A true Swede is never far from water physically (Sweden is peppered with 90,000 lakes and a vast coastline) or, more important, mentally. As an ancient nation of mariners, the love of and fascination with water is second nature to most Swedes. In the summer months, boating and sailing are rarely far from the daily agenda. What

better activity to partner with boating than a bit of fishing? Coupled with their constitutional right to roam freely in the countryside, Swedes see sailing and hunting as an inextricable link to their past and a valuable part of their collective national psyche. Foreigners looking to ingratiate themselves with a Swede could do worse than display skill in handling a boat or catching and cooking a fish over a makeshift fire.

St. Lucia Holiday

In Sweden, December 13th is a bad day to sleep in. On this day the nation awakes early to celebrate an Italian saint from the 6th century, and it's a spectacle not to be missed. For hundreds of years, Swedes have borrowed Saint Lucia as the symbol for their festival of light, a celebration of the turn of winter and the hope of spring. Historically, a young girl from each village dressed in a long white gown tied with a red sash and wearing a crown of lingonberry branches carries lighted candles through the streets, visiting villagers and delivering saffron buns and a symbolic ray of light to the darkened doors of winter. Swedes have adapted their festival; today, offices, factories, and schools nominate their own Lucia. People gather to watch the procession and to sing traditional songs. For most Swedes it is a highly emotive time, reminding them of childhood comforts and of the impending Christmas holiday. Light and warmth from a candle still carry enormous significance in the dark months of winter here.

IF YOU LIKE

Pleasing Your Palate

Many restaurants in Sweden's larger cities offer innovative dishes that combine the superb ingredients and simplicity of traditional Swedish cuisine with Mediterranean, Asian, and Caribbean influences. Whether you're looking for "new Scandinavian," *husmanskost* (home cooking), or traditional Thai, most restaurants offer a *dagens rätt* (daily special) at lunch, an affordable way to sample a range of excellent cuisines.

- **Bon Lloc, Stockholm.** Chef and proprietor Mathias Dahlgren wows customers with Mediterranean-influenced Swedish cuisine inspired by his extensive global travels.

- **Oaxen, Stockholm.** The wild, rocky beauty of Stockholm's archipelago is the perfect backdrop to the refined culinary masterpieces served at what may be Sweden's best restaurant.

- **Mistral, Stockholm.** Securing one of the 18 seats takes some patience, but it's worth it. The artfully presented modern Swedish food is some of the best in town. The emphasis is on local ingredients, like the fish hooked just blocks from the kitchen.

- **Sjömagasinet, Göteborg.** West-coast seafood is the specialty at this converted waterside warehouse. The oak beams, wood floors, and beautifully dressed tables are as lovely as chef Leif Mannerström's creations.

- **Viktor, Umeå.** The clean 1950s interior design, excellent service, and innovative, exquisite contemporary food make Viktor the best restaurant north of Stockholm.

Art Inspirations

Most non-Swedes would say Carl Larsson if asked to name a Swedish artist. In truth, so would many Swedes. No other artist managed to capture the Swedish spirit so completely as this 19th-century master. Other notable Swedish artists include Anders Zorn, Prince Eugen, Tobias Sergel, and Carl Milles. Swedes have a strong history as avid art collectors; in all the major cities you'll find museums and galleries displaying world-class collections.

- **Nationalmuseum, Stockholm.** A stunning limestone building houses one of Sweden's best art collections, made up of about 12,500 works, with an emphasis on Nordic art.

- **Skansen, Stockholm.** Farmhouses, windmills, and churches are just some of the Swedish structures preserved here. Lose yourself in time as you wander reconstructed streets from bygone days.

- **Konstmuseet, Göteborg.** Fans of photography love the Hasselblad Center, but be sure to venture to the top floors, where you'll find works by 19th- and 20th-century Swedish masters.

- **Röhsska Museet, Göteborg.** The ancient manuscripts and tapestries at this museum of applied arts are interesting, but most people head straight for the 20th-century galleries, where they gather around displays to spot items they remember so well from childhood.

- **Carl Larsson Gården, Sundborn.** Sweden's most famous artist lived, worked, and died within the walls of this delightful cottage. The fascinating grounds remain mostly untouched.

The Seafaring Life

At heart, modern Swedes are still seafaring Vikings. Sweden's cultural dependence on boats runs so deep that a popular gift at Christmas is candles containing creosote, providing the comforting scent of dock and hull for when sailors can't be on their boats. In summer, thousands of craft jostle among the islands of the archipelago. Statistics claim there are more than 250,000 boats in the Stockholm archipelago alone.

- **Island Hopping, Archipelago, Stockholm.** Beauty and sheer relaxation don't come any better than this. Whether you hitch a ride or charter your own boat, exploring the 25,000 islands of Stockholm's archipelago is among the greatest Swedish adventures.

- **Vasamuseet, Stockholm.** Those interested in boats will be fascinated by the *Vasa*, a warship that sank on its maiden voyage in 1628 and was raised nearly intact in 1961. The sheer bulk of this man-of-war is awe-inspiring, and the accompanying exhibition offers an interesting insight into maritime life of old.

- **Summers in Gotland.** Sweden's rugged holiday island is the perfect place for swimming, boating, and sea kayaking. Views of the island from the water beat those of the water from the island—and nothing beats a Gotland sunset from a bobbing boat of your own.

- **SS *Mariefred*, Mariefred.** Catch a ride on the world's oldest continuous-service steamship. *Mariefred* has chugged along faithfully for more than 100 years between Stockholm and the town of the ship's name. Still with its original engine and fittings, the boat offers a charming three-hour trip.

Bricks & Beauty

Sweden's churches testify to a time when the country was fervently religious (strong Lutheran values are still evident today in the Swedish work ethic), while its glorious castles and palaces speak of the era before a more widespread social equity. Whether perched on islands or in the middle of grand cities, Sweden's grand edifices tell an important tale of social history.

- **Stadshuset, Stockholm.** Ragnar Östberg's ornate but functional 1923 town-hall building has become an unofficial symbol of Stockholm. A trip to the top of the tower is rewarded by a breathtaking panorama of the city.

- **Kungliga Slottet, Stockholm.** One of the largest royal palaces in Europe has one of the most enviable locations, right on the waterfront overlooking Stockholm's medieval old town. Tour the State Apartments, the Royal Armory, and the Treasury, where the crown jewels are kept.

- **Drottningholms Slott, West of Stockholm.** This delightful confection is full of insights into how mid-18th-century royalty lived. Today's royal family moved here from Stockholm, so if you see the curtains twitching, it's probably them observing how 21st-century subjects live.

- **Skellefteå Landskyrka, Skellefteå, Bothnian Coast.** This striking church is a reminder of northern Sweden's staunch Christian past. Its 800-year-old Romanesque carving of the Virgin is one of the few of its kind left in the world.

- **Leksands Kyrka, Leksand, Dalarna.** Sweden's largest village church is also one of its prettiest. The shaded churchyard opens onto a stunning view across Lake Siljan.

IF YOU LIKE

Taking the Plunge

Beaches in Sweden range from wide and sandy strands in the west to steep and rocky shores in the east, and from ocean-front to lakefront. The area most favored for a sunbathing and wave-frolicking vacation is known as the Swedish Riviera, on the coast south of Göteborg. Wherever you go, a dip in the east's brackish Baltic or the west's wild Atlantic is a bracing experience that will set your pulse racing.

- **Archipelago, Stockholm.** Find a rock, any rock, and take the plunge. Swimming in the archipelago is a uniquely personal act; eschew the crowded beaches and follow the seagulls to an isolated outcrop. After your dip, you can dry as the sun sets over the Baltic.

- **Kallbadhuset Ribersborgsstranden, Malmö.** This beautiful wooden bathing center was built in 1898, when enjoying the waters was considered more of a health benefit than a chance to have fun. Nothing quite beats a quick dip in the waters here, even after all these years.

- **Vitemölle Badhotell, Kivik.** A renovated bath hotel right on the softly rolling sand dunes of Sweden's southern tip, this is the perfect setting for a favorite Swedish ritual: an early-evening swim, a fresh-fried-herring dinner on the hotel veranda, a good night's sleep, and a 6 AM wake-up swim the next morning. Life's never felt so good!

Hardworking Hands

The craft movement seems to have a natural home in Sweden. Historically, handicrafts were an important way to survive here. With such isolated, rural communities, people had to learn to weave, carve, fix, sculpt, and smelt to get by. Today many Swedes have embraced the country's ancient crafts. But Sweden is a country of modernity and progress, too, and many of the best craftsmen use ancient techniques married to cutting-edge design to create something uniquely Swedish.

- **Nusnäs, Dalarna.** This tiny village is home to the Dala horse, the carved wooden animal that started as a toy for local children and went on to become an international symbol of Sweden. Traditionally hand-painted red and richly patterned, you can also opt for one in black, white, or plain, oiled wood.

- **The Kingdom of Glass.** A 113-km (70-mi) stretch of densely forested land is home to Sweden's world-famous glass industry. Visitors here can enjoy superb glass and crystal design and experience glassblowing first-hand before picking up some original examples to take home.

- **Norrbottens Museum, Luleå.** Housing one of the best collections of Sámi ethnography, the museum also has a wonderful shop where you can buy quality Sámi crafts. Pick up carved-bone-handled knives, wooden cups, silver jewelry, and leather straps embroidered with pewter thread.

GREAT
ITINERARY

10 DAYS TO SWEDISH ENLIGHTENMENT

Day 1: Arrival in Stockholm

Stockholm is best explored on foot, so start with a walk around downtown and Gamla Stan, the historic heart of the city. In the afternoon, take in several of the city's museums or head to the serene greenery of Djurgården, a 20-minute walk from the center of town. Fine dining and a night at the opera will complete the day. For a more budget-conscious option, some people-watching over beers in Stureplan is just the ticket.

Logistics: The best way to get downtown from the airport is by the express train, Arlanda Express. Stockholm's metro and bus networks are excellent; tickets are available for single rides, 10 rides, or unlimited travel for 24 or 72 hours. Better still is the Stockholm Card (Stockholmskortet) with 24 or 48 hours of unlimited travel and free entry to over 60 museums included in the price (⇨ Transportation Around Stockholm *in* Stockholm A to Z).

Days 2–5: Royalty, Antiquity & the Archipelago

Don't miss Skansen, Stockholm's fantastic open-air museum, and Drottningholms Slott, home to Sweden's royal family and one of the most delightful palaces in Europe. Also of interest is the view from the top of Stadshuset, the city hall. Spend the afternoon strolling through Sigtuna, Sweden's oldest town, or Uppsala, the site of one of Europe's oldest universities.

At least one afternoon—or a few days, if you have the time—should be spent exploring the archipelago; to do this you can rent a small boat (strong arms required), charter a boat (well in advance), or hop on a ferry between islands (our favorite spots include the towns Vaxholm, Saltsjobaden, and Sandhamn, and the islands Fjäderholmarna, Utö, and Grinda).

Logistics: All this ground can be easily covered by car, although the archipelago is more accessible by water. Ferry transport from Stockholm to the archipelago is reliable and regular (⇨ Boat & Ferry Travel *in* Vaxholm & the Archipelago A to Z). There are many boat charter and rental companies in Stockholm. For information, contact the Swedish Sailing Association (⇨ Boating *in* Stockholm Sports & the Outdoors). For small-boat rental, contact the Swedish Canoeing Association (⇨ Boating *in* Stockholm Sports & the Outdoors). There are daily trains twice per hour between Stockholm and Uppsala (the journey is under an hour). Drottningholms Slott can be reached by ferry from Stockholm's center.

Days 6–8: Driving Dalarna

Pick up a rental car in Stockholm and head northwest to Dalarna. The goal is to circle Lake Siljan. If you have a few days, there are plenty of fun stops along the way (and you can visit Uppsala, if you haven't yet, outside of Stockholm). Some highlights include a visit to a Dala horse factory in Nusnäs; a swim at Sollerön; and a lakeside picnic in front of the beautiful Leksand Kyrka. Be sure to make a detour to see the Carl Larsson Gården, a short drive southeast of Tällberg on route 80, in the village of Sundborn.

Logistics: Driving time between Stockholm and the Dalarna region is about 3 hours. Both Avis and Europcar have one-way drop-off facilities at Dala Airport if you de-

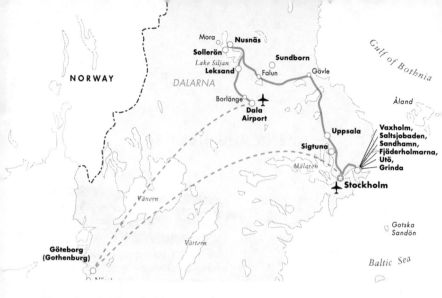

cide to skip the drive back to Stockholm and fly directly out of Dala Airport (⇨ Car Rental *in* Smart Travel Tips).

Days 9–10: Fresh Seafood & Beaches in Göteborg

Fly from Stockholm or from Dala Airport (if you can arrange the rental-car drop-off) to Göteborg (⇨ Air Travel *in* Smart Travel Tips). This is your official welcome to the west coast. Spend the day exploring the city's dock district, the cultural Vasastan neighborhood, and the rejuvenated Haga and Linné areas. Be sure to sample the local fish at one of the city's fantastic restaurants.

The next day, get out of town. Try Näset, a wonderful beach just 7 mi southwest of town, taking Bus 19 (which leaves every 20 minutes from 7 AM to 8 PM daily). A dip in the Atlantic will gear you up for an afternoon of museum-hopping back in town; be sure to check out Röhsska Museet and Konstmuseet.

Logistics: Göteborg's tram system is a cheap and fun way to get around. A Göteborgs Pass (SKr 175 for one day; SKr 295 for two days) includes unlimited public transport, plus entry to many museums around town. If you are traveling on foot (a good way to see this compact city), keep an eye out for trams, which can appear unexpectedly.

TIPS

❶ Speed limits and alcohol levels are strictly enforced by Swedish police.

❷ Many museums are closed on Mondays and are busy in the afternoons with school visits.

❸ Water is plentiful and clean in Sweden. Always carry your bathing suit in case you want to take a dip.

❹ Sweden's constitution upholds the right to roam. Do as the Swedes do and explore any beach, field, forest, lake, or river that strikes your fancy.

❺ Off season and away from major cities, many attractions keep limited hours. Check in advance to be certain.

ON THE
CALENDAR

WINTER	
November	The Stockholm Film Festival brings world-class films, directors, and actors to the city. The Stockholm Open tennis tournament attracts top players for an indoor tournament at the Kungliga Tennishallen. The Stockholm International Horse Show, held at the Globen sports center, is a big draw.
November 11	St. Martin's Day is celebrated primarily in the southern province of Skåne. Roast goose is served, accompanied by *svartsoppa*, a bisque made of goose blood and spices.
December	For each of the four weeks of Advent, which leads up to Christmas, a candle is lighted in a four-prong candelabra.
December 10	Nobel Day sees the presentation of the Nobel prizes by the king of Sweden at a glittering banquet held in Stadshuset, Stockholm's City Hall.
December 13	On Santa Lucia Day young girls are selected to be "Lucias"; they wear candles—today usually electric substitutes—in their hair and sing hymns at ceremonies around the country.
December 24	Christmas Eve is the principal day of the Christmas celebration. Traditional Christmas dishes include ham, rice porridge, and *lutefisk* (dried cod soaked in lye and then boiled).
December 31	New Year's Eve is the Swedes' occasion to set off an astounding array of fireworks. Every household has its own supply, and otherwise quiet neighborhood streets are full of midnight merrymakers.
January 13	Knut signals the end of Christmas festivities and the "plundering" of the Christmas tree: trinkets are removed from the tree, edible ornaments gobbled up, and the tree itself thrown out.
February	A market held in Jokkmokk features both traditional Sámi (Lapp) artifacts and plenty of reindeer. It begins on the first Thursday and runs through Saturday. On Shrove Tuesday special buns called *semlor*—lightly flavored with cardamom and filled with almond paste and whipped cream—are traditionally placed in a dish of warm milk, topped with cinnamon, and eaten.
SPRING	
March (first Sunday)	The Vasalopp Ski Race goes 90 km (56 mi) from Sälen to Mora in Dalarna and attracts entrants from all over the world.
April	On Maundy Thursday, which marks the beginning of the Easter celebrations, girls dress up as witches and hand out "Easter letters"

ON THE CALENDAR

	for small change or candy. *Påskris,* twigs tipped with dyed feathers, decorate homes. On April 30, for the Feast of Valborg, bonfires are lighted to celebrate the end of winter. The liveliest celebrations involve the students of the university cities of Uppsala, 60 km (37 mi) north of Stockholm, and Lund, 16 km (10 mi) north of Malmö.
May	On May 1, Labor Day marches and rallies are held nationwide, and politicians give speeches in town squares. Tjejtrampet, one of the world's largest bicycle races for women, takes place this month, as well.
June	In early June the Restaurant Festival fills Stockholm's Kungsträdgården with booths offering inexpensive international and Swedish cuisine. Also in June is the Stockholm Marathon. Midsummer Eve and Day celebrations are held on the Friday evening and Saturday that fall between June 20 and 26. Swedes raise maypoles decorated with floral garlands and sing, play games, and dance all night long. Traditional celebrations, open to the public, are held every year at Skansen in Stockholm. In mid-June comes the Hultsfred Festival, in southern Sweden. It's the country's largest, and wildest, rock festival, with major acts from all over the world.
June 6	National Day is celebrated with parades, speeches, and band concerts nationwide.
SUMMER July	Since 1983 the Stockholm Jazz Festival has brought in the world's best jazz and blues musicians for a five-day festival of music and good cheer. It's held on Skeppsholmen, on a stage behind the Moderna Museet.
August	Crayfish are a delicacy in Sweden, and the second Wednesday of August marks the Crayfish Premiere, when friends gather to eat them at outdoor parties.

SMART TRAVEL TIPS

Finding out about your destination before you leave home means you won't spend time organizing everyday minutiae once you've arrived. You'll be more streetwise when you hit the ground as well, better prepared to explore the aspects of Sweden that drew you here in the first place. The organizations in this section can provide information to supplement this guide; contact them for up-to-the-minute details, and consult the A to Z sections that end each chapter for facts on the various topics as they relate to Sweden's many regions. Happy landings!

AIR TRAVEL

BOOKING

When you book, look for nonstop flights and remember that "direct" flights stop at least once. Try to avoid connecting flights, which require a change of plane. Two airlines may operate a connecting flight jointly, so ask whether your airline operates every segment of the trip; you may find that the carrier you prefer flies you only part of the way. To find more booking tips and to check prices and make online flight reservations, log on to www.fodors.com.

CARRIERS

To & From Sweden From North America to Stockholm Arlanda Airport, Air Canada has flights with connections through London or Frankfurt; American Airlines has direct flights; Continental has direct flights from Newark, New Jersery; Delta has flights with connections through Paris; Finnair has flights with connections through Helsinki; Icelandair has flights with connections through Reykjavík and Oslo; Lufthansa has flights with connections through Frankfurt; Scandinavian Airlines System (SAS) has direct flights, as well as additional flights with connections through London or Copenhagen (United co-shares with SAS-operated flights).

From the United Kingdom, British Airways has direct flights to Stockholm Arlanda; BMI has direct flights to Stockholm Arlanda and Göteborg Landvetter; Fly Snowflake (an SAS group) has direct flights to Stockholm Arlanda; Ryan Air has direct flights to Stockholm Vasteras and Skavska airports as well as Göteborg City airport, and Scandinavian Airlines

System has direct flights to Stockholm Arlanda and Göteborg Landvetter.

Within Sweden Inside Sweden, Fly Me and Fly Nordic have direct flights from Stockholm Arlanda to Göteborg Landvetter; Malmö Aviation has direct flights from Stockholm City Airport Bromma to Göteborg Landvetter; Malmö Aviation and Scandinavian Airlines System connects all major cities by regular flights.

Airlines & Contacts Air Canada ☎ 888/247–2262 in Canada and the U.S. ⊕ www.aircanada.ca. **American** ☎ 800/433–7300 ⊕ www.aa.com. **British Airways** ☎ 020/88974000 ⊕ www.british-airways.com. **British Midland** ☎ 01332/854000 in the U.K ⊕ www.flybmi.com. **Continental** ☎ 800/231–0856 ⊕ www.continental.com. **Delta** ☎ 800/221–1212 ⊕ www.delta.com. **Finnair** ☎ 800/950–5000 ⊕ www.finnair.com. **Fly Me** ☎ 0313011000 ⊕ www.flyme.com. **Fly Nordic** ☎ 08/52806820 ⊕ www.flynordic.com. **Iceland Air** ☎ 800/223–5500 ⊕ www.icelandair.com. **Lufthansa** ☎ 800/399–5838 ⊕ www.lufthansa.com. **Malmö Aviation** ☎ 406602900 ⊕ www.malmoaviation.se. **Ryan Air** ☎ 0871/246–0000 in the U.K., 0155/202240 in Sweden ⊕ www.ryanair.com. **SAS** ☎ 0770/727727 in Sweden, 020/77344020 in the U.K., 800/345–9684 in the U.S. ⊕ www.scandinavian.net. **United** ☎ 800/241–6522 ⊕ www.united.com.

CHECK-IN & BOARDING

Always **find out your carrier's check-in policy.** Plan to arrive at the airport about 2 hours before your scheduled departure time for domestic flights and 2½ to 3 hours before international flights. You may need to arrive earlier if you're flying from one of the busier airports or during peak air-traffic times. To avoid delays at airport-security checkpoints, try not to wear any metal. Jewelry, belt and other buckles, steel-toe shoes, barrettes, and underwire bras are among the items that can set off detectors.

Assuming that not everyone with a ticket will show up, airlines routinely overbook planes. When everyone does, airlines ask for volunteers to give up their seats. In return, these volunteers usually get a several-hundred-dollar flight voucher, which can be used toward the purchase of another ticket, and are rebooked on the next available flight out. If there are not enough volunteers, the airline must choose who will be denied boarding. The first to get bumped are passengers who checked in late and those flying on discounted tickets, so get to the gate and check in as early as possible, especially during peak periods.

Always **bring a government-issued photo ID** to the airport; even when it's not required, a passport is best.

CUTTING COSTS

The **SAS Visit Scandinavia/Europe Air Pass** offers up to eight flight coupons for one-way travel within and between Scandinavian cities (and participating European countries from the United Kingdom to the Baltic states and as far south as Spain and Portugal). Most one-way tickets for domestic travel within each Scandinavian country cost $69; one-way fares between the Scandinavian countries are usually $80, unless you are venturing into the far north, Lapland, Iceland, or Greenland (these flights range from $122 to $200); fares to other European destinations range from $65 to $165. These passes can be bought only in conjunction with a round-trip ticket between North America and Europe on SAS and must be used within three months of arrival. SAS also provides family fares—children between 2 and 17 and a spouse can receive 50% off the full fare of business-class tickets with the purchase of one full-fare business-class ticket. Contact SAS for information.

The least-expensive airfares to Scandinavia are often priced for round-trip travel and must usually be purchased in advance. Airlines generally allow you to change your return date for a fee; most low-fare tickets, however, are nonrefundable. It's smart to call a number of airlines and check the Internet; when you are quoted a good price, book it on the spot—the same fare may not be available the next day, or even the next hour. Always check different routings and look into using alternate airports. Also, price off-peak flights and red-eye, which may be significantly less expensive than others. Travel agents, especially low-fare specialists (⇨ Discounts & Deals), are helpful.

Consolidators are another good source. They buy tickets for scheduled flights at reduced rates from the airlines, then sell them at prices that beat the best fare available directly from the airlines. (Many also offer reduced car-rental and hotel rates.) Sometimes you can even get your money back if you need to return the ticket. Carefully read the fine print detailing penalties for changes and cancellations, purchase the ticket with a credit card, and confirm your consolidator reservation with the airline.

Consolidators **AirlineConsolidator.com** ☎ 888/468-5385 ⊕ www.airlineconsolidator.com; for international tickets. **Best Fares** ☎ 800/880-1234 ⊕ www.bestfares.com; $59.90 annual membership. **Cheap Tickets** ☎ 800/377-1000 or 800/652-4327 ⊕ www.cheaptickets.com. **Expedia** ☎ 800/397-3342 or 404/728-8787 ⊕ www.expedia.com. **Hotwire** ☎ 866/468-9473 or 920/330-9418 ⊕ www.hotwire.com. **Now Voyager Travel** ☎ 212/459-1616 ⊕ www.nowvoyagertravel.com. **Onetravel.com** ⊕ www.onetravel.com. **Orbitz** ☎ 888/656-4546 ⊕ www.orbitz.com. **Priceline.com** ⊕ www.priceline.com. **Travelocity** ☎ 888/709-5983, 877/282-2925 in Canada, 0870/111-7061 in the U.K. ⊕ www.travelocity.com.

ENJOYING THE FLIGHT

State your seat preference when purchasing your ticket, and then repeat it when you confirm and when you check in. For more legroom, you can request one of the few emergency-aisle seats at check-in, if you're capable of moving obstacles comparable in weight to an airplane exit door (usually between 35 pounds and 60 pounds)—a Federal Aviation Administration requirement of passengers in these seats. Seats behind a bulkhead also offer more legroom, but they don't have underseat storage. Don't sit in the row in front of the emergency aisle or in front of a bulkhead, where seats may not recline. SeatGuru.com has more information about specific seat configurations, which vary by aircraft.

Ask the airline whether a snack or meal is served on the flight. If you have dietary concerns, request special meals when booking. These can be vegetarian, low-cholesterol, or kosher, for example. It's a

good idea to pack some healthful snacks and a small (plastic) bottle of water in your carry-on bag. On long flights, try to maintain a normal routine, to help fight jet lag. At night, get some sleep. By day, eat light meals, drink water (not alcohol), and **move around the cabin** to stretch your legs. For additional jet-lag tips consult *Fodor's FYI: Travel Fit & Healthy* (available at bookstores everywhere).

Smoking policies vary from carrier to carrier. Most airlines prohibit smoking on all their flights; others allow smoking only on certain routes or certain departures. Ask your carrier about its policy.

FLYING TIMES

Flying time from New York to Stockholm is 8 hours. From London's Heathrow Airport flying time to Stockholm is 2¼ hours. From Sydney and major cities in New Zealand, the flight to any Scandinavian country will last more than 20 hours and will require at least one transfer.

HOW TO COMPLAIN

If your baggage goes astray or your flight goes awry, complain right away. Most carriers require that you **file a claim immediately.** The Aviation Consumer Protection Division of the Department of Transportation publishes *Fly-Rights*, which discusses airlines and consumer issues and is available online. You can also find articles and information on mytravelrights.com, the Web site of the nonprofit Consumer Travel Rights Center.

Airline Complaints **Aviation Consumer Protection Division** ✉ U.S. Department of Transportation, Office of Aviation Enforcement and Proceedings, C-75, Room 4107, 400 7th St. SW, Washington, DC 20590 ☎ 202/366-2220 ⊕ airconsumer.ost.dot.gov. **Federal Aviation Administration Consumer Hotline** ✉ For inquiries: FAA, 800 Independence Ave. SW, Washington, DC 20591 ☎ 800/322-7873 ⊕ www.faa.gov.

RECONFIRMING

Check the status of your flight before you leave for the airport. You can do this on your carrier's Web site, by linking to a flight-status checker (many Web booking services offer these), or by calling your carrier or travel agent. Always confirm international flights at least 72 hours ahead of the scheduled departure time.

AIRPORTS

Sweden's major gateway, **Arlanda International Airport**, is 41 km (26 mi) from Stockholm. Göteborg's **Landvetter Airport** is 26 km (16 mi) from the city.

🛈 Airport Information **Arlanda International Airport** ☎ 46/87976100 🌐 www.lfv.se. **Landvetter Airport** ☎ 46/31941100 🌐 www.lfv.se.

BIKE TRAVEL

Cycling is a very popular sport in Sweden, and the south of the country, with its low-lying, flat landscape, is perfect for the more genteel cyclist. All major towns and cities are well provided with cycle paths and designated cycle lanes. Bike-rental costs average around SKr 100 per day. Tourist offices and the Swedish Touring Association have information about cycling package holidays that include bike rentals, overnight accommodations, and meals. The Swedish bicycling organization, Cykelfrämjandet (National Cycle Association), publishes a free English-language guide to cycling trips. Various companies, including Cycling Sweden, offer a variety of cycling tours around the country.

🛈 **Cykelfrämjandet** ✉ Thuleg. 43, 113 53 Stockholm ☎ 08/54591030 Mon.–Thurs. 9–noon 🖷 08/54591039 🌐 www.cykelframjandet.a.se. **Cycling Sweden** ✉ Tranmog. 10, 641 50 Katrineholm ☎ 15055091 🌐 www.cyclingsweden.se. **Swedish Touring Association** (STF) 🗐 Box 25, 101 20 Stockholm ☎ 08/4632200 🖷 08/6781938 🌐 www.meravsverige.se.

BIKES IN FLIGHT

Most airlines accommodate bikes as luggage, provided they are dismantled and boxed; check with individual airlines about packing requirements. Some airlines sell bike boxes, which are often free at bike shops, for about $20 (bike bags can be considerably more expensive). International travelers often can substitute a bike for a piece of checked luggage at no charge; otherwise, the cost is about $100. Most U.S. and Canadian airlines charge $40–$80 each way.

BOAT & FERRY TRAVEL

From the United Kingdom, DFDS Seaways has services departing from Newcastle at 3 PM and arriving in Kristiansand, southern Norway, at 9:15 AM local time before continuing on to Göteborg, where it arrives at 5 PM local time.

DFDS Tor Line has services on its freight liners—with freight taking precedence over passengers—from Immingham, usually departing at 4 AM and arriving in Göteborg at 7 AM local time the next day.

Taking a ferry is not only fun, it is often necessary in Scandinavia. Many companies arrange package trips, some offering a rental car and hotel accommodations as part of the deal. The word *ferry* can be deceptive; generally, those vessels so named are more like small-scale cruise ships, with several dining rooms, sleeping quarters, shopping, pool and sauna, and entertainment.

Silja Line operates massive ferries between Stockholm and Helsinki, departing from Stockholm at 5 PM, with a stop at Mariehamn at 11:55 PM, and arriving at Helsinki at 9:30 AM. Fares range from SKr 50 to SKr 63 without a cabin, depending upon the day, and SKr 120 to SKr 760, depending upon the class of cabin and day. Viking Line also operates large ferries to Helsinki, departing from Stockholm at 4:45 PM with a brief stop at Mariehamn before arriving in Helsinki at 9:55 AM. Fares, without cabins, range from € 32 to € 56, depending upon the day. Unity Line operates a ferry service departing from Ystad at 10 PM and arriving at 7 AM in Świnoujście, Poland, where a mini-bus will be waiting to take you to the historic city of Szczecin, Poland. The fares range from SKr 550 to SKr 860, depending upon the season.ScandLines operates a frequent ferry service on the 20-minute sail between Helsingborg and Helsingør, Denmark. Single fares cost SKr 22 for a foot passenger, and SKr 290 for a car and passengers.

A rewarding way to see Sweden is from the many ferryboats that ply the archipelagos and main lakes. In Stockholm, visitors can buy a special *Båtluffarkort* (Inter Skerries Card, SKr 300) from Waxholmsbolaget.

This card allows you 5 days of unlimited travel on the archipelago ferryboats. (⇨ Boat & Ferry Travel *in* Stockholm A to Z.)

⊞ Major Operators DFDS Seaways ✉ DFDS Seaways Travel Centre, Scandinavia House, Parkeston, Harwich, Essex CO12 4QG ☎ 44/8705-333-111 ⊕ www.dfdsseaways.co.uk. **DFDS Tor Line** ✉ Nordic House, Western Access Rd., Immingham Dock, Immingham, DN402LZ North East Lincolnshire ☎ 44/1469-575231. **ScandLines** ⌖ Dampfærgevej, 10, DK-2100 Copenhagen, Denmark ☎ 45/33-15-15-15 ✉ Knutpunkten 43, 252 78 Helsingborg, Sweden ☎ 46/42186100 ♻ 46/42186000 ⊕ www.scandlines.com. **Silja Line** ✉ Mannerheimintie 2, 00100 Helsinki, Finland ☎ 358/9-18041 ♻ 358/9-1804279 ✉ Kungsg. 2, 111 43 Stockholm, Sweden ☎ 46/86663512 ♻ 46/86119162 ⊕ www.silja.com/english. **Unity Line** ✉ Färjeterminalen, 271 39 Ystad ☎ 46/0411556900 ♻ 46/0411556953 ⊕ www.unityline.pl. **Viking Line** ✉ Mannerheimintie 14, 00100 Helsinki ☎ 358/9-12351 ♻ 358/9-647075 ⊕ www.vikingline.fi.

CAR FERRIES

Travel by car in Scandinavia often necessitates travel by ferry. Some well-known vehicle and passenger ferries run between Copenhagen, Denmark, and Malmö, Sweden; between Helsingør, Denmark, and Helsingborg, Sweden; between Copenhagen and Göteborg, Sweden; and between Stockholm, Sweden, and Helsinki, Finland. The Helsingør/Helsingborg ferry (ScandLines) takes only 20 minutes. Round-trip fares are cheapest.

⊞ Color Line ⌖ Box 30, DK-9850 Hirsthals, Denmark ☎ 45/99-56-20-00 ♻ 45/99-56-20-20 ✉ Hjortneskaia, Box 1422 Vika, N-0115 Oslo, Norway ☎ 47/22-94-44-00 ♻ 47/22-83-04-30 ✉ Color Scandi Line, Torksholmen, 45 200 Strømstad, Sweden ☎ 46/52662000 ♻ 46/52614669 ✉ Color Line GmbH, Postfach 6080, 24121 Kiel, Germany ☎ 49/431-7300-300 ♻ 49/431-7300-400 ⊕ www.colorline.no. **ScandLines** ⌖ Dampfærgevej, 10, DK-2100 Copenhagen, Denmark ☎ 45/33-15-15-15 ✉ Knutpunkten 43, 252 78 Helsingborg, Sweden ☎ 46/42186100 ♻ 46/42186000 ⊕ www.scandlines.com.

BUS TRAVEL

There is excellent bus service between all major towns and cities. Consult the *Yellow Pages* under "Bussresearrangörer" for the telephone numbers of the companies concerned. Recommended are the services offered to different parts of Sweden from Stockholm by Swebus. When buying a single ticket for local bus journeys, it is usual to pay the driver on boarding. Coupons or multiple tickets for longer journeys should be purchased before your journey from the relevant bus company.

⊞ Svenska Buss ☎ 0771/676767 ⊕ www.svenskabuss.se. **Swebus Express** ☎ 0200/218218 ⊕ www.swebusexpress.se.

BUSINESS HOURS

BANKS & OFFICES

Banks are officially open weekdays 9:30–3, but many stay open until 5 on most weekdays and until 6 on Thursday. The bank at Arlanda International Airport is open every day with extended hours, and the Forex and Valuta Specialisten currency-exchange offices also have extended hours. Most banks operate a numbered-ticket system for lining up: take a number and wait your turn. Ticket machines are always near a bank's doors. Make exchanging money your first task to avoid a frustratingly long wait. More and more Swedes use Internet banking for daily cash transactions, and, strange as it may seem, it is not uncommon to come across cashless bank branches. These are more often found in smaller towns and villages, so it is worth checking before traveling.

MUSEUMS & SIGHTS

The opening times for museums vary widely, but most are open from 10 to 4 Tuesday–Sunday. Consult the guide in *På Stan,* the entertainment supplement published in *Dagens Nyheter's* Friday edition, or *What's On,* a monthly entertainment listings guide published in Swedish and English by the Swedish tourism authorities. It's available for free at hotels, tourist centers, and some restaurants.

⊞ På Stan ⊕ www.dn.se/pastan. **What's On** ⊕ www.stockholmtown.se ⊕ www.stockholmsmuseer.com.

SHOPS

Shops are generally open weekdays from 9, 9:30, or 10 until 6 and Saturday from 10 to 1 or 4. Most large department stores stay open later in the evening, and some open on Sunday. Several supermarkets open on Sunday, and there are a number of late-night food shops, such as the 7-Eleven chain. Systembolaget, Sweden's only place to buy alcohol, is open weekdays from 10 to 6, with extended hours until 7 on Thursday and Saturday from 10 to 2. Most Systembolaget display their product behind glass. Customers take a numbered ticket and order at a counter from which their choice is collected when their number is called. Unless time is very definitely on your hands, avoid buying alcohol on a Friday, when the wait can be as long as an hour.

CAMERAS & PHOTOGRAPHY

The *Kodak Guide to Shooting Great Travel Pictures* (available at bookstores everywhere) is loaded with tips.

🖪 Photo Help **Kodak Information Center** ☎ 800/242-2424 ⊕ www.kodak.com.

EQUIPMENT PRECAUTIONS

Don't pack film or equipment in checked luggage, where it is much more susceptible to damage. X-ray machines used to view checked luggage are extremely powerful and therefore are likely to ruin your film. Try to ask for hand inspection of film, which becomes clouded after repeated exposure to airport X-ray machines, and keep videotapes and computer disks away from metal detectors. Always keep film, tape, and computer disks out of the sun. Carry an extra supply of batteries, and be prepared to turn on your camera, camcorder, or laptop to prove to airport security personnel that the device is real.

CAR RENTAL

Major car-rental companies such as Avis, Budget, Europcar, and Hertz have facilities in all major towns and cities as well as at airports. Various service stations also offer car rentals, including Q8, Shell, Statoil, and Texaco. See the *Yellow Pages* under "Biluthyrning" for telephone numbers and addresses. Renting a car is a speedy business in Sweden, with none of the usual lengthy documentation and vehicle checks; show your passport, license, and credit card, pick up the key, and away you go.

Although this is a plus if you are in a hurry, if you feel more comfortable being shown around your car before you drive, just ask and most companies will oblige.

Rates in Stockholm begin at $75 a day and $190 a week for a manual-drive economy car without air-conditioning and with unlimited mileage. This does not include tax on car rentals, which is 25% in Sweden. A service charge also is usually added, which ranges from $15 to $25.

🚗 **Alamo** ☎ 800/522-9696 ⊕ www.alamo.com. **Avis** ☎ 800/331-1084, 800/879-2847 in Canada, 0870/606-0100 in the U.K., 02/9353-9000 in Australia, 09/526-2847 in New Zealand ⊕ www.avis.com. **Budget** ☎ 800/527-0700 ⊕ www.budget.com. **Dollar** ☎ 800/800-6000, 0800/085-4578 in the U.K. ⊕ www.dollar.com. **Europcar** ☎ 877/940-6900, 0870/607-5000 in the U.K. ⊕ www.europcar.com. **Hertz** ☎ 800/654-3001, 800/263-0600 in Canada, 0870/844-8844 in the U.K., 02/9669-2444 in Australia, 09/256-8690 in New Zealand ⊕ www.hertz.com. **National Car Rental** ☎ 800/227-7368 ⊕ www.nationalcar.com.

CUTTING COSTS

For a good deal, book through a travel agent who will shop around. Do look into wholesalers, companies that do not own fleets but rent in bulk from those that do and often offer better rates than traditional car-rental operations. Prices are best during off-peak periods. Rentals booked through wholesalers often must be paid for before you leave home.

🚗 Wholesalers **Auto Europe** ☎ 800/223-5555 or 207/842-2000 🖷 207/842-2222 ⊕ www.autoeurope.com. **Destination Europe Resources** (DER) ✉ 9501 W. Devon Ave., Rosemont, IL 60018 ☎ 800/782-2424 🖷 800/282-7474. **Europe by Car** ☎ 800/223-1516 or 212/581-3040 🖷 212/246-1458 ⊕ www.europebycar.com. **Kemwel** ☎ 877/820-0668 or 800/678-0678 🖷 207/842-2124 or 866/726-6726 ⊕ www.kemwel.com.

INSURANCE

When driving a rented car you are generally responsible for any damage to or loss of the vehicle. Collision policies that car-rental companies sell for European rentals typically do not cover stolen vehicles. Before you rent—and purchase collision or theft coverage—see what coverage you already have under the terms of your personal auto-insurance policy and credit cards.

REQUIREMENTS & RESTRICTIONS

Ask about age requirements: Several countries require drivers to be over 20 years old, but some car-rental companies require that drivers be at least 25. In Scandinavia your own driver's license is acceptable for a limited time; check with the country's tourist board before you go. An International Driver's Permit is a good idea; it's available from the American or Canadian Automobile Association or, in the United Kingdom, from the Automobile Association or Royal Automobile Club.

SURCHARGES

Before you pick up a car in one city and leave it in another, ask about drop-off charges or one-way service fees, which can be substantial. Also inquire about early-return policies; some rental agencies charge extra if you return the car before the time specified in your contract while others give you a refund for the days not used. Most agencies note the tank's fuel level on your contract; to avoid a hefty refueling fee, return the car with the same tank level. If the tank was full, refill it just before you turn in the car, but be aware that gas stations near the rental outlet may overcharge. It's almost never a deal to buy a tank of gas with the car when you rent it; the understanding is that you'll return it empty, but some fuel usually remains.

CAR TRAVEL

Your driver's license may not be recognized outside your home country. International driving permits (IDPs) are available from the American and Canadian automobile associations and, in the United Kingdom, from the Automobile Association and Royal Automobile Club. These international permits, valid only in conjunction with your regular driver's license, are universally recognized; having one may save you a problem with local authorities.

The Øresundsbron, the new 8-km (5-mi) bridge between Malmö and Copenhagen, simplifies car travel and makes train connections possible between the two countries. Ferry service is cheaper but slower—it takes 45 minutes to make the crossing.

Sweden has an excellent highway network of more than 80,000 km (50,000 mi). The fastest routes are those with numbers prefixed with an *E* (for "European"), some of which are the equivalent of American highways or British motorways. The size of the country compared to its population means that most roads are relatively traffic free. However, rush hour around major cities can bring traffic jams and holdups of frustrating proportions.

Also be aware that there are relatively low legal blood-alcohol limits and tough penalties for driving while intoxicated in Scandinavia; Sweden, Iceland, and Finland have zero-tolerance laws. Penalties include license suspension and fines or imprisonment, and the laws are sometimes enforced by random police roadblocks in urban areas on weekends. In addition, an accident involving a driver who has an illegal blood-alcohol level usually voids all insurance agreements, making the driver responsible for all medical bills and collision damage.

In a few remote areas in northern Sweden, road conditions can be unpredictable, and careful planning is required for safety's sake. Several mountain and highland roads in these areas close in winter—when driving in such remote areas, especially in winter, it is best to let someone know your travel plans. It is also wise to **use a four-wheel-drive vehicle** and to **travel with at least one other car** in these areas.

AUTO CLUBS

In Australia **Australian Automobile Association** ☎ 02/6247-7311 ⊕ www.aaa.asn.au.

In Canada **Canadian Automobile Association (CAA)** ☎ 613/247-0117 ⊕ www.caa.ca.

In New Zealand **New Zealand Automobile Association** ☎ 09/377-4660 ⊕ www.aa.co.nz.

In the U.K. **Automobile Association (AA)** ☎ 0870/600-0371 ⊕ www.theaa.com. **Royal Automobile Club (RAC)** ☎ 0800/731-7090 for membership, 0845/300-0755 for insurance ⊕ www.rac.co.uk.

In the U.S. **American Automobile Association** ☎ 800/564-6222.

EMERGENCY SERVICES

The emergency number for the European Union is 112. The Sweden-specific emergency number is 90000. The Larmtjänst organization, run by a confederation of Swedish insurance companies, provides a 24-hour breakdown service. Its phone numbers are listed in the *Yellow Pages*.

GASOLINE

Sweden has some of the highest gasoline rates in Europe, about SKr 10.74 per liter (about SKr 40 per gallon). Lead-free gasoline is readily available. Gas stations are self-service: pumps marked SEDEL are automatic and accept SKr 20 and SKr 100 bills; pumps marked KASSA are paid for at the cashier; the KONTO pumps are for customers with credit cards.

PARKING

Parking meters and, increasingly, timed ticket machines operate in larger towns, usually between 8 AM and 6 PM. The fee varies from about SKr 6 to SKr 35 per hour. Parking garages in urban areas are mostly automated, often with machines that accept credit cards; LEDIGT on a garage sign means space is available. Many streets in urban areas are cleaned weekly at a designated time on a designated day, during which time parking is not allowed, not even at meters. Times are marked on a yellow sign at each end of the street. Try to avoid getting a parking ticket, which can come with fines of SKr 300–SKr 700.

ROAD CONDITIONS

All main and secondary roads are well surfaced, but some minor roads, particularly in the north, are gravel.

ROAD MAPS

If you plan on extensive road touring, consider buying the *Vägatlas över Sverige,* a detailed road atlas published by the Mötormännens Riksförbund, available at bookstores for around SKr 300.

RULES OF THE ROAD

Drive on the right, and—no matter where you sit in a car—seat belts are mandatory. You must also have at least low-beam headlights on at all times. Cars rented or bought in Sweden will have automatic headlights, which are activated every time the engine is switched on. Signs indicate five basic speed limits, ranging from 30 kph (19 mph) in school or playground areas to 110 kph (68 mph) on long stretches of E roads.

CHILDREN IN SWEDEN

In Sweden children are to be seen *and* heard and are genuinely welcome in most public places. This includes restaurants and bars, most of which will offer baby and infant chairs.

If you are renting a car, don't forget to arrange for a car seat when you reserve. For general advice about traveling with children, consult *Fodor's FYI: Travel with Your Baby* (available in bookstores everywhere).

DISCOUNTS

Children are entitled to discount tickets (often as much as 50% off) on buses, trains, and ferries throughout Scandinavia, as well as reductions on special City Cards. A parent with a buggy or stroller travels free on local buses in Sweden's towns and cities. On SAS children ages 2–12 pay 75% of an adult round-trip airfare; children under 2 pay 10%. There are no restrictions on children's fares when booked in economy class. "Family fares," available only in business class, are also worth looking into (⇨ Cutting Costs *under* Air Travel).

With the Scanrail Pass (⇨ Train Travel)— good for rail journeys throughout Scandinavia—children under age 4 travel free (on lap); those ages 4–11 pay half fare, and those ages 12–25 can get a Scanrail Youth Pass, providing a 25% discount off the adult fare.

FLYING

If your children are two or older, ask about children's airfares. As a general rule, infants under two not occupying a seat fly at greatly reduced fares or even for free. But if you want to guarantee a seat for an infant, you have to pay full fare. Consider flying during off-peak days and times; most airlines will grant an infant a seat without a ticket if there are available seats.

When booking, confirm carry-on allowances if you're traveling with infants. In general, for babies charged 10% to 50% of the adult fare you are allowed one carry-on bag and a collapsible stroller; if the flight is full, the stroller may have to be checked or you may be limited to less.

Experts agree that it's a good idea to use safety seats aloft for children weighing less than 40 pounds. Airlines set their own policies: if you use a safety seat, U.S. carriers usually require that the child be ticketed, even if he or she is young enough to ride free, because the seats must be strapped into regular seats. And even if you pay the full adult fare for the seat, it may be worth it, especially on longer trips. Do **check your airline's policy about using safety seats during takeoff and landing.** Safety seats are not allowed everywhere in the plane, so get your seat assignments as early as possible.

When reserving, request children's meals or a freestanding bassinet (not available at all airlines) if you need them. But note that bulkhead seats, where you must sit to use the bassinet, may lack an overhead bin or storage space on the floor.

For all airlines servicing Scandinavia, it is necessary to reserve children's and infant meals at least 24 hours in advance; travel of an unaccompanied minor should be confirmed at least three days prior to the flight.

LODGING
Most hotels in Scandinavia allow children under a certain age to stay in their parents' room at no extra charge, but others charge for them as extra adults; be sure to find out the cutoff age for children's discounts.

SIGHTS & ATTRACTIONS
Places that are especially appealing to children are indicated by a rubber-duckie icon (🐤) in the margin.

CONSUMER PROTECTION
Whether you're shopping for gifts or purchasing travel services, **pay with a major credit card** whenever possible, so you can cancel payment or get reimbursed if there's a problem (and you can provide documentation). If you're doing business with a

particular company for the first time, contact your local Better Business Bureau and the attorney general's offices in your state and (for U.S. businesses) the company's home state as well. Have any complaints been filed? Finally, if you're buying a package or tour, always consider travel insurance that includes default coverage (⇨ Insurance).

🗂 BBBs **Council of Better Business Bureaus** ✉ 4200 Wilson Blvd., Suite 800, Arlington, VA 22203 ☎ 703/276-0100 🖷 703/525-8277 ⊕ www.bbb.org.

CRUISE TRAVEL
You can go on one of the highly popular cruises of the Göta Canal, which traverse rivers, lakes, and, on the last lap, the Baltic Sea. A lovely waterway, the Göta Canal with its 65 locks links Göteborg, on the west coast, with Stockholm, on the east. Cruise participants travel on fine old steamers, some of which date back almost to the canal's opening, in 1832. The oldest and most desirable is the *Juno*, built in 1874. Prices start at SKr 6,100 for a bed in a double cabin. For more information contact the Göta Canal Steamship Company.

To learn how to plan, choose, and book a cruise-ship voyage, consult *Fodor's FYI: Plan & Enjoy Your Cruise* (available in bookstores everywhere).

🗂 **Göta Canal Steamship Company** 🛳 Pusterviksgatan 13, SE413-01 Göteborg ☎ 03/1806315 🖷 03/1158311 ⊕ www.gotacanal.se.

CUSTOMS & DUTIES
When shopping abroad, keep receipts for all purchases. Upon reentering the country, **be ready to show customs officials what you've bought.** Pack purchases together in an easily accessible place. If you think a duty is incorrect, appeal the assessment. If you object to the way your clearance was handled, note the inspector's badge number. In either case, first ask to see a supervisor. If the problem isn't resolved, write to the appropriate authorities, beginning with the port director at your point of entry.

IN AUSTRALIA
Australian residents who are 18 or older may bring home A$900 worth of souvenirs and gifts (including jewelry), 250

cigarettes or 250 grams of cigars or other tobacco products, and 2.25 liters of alcohol (including wine, beer, and spirits). Residents under 18 may bring back A$450 worth of goods. If any of these individual allowances are exceeded, you must pay duty for the entire amount (of the group of products in which the allowance was exceeded). Members of the same family traveling together may pool their allowances. Prohibited items include meat products. Seeds, plants, and fruits need to be declared upon arrival.

Australian Customs Service ⌖ Customs House, 10 Cooks River Dr., Sydney International Airport, Sydney, NSW 2020 ☎ 1300/363263 or 02/6275-6666, 1800/020-504 or 02/8334-7444 quarantine-inquiry line 🖷 02/8339-6714 ⌖ www.customs.gov.au.

IN CANADA

Canadian residents who have been out of Canada for at least seven days may bring in C$750 worth of goods duty-free. If you've been away fewer than seven days but more than 48 hours, the duty-free allowance drops to C$200. If your trip lasts 24 to 48 hours, the allowance is C$50; if the goods are worth more than C$50, you must pay full duty on all of the goods. You may not pool allowances with family members. Goods claimed under the C$750 exemption may follow you by mail; those claimed under the lesser exemptions must accompany you. Alcohol and tobacco products may be included in the seven-day and 48-hour exemptions but not in the 24-hour exemption. If you meet the age requirements of the province or territory through which you reenter Canada, you may bring in, duty-free, 1.5 liters of wine *or* 1.14 liters (40 imperial ounces) of liquor *or* 24 12-ounce cans or bottles of beer or ale. Also, if you meet the local age requirement for tobacco products, you may bring in, duty-free, 200 cigarettes, 50 cigars or cigarillos, and 200 grams of tobacco. You may have to pay a minimum duty on tobacco products, regardless of whether or not you exceed your personal exemption. Check ahead of time with the Canada Border Services Agency or the Department of Agriculture for policies regarding meat products, seeds, plants, and fruits.

You may send an unlimited number of gifts (only one gift per recipient, however) worth up to C$60 each duty-free to Canada. Label the package UNSOLICITED GIFT—VALUE UNDER $60. Alcohol and tobacco are excluded.

Canada Border Services Agency ✉ Customs Information Services, 191 Laurier Ave. W, 15th fl., Ottawa, Ontario K1A 0L5 ☎ 800/461-9999 in Canada, 204/983-3500, 506/636-5064 ⌖ www.cbsa.gc.ca.

IN NEW ZEALAND

All homeward-bound residents may bring back NZ$700 worth of souvenirs and gifts; passengers may not pool their allowances, and children can claim only the concession on goods intended for their own use. For those 17 or older, the duty-free allowance also includes 4.5 liters of wine or beer; one 1,125-ml bottle of spirits; and either 200 cigarettes, 250 grams of tobacco, 50 cigars, *or* a combination of the three up to 250 grams. Meat products, seeds, plants, and fruits must be declared upon arrival to the Agricultural Services Department.

New Zealand Customs ✉ Head office: The Customhouse, 17-21 Whitmore St., Box 2218, Wellington ☎ 0800/428786 or 09/300-5399 ⌖ www.customs.govt.nz.

IN SWEDEN

Travelers 21 or older entering Sweden from non-EU countries may import duty-free 1 liter of liquor and 2 liters of fortified wine; 2 liters of wine or 15 liters of beer; 200 cigarettes or 100 grams of cigarillos or 50 cigars or 250 grams of tobacco; 50 grams of perfume; ¼ liter of aftershave; and other goods whose total value does not exceed SKr 1,700. Travelers from the United Kingdom or other EU countries may import duty-free 1 liter of liquor or 3 liters of fortified wine; 5 liters of wine; 15 liters of beer; 300 cigarettes or 150 cigarillos or 75 cigars or 400 grams of tobacco; and other goods, including perfume and aftershave, of any value.

IN THE U.K.

If you are a U.K. resident and your journey was wholly within the European

Union, you probably won't have to pass through customs when you return to the United Kingdom. If you plan to bring back large quantities of alcohol or tobacco, check EU limits beforehand. In most cases, if you bring back more than 200 cigars, 3,200 cigarettes, 400 cigarillos, 3 kilograms of tobacco, 10 liters of spirits, 110 liters of beer, 20 liters of fortified wine, and/or 90 liters of wine, you have to declare the goods upon return.

🄵 **HM Customs and Excise** ✉ Portcullis House, 21 Cowbridge Rd. E, Cardiff CFll 9SS ☎ 0845/010–9000 or 0208/929–0152 advice service, 0208/929–6731 or 0208/910–3602 complaints ⊕ www.hmce.gov.uk.

IN THE U.S.

U.S. residents who have been out of the country for at least 48 hours may bring home, for personal use, $800 worth of foreign goods duty-free, as long as they haven't used the $800 allowance or any part of it in the past 30 days. This exemption may include 1 liter of alcohol (for travelers 21 and older), 200 cigarettes, and 100 non-Cuban cigars. Family members from the same household who are traveling together may pool their $800 personal exemptions. For fewer than 48 hours, the duty-free allowance drops to $200, which may include 50 cigarettes, 10 non-Cuban cigars, and 150 ml of alcohol (or 150 ml of perfume containing alcohol). The $200 allowance cannot be combined with other individuals' exemptions, and if you exceed it, the full value of all the goods will be taxed. Antiques, which U.S. Customs and Border Protection defines as objects more than 100 years old, enter duty-free, as do original works of art done entirely by hand, including paintings, drawings, and sculptures. This doesn't apply to folk art or handicrafts, which are in general dutiable.

You may also send packages home duty-free, with a limit of one parcel per addressee per day (except alcohol or tobacco products or perfume worth more than $5). You can mail up to $200 worth of goods for personal use; label the package PERSONAL USE and attach a list of its contents and their retail value. If the package contains your used personal belongings, mark it AMERICAN GOODS RETURNED to avoid paying duties. You may send up to $100 worth of goods as a gift; mark the package UNSOLICITED GIFT. Mailed items do not affect your duty-free allowance on your return.

To avoid paying duty on foreign-made high-ticket items you already own and will take on your trip, register them with a local customs office before you leave the country. Consider filing a Certificate of Registration for laptops, cameras, watches, and other digital devices identified with serial numbers or other permanent markings; you can keep the certificate for other trips. Otherwise, bring a sales receipt or insurance form to show that you owned the item before you left the United States.

For more about duties, restricted items, and other information about international travel, check out U.S. Customs and Border Protection's online brochure, *Know Before You Go*. You can also file complaints on the U.S. Customs and Border Protection Web site, listed below.

🄵 **U.S. Customs and Border Protection** ✉ For inquiries and complaints, 1300 Pennsylvania Ave. NW, Washington, DC 20229 ⊕ www.cbp.gov ☎ 877/227–5551 or 202/354–1000.

DISABILITIES & ACCESSIBILITY

Facilities for travelers with disabilities in Scandinavia are generally good, and most major tourist offices offer special booklets and brochures on travel and accommodations. Most Scandinavian countries have organizations that offer advice to travelers with disabilities and can give information on public and local transportation, sights and museums, hotels, and special-interest tours. Notify and make all local and public transportation and hotel reservations in advance to ensure a smooth trip.

🄵 Local Resources **DHR De Handikappades Riksförbund** ✉ Box 47305, Katrinebergsvägen 6, 100 74 Stockholm, Sweden ☎ 46/86858000 ⊕ www.dhr.se/english.htm.

LODGING

Best Western in Stockholm has properties with wheelchair-accessible rooms. If wheelchair-accessible rooms on other floors are not available, ground-floor rooms are provided.

▸ Wheelchair-Friendly Chain **Best Western** 📞 800/528-1234.

RESERVATIONS

When discussing accessibility with an operator or reservations agent, ask hard questions. Are there any stairs, inside *or* out? Are there grab bars next to the toilet *and* in the shower/tub? How wide is the doorway to the room? To the bathroom? For the most extensive facilities meeting the latest legal specifications, opt for newer accommodations. If you reserve through a toll-free number, consider also calling the hotel's local number to confirm the information from the central reservations office. Get confirmation in writing when you can.

SIGHTS & ATTRACTIONS

Although most major attractions in Stockholm present no problems, winding cobblestone streets, especially in the Gamla Stan (Old Town), may be challenging for travelers with disabilities.

TRANSPORTATION

The U.S. Department of Transportation Aviation Consumer Protection Division's online publication *New Horizons: Information for the Air Traveler with a Disability* offers advice for travelers with a disability, and outlines basic rights. Visit DisabilityInfo.gov for general information.

With advance notice most airlines, buses, and trains can arrange assistance for those requiring extra help with boarding. Contact each company you will be using at least one week in advance or, ideally, when you book.

Confirming ahead is especially important when planning travel to less-populated regions. Not all of the smaller planes and ferries often used in such areas are accessible.

▸ Information & Complaints **Aviation Consumer Protection Division** (⇨ Air Travel) for airline-related problems; ⊕ airconsumer.ost.dot.gov/publications/horizons.htm for airline travel advice and rights. **Departmental Office of Civil Rights** ⊠ For general inquiries, U.S. Department of Transportation, S-30, 400 7th St. SW, Room 10215, Washington, DC 20590 📞 202/366-4648, 202/366-8538 TTY 🖶 202/366-9371 ⊕ www.dotcr.ost.dot.gov. **Disability Rights Section** ⊠ NYAV, U.S. Department of Justice, Civil Rights Division, 950 Pennsylvania Ave. NW, Washington, DC 20530 📞 800/514-0301, 202/514-0301 ADA information line, 800/514-0383 TTY, 202/514-0383 TTY ⊕ www.ada.gov. **U.S. Department of Transportation Hotline** 📞 For disability-related air-travel problems, 800/778-4838 or 800/455-9880 TTY.

TRAVEL AGENCIES

In the United States, the Americans with Disabilities Act requires that travel firms serve the needs of all travelers. Some agencies specialize in working with people with disabilities.

▸ Travelers with Mobility Problems **Access Adventures/B. Roberts Travel** ⊠ 1876 East Ave., Rochester, NY 14610 📞 800/444-6540 ⊕ www.brobertstravel.com, run by a former physical-rehabilitation counselor. **CareVacations** ⊠ No. 5, 5110-50 Ave., Leduc, Alberta T9E 6V4, Canada 📞 877/478-7827 or 780/986-6404 🖶 780/986-8332 ⊕ www.carevacations.com, for group tours and cruise vacations. **Flying Wheels Travel** ⊠ 143 W. Bridge St., Box 382, Owatonna, MN 55060 📞 507/451-5005 🖶 507/451-1685 ⊕ www.flyingwheelstravel.com.

DISCOUNTS & DEALS

Be a smart shopper and compare all your options before making decisions. A plane ticket bought with a promotional coupon from travel clubs, coupon books, and direct-mail offers or purchased on the Internet may not be cheaper than the least-expensive fare from a discount ticket agency. And always keep in mind that what you get is just as important as what you save.

DISCOUNT RESERVATIONS

To save money, look into discount reservations services with Web sites and toll-free numbers, which use their buying power to get a better price on hotels, airline tickets (⇨ Air Travel), even car rentals. When booking a room, always **call the hotel's local toll-free number** (if one is available) rather than the central reservations number—you'll often get a better price. Always ask about special packages or corporate rates.

When shopping for the best deal on hotels and car rentals, look for guaranteed exchange rates, which protect you against a falling dollar. With your rate locked in, you won't pay more, even if the price goes up in the local currency.

Hotel Rooms **Accommodations Express** ☎ 800/444-7666 or 800/277-1064. **Hotels.com** ☎ 800/246-8357 ⊕ www.hotels.com. **Steigenberger Reservation Service** ☎ 800/223-5652 ⊕ www.srs-worldhotels.com. **Turbotrip.com** ☎ 800/473-7829 ⊕ w3.turbotrip.com.

PACKAGE DEALS

Don't confuse packages and guided tours. When you buy a package, you travel on your own, just as though you had planned the trip yourself. Fly/drive packages, which combine airfare and car rental, are often a good deal. In cities, ask the local visitor's bureau about hotel and local transportation packages that include tickets to major museum exhibits or other special events. If you **buy a rail/drive pass,** you may save on train tickets and car rentals. All Eurail-Pass holders get a discount on Eurostar fares through the Channel Tunnel and often receive reduced rates for buses, hotels, ferries, sightseeing cruises, and car rentals. Also check rates for Scanrail Passes (⇨ Train Travel).

EATING & DRINKING

Sweden's major cities offer a full range of dining choices, from traditional to international restaurants. Outside the cities, restaurants are usually more local in influence, and most use good, fresh ingredients. Investments in training and successes in international competitions have spurred restaurant quality to fantastic heights in Sweden, and it easily competes with other major European countries in the gourmet stakes. It is worth remembering, though, that for many years eating out was prohibitively expensive for many Swedes, giving rise to a home socializing culture that still exists today. For this reason many smaller towns and rural areas are bereft of anything approaching a varied restaurant scene. The restaurants we list are the cream of the crop in each price category. Properties indicated by an ✕☷ are lodging

establishments whose restaurant warrants a special trip.

CUTTING COSTS

Restaurant meals are big-ticket items throughout Scandinavia, but there are ways to keep the cost of eating down. Take full advantage of the large buffet breakfast often included in the cost of a hotel room. At lunch look for a "menu" that offers a two- or three-course meal for a set price, often including bread and salad, or limit yourself to a hearty appetizer. Some restaurants now include a trip to the salad bar in the dinner price. At dinner pay careful attention to the price of wine and drinks, since the high tax on alcohol raises these costs considerably. For more information on affordable eating, *see* Money Matters.

CATEGORY	COST*
$$$$	over SKr 420
$$$	SKr 250–SKr 420
$$	SKr 150–SKr 250
$	SKr 100–SKr 150
¢	under SKr 100

per person for a main course at dinner

MEALS & SPECIALTIES

The surrounding oceans and plentiful inland lakes and streams provide Scandinavian countries with an abundance of fresh fish and seafood: salmon, herring, trout, and seafood delicacies are mainstays and are prepared in countless ways. Elk, deer, reindeer, and lamb feed in relatively unspoiled areas in Iceland and northern Norway, Sweden, and Finland and have the succulent taste of wild game. Berries and mushrooms are still harvested from the forests; sausage appears in a thousand forms, as do potatoes and other root vegetables such as turnips, radishes, rutabagas, and carrots. Some northern tastes may seem a bit unusual, such as the fondness for pickled and fermented fish—to be sampled carefully at first—and a universal obsession with sweet pastries, ice cream, and chocolate.

Also novel for the visitor might be the use of fruit in main dishes and soups, of sour milk on breakfast cereal, and of preserved fish paste as a spread for crackers, along with the ever-present tasty whole-grain crispbreads and hearty ryes. The Swedish *smörgåsbord* (a kind of buffet meal) is less common these days but is still the traveling diner's best bet for a good meal. A smörgåsbord usually comes with a wide range of cheeses, fresh fish, and vegetables alongside meat and breads and other starches.

MEALTIMES
Unless otherwise noted, the restaurants listed in this guide are open daily for lunch and dinner.

Most Swedes take all their meals early, particularly outside urban areas. It is not uncommon for lunch to be taken at 11 AM and dinner at 6 PM. For this reason many restaurants close their kitchens earlier than their southern European counterparts. Lovers of late dining should stick to the cities.

RESERVATIONS & DRESS
Reservations are always a good idea; we mention them only when they're essential or not accepted. Book as far ahead as you can, and reconfirm as soon as you arrive. (Large parties should always call ahead to check the reservations policy.) We mention dress only when men are required to wear a jacket or a jacket and tie.

WINE, BEER & SPIRITS
In Scandinavia the markup on alcoholic beverages by restaurants is often very high—with drinks selling for as much as four times the standard retail price.

ELECTRICITY
To use electric-powered equipment purchased in the United States or Canada, **bring a converter and adapter.** The electrical current in Scandinavia is 220 volts, 50 cycles alternating current (AC); wall outlets take Continental-type plugs, with two round prongs.

If your appliances are dual-voltage, you'll need only an adapter. Don't use 110-volt outlets marked FOR SHAVERS ONLY for high-wattage appliances such as blow-dryers. Most laptops operate equally well on 110 and 220 volts and so require only an adapter.

EMBASSIES
🏠 Australia ✉ Sergels torg 12 ☎ 08/6132900 ⊕ www.sweden.embassy.gov.au.
🏠 Canada ✉ Tegelbacken 4, Box 16129, 103 23 Stockholm ☎ 08/4533000.
🏠 New Zealand ✉ Sturplan 2, Stockholm ☎ 08/6112625.
🏠 U.K. ✉ Skarpög. 68, 115 93 Stockholm ☎ 08/6713000 ⊕ www.britishembassy.se.
🏠 U.S. ✉ Strandv. 101, Dag Hammarskjölds väg 31, 115 89 Stockholm ☎ 08/7835300 ⊕ stockholm.usembassy.gov.

EMERGENCIES
Anywhere in Sweden, dial 112 for emergency assistance.

GAY & LESBIAN TRAVEL
🏠 Gay- & Lesbian-Friendly Travel Agencies **Different Roads Travel** ✉ 1017 N. LaCienega Blvd., Suite 308, West Hollywood, CA 90069 ☎ 800/429–8747 or 310/289–6000 (Ext. 14 for both) 🖷 310/855–0323 ✎ lgernert@tzell.com. **Kennedy Travel** ✉ 130 W. 42nd St., Suite 401, New York, NY 10036 ☎ 800/237–7433 or 212/840–8659 🖷 212/730–2269 ⊕ www.kennedytravel.com. **Now, Voyager** ✉ 4406 18th St., San Francisco, CA 94114 ☎ 800/255–6951 or 415/626–1169 🖷 415/626–8626 ⊕ www.nowvoyager.com. **Skylink Travel and Tour/Flying Dutchmen Travel** ✉ 1455 N. Dutton Ave., Suite A, Santa Rosa, CA 95401 ☎ 800/225–5759 or 707/546–9888 🖷 707/636–0951; serving lesbian travelers.

HOLIDAYS
In general, all Scandinavian countries celebrate New Year's Eve and New Year's Day, Good Friday, Easter Sunday and Easter Monday, May Day (May 1; celebrated as Labor Day in many countries), Midsummer Eve and Midsummer Day (over the weekend that falls between June 20 and June 26), and Christmas (as well as Christmas Eve and Boxing Day, the day after Christmas. In addition, Sweden has the following holidays: Epiphany, January 6; Ascension (39th day after Easter); and All Saints' Day (observed the first Saturday after October 30).

On major holidays such as Christmas, most shops close or operate on a Sunday schedule. On the eves of such holidays, many shops are also closed all day or are open with reduced hours.

On May Day the city centers are usually full of people, celebrations, and parades. During midsummer, at the end of June, locals flock to the lakes and countryside to celebrate the beginning of long summer days with bonfires and other festivities.

INSURANCE

The most useful travel-insurance plan is a comprehensive policy that includes coverage for trip cancellation and interruption, default, trip delay, and medical expenses (with a waiver for preexisting conditions).

Without insurance you'll lose all or most of your money if you cancel your trip, regardless of the reason. Default insurance covers you if your tour operator, airline, or cruise line goes out of business—the chances of which have been increasing. Trip-delay covers expenses that arise because of bad weather or mechanical delays. Study the fine print when comparing policies.

If you're traveling internationally, a key component of travel insurance is coverage for medical bills incurred if you get sick on the road. Such expenses aren't generally covered by Medicare or private policies. U.K. residents can buy a travel-insurance policy valid for most vacations taken during the year in which it's purchased (but check preexisting-condition coverage). British and Australian citizens need extra medical coverage when traveling overseas.

Always **buy travel policies directly from the insurance company**; if you buy them from a cruise line, airline, or tour operator that goes out of business you probably won't be covered for the agency or operator's default, a major risk. Before making any purchase, review your existing health and home-owner's policies to find what they cover away from home.

🖪 Travel Insurers In the United States: **Access America** ✉ 2805 N. Parham Rd., Richmond, VA 23294 ☎ 800/284-8300 📠 800/346-9265 or 804/673-1469 ⊕ www.accessamerica.com. **Travel Guard International** ✉ 1145 Clark St., Stevens Point, WI 54481 ☎ 800/826-1300 or 715/345-1041 📠 800/955-8785 or 715/345-1990 ⊕ www.travelguard.com. 🖪 In the United Kingdom: **Association of British Insurers** ✉ 51 Gresham St., London EC2V 7HQ ☎ 020/76003333 📠 020/76968999 ⊕ www.abi.org.uk. In Canada: **RBC Insurance** ✉ 6880 Financial Dr., Mississauga, Ontario L5N 7Y5 ☎ 800/387-4357 or 905/816-2559 📠 888/298-6458 ⊕ www.rbcinsurance.com. In Australia: **Insurance Council of Australia** ✉ Level 3, 56 Pitt St., Sydney, NSW 2000 ☎ 02/9253-5100 📠 02/9253-5111 ⊕ www.ica.com.au. In New Zealand: **Insurance Council of New Zealand** ✉ Level 7, 111-115 Customhouse Quay, Box 474, Wellington ☎ 04/472-5230 📠 04/473-3011 ⊕ www.icnz.org.nz.

LANGUAGE

Swedish is closely related to Danish and Norwegian. After *z,* the Swedish alphabet has three extra letters, *å, ä,* and *ö,* something to bear in mind when using the phone book. Another phone-book alphabetical oddity is that *v* and *w* are interchangeable; Wittström, for example, comes before Vittviks, not after. And after all that, you'll be happy to know that most Swedes are happy to speak English.

LODGING

The lodgings we list are the cream of the crop in each price category. We always list the facilities that are available—but we don't specify whether they cost extra: when pricing accommodations, always ask what's included and what costs extra.

Sweden offers a variety of accommodations, from simple bed-and-breakfasts, campsites, and hostels to hotels of the highest international standard. In the larger cities lodging ranges from first-class business hotels run by SAS, Sheraton, and Scandic to good-quality tourist-class hotels, such as RESO, Best Western, Scandic Budget, and Sweden Hotels, to a wide variety of single-entrepreneur hotels. In the countryside look for independently run inns and motels, known as guesthouses. In addition, farm holidays increasingly have become available to tourists, and Sweden has organizations that can help plan stays in the countryside.

Before you leave home, **ask your travel agent about discounts** (⇨ Hotels *under* Lodging), including summer hotel checks for Best Western, Scandic, and Inter Nor hotels, and enormous year-round rebates at SAS hotels for travelers over 65. All EuroClass (business-class) passengers can get discounts of at least 10% at SAS hotels when they book through SAS.

Two things about hotels usually surprise North Americans: the relatively limited dimensions of Scandinavian beds and the generous size of Scandinavian breakfasts. Scandinavian double beds are often about 60 inches wide or slightly less, close in size to the U.S. queen size. King-size beds (72 inches wide) are difficult to find and, if available, require special reservations.

Older hotels may have some rooms described as "double" that in fact have one double bed plus one foldout sofa big enough for two people. This arrangement is occasionally called a combi-room but is being phased out.

Many older hotels, particularly the country inns and independently run smaller hotels in the cities, do not have private bathrooms. Inquire about this ahead of time if this is important to you.

Scandinavian breakfasts resemble what many people would call lunch, usually including breads, cheeses, marmalade, hams, lunch meats, eggs, juice, cereal, milk, and coffee. Generally, the farther north you go, the larger the breakfasts become.

Make reservations whenever possible. Even countryside inns, which usually have space, are sometimes packed with vacationing Europeans.

Assume that hotels operate on the European Plan (EP, with no meals) unless we specify that they use the Continental Plan (CP, with a Continental breakfast), Breakfast Plan (BP, with a full breakfast), Modified American Plan (MAP, with breakfast and dinner), or the Full American Plan (FAP, with all meals).

CATEGORY	COST*
$$$$	over SKr 2,900
$$$	SKr 2,300–SKr 2,900
$$	SKr 1,500–SKr 2,300
$	SKr 1,000–SK2 1,500
¢	under SKr 1,000

All prices are for two people in a standard double room.

APARTMENT & VILLA [OR HOUSE] RENTALS

If you want a home base that's roomy enough for a family and comes with cooking facilities, consider a furnished rental. These can save you money, especially if you're traveling with a group. Home-exchange directories sometimes list rentals as well as exchanges.

With 250 chalet villages with high standards, Sweden enjoys popularity with its chalet accommodations, often arranged on the spot at tourist offices. Many are organized under the auspices of the Swedish Touring Association (STF). DFDS Seaways in Göteborg arranges package deals that combine a ferry trip from Britain across the North Sea and a stay in a chalet village.

International Agents **Hideaways International** ✉ 767 Islington St., Portsmouth, NH 03801 ☎ 800/843-4433 or 603/430-4433 🖷 603/430-4444 ⊕ www.hideaways.com, annual membership $185. Rental Contacts **DFDS Seaways** ☎ 08705/333-111 within the U.K. **Swedish Touring Association** ☎ 08/4632100 🖷 08/6781938 ⊕ www.meravsverige.se.

CAMPING

There are 760 registered campsites nationwide, many close to uncrowded swimming places and with fishing, boating, or canoeing; they may also offer bicycle rentals. Prices range from SKr 70 to SKr 130 per 24-hour period. Many campsites also offer accommodations in log cabins at various prices, depending on the facilities offered. Most are open between June and September, but about 200 remain open in winter for skiing and skating enthusiasts. Sveriges Campingvårdernas Riksförbund (Swedish Campsite Owners' Association or SCR) publishes, in English, an abbreviated list of sites; contact the office for a free copy.

Sveriges Campingvårdernas Riksförbund 🕮 Box 255, 451 17 Uddevalla ☎ 0522/642440 🖷 0522/642430 ⊕ www.camping.se.

CUTTING COSTS

Ask about high and low seasons when making reservations since different countries define their tourist seasons differently. Some hotels lower prices during tourist season, whereas others raise them during the same period. In Sweden many hotels offer lower prices on weekends and during the summer months, some by as much as 50%.

If you are visiting a city in Sweden it is worth looking at accommodation outside the city limits. This is where you will find the best budget lodging and good transport links and the relatively small Swedish cities means a trip downtown never takes too long.

Hotels in Sweden offer Inn Checks, or prepaid hotel vouchers, for accommodations ranging from first-class hotels to country cottages. These vouchers, which must be purchased from travel agents or from the Scandinavian Tourist Board before departure, are sold individually and in packets for as many nights as needed and offer savings of up to 50%. Most countries also offer summer bargains for foreign tourists; winter bargains can be even greater. For further information about Scandinavian hotel vouchers, contact the Scandinavian Tourist Board.

ProSkandinavia checks can be used in 400 hotels across Scandinavia (excluding Iceland) for savings up to 50% for reservations made usually no earlier than 24 hours before arrival, although some hotels allow earlier bookings. One check costs € 38. Two checks will pay for a double room at a hotel, one check for a room in a cottage. The checks can be bought at many travel agencies in Scandinavia or ordered from **ProSkandinavia** (✉ Akersgt. 11, N-0158 Oslo, Norway ☎ 47/22–41–13–13 🖷 47/22–42–06–57 ⊕ www.proskandinavia. no).

FARM & COTTAGE HOLIDAYS

The old-fashioned farm or countryside holiday, long a staple for Scandinavian city dwellers, is becoming increasingly available to tourists. In general, you can choose to stay on the farm itself and even participate in daily activities, or you can opt to rent a private housekeeping cottage. Contact the local tourist board or Swedish Farm Holidays for details.

🏠 **Swedish Farm Holidays** 🏠 Box 8, 668 21 Ed, Sweden ☎ 46/53412075 🖷 46/53461011 ⊕ www.bopalantgard.org. **Upplev Landet** 🏠 105 33 Stock-

holm, Sweden ☎ 771/573–573 ⊕ www.upplevlandet. se ⊕ www.stugguiden.se.

HOME EXCHANGES

If you would like to exchange your home for someone else's, join a home-exchange organization, which will send you its updated listings of available exchanges for a year and will include your own listing in at least one of them. It's up to you to make specific arrangements.

🏠 Exchange Clubs **HomeLink USA** ✉ 2937 N.W. 9th Terr., Wilton Manors, FL 33311 ☎ 800/638-3841 or 954/566-2687 🖷 954/566-2783 ⊕ www. homelink.org; $75 yearly for a listing and online access; $45 additional to receive directories. **Intervac U.S.** ✉ 30 Corte San Fernando, Tiburon, CA 94920 ☎ 800/756-4663 🖷 415/435-7440 ⊕ www. intervacus.com; $128 yearly for a listing, online access, and a catalog; $68 without catalog.

HOSTELS

No matter what your age, you can save on lodging costs by staying at hostels. In some 4,500 locations in more than 70 countries around the world, Hostelling International (HI), the umbrella group for a number of national youth-hostel associations, offers single-sex, dorm-style beds and, at many hostels, rooms for couples and family accommodations. Membership in any HI national hostel association, open to travelers of all ages, allows you to stay in HI-affiliated hostels at member rates; one-year membership is about $28 for adults (C$35 for a two-year minimum membership in Canada, £15 in the United Kingdom, A$52 in Australia, and NZ$40 in New Zealand); hostels charge about $10–$30 per night. Members have priority if the hostel is full; they're also eligible for discounts around the world, even on rail and bus travel in some countries.

🏠 Organizations **Hostelling International–USA** ✉ 8401 Colesville Rd., Suite 600, Silver Spring, MD 20910 ☎ 301/495-1240 🖷 301/495-6697 ⊕ www. hiusa.org. **Hostelling International–Canada** ✉ 205 Catherine St., Suite 400, Ottawa, Ontario K2P 1C3 ☎ 800/663-5777 or 613/237-7884 🖷 613/237-7868 ⊕ www.hihostels.ca. **YHA England and Wales** ✉ Trevelyan House, Dimple Rd., Matlock, Derbyshire DE4 3YH, U.K. ☎ 0870/870-8808, 0870/770-8868, or 0162/959-2600 🖷 0870/770-6127

⊕ www.yha.org.uk. **YHA Australia** ⊠ 422 Kent St., Sydney, NSW 2001 ☎ 02/9261-1111 🖷 02/9261-1969 ⊕ www.yha.com.au. **YHA New Zealand** ⊠ Level 1, Moorhouse City, 166 Moorhouse Ave., Box 436, Christchurch ☎ 0800/278299 or 03/379-9970 🖷 03/365-4476 ⊕ www.yha.org.nz.

HOTELS

Major hotels in larger cities cater mainly to business clientele and can be expensive; weekend rates are more reasonable and can even be as low as half the normal price. Prices are normally on a per-room basis and include all taxes and service charges and usually breakfast. Apart from the more modest inns and the cheapest budget establishments, private baths and showers are standard.

Whatever their size, almost all Swedish hotels provide scrupulously clean accommodations and courteous service. Since many Swedes go on vacation in July and through early August, make your hotel reservations in advance, especially if staying outside the city areas during that time. Some hotels close during the winter holidays as well; call ahead for information.

An official annual guide, *Hotels in Sweden,* published by and available free from the Swedish Travel and Tourism Council, gives comprehensive information about hotel facilities and prices. Countryside Hotels comprises 35 select resort hotels, some of them restored manor houses or centuries-old inns. Hotellcentralen is an independent agency that makes advance telephone reservations for any Swedish hotel at no cost. The Sweden Hotels group has about 100 independently owned hotels and its own classification scheme—with a letter assigned according to a hotel's facilities.

Major hotel groups like Best Western, Radisson SAS, RESO, Scandic, and Sweden Hotels also have their own central reservations services.

🚩 **Countryside Hotels** ⌂ Store Wäsby, 194 37 Upplands Väsby ☎ 8590/32732 🖷 8590/340 59 ⊕ www.countrysidehotels.se. **Hotellcentralen** ⊠ Centralstation, 111 20 ☎ 08/50828508 🖷 08/7918666. **Radisson SAS** ☎ 888/201-1718 in the U.S. and Canada, 800/374411 in the U.K. ⊕ www.

radisson.com. **Scandic** ☎ 08/51751700 ⊕ www.scandic-hotels.se. **Sweden Hotels** ☎ 020/770000. 🚩 Toll-Free Numbers **Best Western** ☎ 800/780-7234 in the U.S. and Canada, 800/393130 in the U.K. ⊕ www.bestwestern.com. **Choice** ☎ 877/424-6423 in the U.S. and Canada, 800/444444 in the U.K. ⊕ www.choicehotels.com. **Comfort Inn** ☎ 877/424-6423 in the U.S. and Canada, 800/444444 in the U.K. ⊕ www.choicehotels.com. **Hilton** ☎ 800/445-8667 in the U.S. and Canada, 08705/909-090 in the U.K. ⊕ www.hilton.com. **Holiday Inn** ☎ 800/315-2621 ⊕ www.ichotelsgroup.com. **Quality Inn** ☎ 800/424-6423 ⊕ www.choicehotels.com. **Sheraton** ☎ 877/477-4674 in the U.S. and Canada, 0870/400-9670 in the U.K. ⊕ www.starwood.com/sheraton.

MAIL & SHIPPING

POSTAL RATES

Postcards and letters up to 20 grams can be mailed for SKr 8 within Sweden, SKr 10 to destinations within Europe, and SKr 10 to the United States and all other countries.

MONEY MATTERS

Prices throughout this guide are given for adults. Substantially reduced fees are almost always available for children, students, and senior citizens. For information on taxes, *see* Taxes.

Here is an idea what you'll pay for food and drink in Sweden: a cup of coffee, SKr 25–SKr 35; a beer, SKr 40–SKr 55; a mineral water, SKr 12–SKr 25; a cheese roll, SKr 25–SKr 50; pepper steak à la carte, SKr 120–SKr 190; a cheeseburger, SKr 60; and pizza, starting at SKr 40.

Be aware that sales taxes can be very high, but foreigners can get some refunds by shopping at tax-free stores (⇨ Taxes). City Cards can save you transportation and entrance fees in many of the larger cities.

You can **reduce the cost of food by planning.** Breakfast is often included in your hotel bill; if not, you may wish to buy fruit, sweet rolls, and a beverage for a picnic breakfast. Electrical devices for hot coffee or tea should be bought abroad. When purchasing, make sure they conform to the local current.

Opt for a restaurant lunch instead of dinner, since the latter tends to be significantly more expensive. Instead of beer or wine, **drink tap water**—liquor can cost four times the price of the same brand in a store—but do specify tap water, as the term *water* can refer to soft drinks and bottled water, which are also expensive. Throughout Scandinavia the tip is included in the cost of your meal.

In most of Scandinavia, liquor and strong beer (over 3% alcohol) can be purchased only in state-owned shops, at very high prices, during weekday business hours, usually 9:30–6, and in some areas on Saturday until mid-afternoon. A midsize bottle of whiskey in Sweden, for example, can easily cost SKr 250 (about $35). Weaker beers and ciders are usually available in grocery stores in Scandinavia.

ATMS

The 1,200 or so blue Bankomat cash dispensers nationwide have been adapted to take some foreign cards, including Master-Card, Visa, and bank cards linked to the Cirrus network. You may encounter some complications on remote machines. It's best to use those that are next to major bank offices. For more information contact Bankomatcentralen in Stockholm or your local bank. American Express has cash and traveler's check dispensers; there's also an office at Stockholm's Arlanda Airport.

🖪 **American Express** ✉ Birger Jarlsg. 1 ☎ 020/793211 toll-free. **Bankomatcentralen/CEK AB** ☎ 08/7255700.

CREDIT CARDS

Throughout this guide, the following abbreviations are used: **AE,** American Express; **DC,** Diners Club; **MC,** MasterCard; and **V,** Visa.

CURRENCY

The unit of currency is the krona (plural kronor), which is divided into 100 öre and is written as SKr or SEK. Coins come in SKr 1, SKr 5, and SKr 10. Bank notes come in denominations of SKr 20, SKr 50, SKr 100, SKr 500, and SKr 1,000. **At press time the exchange rates for the krona** were SKr 7.9 to the U.S. dollar, SKr 6.7 to the Canadian dollar, SKr 13.8 to the British pound sterling, SKr 9.4 to the euro, SKr 5.9 to the Australian dollar, SKr 5.5 to the New Zealand dollar, and SKr 1.2 to the South African rand.

CURRENCY EXCHANGE

Traveler's checks and foreign currency can be exchanged at banks all over Sweden and at post offices displaying the NB EX-CHANGE sign. Be sure to have your passport with you when exchanging money at a bank.

For the most favorable rates, **change money through banks.** Although ATM transaction fees may be higher abroad than at home, ATM rates are excellent because they're based on wholesale rates offered only by major banks. You won't do as well at exchange booths in airports or rail and bus stations, in hotels, in restaurants, or in stores. To avoid lines at airport exchange booths, get a bit of local currency before you leave home.

🖪 Exchange Services **International Currency Express** ✉ 427 N. Camden Dr., Suite F, Beverly Hills, CA 90210 ☎ 888/278-6628 orders 🖷 310/278-6410 ⊕ www.foreignmoney.com. **Travel Ex Currency Services** ☎ 800/287-7362 orders and retail locations ⊕ www.travelex.com.

TRAVELER'S CHECKS

Do you need traveler's checks? It depends on where you're headed. If you're going to rural areas and small towns, go with cash; traveler's checks are best used in cities. Lost or stolen checks can usually be replaced within 24 hours. To ensure a speedy refund, buy your own traveler's checks—don't let someone else pay for them: irregularities like this can cause delays. The person who bought the checks should make the call to request a refund.

PACKING

In your carry-on luggage, pack an extra pair of eyeglasses or contact lenses and enough of any medication you take to last a few days longer than the entire trip. You may also ask your doctor to write a spare prescription using the drug's generic name, as brand names may vary from country to country. In luggage to be checked, **never pack prescription drugs, valuables, or un-**

developed film. And don't forget to carry with you the addresses of offices that handle refunds of lost traveler's checks. Check *Fodor's How to Pack* (available at online retailers and bookstores everywhere) for more tips.

To avoid customs and security delays, carry medications in their original packaging. Don't pack any sharp objects in your carry-on luggage, including knives of any size or material, scissors, nail clippers, and corkscrews, or anything else that might arouse suspicion.

To avoid having your checked luggage chosen for hand inspection, don't cram bags full. The U.S. Transportation Security Administration suggests packing shoes on top and placing personal items you don't want touched in clear plastic bags.

CHECKING LUGGAGE

You're allowed to carry aboard one bag and one personal article, such as a purse or a laptop computer. Make sure what you carry on fits under your seat or in the overhead bin. Get to the gate early, so you can board as soon as possible, before the overhead bins fill up.

Baggage allowances vary by carrier, destination, and ticket class. On international flights, you're usually allowed to check two bags weighing up to 70 pounds (32 kilograms) each, although a few airlines allow checked bags of up to 88 pounds (40 kilograms) in first class. Some international carriers don't allow more than 66 pounds (30 kilograms) per bag in business class and 44 pounds (20 kilograms) in economy. If you're flying to or through the United Kingdom, your luggage cannot exceed 70 pounds (32 kilograms) per bag. On domestic flights, the limit is usually 50 to 70 pounds (23 to 32 kilograms) per bag. In general, carry-on bags shouldn't exceed 40 pounds (18 kilograms). Most airlines won't accept bags that weigh more than 100 pounds (45 kilograms) on domestic or international flights. Expect to pay a fee for baggage that exceeds weight limits. Check baggage restrictions with your carrier before you pack.

Airline liability for baggage is limited to $2,500 per person on flights within the United States. On international flights it amounts to $9.07 per pound or $20 per kilogram for checked baggage (roughly $640 per 70-pound bag), with a maximum of $634.90 per piece, and $400 per passenger for unchecked baggage. You can buy additional coverage at check-in for about $10 per $1,000 of coverage, but it often excludes a rather extensive list of items, shown on your airline ticket.

Before departure, itemize your bags' contents and their worth, and label the bags with your name, address, and phone number. (If you use your home address, cover it so potential thieves can't see it readily.) Include a label inside each bag and **pack a copy of your itinerary.** At check-in, make sure each bag is correctly tagged with the destination airport's three-letter code. Because some checked bags will be opened for hand inspection, the U.S. Transportation Security Administration recommends that you leave luggage unlocked or use the plastic locks offered at check-in. TSA screeners place an inspection notice inside searched bags, which are resealed with a special lock.

If your bag has been searched and contents are missing or damaged, file a claim with the TSA Consumer Response Center as soon as possible. If your bags arrive damaged or fail to arrive at all, file a written report with the airline before leaving the airport.

🔁 **Complaints U.S. Transportation Security Administration Contact Center** ☎ 866/289-9673 ⊕ www.tsa.gov.

PASSPORTS & VISAS

When traveling internationally, carry your passport even if you don't need one. Not only is it the best form of ID, but it's also being required more and more. As of December 31, 2005, for instance, Americans need a passport to reenter the country from Bermuda, the Caribbean, and Panama. Such requirements also affect reentry from Canada and Mexico by air and sea (as of December 31, 2006) and land (as of December 31, 2007). **Make two photocopies of the data page** (one for someone at home and another for you, carried separately from your passport). If you lose your passport, promptly call the nearest embassy or consulate and the local police.

U.S. passport applications for children under age 14 require consent from both parents or legal guardians; both parents must appear together to sign the application. If only one parent appears, he or she must submit a written statement from the other parent authorizing passport issuance for the child. A parent with sole authority must present evidence of it when applying; acceptable documentation includes the child's certified birth certificate listing only the applying parent, a court order specifically permitting this parent's travel with the child, or a death certificate for the non-applying parent. Application forms and instructions are available on the Web site of the U.S. State Department's Bureau of Consular Affairs (⊕ www.travel.state.gov).

ENTERING SCANDINAVIA
All U.S. citizens, even infants, need only a valid passport to enter any Scandinavian country for stays of up to three months.

PASSPORT OFFICES
The best time to apply for a passport or to renew is in fall and winter. Before any trip, check your passport's expiration date, and, if necessary, renew it as soon as possible.

🔢 Australian Citizens **Passports Australia** Australian Department of Foreign Affairs and Trade 🖀 131-232 ⊕ www.passports.gov.au.

🔢 Canadian Citizens **Passport Office** ✉ To mail in applications: 70 Cremazie St., Gatineau, Québec J8Y 3P2 🖀 800/567-6868 or 819/994-3500 ⊕ www.ppt.gc.ca.

🔢 New Zealand Citizens **New Zealand Passports Office** 🖀 0800/225050 or 04/474-8100 ⊕ www.passports.govt.nz.

🔢 U.K. Citizens **U.K. Passport Service** 🖀 0870/521-0410 ⊕ www.passport.gov.uk.

🔢 U.S. Citizens **National Passport Information Center** 🖀 877/487-2778, 888/874-7793 TDD/TTY ⊕ www.travel.state.gov.

SENIOR-CITIZEN TRAVEL
To qualify for age-related discounts, mention your senior-citizen status up front when booking hotel reservations (not when checking out) and before you're seated in restaurants (not when paying the bill). Be sure to have identification on hand. When renting a car, ask about promotional car-rental discounts, which can be cheaper than senior-citizen rates.

TRAIN TRAVEL
Seniors over 60 are entitled to discount tickets (often as much as 50% off) on buses, trains, and ferries throughout Scandinavia, as well as reductions on special City Cards. Eurail offers discounts on Scanrail and Eurail train passes (⇨ Train Travel).

🔢 Educational Programs **Elderhostel** ✉ 11 Ave. de Lafayette, Boston, MA 02111 🖀 877/426-8056, 978/323-4141 international callers, 877/426-2167 TTY 🖳 877/426-2166 ⊕ www.elderhostel.org. **Interhostel** ✉ University of New Hampshire, 6 Garrison Ave., Durham, NH 03824 🖀 800/733-9753 or 603/862-1147 🖳 603/862-1113 ⊕ www.learn.unh.edu.

SHOPPING
Prices in Scandinavia are never low, but quality is high, and specialties are sometimes less expensive here than elsewhere. Scandinavian design in both furniture and glassware is world renowned. Swedish crystal, Icelandic sweaters, Danish Lego blocks and furniture, Norwegian furs, and Finnish fabrics—these are just a few of the items to look for. Keep an eye out for sales, called *rea* in Swedish. Most shops in Sweden will gift-wrap items for you if you ask.

SPORTS & OUTDOORS
BOATING & SAILING
Swedes love to be on the water, whether sailing in the Stockholm archipelago or kayaking along the rocky west coast. Swedish Touring Association (STF) publishes a Swedish-language annual guide to all the country's marinas. Svenska Kanotförbundet (Swedish Canoeing Association) publishes a similar booklet. For information on sailing throughout the country, including information on how to rent or charter boats yourself, contact the Svenska Seglarförbundet (Swedish Sailing Association).

🔢 **Svenska Kanotförbundet** (Swedish Canoeing Association) ✉ Idrotts Hus, 123 87 Farsta 🖀 08/6056565 ⊕ www.svenskidrott.se/kanot. **Svenska**

Seglarförbundet (Swedish Sailing Association)
✉ Af Pontins väg 6, 115 21 Stockholm ☎ 08/4590990
⊕ www.ssf.se.

GOLF

Sweden has 365 golf clubs; you can even play by the light of the midnight sun at Boden, in the far north, and there are a number of ice courses, too, offering winter challenges. Wherever you play, all Swedish golf courses require you to show a handicap certificate. Svenska Golfförbundet (the Swedish Golfing Association) publishes an annual guide in Swedish; it costs around SKr 100, including postage.

🗹 **Svenska Golfförbundet** ⊕ Box 84, 182 11 Danderyd ☎ 08/6221500 🖶 08/7558439 ⊕ www.golf.se.

SKIING

There are plenty of downhill and cross-country facilities in Sweden. The best-known resorts are in the country's western mountains: Åre, in the north, with 29 lifts; Idre Fjäll, to the south of Åre, offering accommodations for 10,000; and Sälen, in the folklore region of Dalarna. You can ski through May at Riksgränsen, in the far north. Most of Sweden's skiing resorts also offer a host of other winter activities, from skating to ice fishing, for the non-skiers in the family.

TENNIS

Tennis is popular throughout the country, and courts are fairly easy to find. Contact Svenska Tennisförbundet (Swedish Tennis Association) for information.

🗹 **Svenska Tennisförbundet** ✉ Lidingöv. 75, Box 27915, 115 94 Stockholm ☎ 08/6679770 🖶 08/6646606 ⊕ www.tennis.se.

STUDENTS IN SCANDINAVIA

🗹 **IDs & Services STA Travel** ✉ 10 Downing St., New York, NY 10014 ☎ 800/777-0112 24-hr service center, 212/627-3111 🖶 212/627-3387 ⊕ www.sta.com. **Travel Cuts** ✉ 187 College St., Toronto, Ontario M5T 1P7, Canada ☎ 800/592-2887 in the U.S., 866/246-9762 or 416/979-2406 in Canada 🖶 416/979-8167 ⊕ www.travelcuts.com.

TAXES

VALUE-ADDED TAX

All hotel, restaurant, and departure taxes and the value-added tax (V.A.T., called *moms* all over Scandinavia) are automatically included in prices. The V.A.T. is 25%; non-EU residents can obtain a 15% refund on goods of SKr 200 or more. To receive your refund at any of the 15,000 stores that participate in the tax-free program, you'll be asked to fill out a form and show your passport. The form can then be turned in at any airport or ferry customs desk. Keep all your receipts and tags; occasionally, customs authorities ask to see your purchases, so pack them where they will be accessible.

Note: Tax-free sales of alcohol, cigarettes, and other luxury goods have been abolished among EU countries, with Sweden, Finland, and Denmark among the last to adopt these regulations. Finland's Åland Islands have some special rights under the EU and therefore allow tax-free sales for ferries in transit through its ports. All Sweden–Finland ferry routes now pass through the islands, de facto continuing the extremely popular tax-free sales for tourists. Air travel to the Scandinavia EU member states (Sweden, Finland, Denmark), as well as Norway, no longer allows tax-free sales.

When making a purchase, **ask for a V.A.T. refund form** and find out whether the merchant gives refunds—not all stores do, nor are they required to. Have the form stamped like any customs form by customs officials when you leave the country or, if you're visiting several European Union countries, when you leave the EU. Be ready to show customs officials what you've bought (pack purchases together, in your carry-on luggage); budget extra time for this. After you're through passport control, take the form to a refund-service counter for an on-the-spot refund (which is usually the quickest and easiest option), or mail it to the address on the form (or the envelope with it) after you arrive home.

A service processes refunds for most shops. You receive the total refund stated on the form. Global Refund is a Europe-wide service with 210,000 affiliated stores and more than 700 refund counters—located at major airports and border crossings. Its refund form is called a Tax Free

Check. The service issues refunds in the form of cash, check, or credit-card adjustment. If you don't have time to wait at the refund counter, you can mail in the form to an office in Europe or Canada instead.
🄵 V.A.T. Refunds **Global Refund Canada** 🄳 Box 2020, Station Main, Brampton, Ontario L6T 3S3 ☎ 800/993-4313 🖷 905/791-9078 ⊕ www.globalrefund.com.

TELEPHONES
Post offices do not have telephone facilities, but there are plenty of pay phones. Long-distance calls can be made from special telegraph offices called Telebutik, marked TELE.

AREA & COUNTRY CODES
The country code for Sweden is 46. Swedish phone numbers vary in their number of digits. When dialing a Sweden number from abroad, drop the initial "0" from the local area code. The country code is 1 for the United States and Canada, 61 for Australia, 64 for New Zealand, and 44 for the United Kingdom.

DIRECTORY & OPERATOR ASSISTANCE
🄵 **Directory Assistance** ☎ 118118, 118119 for international calls. **Operator Assistance** ☎ 90200, 0018 for international calls.

INTERNATIONAL CALLS
To make an international call, dial 00, followed by the country code and then your number. Access codes for various international companies are listed below.

LOCAL CALLS
A local call costs a minimum of SKr 2. For calls outside the locality, dial the area code (see telephone directory). Public phones are of three types: one takes SKr 1 and SKr 5 coins (newer public phones also accept SKr 10 coins); another takes only credit cards; and the last takes only the prepaid Telefonkort (telephone card).

LONG-DISTANCE SERVICES
AT&T, MCI, and Sprint access codes make calling long-distance relatively convenient, but you may find the local access number blocked in many hotel rooms. First ask the hotel operator to connect

you. If the hotel operator balks, ask for an international operator, or dial the international operator yourself. One way to improve your odds of getting connected to your long-distance carrier is to travel with more than one company's calling card (a hotel may block Sprint, for example, but not MCI). If all else fails, call from a pay phone. If you are traveling for a longer period of time, consider renting a cell phone from a local company.
🄵 Access Codes **AT&T Direct** ☎ 020/795611. **MCI WorldPhone** ☎ 020/0895438. **Sprint International Access** ☎ 020/799011.

MOBILE PHONES
Scandinavia has been one of the world leaders in mobile phone development; nearly half of all Scandinavians own a cellular phone. Although standard North American cellular phones will not work in Scandinavia, most Scandinavian capitals have several companies that rent cellular phones to tourists. Contact the local tourist offices for details.

PHONE CARDS
A Telefonkort, available at Telebutik, Pressbyrån (large blue-and-yellow newsstands), or hospitals, costs SKr 35, SKr 60, or SKr 100. If you're making numerous domestic calls, the card saves money. Many pay phones in downtown Stockholm and Göteborg take only these cards, so it's a good idea to carry one.

TIME
Sweden is one hour ahead of Greenwich mean time (GMT) and six hours ahead of eastern standard time (EST).

TIPPING
In addition to the 12% value-added tax, most hotels usually include a service charge of 15%; it is not necessary to tip unless you have received extra services. Similarly, a service charge of 13% is usually included in restaurant bills. It is a custom, however, to leave small change when buying drinks. Taxi drivers and hairdressers expect a tip of about 10%.

TOURS & PACKAGES
Because everything is prearranged on a prepackaged tour or independent vacation,

you spend less time planning—and often get it all at a good price.

BOOKING WITH AN AGENT

Travel agents are excellent resources. But it's a good idea to collect brochures from several agencies, as some agents' suggestions may be influenced by relationships with tour and package firms that reward them for volume sales. If you have a special interest, find an agent with expertise in that area. The American Society of Travel Agents (ASTA) has a database of specialists worldwide; you can log on to the group's Web site to find one near you.

Make sure your travel agent knows the accommodations and other services of the place being recommended. Ask about the hotel's location, room size, beds, and whether it has a pool, room service, or programs for children, if you care about these. Has your agent been there in person or sent others whom you can contact?

Do some homework on your own, too: local tourism boards can provide information about lesser-known and small-niche operators, some of which may sell only direct.

BUYER BEWARE

Each year consumers are stranded or lose their money when tour operators—even large ones with excellent reputations—go out of business. So check out the operator. Ask several travel agents about its reputation, and try to **book with a company that has a consumer-protection program.** (Look for information in the company's brochure.) In the United States, members of the United States Tour Operators Association are required to set aside funds (up to $1 million) to help eligible customers cover payments and travel arrangements in the event that the company defaults. It's also a good idea to choose a company that participates in the American Society of Travel Agents' Tour Operator Program; ASTA will act as mediator in any disputes between you and your tour operator.

Remember that the more your package or tour includes, the better you can predict the ultimate cost of your vacation. Make sure you know exactly what is covered, and beware of hidden costs. Are taxes, tips, and transfers included? Entertainment and excursions? These can add up.

🔽 Tour-Operator Recommendations **American Society of Travel Agents** (⇨ Travel Agencies). **CrossSphere–The Global Association for Packaged Travel** ✉ 546 E. Main St., Lexington, KY 40508 ☎ 800/682–8886 or 859/226–4444 🖷 859/226–4414 ⊕ www.CrossSphere.com. **United States Tour Operators Association** (USTOA) ✉ 275 Madison Ave., Suite 2014, New York, NY 10016 ☎ 212/599–6599 🖷 212/599–6744 ⊕ www.ustoa.com.

SIGHTSEEING TOURS

Stockholm Sightseeing runs a variety of sightseeing tours of Stockholm. Also contact local tourist offices.

🔽 **Stockholm Sightseeing** ✉ Skeppsbron 22 ☎ 08/57814020 ⊕ www.stockholmsightseeing.com.

TRAIN TRAVEL

From London the British Rail European Travel Center can be helpful in arranging connections to Sweden's SJ (Statens Järnvägar, ⊕ www.sj.se), the state railway.

SJ has a highly efficient network of comfortable electric trains. On nearly all long-distance routes there are buffet cars and, on overnight trips, sleeping cars and couchettes in both first- and second class. Seat reservations are advisable, and on some trains—indicated with *R, IN,* or *IC* on the timetable—they are compulsory. An extra fee of SKr 15 is charged to reserve a seat on a trip of less than 150 km (93 mi); on longer trips there is no extra charge. Reservations can be made right up to departure time. The high-speed X2000 train has been introduced on several routes; the Stockholm–Göteborg run takes just under three hours. Travelers younger than 19 years travel at half fare. Up to two children younger than 12 years may travel free if accompanied by an adult.

CUTTING COSTS

To save money, **look into rail passes.** But be aware that if you don't plan to cover many miles, you may come out ahead by buying individual tickets.

SJ cooperates with a number of local traffic systems, allowing you to buy one ticket, called a Tågplusbiljett, that works on trains, buses, and subways. Speak with the reservations people about what kind of combination you are interested in and where you'd like to travel. The Eurail and InterRail passes are both valid in Sweden. SJ also organizes reduced-cost package trips in conjunction with local tourist offices. Details are available at any railway station or from SJ.

Consider a Scanrail Pass, available for travel in Denmark, Sweden, Norway, and Finland for second-class train travel: you may have 5 days of unlimited travel in any two-month period ($291), 10 days of unlimited travel in two months ($390), or 21 consecutive days of unlimited train travel ($453). With the Scanrail Pass you also enjoy travel bonuses, including free or discounted ferry, boat, and bus travel and a Hotel Discount Card that allows 10%–30% off rates for select hotels June–August.

Passengers ages 12–25 can **buy Scanrail Youth Passes** ($203 second class, for 5 travel days in two months; $273 for 10 travel days in two months; $316 for 21 days of unlimited travel).

Those over age 60 can **take advantage of the Scanrail Senior Pass,** which offers the travel bonuses of the Scanrail Pass and discounted travel ($258 second class, 5 days; $348, 10 days; $400, for 21 consecutive days). Buy Scanrail Passes through Rail Europe and travel agents.

For car and train travel, price the Scanrail 'n Drive Pass: in two months you can get five days of unlimited train travel and two days of car rental (choice of three car categories) with unlimited mileage in Denmark, Norway, and Sweden. You can purchase extra car-rental days. Individual rates for two adults traveling together (economy car $399, compact car $439, intermediate car $449, all options with second-class train travel) are considerably lower (about 25%) than those for single adults; the third or fourth person sharing the car needs to purchase only a Scanrail Pass.

In Scandinavia you can **use EurailPasses,** which provide unlimited first-class rail travel, in all of the participating countries for the duration of the pass. If you plan to

rack up the miles, get a standard pass. These are available for 15 days ($588), 21 days ($762), one month ($946), two months ($1,338), and three months ($1,654). Eurail- and EuroPasses are available through travel agents and Rail Europe.

If you are an adult traveling with a youth under age 26 and/or a senior, **consider buying a EurailSaver Pass**; this entitles you to second-class train travel at the discount youth or senior fare, provided that you are traveling with the youth or senior at all times. A Saver pass is available for $498 (15 days), $648 (21 days), $804 (one month), $1,138 (two months), and $1,408 (three months).

In addition to standard EurailPasses, **ask about special rail-pass plans.** Among these are the Eurail YouthPass (for those under age 26), a Eurail FlexiPass (which allows a certain number of travel days within a set period), the Euraildrive Pass, and the EuroPass Drive (which combines travel by train and rental car).

Whichever pass you choose, remember that you must **purchase your pass before you leave** for Europe.

Many travelers assume that rail passes guarantee them seats on the trains they wish to ride. Not so. You need to **book seats ahead even if you are using a rail pass**; seat reservations are required on some European trains, particularly high-speed trains, and are a good idea on trains that may be crowded—particularly in summer on popular routes. You will also need a reservation if you purchase sleeping accommodations.

🚆 Where to Buy Rail Passes **Rail Europe** ☎ 877/ 257-2887 in the U.S., 800/361-RAIL in Canada ⊕ www.raileurope.com ☎ 08708/371371 in the U.K. ⊕ www.raileurope.co.uk.

TRAVEL AGENCIES

A good travel agent puts your needs first. Look for an agency that has been in business at least five years, emphasizes customer service, and has someone on staff who specializes in your destination. In addition, **make sure the agency belongs to a professional trade organization.** The American Society of Travel Agents (ASTA) has more than 10,000 members in some 140 countries, enforces a strict code of ethics, and will step in to mediate agent-client disputes involving ASTA members. ASTA also maintains a directory of agents on its Web site; ASTA's TravelSense.org, a trip planning and travel advice site, can also help to locate a travel agent who caters to your needs. (If a travel agency is also acting as your tour operator, *see* Buyer Beware *in* Tours & Packages.)

🔳 Local Agent Referrals **American Society of Travel Agents (ASTA)** ✉ 1101 King St., Suite 200, Alexandria, VA 22314 ☎ 800/965-2782 24-hr hotline, 703/739-2782 🖨 703/684-8319 ⊕ www.astanet.com and www.travelsense.org. **Association of British Travel Agents** ✉ 68-71 Newman St., London W1T 3AH ☎ 020/76372444 🖨 020/76370713 ⊕ www.abta.com. **Association of Canadian Travel Agencies** ✉ 130 Albert St., Suite 1705, Ottawa, Ontario K1P 5G4 ☎ 613/237-3657 🖨 613/237-7052 ⊕ www.acta.ca.**Australian Federation of Travel Agents** ✉ Level 3, 309 Pitt St., Sydney, NSW 2000 ☎ 02/9264-3299 or 1300/363-416 🖨 02/9264-1085 ⊕ www.afta.com.au. **Travel Agents' Association of New Zealand** ✉ Level 5, Tourism and Travel House, 79 Boulcott St., Box 1888, Wellington 6001 ☎ 04/499-0104 🖨 04/499-0786 ⊕ www.taanz.org.nz.

VISITOR INFORMATION

Learn more about foreign destinations by checking government-issued travel advisories and country information.

🔳 **Stockholm Information Service** (Sverigehuset) ✉ Hamng. 27, Box 7542, 103 93 Stockholm ☎ 08/50828500 ⊕ www.stockholmtown.com. **Swedish Travel and Tourism Council** ✉ 5 Upper Montague St., London W1H2AG ☎ 020/71086168 in the U.K. 🖨 020/77245872 ✉ 655 3rd Ave., 18th fl. New York,

NY 10017 ☎ 212/885-9700 🖨 212/885-9710 ✉ Box 3030, Kungsg. 36, 103 61 Stockholm ☎ 08/7255500 or 08/7891000 🖨 08/7891031.

🔳 Government Advisories **U.S. Department of State** ✉ Bureau of Consular Affairs, Overseas Citizens Services Office, 2201 C St. NW, Washington, DC 20520 ☎ 888/407-4747 or 317/472-2328 for interactive hotline, 202/647-5225 ⊕ www.travel.state.gov. **Consular Affairs Bureau of Canada** ☎ 800/267-6788 or 613/944-6788 ⊕ www.voyage.gc.ca. **U.K. Foreign and Commonwealth Office** ✉ Travel Advice Unit, Consular Directorate, Old Admiralty Bldg. London SW1A 2PA ☎ 0870/606-0290 or 020/70081500 ⊕ www.fco.gov.uk/travel. **Australian Department of Foreign Affairs and Trade** ☎ 300/139-281 travel advisories, 02/6261-1299 Consular Travel Advice ⊕ www.smartraveller.gov.au or www.dfat.gov.au. **New Zealand Ministry of Foreign Affairs and Trade** ☎ 04/439-8000 ⊕ www.mft.govt.nz.

WEB SITES

Do check out the World Wide Web when planning your trip. You'll find everything from weather forecasts to virtual tours of famous cities. Be sure to visit Fodors.com (⊕ www.fodors.com), a complete travel-planning site. You can research prices and book plane tickets, hotel rooms, rental cars, vacation packages, and more. In addition, you can post your pressing questions in the Travel Talk section. Other planning tools include a currency converter and weather reports, and there are loads of links to travel resources.

SWEDISH RESOURCES

Swedish Travel & Tourism Council (⊕ www.visitsweden.org). **City of Stockholm** (⊕ www.stockholm.se/english).

Stockholm

WORD OF MOUTH

"I thought the Vasamuseet was incredible. The low lighting gave it a spooky feel. I kept expecting ghosts of pirates and sailors to swarm the decks."
—indytravel

"Stockholm's public transportation is wonderful, but it's not cheap. It's well worth it to get a multi-day pass or buy a strip of tickets, which is slightly cheaper than paying per ride."
—KT

"Millesgarden has a wonderful cliff-top setting. We didn't know much about Carl Milles before we went, but we loved his work—sculpture displayed on terraces and around fountains—and it was a good fit for our divergent intersests."
—sprin2

Updated by
Rob Hincks

STOCKHOLM IS A CITY IN THE FLUSH OF ITS SECOND YOUTH. In the last 10 years Sweden's capital has emerged from its cold, Nordic shadow to take the stage as a truly international city. What started with entry into the European Union in 1995, and continued with the extraordinary IT boom of the late 1990s, is still happening today as Stockholm gains even more global confidence. Stockholm's 1 million or so inhabitants have, almost as one, realized that their city is one to rival Paris, London, New York, or any other great metropolis.

With this realization comes change. Stockholm has become a city of design, fashion, innovation, technology, and world-class food, pairing homegrown talent with international standard. The streets are flowing with a young and confident population keen to drink in everything the city has to offer. You can sense this energy in the gossiping crowds that pack the street cafés and restaurant terraces, discussing life over an espresso and from behind designer sunglasses; you can hear it in the laughter of laid-back weekenders in the city's many open spaces; and it seems you can buy it in the shops, which are full to bursting with cutting-edge Swedish products. The glittering feeling of optimism, success, and living in the "here and now" is rampant in Stockholm.

Of course, not everyone is looking to live so much in the present; luckily, Stockholm also has plenty of history. Positioned where the waters of Lake Mälaren rush into the Baltic, Stockholm has been an important Baltic trading site and an international city of some wealth for centuries.

Built on 14 small islands joined by bridges crossing open bays and narrow channels, Stockholm boasts the story of its history in its glorious medieval old town, grand palaces, ancient churches, sturdy edifices, public parks, and 19th-century museums—its history is soaked into the very fabric of its airy boulevards, built as a public display of trading glory.

From the first written mention of the city, in 1252, to the last word on Swedish street fashion today, Stockholm is a world capital in the truest sense. The city invites you to explore the way back when, enjoy the now, and fancy the near future.

EXPLORING STOCKHOLM

Much of Stockholm's beauty comes from its water. In the same way that Venice is unquestionably defined by its lagoon, so too is Stockholm mapped and interpreted by its archipelago landscape. For the inhabitants there's a tribal status to each of the islands. Residents of Södermalm are fiercely proud of their rather bohemian settlement, while those who call Gamla Stan home will tell you that there is nowhere else like it. But for the visitor, Stockholm's islands have a more practical, less passionate meaning: they help to dissect the city, both in terms of history and in terms of Stockholm's different characteristics, conveniently packaging the capital into easily handled, ultimately digestible, areas.

The central island of Gamla Stan wows visitors with its medieval beauty, winding, narrow lanes, cellar bars, and small café-lined squares. Directly to the east is the small island of Skeppsholmen. To the south, Södermalm challenges with contemporary boutiques, hip hangouts, and left-of-center sensibilities. North of Gamla Stan is Norrmalm, the financial and business heart of the city, and a reliable, solid, international face of Stockholm. Travel west and you'll find Kungsholmen, site of the Stadshuset (City Hall), where you'll find the first signs of residential leafiness and one of Stockholm's newly hip enclaves. Turn east from Norrmalm and Östermalm awaits, an old residential neighborhood with the most money, the most glamorous people, the most tantalizing shops, and the most expensive street on the Swedish Monopoly board. Finally, between Östermalm and Södermalm lies the island of Djurgården, once a royal game preserve, now the site of lovely parks and museums; it's a place to come to recharge and regroup before you hit the more lively parts of town again.

Modern Stockholm

The area bounded by Stadshuset, Hötorget, Stureplan, and the Kungliga Dramatiska Teatern (nicknamed Dramaten) is essentially Stockholm's downtown, where the city comes closest to feeling like a bustling metropolis. Shopping, nightlife, business, traffic, dining, festivals—all are at their most intense in this part of town. Much of this area was razed to the ground in the 1960s as part of a social experiment to move people to the new suburbs. What came in its place, a series of modernist buildings, concrete public spaces, and pedestrianized walkways, garners support and derision in equal measure. Whatever your reaction, it is part of Stockholm's unique personality and should not be missed.

a good
walk

Stockholm's symbol of power, **Stadshuset** ❶ ➤, is a perfect place to begin your walk. Cross the bridge to Klara Mälarstrand and follow the waterfront to Drottninggatan. Take a left and continue north along this crowded pedestrian street, a purposeful shop-lined artery that cuts right through the center of the city. It is broken only once, by modern Stockholm's heart, **Sergels Torg** ❷. The **Kulturhuset** ❸ is in the imposing glass building on the southern side of Sergels Torg. Continue along Drottninggatan, stopping at the market-filled **Hötorget** ❹. The intersection of Kungsgatan and Sveavägen, where the Konserthuset (Concert Hall) stands, is one of the busiest pedestrian crossroads in town.

Head north on Sveavägen for a brief detour to see the spot where Prime Minister Olof Palme was assassinated in 1986. A plaque has been laid on the right-hand side of the street, just before the intersection with Olof Palmes Gata; his grave is in Adolf Fredrik's Kyrkogård, a few blocks farther on. This is the perfect place to cut back to Drottninggatan, heading southwest along Kammakargatan. Drottninggatan changes here; the crowds thin, as do the more touristy shops. Instead, the area's locals go about their business, dropping off dry cleaning, chatting in cafés, and popping into bookshops. Eventually you will reach Odengatan. On your right will be the magnificent **Stockholms Stadsbiblioteket** ❺. Find your way (from Odengatan to Sveavägen) onto Döbelnsgatan, a peaceful and pleasant residential street and head south. Turn right up Tegnérgatan to find **Strindbergsmuseet**

4 <

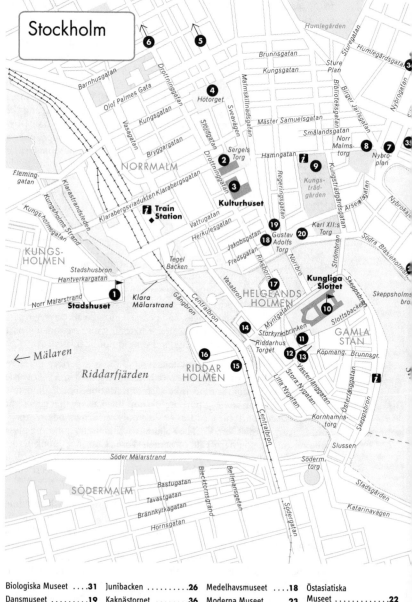

Stockholm

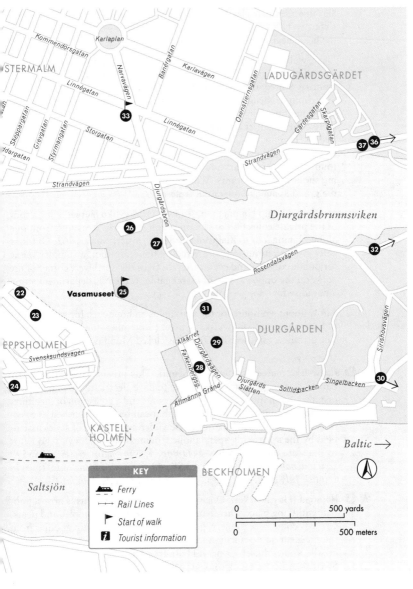

KEY

🚢 Ferry

├─┤ Rail Lines

► Start of walk

🛈 Tourist information

0 _____ 500 yards

0 _____ 500 meters

Saltsjön

Baltic →

Blå Tornet ⑥, where playwright August Strindberg lived from 1908 to 1912. Return to Hötorget by way of Sveavägen, a riot of sound and activity after the head-clearing peace of Döbelnsgatan.

Next, walk east along Kungsgatan, one of Stockholm's main shopping streets, to Stureplan. On this street is Sturegallerian, an elegant mall. In front of Sturegallerian is Svampen (the mushroom), a little piece of Stockholm's social history. The fungus-shape pay-phone shelter has been a meeting point for years: "I'll see you by Svampen at eight o'clock." Here countless first dates have met, lifelong friendships have formed, and likely more than a few hearts have been broken. Head southeast along Birger Jarlsgatan—named for the nobleman generally credited with founding Stockholm around 1252—where there are still more interesting shops and restaurants. When you reach Nybroplan, take a look at the grand **Kungliga Dramatiska Teatern** ⑦.

Heading west up Hamngatan, stop in at **Hallwylska Museet** ⑧ for a tour of the private collection of Countess von Hallwyl's treasures. Continue along Hamngatan to **Kungsträdgården** ⑨, a park since 1562. Outdoor cafés and restaurants are clustered by this leafy spot, a summer venue for public concerts and events. Across from the northwest corner of the park, on the opposite side of Hamngatan, is the NK department store, a paradise for shoppers of all persuasions.

TIMING   Allow about 4½ hours for the walk, plus an hour each for guided tours of Stadshuset and Hallwylska Museet (September–June, Sunday only). The Strindbergsmuseet Blå Tornet is closed Monday.

What to See

⑧ **Hallwylska Museet** (Hallwyl Museum). This private late-19th-century palace, one of the first in Stockholm to have electricity and a telephone installed, has imposing wood-panel rooms and a collection of furniture, paintings, and musical instruments that can be best described as eclectic. The palace is decked out in a bewildering mélange of styles assembled by the apparently spendaholic Countess von Hallwyl, who left it to the state on her death. ⊠ *Hamng. 4, Norrmalm* ☎ *08/51955599* ⊕ *www.hallwylskamuseet.se* 🖻 *SKr 40* ☉ *Guided tours only. Tours in English July and Aug., Tues.–Sun. at 1; Sept.–June, Sun. at 1.*

★ ④ **Hötorget** (Hay Market). Once the city's hay market, this is now a popular gathering place where you're more likely to find apples and pears. Crowds come here to meet, gossip, hang out, or pick up goodies from the excellent outdoor fruit-and-vegetable market. Also lining the square are the Konserthuset (Concert Hall), fronted by a magnificent statue by Swedish-American sculptor Carl Milles, the PUB department store, and a multiscreen cinema Filmstaden Sergel. ⊠ *On the corner of Kungsgatan and Sveaväg, Norrmalm.*

need a break?   Duck into the food hall **Kungshallen** (⊠ Hötorget opposite Filmstaden Sergel, Norrmalm ☎ 08/218005) for a lightning tour of global cuisines at the crowded food stalls, including some wonderful Turkish meze. Or get a window table at the café inside Filmstaden Sergel.

☾ ❸ **Kulturhuset** (Culture House). Since it opened in 1974, architect Peter Celsing's cultural center, a glass-and-stone monolith on the south side of Sergels Torg, has become a symbol of modernism in Sweden. Stockholmers are divided on the aesthetics of this building—most either love it or hate it. Here there are exhibitions for children and adults, a library, a theater, a youth center, an exhibition center, and a restaurant. Head to Café Panorama, on the top floor, to savor traditional Swedish cuisine and a great view of Sergels Torg down below. ⊠ *Sergels Torg 3, City* ☎ *08/50831508* ⊕ *www.kulturhuset.se.*

❼ **Kungliga Dramatiska Teatern** (Royal Dramatic Theater). Locally known as Dramaten, the national theater stages works by the likes of Strindberg and other playwrights of international stature in a grand appealing building whose facade and gilded statuary look out over the city harbor. The theater gave its first performance in 1788, when it was located at Bollhuset on Slottsbacken, next to the Royal Palace. It later moved to Kungsträdgården, spent some time in the Opera House, and ended up at its present location in 1908. Performances are in Swedish. ⊠ *Nybroplan, Östermalm* ☎ *08/6670680* ⊕ *www.dramaten.se.*

☾ ❾ **Kungsträdgården** (King's Garden). This is one of Stockholm's smallest yet most central parks. Once the royal kitchen garden, it now hosts a large number of festivals and events each season. The park has numerous cafés and restaurants, a playground, and, in winter, an ice-skating rink. In 2004 the park saw the removal of almost every large tree from the area—they were diseased due to bad pruning techniques in the 1960s, apparently—but work is underway to reverse the damage. The park still manages to retain an air of quiet sanctuary, even without so much foliage. ⊠ *Between Hamng. and the Operan.*

❷ **Sergels Torg.** Named after Johan Tobias Sergel (1740–1814), one of Sweden's greatest sculptors, this busy junction in Stockholm's center is dominated by modern, functional buildings and a sunken pedestrian square with subterranean connections to the rest of the neighborhood. Visitors are often put off by its darkened covered walkways and youths in hooded tops, but it is relatively safe and a great place to witness some real Stockholm street life.

► ❶ **Stadshuset** (City Hall). The architect Ragnar Östberg, one of the
FodorśChoice founders of the National Romantic movement, completed Stockholm's
★ city hall in 1923. Headquarters of the city council, the building is functional but ornate: its immense **Blå Hallen** (Blue Hall) is the venue for the annual Nobel Prize dinner, Stockholm's principal social event. Take a trip to the top of the 348-foot tower, most of which can be achieved by elevator, to enjoy a breathtaking panorama of the city and Riddarfjärden. ⊠ *Hantverkarg. 1, Kungsholmen* ☎ *08/50829058* ⊕ *www.stockholm.se* ▨ *SKr 60, tower SKr 20* ☉ *Guided tours only. Tours in English, June–Aug., daily 10, 11, noon, 2, and 3; Sept., daily 10, noon and 2; Oct.–May, daily 10 and noon. Tower open May–Sept., daily 10–4.30.*

need a
break?
After climbing the Stadshuset tower, relax on the fine grass terraces that lead down to the bay and overlook Lake Mälaren. Or have lunch in **Stadshuskällaren** (City Hall Cellar; ☎ 08/6505454), where the annual Nobel Prize banquet is held. You can also head a few blocks down Hantverkargatan to find several good small restaurants.

❺ Stockholms Stadsbiblioteket (Stockholm City Library). Libraries aren't always a top sightseeing priority, but the Stockholm City Library is among the most captivating buildings in town. Designed by the famous Swedish architect E. G. Asplund and completed in 1928, the building's cylindrical, galleried main hall gives it the appearance of a large birthday cake. Inside is an excellent "information technology" center with free Internet access—and lots of books too. ⊠ *Sveav. 73, Vasastan* ☎ *08/50831100* ⊕ *www.ssb.stockholm.se* ☉ *Mon.–Thurs. 9–9, Fri. 9–7, and weekends noon–4.*

★ **❻ Strindbergsmuseet Blå Tornet** (Strindberg Museum, Blue Tower). Hidden away over a grocery store, this museum is dedicated to Sweden's most important author and dramatist, August Strindberg (1849–1912), who resided here from 1908 until his death four years later. The interior has been expertly reconstructed with authentic furnishings and other objects, including one of his pens. The museum also houses a library, printing press, and picture archives, and it is the setting for literary, musical, and theatrical events. ⊠ *Drottningg. 85, Norrmalm* ☎ *08/4115354* ⊕ *www.strindbergsmuseet.se* ☒ *SKr 40* ☉ *Tues.–Sun. noon–4.*

need a
break?
Peace and quiet come in rare doses in modern cities, so take the chance to get some at **Centralbadet** (⊠ Drottningg. 88, Norrmalm ☎ 08/241081), a classic 19th-century bathhouse. No need to bring your swimming costume though. Just relax in the secluded, tree-shaded courtyard with a cup of tea, a light snack, some very pleasant lunch—or maybe just the Sunday paper.

Gamla Stan & Skeppsholmen

Gamla Stan (Old Town) sits between two of Stockholm's main islands, and is the site of the medieval city. Just east of Gamla Stan is the island of Skeppsholmen, whose narrow, twisting cobble streets are lined with superbly preserved old buildings. As the site of the original Stockholm, this area is rich in history and, understandably, a magnet for tourists. Consequently there are plenty of substandard shops and restaurants ready to take your money in return for shoddy goods and bad food. Therefore, caution is advised. Because of this, locals often make a big show of dismissing the area as a tourist trap, but don't believe them. Secretly they love Gamla Stan and Skeppsholmen. And who wouldn't? With its divine hideaway alleys and bars, gorgeous architecture, specialty shops, and great restaurants, it's impossible to resist. Find out where the locals go and do likewise; you'll be privy to one of the most charming places in town.

a good
walk
Start at the waterfront edge of Kungsträdgården. Stand for a moment with the park behind you and look out. This is one of the most beauti-

ful views of Stockholm, especially if the sun is shining. Walk across Strömsbron to the magnificent **Kungliga Slottet** ⑩ ⌐, where you can see the changing of the guard at noon every day—a spectacle which, although formal, lacks the cold stiffness of London's changing of the guard, reflecting the relaxed formality that pervades much of Swedish life. Walk up the sloping cobblestone drive called Slottsbacken and bear right past the Obelisk (which was built by King Gustav III in honor of the people of Stockholm) to find the main entrance to the palace. Stockholm's 15th-century Gothic cathedral, **Storkyrkan** ⑪, stands at the top of Slottsbacken, but its entrance is at the other end, on Trångsund.

Following Källargränd from the Obelisk or Trångsund from Storkyrkan, you will reach the small square called **Stortorget** ⑫, marvelously atmospheric amid magnificent old merchants' houses. Stockholm's Börshuset (Stock Exchange), which currently houses the **Nobelmuseet** ⑬, fronts the square. You are right in the heart of old Stockholm now. Prepare for an onslaught to the senses, as history, culture, and a dash of old Europe come thick and fast around here.

Walk past Svartmangatan's many ancient buildings, including the Tyska Kyrkan, or German Church, with its resplendent oxidized copper spire and airy interior. Continue along Svartmangatan and take a right on Tyska Stallplan to Prästgatan, and just to your left will be Mårten Trotzigs Gränd; this lamplit alley stairway leads downhill to Järntorget. From here, take Västerlånggatan back north across Gamla Stan, checking out the pricey fashion boutiques, galleries, and souvenir shops along the way.

Cut down Storkyrkobrinken to the 17th-century Dutch baroque **Riddarhuset** ⑭. A short walk takes you over Riddarholmsbron to Riddarholmen—Island of Knights—on which stands **Riddarholmskyrkan** ⑮. Also on Riddarholmen is the white 17th-century palace that houses the **Svea Hovrätt** ⑯. Returning across Riddarholmsbron, take Myntgatan back toward Kungliga Slottet and turn left onto Stallbron and cross the bridge. You'll then pass through the refurbished stone **Riksdagshuset** ⑰ on Helgeandsholmen, Holy Ghost Island. Another short bridge returns you to the mainland and Drottninggatan; take a right onto Fredsgatan and walk until you reach **Medelhavsmuseet** ⑱, on the left, just before Gustav Adolfs Torg. Right there on the square is the **Dansmuseet** ⑲.

The **Operan** ⑳ occupies the waterfront between Gustav Adolfs Torg and Karl XII's Torg (part of Kungsträdgården). A little farther along, on Södra Blasieholmshamn, a host of tour boats dock in front of the stately Grand Hotel. Pass the Grand and visit the **Nationalmuseum** ㉑. Cross the footbridge to the island of Skeppsholmen, a hotspot for museum lovers. Here you will find the **Östasiatiska Museet** ㉒, with a fine collection of Buddhist art, the **Moderna Museet** ㉓, which is in the same complex that houses the **Arkitekturmuseet.** and, to the southwest, **Svensk Form** ㉔, a design museum. The adjoining island, Kastellholmen, is a pleasant place for a stroll, especially on a summer evening, when views of the Baltic harbor and the lights of Djurgården's parks are served up with a warm, salty breeze and the promise of another fine day tomorrow.

STOCKHOLM'S ARCHITECTURAL PROCESSION

AS IN MANY OTHER SWEDISH CITIES, *a single afternoon walk in Stockholm offers a journey through centuries of architectural change and innovation. There are, of course, the classics. Take Kungliga Slottet (Royal Palace) on Gamla Stan. Designed by Nicodemus Tessin the Younger and built between 1690 and 1704, it's a rather austere palace—no domes, no great towers—and yet it commands a certain respect sitting so regally over the water. Nearby, on Riddarholmen, observe the gorgeous, medieval Riddarholmskyrkan (Riddarholm Church), with its lattice spire pointed toward the heavens. And let's not forget Drottningholms Slott, just west of the city, a 17th-century châteauesque structure—designed by Tessin the Elder and finished by his son—that has been the home of the royal family since 1981. Also at Drottningholm is the Court Theater (1766), which, remarkably, still contains its original interior and fully functional stage machinery.*

Stadshuset (City Hall) is also a must-see. Completed in 1923, the building contains more than 8 million bricks and 19 million gilded mosaic tiles. Each year the Nobel Prize ceremony is held in the building's Blå Hallen (Blue Hall). Built a few years later is Stadsbiblioteket (City Library), designed by Eric Gunnar Asplund—one of Sweden's most renowned architects. The library's eye-pleasing yet simple design foreshadows the funkis (functionalist) movement that Gunnar helped spearhead in the 1920s and '30s.

Skattehuset (Tax House), also known as Skatteskrapan (a play on the word "skyscraper"), is hard to miss, looming mercilessly as it does over Södermalm. Completed in the early 1950s as part of an attempt to consolidate the nation's tax

offices, the singularly dull, gray, 25-story building is often criticized for having ruined the southern skyline of Stockholm.

Farther south, another architectural oddity plagues—or enhances, depending on whom you ask—the skyline. Globen (the Globe), the world's largest spherical building, looks something like a colossal golf ball. Unveiled in 1988, it's the main arena in Stockholm for indoor sporting events and rock concerts. Despite debates concerning its aesthetics (or lack thereof), a look at the cables and beams inside reveals Globen's architecture marvel.

Another much-debated architectural undertaking is Hötorgscity, across from the highly influential Kulturhuset at Sergels Torg. Constructed in the mid-'50s, Hötorgscity was built to house retail stores and offices to bring more commerce to downtown Stockholm. The project failed, and a significant chunk of historic Stockholm was lost. The buildings were shut down in the '70s, but today there is a renewed interest in the top floors of the buildings, especially among young business owners.

What is most striking about the buildings that make up Stockholm's architectural portfolio is their diversity. Centuries of history involving both failures and successes are reflected in the styles that make up the city's skyline. Every building in Stockholm, new or old, tells a story.

TIMING Allow three hours for the walk, double that if you want to tour the various parts of the palace. The Nationalmuseum and Östasiatiska Museet will take up to an hour each to view. Note that Kungliga Slottet is closed Monday off-season, and Arkitekturmuseet, Dansmuseet, Medelhavsmuseet, Moderna Museet, Nationalmuseum, Svensk Form, and Östasiatiska Museet are always closed Monday. The Riddarhuset is open weekdays only; off-season, hit the Riddarholmskyrkan on a Wednesday or weekend.

What to See

Arkitekturmuseet. The Museum of Architecture uses models, photos, and drawings to tell the long and interesting story of Swedish architecture. Certain buildings shed light on specific periods, including the Stockholm Town Hall, Vadstena Castle, and the Helsingborg Concert House. The museum also hosts lectures, debates, and architectural tours of the city. ⊠ *Skeppsholmen* ☎ *08/58727000* ⊕ *www.arkitekturmuseet. se* ⊠ *Free* ⊙ *Tues. and Wed. 10–8, Thurs.–Sun. 10–6.*

❶❾ Dansmuseet (Museum of Dance). Close to the Royal Opera House, the Museum of Dance has a permanent collection that examines dance, theater, and art from Asia, Africa, and Europe. Such artists as Fernand Léger, Francis Picabia, Giorgio de Chirico, and Jean Cocteau are represented in the exhibitions. The Rolf de Maré Study Centre has a vast collection of dance reference materials, including about 4,000 books and 3,000 videos. ⊠ *Gustav Adolfs Torg 22–24, City* ☎ *08/4417650* ⊕ *www. dansmuseet.nu* ⊠ *SKr 50* ⊙ *Tues.–Fri. 11–4, weekends noon–4.*

Järntorget (Iron Square). Named after its original use as an iron and copper marketplace, this square was also the site of public executions. ⊠ *Intersection of Västerlångg and Österlångg, Gamla Stan.*

off the
beaten
path

KATARINAHISSEN – Built in 1935, this marvel of engineering is the passageway home for hundreds who live in the former working-class Mosebacke area of Södermalm. The construction is reminiscent of a railway carriage protruding from the cliff face that fronts Södermalm, supported at one end by a giant wrought-iron-girdered leg. The leg holds an elevator which will take you to a walkway that affords magnificent views over Gamla Stan and across the water to Djurgården. Follow the walkway to Mosebacke torg, a leafy, peaceful square built in 1857—it's an ideal place to drift off a little and clear your head. ⊠ *Slussen, Södermalm* ⊠ *SKr 5 each way* ⊙ *Mon.–Sat. 7.30–10, Sun. 10–10.*

▶ **❶⓿ Kungliga Slottet** (Royal Palace). Designed by Nicodemus Tessin, the Royal
Fodor's Choice Palace was completed in 1760 and replaced the previous palace that had
★ burned here in 1697. Just three weeks after the fire, Tessin—who had also designed the previous incarnation, submitted his drawings for the new palace to the Swedish government. The rebuilding was finally completed, exactly according to Tessin's designs, 60 years later. The four facades of the palace each have a distinct style: the west is the king's, the east the queen's, the south belongs to the nation, and the north represents royalty in general. Watch the changing of the guard in the curved terrace entrance, and

view the palace's fine furnishings and Gobelin tapestries on a tour of the **Representationsvän** (State Apartments). To survey the crown jewels, which are no longer used in this self-consciously egalitarian country, head to the **Skattkammaren** (Treasury). The **Livrustkammaren** (Royal Armory) has an outstanding collection of weaponry, coaches, and royal regalia. Entrances to the Treasury and Armory are on the Slottsbacken side of the palace. ⊠ *Gamla Stan* ☎ *08/4026130* ⊕ *www.royalcourt.se* 🎫 *State Apartments SKr 80, Treasury SKr 80, Royal Armory SKr 80, combined ticket for all areas SKr 120* ☉ *State Apartments and Treasury May–Aug., daily 10–4; Sept.–Apr., Tues.–Sun. noon–3. Armory May–Aug., daily 11–4; Sept.–Apr., Tues.–Sun. 11–4.*

🔞 **Medelhavsmuseet** (Mediterranean Museum). During the 1700s this building housed the Royal Courts. Then, in the early 1900s, the vast interior of the building was redesigned to resemble the Palazzo Bevilaqua in Bologna, Italy. The collection has a good selection of art from Asia as well as from ancient Egypt, Greece, and Rome. In the Gold Room you can see fine gold, silver, and bronze jewelry from the Far East, Greece, and Rome. ⊠ *Fredsg. 2, City* ☎ *08/51955380* ⊕ *www. medelhavsmuseet.se* 🎫 *Free* ☉ *Tues. and Wed. 11–8, Thurs. and Fri. 11–4, weekends noon–5.*

★ ㉓ **Moderna Museet** (Museum of Modern Art). Reopened in its original venue on Skeppsholmen following extensive treatment for moisture problems, the museum's excellent collection includes works by Picasso, Kandinsky, Dalí, Brancusi, and other international artists. You can also view examples of significant Swedish painters and sculptors and an extensive section on photography. The building itself is striking. Designed by the well-regarded Spanish architect Rafael Moneo, it has seemingly endless hallways of blond wood and walls of glass. ⊠ *Skeppsholmen, City* ☎ *08/51955200* ⊕ *www.modernamuseet.se* 🎫 *Free* ☉ *Tues. and Wed. 10–8, Thurs.–Sun. 10–6.*

㉑ **Nationalmuseum.** The museum's collection of paintings and sculptures **FodorśChoice** is made up of about 12,500 works. The emphasis is on Swedish and ★ Nordic art, but other areas are well represented. Look especially for some fine works by Rembrandt. The print and drawing department is also impressive, with a nearly complete collection of Edouard Manet prints. ⊠ *Södra Blasieholmshamnen, City* ☎ *08/51954428* ⊕ *www. nationalmuseum.se* 🎫 *Free* ☉ *Jan.–Aug., Tues. 11–8, Wed.–Sun. 11–5; Sept.–Dec., Tues. and Thurs. 11–8, Wed., Fri., and weekends 11–5.*

need a break? The inner courtyard of the Nationalmuseum houses **Atrium** (⊠ Södra Blasieholmshamnen, City ☎ 08/6113430), a contemporary and stunning lunch restaurant and café. The tasty fixed-price lunches are an excellent value.

🔞 **Nobelmuseet.** The Swedish Academy meets at Börshuset (the Stock Exchange) every year to decide the winner of the Nobel Prize for literature. The building is also the home of the Nobel Museum. Along with exhibits on creativity's many forms, the museum displays scientific models, shows films, and has a full explanation of the process of choosing prizewinners. The museum does a good job covering the controversial selections made over the years. It's a must for Nobel Prize hopefuls and others. ⊠ *Börshuset, Stortorget, Gamla Stan* ☎ *08/232506* ⊕ *www. nobelprize.org/nobelmuseum* ⊠ *SKr 50* ⊙ *Wed.–Mon. 10–5, Tues. 10–8.*

20 **Operan** (Opera House). Stockholm's baroque Opera House is almost more famous for its restaurants and bars than for its opera and ballet productions, but that doesn't mean an evening performance should be missed. There's not a bad seat in the house. For just SKr 35 you can even get a listening-only seat (with no view). Still, its food and drink status can't be denied. It has been one of Stockholm's artistic and literary watering holes since the first Operakällaren restaurant opened on the site in 1787. ⊠ *Gustav Adolfs Torg, City* ☎ *08/248240* ⊕ *www.operan.se.*

22 **Östasiatiska Museet** (Museum of Far Eastern Antiquities). If you have an affinity for Asian art and culture, don't miss this impressive collection of Chinese and Japanese Buddhist sculptures and artifacts. Although some exhibits are displayed with little creativity, the pieces themselves are always worthwhile. The more than 100,000 pieces that make up the holdings here include many from China's Neolithic and Bronze ages. ⊠ *Skeppsholmen, City* ☎ *08/51955750* ⊕ *www.mfea.se* ⊠ *Free* ⊙ *Tues. 11–8, Wed.–Sun. 11–5.*

15 **Riddarholmskyrkan** (Riddarholm Church). Dating from 1270, the Grey Friars monastery is the second-oldest structure in Stockholm, and has been the burial place for Swedish kings for more than 400 years. The redbrick structure, distinguished by its delicate iron-fretwork spire, is rarely used for services: it's more like a museum now. The most famous figures interred within are King Gustavus Adolphus, hero of the Thirty Years' War, and the warrior King Karl XII, renowned for his daring invasion of Russia, who died in Norway in 1718. The most recent of the 17 Swedish kings to be put to rest here was Gustav V, in 1950. The different rulers' sarcophagi, usually embellished with their monograms, are visible in the small chapels dedicated to the various dynasties. ⊠ *Riddarholmen* ☎ *08/4026130* ⊠ *SKr 20* ⊙ *May–Aug., daily 10–4; Sept., weekends noon–3.*

14 **Riddarhuset.** Completed in 1674, the House of Nobles was used for parliamentary assemblies and administration during the four-estate parliamentary period that lasted until 1866. Since then Swedish nobility have continued to meet here every three years for administrative meetings. Hanging from its walls are 2,325 escutcheons, representing all the former noble families of Sweden. The building has excellent acoustic properties and is often used for concerts. ⊠ *Riddarhustorget 10, Gamla Stan* ☎ *08/7233990* ⊕ *www.riddarhuset.se* ⊠ *SKr 40* ⊙ *Weekdays 11:30–12:30.*

17 **Riksdagshuset** (Parliament Building). When in session, the Swedish Parliament meets in this 1904 building. Above the entrance, the architect placed sculptures of a peasant, a burgher, a clergyman, and a nobleman. Take a tour of the building not only to learn about Swedish government but also to see the art within. In the former First Chamber are murals by Otte Sköld illustrating different periods in the history of Stockholm, and in the current First Chamber a massive tapestry by Elisabet Hasselberg Olsson, *Memory of a Landscape,* hangs above the podium. ✉ *Riksg. 3A, Gamla Stan* ☎ *08/7864000* ⊕ *www.riksdagen.se* ✉ *Free* ☉ *Tours in English late June–late Aug., weekdays 12:30 and 2; late Aug.–late June, weekends 1:30. Call ahead for reservations.*

⑪ Storkyrkan. Swedish kings were crowned in the 15th-century Great Church as late as 1907. Today its main attractions are a dramatic wooden statue of St. George slaying the dragon, carved by Bernt Notke of Lübeck in 1489, and the *Parhelion* (1520), the oldest-known painting of Stockholm. ✉ *Trångsund 1, Gamla Stan* ☎ *08/7233016* ☉ *Sept.–Apr., daily 9–4; May–Aug., daily 9–6.*

⑫ Stortorget (Great Square). Here in 1520 the Danish king Christian II ordered a massacre of Swedish noblemen. The slaughter paved the way for a national revolt against foreign rule and the founding of Sweden as a sovereign state under King Gustav Vasa, who ruled from 1523 to 1560. One legend holds that if it rains heavily enough on the anniversary of the massacre, the old stones still run red. ✉ *Near Kungliga Slottet, Gamla Stan.*

need a break? The tall, thin building that houses the café **Kaffekoppen** (✉ Stortorget 18–20, Gamla Stan ☎ 08/203170) graces countless postcards of the city. And beautiful it is. Even better, though, is to head for the inviting, dim cellar to indulge in sandwiches, coffee, cakes, and pastries. You can write your postcards between bites.

⑯ Svea Hovrätt (Swedish High Court). The Swedish High Court commands a prime site on the island of Riddarholmen, on a quiet and restful quayside. Though it's closed to the public, you can sit on the water's edge nearby and watch the boats on Riddarfjärden (Bay of Knights) and, beyond it, Lake Mälaren. From here you can see the stately arches of Västerbron (West Bridge) in the distance, the southern heights, and above all, the imposing profile of City Hall, which appears almost to be floating on the water. At the quay you may see one of the Göta Canal ships.

㉔ Svensk Form (Swedish Form). This museum emphasizes the importance of Swedish form and design, although international works and trends are also covered. Exhibits include everything from chairs to light fixtures to cups, bowls, and silverware. Find out why Sweden is considered a world leader in industrial design. Every year the museum gives out a prestigious and highly coveted design award called Utmärkt Svenskt Form (Outstanding Swedish Design). The winning objects are then exhibited in fall. ✉ *Holmamiralens väg 2, Skeppsholmen, City* ☎ *08/4633130* ⊕ *www.svenskform.se* ✉ *SKr 20* ☉ *Tues.–Sun. noon–5.*

Djurgården & Skansen

Throughout history, Djurgården has been Stockholm's pleasure island. There was time when only the king could enjoy this enormous green space, and enjoy it he did. Today Stockholmers of all persuasions come here to breathe some fresh air, visit the island's many museums, stroll through the forests and glades, get their pulses racing at the Gröna Lund amusement park, or just relax by the water and watch the boats sail by.

a good
walk

You can approach Djurgården from the water aboard the small ferries that leave from Slussen at the southern end of Gamla Stan. In summer, ferries also leave from Nybrokajen, or New Bridge Quay, in front of the Kungliga Dramatiska Teatern. Alternatively, starting at the theater, stroll down the grandiose residential strip of Strandvägen—taking in the magnificent old sailing ships, the fine views over the harbor and the ornately luxurious apartment buildings—and cross Djurgårdsbron, or Djurgården Bridge, to the island. Your first port of call should be the **Vasamuseet** ㉕ ▶, with its dramatic display of splendid 17th-century warships. If you have children in tow, be sure to visit **Junibacken** ㉖, just off Djurgårdsbron. Return to Djurgårdsvägen to find the entrance to the **Nordiska Museet** ㉗, worth a visit for insight into Swedish folklore.

Continue on Djurgårdsvägen to the amusement park **Gröna Lund Tivoli** ㉘, where Stockholmers of all ages come to play. Beyond the park, cross Djurgårdsvägen to **Skansen** ㉙.

From Skansen continue on Djurgårdsvägen to Prins Eugens Väg and follow the signs to the beautiful late-19th-century **Waldemarsudde** ㉚. On the way back to Djurgårdsbron, take the small street called Hazeliusbacken around to the charmingly archaic **Biologiska Museet** ㉛. From the museum walk toward Djurgårdsbron and then take a right on Rosendalsvägen. Signs on this street lead to **Rosendals Trädgården** ㉜, which has beautiful gardens and a delightful café. From here you can stroll back along the water toward the city.

TIMING This is one part of Stockholm you won't want to rush through. Allow half a day for this tour, unless you're planning to turn it into a full-day event with lengthy visits to Skansen, Junibacken, and Gröna Lund Tivoli, plus a bit more time for treating yourself to some tempting ice-cream breaks on the grass or a snooze in the shade of a tree. The Vasamuseet warrants two hours, the Nordiska needs an hour, and the Biologiska museum and Waldemarsudde require about an hour. Gröna Lund Tivoli is closed from mid-September to late April. The Biologiska Museet and Waldemarsudde are closed Monday.

What to See

🖰 ㉛ **Biologiska Museet** (Biological Museum). The Biological Museum, in the shadow of Skansen, exhibits preserved animals in various simulated environments. The museum itself, unchanged since its 19th-century opening, is a delightful look into the past. ⊠ *Hazeliusporten, Djurgården* ☎ *08/4428215* ⊕ *www.skansen.se* ⊠ *SKr 30* ⊙ *Apr.–Sept., daily 11–4; Oct.–Mar., Tues.–Sun. 11–3.*

🖰 ㉘ **Gröna Lund Tivoli.** Smaller than Copenhagen's Tivoli or Göteborg's Liseberg, this amusement park has managed to retain much of its historical charm, while making room for some modern, hair-raising rides among the pleasure gardens, amusement arcades, and restaurants. If you're feeling especially daring, try the Power Tower. At 350 feet, it's Europe's tallest free-fall amusement-park ride and one of the best ways to see Stockholm, albeit for about three seconds, before you plummet. There isn't an adult who grew up in Stockholm who can't remember the annual excitement of Gröna Lund's April opening. Go and you will see why. ✉ *Allmänna Gränd 9, Djurgården* ☎ *08/58750100* ⊕ *www.tivoli.se* 🖾 *SKr 60, not including tickets or passes for rides* ☉ *Late Apr.–mid-Sept., daily. Hrs vary but are generally noon–11 PM. Call ahead for specific information.*

★ ☸ ㉖ **Junibacken.** In this storybook house you travel in small carriages through the world of children's book writer Astrid Lindgren, creator of the irrepressible character Pippi Longstocking, among others. Lindgren's tales come alive as various scenes are revealed. Parents can enjoy a welcome moment of rest after the mini-train ride as the children lose themselves in the near-life-size model of Pippi Longstocking's house. It's perfect for children ages five and up. ✉ *Galärvarsv., Djurgården* ☎ *08/58723000* ⊕ *www.junibacken.se* 🖾 *SKr 95* ☉ *Jan.–May and Sept.–Dec., Tues. to Fri. 10–5, weekends 9–6; June and Aug. daily 10–5; July daily 9–6.*

☸ ㉗ **Nordiska Museet** (Nordic Museum). An imposing late-Victorian structure housing peasant costumes from every region of the country and exhibits on the Sámi (pronounced *sah*-mee)—Lapps, the formerly seminomadic reindeer herders who inhabit the far north—and many other aspects of Swedish life. Families with children should visit the delightful "village life" play area on the ground floor. ✉ *Djurgårdsv. 6–16, Djurgården* ☎ *08/51954600* ⊕ *www.nordiskamuseet.se* 🖾 *SKr 60* ☉ *Mon.–Fri. 10–4, weekend 11–5.*

㉜ **Rosendals Trädgården** (Rosendal's Garden). This gorgeous slice of greenery is a perfect place to spend a few hours on a late summer afternoon. When the weather's nice, people flock to the garden café, which is in one of the greenhouses, to enjoy tasty pastries and salads made from the locally grown vegetables. Pick your own flowers from the vast flower beds (paying by weight), stroll through the creative garden displays, or take away produce from the farm shop. ✉ *Rosendalsterrassen 12, Djurgården* ☎ *08/54581270* 🖾 *Free* ☉ *May–Sept., weekdays 11–5, weekends 11–6; Oct.–Apr. call ahead for specific information.*

Fodor'sChoice
★

★ ☸ ㉙ **Skansen.** The world's first open-air museum, Skansen was founded in 1891 by philologist and ethnographer Artur Hazelius, who is buried here. He preserved examples of traditional Swedish architecture brought from all parts of the country, including farmhouses, windmills, barns, a working glassblower's hut, and churches. Not only is Skansen a delightful trip out of time in the center of a modern city, but it also provides insight into the life and culture of Sweden's various regions. In addition, the park has a zoo, carnival area, aquarium, theater, and cafés. You might see a wedding in the old church, complete with horse-drawn carriage; you can have a go at threshing wheat in the old mill; you'll probably laugh at the clapping seals in the zoo; and you'll almost certainly want to come back again. ✉ *Djurgårdsslätten 4951, Djurgår-*

den ☎ *08/4428000* ⊕ *www.skansen.se* 🕮 *Park and zoo: Sept.–Apr. SKr 50; May–Aug. SKr 70. Aquarium SKr 60* ☉ *Oct.–Apr., daily 10–4; May, daily 10–8; June–Aug., daily 10–10; Sept., daily 10–5.*

need a break? The **Cirkus Theater** (⊠ Djurgårdsslätten, Djurgården ☎ 08/58798750), on Hazeliusbacken right near the entrance to Skansen, has a lovely terrace café, where you can soak up some rays over a cold beer, a glass of wine, or a frothy cappuccino. If you want something a bit more hearty, head to **Hasselbacken Hotel** (⊠ Hazeliusbacken 20, Djurgården ☎ 08/51734300) (the birthplace of the well-known eponymous crispy potato dish), where you can dine on the terrace.

★ ▶ ㉕ **Vasamuseet** (Vasa Museum). The warship *Vasa* sank 10 minutes into its maiden voyage in 1628, consigned to a watery grave until it was raised from the seabed in 1961. Its hull was preserved by the Baltic mud, free of the worms that can eat through ships' timbers. Now largely restored to her former glory (however short-lived it may have been), the man-of-war resides in a handsome museum. The sheer size of this cannon-laden hulk inspires awe and fear in equal measure. The political history of the world may have been different had she made it out of harbor. Daily tours are available year-round. ⊠ *Galärvarsv., Djurgården* ☎ *08/51954800* ⊕ *www.vasamuseet.se* 🕮 *SKr 80* ☉ *Thurs.–Tues. 10–5, Wed. 10–8.*

㉚ **Waldemarsudde.** This estate, Djurgården's gem, was bequeathed to the Swedish people by Prince Eugen upon his death, in 1947. It maintains an important collection of Nordic paintings from 1880 to 1940, in addition to the prince's own works. The rather grand stone terrace, situated above the entrance to Stockholm's harbor, is the perfect spot to perch and watch passing boats. ⊠ *Prins Eugens väg 6, Djurgården* ☎ *08/54583700* ⊕ *www.waldemarsudde.com* 🕮 *SKr 80* ☉ *May–Aug., Tues., Wed., and Fri.–Sun. 11–5, Thurs. 11–8; Sept.–Apr., Tues., Wed., and Fri. 11–4, Thurs. 11–8, weekends 11–4.*

Östermalm & Kaknästornet

Marked by waterfront rows of Renaissance buildings with palatial rooftops and ornamentation, Östermalm is a quietly regal residential section of central Stockholm. History and money are steeped into the very bricks and mortar of its elegant streets, which are lined with museums, fine shopping, and exclusive restaurants. On Strandvägen, or Beach Way, the boulevard that follows the harbor's edge from the busy downtown area to the staid diplomatic quarter, you can choose one of three routes. The waterside walk, with its splendid views of the city harbor, bustles with tour boats and sailboats. Parallel to the walk (away from the water) is a tree-shaded walking and bike path. Walk, rollerblade, or ride a bike down the middle, and you just might meet the occasional horseback rider, properly attired in helmet, jacket, and high polished boots. Take the route farthest from the water, and you will walk past upscale shops and expensive restaurants.

a good walk

Walk east from the Kungliga Dramatiska Teatern, in Nybroplan, along Strandvägen until you get to Djurgårdsbron, the ornate little bridge that leads to the island of Djurgården. Resist going to the park, and instead turn left up Narvavägen and walk along the right-hand side until you reach Oscars Kyrka. Cross the street and continue up the left side until you reach the **Historiska Museet** ③③ ►. From here it's only a short walk farther up Narvavägen to Karlaplan, a pleasant circular park with a fountain. Go across or around the park to find Karlavägen. Heading northwest along this long boulevard, you'll pass by many small shops and galleries. At Nybrogatan turn left (this intersection is beyond the limits of the Stockholm map). Be sure to take some time to check out the exclusive furniture stores on your way down to **Östermalmstorg** ③④, where there's an excellent indoor food market. Cut across the square and take a right down Sibyllegatan to the **Musik Museet** ③⑤, installed in the city's oldest industrial building. Within the same block is the **Armémuseum.** Then go back to Nybroplan, where you can catch Bus 69 going east to **Kaknästornet** ③⑥ for a spectacular view of Stockholm from the tallest tower in Scandinavia. From here walk back toward town along Djurgårdsbrunnsvägen until you reach **Tekniska Museet** ③⑦, a particularly good stop if you have kids in tow. If you still have a bit of energy left, you can continue down Djurgårdsbrunnsvägen to see Diplomatstaden, or Diplomat Town. Much fun is to be had wandering the leafy streets of this small waterside gathering of foreign ambassadors' grand mansions.

TIMING   This tour requires a little more than a half day. You'll want to spend about an hour in each of the museums. The bus ride from Nybroplan to Kaknästornet takes about 15 minutes, and the tower merits another half hour. Check ahead for Monday closings in the off-season.

What to See

Armémuseum. The large Military Museum covers everything from Sweden's early might as a kingdom to its unique, neutral military position during the 20th century. The castle guards and military band marches from this square every day on its walk to the Royal Palace on Gamla Stan. ⊠ *Riddarg. 13, Östermalm* ☏ *08/5196300* ⊕ *www.armemuseum. org* ⊠ *Free* ⊙ *Tues. 11–8, Wed.–Sun. 11–4.*

need a break?

For some of the best baguettes and croissants outside Paris, stop by **Riddarbageriet** (⊠ Riddarg. 15, Östermalm) near the Armémuseum. Bread in Stockholm doesn't get any better than this: they deliver to the king and queen and many of the city's best restaurants. You can also get great coffee, sandwiches, and pastries. If you like the food, you can buy the recipe book (in Swedish only). The bakery is closed in July.

► ③③   **Historiska Museet** (Museum of National Antiquities). Viking treasures and the Gold Room are the main draw, but well-presented temporary exhibitions also cover various periods of Swedish history. The gift shop here is excellent. ⊠ *Narvav. 13–17, Östermalm* ☏ *08/51955600* ⊕ *www.historiska.se* ⊠ *Free* ⊙ *Daily 10–5.*

36 Kaknästornet (Kaknäs TV Tower). The 511-foot-high Kaknäs radio and television tower, completed in 1967, is the tallest building in Scandinavia. Surrounded by satellite dishes, it is also used as a linkup station for a number of Swedish satellite TV channels and radio stations. Eat a meal in a restaurant 426 feet above the ground and enjoy panoramic views of the city and the archipelago. ⊠ *Mörkakroken off Djurgårdsbrunnsv., Djurgården* ☎ *08/6672180* ⊠ *SKr 30* ☉ *June–Aug., daily 9 AM–10 PM; Sept.–May, daily 10–9.*

off the beaten path

MILLESGÅRDEN – This gallery and sculpture garden north of the city is dedicated to the property's former owner, American-Swedish sculptor Carl Milles (1875–1955) and is one of the most magical places in Stockholm. On display throughout the property are Milles's own unique works, and inside the main building, once his house, is his private collection. On the terrace is the beautiful Anne's House, designed by famous Austrian designer Josef Frank, where Milles spent the final years of his life. The setting is exquisite: sculptures top columns on terraces in a magical garden high above the harbor and the city. Millesgården can be easily reached via subway to Ropsten, where you catch the Lidingö train and get off at Herserud, the second stop. The trip takes about 30 minutes. ⊠ *Carl Milles väg 2, Lidingö* ☎ *08/4467580* ⊕ *www.millesgarden.se* ⊠ *SKr 80* ☉ *May–Sept., daily 11–5; Oct.–Apr., Tues.–Fri. noon–4, weekends 11–5.*

☾ 35 Musik Museet. Inside what was the military's bread bakery from the 17th century to the mid-1900s, the Music Museum has more than 6,000 instruments in its collection, with the focus on pieces from 1600 to 1850. Its 18th-century woodwind collection is internationally renowned. The museum also holds jazz, folk, and world-music concerts. Children are allowed to touch and play some of the instruments, and the motion-sensitive "Sound Room" lets you produce musical effects simply by gesturing and moving around. ⊠ *Sibylleg. 2, Östermalm* ☎ *08/51955490* ⊕ *www.musikmuseet.se* ⊠ *Free* ☉ *Tues.–Sun. 11–4.*

34 Östermalmstorg. The market square and its neighboring streets represent old, established Stockholm. **Saluhall** is more a collection of boutiques than an indoor food market; the fish displays can be especially intriguing. At the other end of the square, **Hedvig Eleonora Kyrka**, a church with characteristically Swedish faux-marble painting throughout its wooden interior, is the site of frequent lunchtime concerts in spring and summer. ⊠ *Nybrog. at Humlegårdsg., Östermalm.*

need a break?

The little restaurants inside the **Saluhall** (⊠ Östermalmstorg, Östermalm) offer everything from takeout coffee to sit-down meals. One of the best bets is **Lisa Elmquist** (☎ 08/55340410), next to the market's fish stall. It is highly recommended for a bite of lobster, an oyster or four, and a glass of chardonnay.

☾ 37 Tekniska Museet. Only a 10-minute bus ride from the city, the Museum of Science and Technology is a place of wonderment for kids of all ages. Start in the huge Machinery Hall displaying cars, bicycles, a climb-aboard steam train, and even airplanes. Follow this to the robot room, then the TV studio, and, finally, head to the awesome Teknorama, the museum's science center, where you can learn more about the natural sciences and technology. There's a café that does a mean dish of pancakes with cream and jelly, as well as a gift shop. ⊠ *Museiv. 7, Djurgårdsbrunnsv., Djurgården* ☎ *08/4505600* ⊕ *www.tekniskamuseet.se* ⊠ *SKr 60; free Wed. night* ☉ *Mon., Tues., Thurs., and Fri. 10–5; Wed. 10–8; weekends 11–5.*

Outside the City

There are a number of excellent sites only a short bus or subway ride from the city center, many of which can be combined. Stockholm's city environs very quickly become greener as you leave the bustling center. Trips to nearly all these places could be done in a morning or afternoon and even added on to the other walks. Most are excellent ways to experience Sweden's delightful countryside.

What to See

Fodor'sChoice ★ **Bergianska Trädgården.** The beautiful Bergianska Botanical Gardens, on a peninsula extending out into the small bay of Brunnsvik, are a welcome respite from the city. They are only a short subway ride away. Paths weave along the water in the open park area. Visit Edvard Anderson's modern Växthus (Greenhouse) for its impressive Mediterranean and tropical environments. The century-old Victoriahuset (Victoria House) contains tropical plants as well, and has one of the best collections of water plants in the world. ⊠ *Frescativ. near university, Universitet* ☎ *08/54591700* ⊕ *www.bergianska.se* ⊠ *Park free, Greenhouse SKr 40, Victoria House SKr 10* ☉ *Park daily yr-round; Victoria House May–Sept., daily 11–4, weekends 11–5; Greenhouse daily 11–5.*

Fjärilshuset (Butterfly and Bird House). After a short bus ride and a walk through the magnificent Haga Park, you could be in a room filled with hundreds of tropical butterflies. In the bird room, hundreds of birds of 40 species fly freely. The Haga Park itself is impressive and worth a lengthy stroll, but be sure to combine it with a trip to this oasis. ⊠ *Take Bus 515 from the Odenplan subway stop. Haga* ☎ *08/7303981* ⊕ *www.fjarilshuset.se* ⊠ *SKr 70* ☉ *Apr.–Sept., Tues.–Fri. 10–4, weekends 11–5:30; Oct.–Mar., Tues.–Fri. 10–3, weekends 11–4.*

☾ **Naturhistoriska Riksmuseet and Cosmonova** (Museum of Natural History). Founded in 1739 by the famous Swedish botanist Linnaeus and his colleagues at the Science Academy, the museum has been in its present location near the university since 1916. The last decade has brought much rebuilding and other improvements. Exhibits include "Life in Water," "Marvels of the Human Body," and "Space Adventure." Cosmonova shows science and nature films in Sweden's only IMAX theater. The subway ride to the Universitet stop takes less than 10 minutes from the city center. ⊠ *Frescativ. 40, Universitet* ☎ *08/51954040* ⊕ *www.nrm.se* ⊠ *Free* ☉ *Fri.–Wed. 10–7, Thurs. 10–8. Cosmonova mid-May–end of May, Aug., and Sept., Tues.–Sun. 12–5; June and July, daily 10–7.*

Tyresö Slott (Tyresö Castle). After a 20-minute bus ride from southern Stockholm, you'll find yourself in the gorgeous, romantic gardens that surround this castle, built in the 1660s. The Nordic Museum led the renovations that restored the grounds to their late-1800s glory. The main building is filled with elaborate salons, libraries, and studies, and the west wing has a nice café and restaurant. Be sure to leave time for both the castle and gardens. ✉ *Take Bus 805 from Gullmarsplan to Tyresö Slott Tyresö* ☎ *08/7700178* ⊕ *www.nordiskamuseet.se/slott* 🎫 *SKr 80* ☉ *Sept. and Oct., daily 11–3; June 22–Aug. 19, Tues.–Sun. 11–4. Tours at noon, 1, and 2. Closed end of Aug.*

Ulriksdals Slott (Ulriksdals Castle). Construction on the castle began in 1640, but it was during the first half of the 1700s that the castle took on the look that it has today. Built in the Renaissance style, the castle is most closely associated with King Gustav Adolf and Queen Louise, who in 1923 added a famous living room designed by Carl Malmsten. The Dutch Renaissance chapel from the mid-1800s is still used for masses, weddings, and concerts. Entrance is by guided tour only. ✉ *Take Bus 503 from Bergshamra subway stop, on the Red Line. Ulriksdal* ☎ *08/ 4026130* ⊕ *www.royalcourt.se/ulriksdal* 🎫 *SKr 50* ☉ *June–Aug., guided tours at noon, 1, 2, and 3; Sept.–May by appointment only.*

WHERE TO EAT

Stockholm's restaurant scene rivals that of any major European capital, with upscale restaurants offering creative menus at trendy, modern locations. The best combine foreign innovations with Sweden's high-quality raw ingredients. The city's top restaurants will charge accordingly, but you aren't likely to leave disappointed. Of course, there are also plenty of less expensive restaurants with traditional Swedish cooking. Among Swedish dishes, the best bets are wild game and fish, particularly salmon, and the smorgasbord buffet, which usually offers a good variety at an inexpensive price. Reservations are often necessary on weekends.

Prices

WHAT IT COSTS In Swedish Kronor				
	$$$$	**$$$**	**$$**	**$**	**¢**
AT DINNER	over 420	250–420	150–250	100–150	under 100

Prices are for a main course at dinner.

Downtown Stockholm & Beyond

$$$–$$$$ ✕ **Edsbacka Krog.** Chef Christer Lindström is the hot ticket behind the stoves of this ancient coaching inn just outside town; he produces rarefied feasts, classically French in technique, using fresh local ingredients. Critics bemoan the formality and the hush of this place, while fans focus on the exceptional food and faultless service. Don't expect anything too contemporary (inside you'll find old-style luster and exposed beams), but do expect near-perfection. ✉ *Sollentunav. 220, Sollentuna* ☎ *08/ 963300* ▤ *AE, DC, MC, V* ✪ *Closed Sun. and Mon.*

$$$–$$$$ ✕ **Restaurangen.** Flavor is the driving force behind this hip restaurant. As a pleasant sideline it's also great fun to eat here. You build three-, five-, or seven-course meals from 20 flavors, 15 of which are salty and 5 of which are sweet. Each flavor has a letter next to it that corresponds to a list of wines by the glass that are recommended to best complement it. A large box of cutlery appears, to cover all your choices, and the wine is lined up with an identifying label on each glass. Dig in, share, mix and match and, most important, have fun. The food is considered contemporary Asian, but French, Spanish, and Swedish all appear too. The achingly cool interior was created by three students from Stockholm's prestigious Beckman's School of Design. ✉ *Oxtorgsg. 14, City* ☎ *08/ 220952* ▤ *AE, DC, MC, V* ✪ *Closed Sun.*

★ **$$$–$$$$** ✕ **Wedholms Fisk.** Noted for its fresh seafood dishes, Wedholms Fisk is appropriately set by a bay in Stockholm's center. High ceilings, large windows, and tasteful modern paintings from the owner's personal collection create a spacious, sophisticated space. The traditional Swedish cuisine, which consists almost exclusively of seafood, is simple but outstanding. The menu is divided by fish type, with a number of dish options for each type of fish, such as monkfish with a porcini cream sauce and a warm bean salad. ✉ *Nybrokajen 17, City* ☎ *08/6117874* ▤ *AE, DC, MC, V* ✪ *Closed Sun. and July.*

$$–$$$$ ✕ **Operakällaren.** Open since 1787, the haughty grande dame of Stockholm is more a Swedish institution than a seat of gastronomic distinction. Thick carpeting, shiny polished brass, and handsome carved-wood chairs and tables fill what is almost certainly one of Europe's most amazing dining rooms. The crystal chandeliers are said to be Sweden's finest, and the high windows on the south side have magnificent views of the Royal Palace. The restaurant is famed for its seasonal smorgasbord, offered at Christmas. Coveted selections include marinated herring, reindeer, elk, and ice cream with cloudberry sauce. In summer the veranda opens as the Operabryggan Café, facing Kungsträdgården and the waterfront. Around the corner in the same building is the restaurant's *backficka*, a pleasantly active bar/restaurant with a less expensive menu. ✉ *Operahuset, Jakobs Torg 2, City* ☎ *08/6765800* ⌖ *Reservations essential* 🔯 *Jacket and tie* ▤ *AE, DC, MC, V* ✪ *Main dining room closed Sun.–Tues. and July. No lunch.*

$$$ ✕ **Bon Lloc.** With an elegant and spacious dining area and a creative
Fodor'sChoice Mediterranean-influenced menu, Bon Lloc has established itself as one
★ of the hottest restaurants in town. The menu uses common ingredients like ham and cod to create dishes that recall Catalonia as much as Sweden. The extensive wine list offers an excellent selection of European wines. The interior's light-brown wood and mosaic tiles allude to Mediterranean styles while still evoking Swedish simplicity, much as the food does. ✉ *Regeringsg. 111, Norrmalm* ☎ *08/6606060* ⌖ *Reservations essential* ▤ *AE, DC, MC, V* ✪ *Closed Sun. No lunch.*

$$$ ✕ **Fredsgatan 12.** The government crowd files into this funky restaurant
Fodor'sChoice at lunch; a more casual yet stylish crowd arrives at night. All come here
★ to enjoy what is some of the best food in town. The young chef, Melker

SWEDISH GASTRONOMY

GASTRONOMY IN SWEDEN has recently come through what can only be described as turbulent times. For 15 years there was a struggle between two forces. On the one hand was Sweden's traditional home-cooked food with its rich flavors, heavy sauces, and emphasis on meat and simple fish. On the other hand was the emerging young blood of Swedish cuisine, fired by international influence, hungry for creativity, and driven by quality. In a result that is time-honored in Sweden, both parties came out as victors.

Twenty years ago Sweden was a closed book food-wise. Its tables were still laden with the kind of food that had been eaten for years: meatballs, sausage, smoked pork, fried herring, boiled beets, potatoes, pea soup, and onion sauce, among the other usual suspects. A Swedish colleague of mine once remarked that growing up in Sweden in the '70s, it was safe to assume that anything fun you asked for you were not allowed to have. The unknown, it seems, was best left that way—and this philosophy extended into the kitchen.

You can't keep the curious revolutionaries at bay forever, and Sweden's young chefs wanted something different, something to call their own. With this in mind, many went abroad to explore the flavors of other countries, visit foreign chefs, and work in faraway restaurants.

Swedish chefs are a smart bunch. They knew that their own land offered a bounty rarely matched for quality and freshness. Sweden's vast open spaces could offer wild mushrooms, lingonberries, cloudberries, wild strawberries, game, fish, and plenty of grazing land to produce fine meats. So they brought their new inspiration back home. A new Swedish cuisine was born, using the excitement of global flavors with the purity of Swedish ingredients.

The Swedish restaurant industry took note, and a drive was implemented to spread the word of this pioneering cuisine. With typical Swedish Lutheran resolve, money was invested in training new chefs. The Swedish culinary team stormed the world stage, picking up gold medals wherever they went. Sweden's chefs were gaining as much notoriety as the Swedish Chef had at the hands of Muppet creator Jim Henson, only this time for completely different reasons.

Sweden's new culinary regime didn't stay settled for long. It was only natural that a people so fond of tradition could stay away from their meatballs and sausage for only so long. They wanted their old food back, but they wanted it back on their terms. They had tasted quality and innovation, and they liked it.

Today Sweden's restaurants and home kitchens offer a happy mix of old and new. Restaurants that wow diners with rabbit and fennel mille-feuille with a citrus and mustard jus will just as happily offer organic, grass-fed beef meatballs with cream sauce and new-season potato puree. Supermarket shelves are filled with Swedish sausages stacked right next to fresh sushi.

Swedes who just a few years ago publicly dismissed their national dishes for the newer cuisine now fully embrace them. The classic Thursday dish of pea soup is now proudly brandished at outdoor cafés by Swedish diners—as long as they have an espresso and biscotti to finish the meal, of course.

— Rob Hincks

Andersson, works his magic, creating Swedish-, Asian-, and European-inspired dishes that defy convention and positively demand enjoyment. The menu offers creative combinations, such as chicken with eucalyptus or lamb with dill, licorice, and carrots. When ordering a cocktail, choose a flavor such as mint and sugar or lemon-cherry and then an alcohol of your choice with which to mix it. From the bar you can get a nice view into the kitchen of this popular restaurant—always a good sign of a place that values its food. ⊠ *Fredsg. 12, City* ☎ *08/248052* ⊟ *AE, DC, MC, V* ⊘ *Closed Sun. No lunch.*

$$$ ✕ **Ulriksdals Wärdshus.** The weekend lunchtime smorgasbord at this country inn can't be beat. Built in the park of an 18th-century palace in 1868, the beautiful glassed-in dining room, accented with light floral patterns and mint-green seat covers, overlooks orchards and a peaceful lake. It's an expensive restaurant, but the impeccable service and outstanding cuisine make the splurge worthwhile. Menu highlights include terrine of foie gras with rhubarb and cardamom or halibut with asparagus and sorrel. The restaurant's cellar is listed in Guinness world records as the most complete in the world. There are more than 500 bottles of the top six Bordeaux chateaux from the 20th century, nearly one for every year for every wine. ⊠ *Ulriksdals Slottspark, Solna* ☎ *08/850815* ⚲ *Reservations essential* ⊟ *AE, DC, MC, V* ⊘ *No dinner Sun.*

★ **$$$** ✕ **Vasa Eggen.** An exquisite dining room offering the real feeling of being hidden away makes this haunt a top choice among Stockholmers. Vasa Eggen is less talked about than Stockholm's other great restaurants, but no less fabulous. The food is strikingly modern, blending French and Asian techniques with top-quality local ingredients. Fans of the visual will love the clean, simple lines and the natural tones of the restaurant, which are perfectly juxtaposed by a statement-making stained-glass ceiling dome. ⊠ *Birger Jarlsg. 29, Östermalm* ☎ *08/216169* ⚲ *Reservations essential* ⊟ *AE, DC, MC, V* ⊘ *Closed Sun. No lunch Sat.*

★ **$$–$$$** ✕ **Lux.** The former Electrolux household appliance factory is now an industrial-chic restaurant; hence the name. Simple wood furniture and white-cloth tables contrast nicely with the exposed brick and wrought iron of the former work space. Light floods the restaurant through enormous windows during the day. At night the space is more subdued. Young chefs Henrik Norström and Peter Johansson work the stoves here, producing fresh, light, and innovative modern European food, using excellent local ingredients, many of which have their source listed on the menu. ⊠ *Primusg. 116, Lilla Essingen* ☎ *08/6190190* ⚲ *Reservations essential* ⊟ *AE, DC, MC, V* ⊘ *Closed Mon. No lunch weekends.*

$$–$$$ ✕ **Riche.** This Stockholm establishment was for many years an exclusive club. Today the elegance and style remain, but the diners are from a much broader pool. Eat in the casual glassed-in veranda on wicker chairs, or move inside to the main dining room for more formal dining. For the ultimate in posh tradition, book a table at the Teatergrillen, in the back: members of the Swedish royal family are fans, too. All three sections serve Swedish and French cuisine. Upstairs is a chill-out space where DJs play late night and you can buy simple *smørrebrød* (open-face sandwiches) until 2 AM. ⊠ *Birger Jarlsg. 4, Östermalm* ☎ *08/54503560* ⊟ *AE, DC, MC, V* ⊘ *Closed Sun.*

$$–$$$ ✕ **Stallmästaregården.** A historic old inn with an attractive courtyard and garden, Stallmästaregården is in Haga Park, just north of Norrtull, about 15 minutes by car or bus from the city center. Fine summer meals are served on a tented terrace overlooking the waters of Brunnsviken. Specialties include poached fillet of Dover sole with black *tagliolini* and lobster sauce and simple, but delightfully fresh, seafood platters. ⊠ *Norrtull near Haga; take Bus 52 to Stallmästaregården. Haga* ☎ *08/6101300* ⊟ *AE, DC, MC, V* ⊙ *Closed Sun.*

$$–$$$ ✕ **Ulla Winbladh.** Since 1897 this fine old inn on the island paradise of Djurgården has been serving classic Swedish dishes to its happy customers. In 2004 a team of young investors took the place over and nothing has changed—well, almost nothing. The restaurant remains a maze of several small dining rooms, some with exposed brick walls and scrubbed wood tables, others with softly upholstered chairs, Swedish linen on the tables, and every inch of wall space taken up by pictures. Sculptures and other artwork dot the entire restaurant, and the warm orange glow of the chandeliers oozes through tiny, cross-paned windows. All that has changed is the food. There are still plenty of native classics, but the young investors have seen fit to put out some delicious modern Italian cuisine, as well. So far, no one has complained. ⊠ *Rosendalsv. 8, Djurgården* ☎ *08/6630571* ⌲ *Reservations essential* ⊟ *AE, DC, MC, V.*

$–$$$ ✕ **Storstad.** A lighter and less expensive menu is served in the bar area of this popular hangout, which looks out on the street through wide arching windows. In the sparse but inviting dining room in the back you might try the sweet-corn soup with truffle pasta and Parmesan cheese before moving on to meat specialties such as fried duck breast with honey-baked beets, mushroom spring rolls, and port syrup. The wine list is excellent and especially strong on French and Californian wines. ⊠ *Odeng. 41, Vasastan* ☎ *08/6733800* ⌲ *Reservations essential* ⊟ *AE, DC, MC, V* ⊙ *Closed Sun. No lunch.*

¢–$$$ ✕ **Tranan.** There's something about Tranan that makes you want to go back. The food is Swedish with a touch of French and is consistently very good. The stark walls covered with old movie posters and the red-and-white-checked tablecloths are reminders of the days when it was a workingman's beer parlor. Try the *biff rydberg,* a fillet of beef, fried potatoes, horseradish, and egg yolk—it's a Swedish classic. The bar downstairs has DJs and live music; it gets packed to bursting on weekends. ⊠ *Karlbergsv. 14, Vasastan* ☎ *08/52728100* ⊟ *AE, DC, MC, V* ⊙ *No lunch weekends.*

$$ ✕ **Lisa På Udden.** Fish is the order of the day at this light and airy waterside restaurant on Stockholm's beautiful Djurgården island. The spacious modern interior is decked out in very Scandinavian style: wood floors, simple wood furniture, and primary colors. The main draw, though, is the view across the water, through the restaurant's glass facade. The tables fill up, especially on weekends, so turn up early or late to secure one for yourself. ⊠ *Biskopsv. 9, Djurgården* ☎ *08/6609475* ⊟ *MC, V.*

★ **$$** ✕ **Prinsen.** Still in the same location as when it opened in 1897, the Prince serves both traditional and modern Swedish cuisine, but it is for the traditional that most people go. The interior is rich with mellow, warm lighting; dark-wood paneling; and leather chairs and booths. The staff is as delightfully starched as the white aprons they wear. On the walls are black-and-white oil paintings of famous people done by one of the long-serving staff members, as well as paintings by local artists that came into the restaurant's possession when they were used as payment to settle tabs. The restaurant is rightly known for its scampi salad and *Wallenbergare,* a classic dish of veal, cream, and peas. Downstairs are a bar and a space for larger parties. ⊠ *Mäster Samuelsg. 4, City* ☎ *08/ 6111331* ▤ *AE, DC, MC, V* ⊘ *No lunch weekends.*

$$ ╳ **Rolfs Kök.** Small and modern, Rolfs is a casual restaurant serving excellent Swedish-French cuisine to an eclectic mix of businesspeople and theater and arts folks. The salt and pepper shakers hang on hooks on the wall above each table. Go for the lingonberry-glazed reindeer fillet with cauliflower; root vegetables and smoked chili pepper; or a feta cheese salad with lime, soy, and chili-fried chicken. ⊠ *Tegnérg. 41, Norrmalm* ☎ *08/101696* ▤ *AE, DC, MC, V* ⊘ *No lunch weekends.*

$$ ╳ **Stockholms Matvarufabriken.** Although it's a bit hard to find, tucked away as it is on a side street, Stockholm's Food Factory is well worth seeking out. The popular bistro restaurant, serving French, Italian, and Swedish cuisine, is packed full on the weekends as young and old come to enjoy the exposed-brick, candlelight-infused dining room and the varied menu. Here omelets are taken to new levels with ingredients such as truffles and asparagus; the choices when it comes to fresh seafood are excellent. Brown-paper tablecloths and kitchen cloths used as napkins set the informal tone. ⊠ *Idung. 12, Vasastan* ☎ *08/320704* ▤ *AE, DC, MC, V* ⊘ *No lunch.*

$$ ╳ **Sturehof.** This massive complex of a restaurant with two huge bars is a complete social, architectural, and dining experience amid wood paneling, leather chairs and sofas, and distinctive lighting fixtures. There's a bar directly facing Stureplan where you can sit on a summer night and watch Stockholmers gather at the nearby Svampen (the mushroomlike concrete structure that has been the city's meeting point for years). In the elegant dining room fine Swedish cuisine is offered. Upstairs is the O-Bar, a dark and smoky lounge filled well into the night with young people and loud music. ⊠ *Stureplan 2, City* ☎ *08/4405730* ▤ *AE, DC, MC, V.*

$$ ╳ **Wasahof.** Across the street from Vasaparken, and just a short walk from Odenplan, Wasahof feels like an authentic bistro, but the cooking actually mixes Swedish, French, and Italian recipes. The pleasantly rustic space and good food have attracted all kinds of culturati—actors, writers, journalists—for some time. Seafood is a specialty here—this is the place in Stockholm to get oysters. ⊠ *Dalag. 46, Vasastan* ☎ *08/323440* ▤ *AE, DC, MC, V* ⊘ *Closed Sun.*

$–$$ ╳ **Dramatenrestaurangen Frippe.** Connected to Lillascenen, the smaller stage that's behind the Royal National Theater, this is the perfect place to grab a bite before a performance. One wall is covered in black-and-white photos of the theater's most famous actors, and posters of major productions line the bar, behind which is the open kitchen. Bar stools along the window allow for great people-watching. The food is a modern take on *husmanskost,* traditional Swedish cooking. Try the classic Isterband sausage with creamy parsley potatoes. ⊠ *Nybrog./Almlöfsg., City* ☎ *08/6656142* ▤ *MC, V* ⊗ *No lunch weekends.*

$–$$ ⨯ **East.** Just off Stureplan, East is one of the city's culinary hot spots, offering enticing contemporary pan-Asian fare from Thailand, Japan, Korea, and Vietnam. Order a selection of appetizers to get a sampling of this cross-cultural cooking. East is a perfect spot to have dinner before a night on the town. Try the Luxor: chicken, tiger shrimp, and egg noodles with peanuts, mint leaves, and coconut sauce. The bar area at this vibrant restaurant turns into a miniclub at night, with soul and hip-hop on the turntables. ⊠ *Stureplan 13, Norrmalm* ☎ *08/6114959* ▤ *AE, DC, MC, V* ⊗ *No lunch weekends.*

$–$$ ⨯ **Halv trappa plus gård.** This hip restaurant is exactly what its name suggests: two half floors plus a pleasant courtyard. The retro vibe here harks back to the '70s. The menu emphasizes fish, most of it done with a Mediterranean flair. The staff is good-hearted and professional. When possible, eat in the courtyard, but book a table, since there are only 10 out there. ⊠ *Lästmakarg. 3, City* ☎ *08/6781050* ▤ *AE, DC, MC, V* ⊗ *Closed Sun. No lunch.*

$–$$ ⨯ **Kjellsons.** This pleasant hub is a bar first and a restaurant second, but this doesn't mean the menu is short on high-caliber dishes (to say nothing of fine drinks). Appetizers include an excellent pea soup (a Swedish tradition) and a delicious avocado-and-smoked-ham salad—most of the fare is traditional Swedish. And be sure to ask for a basket of cracker bread—it comes with a tube of the famous caviar. In summer there's outdoor seating. ⊠ *Birger Jarlsg. 36, City* ☎ *08/6110045* ▤ *AE, DC, MC, V.*

¢–$$ ⨯ **Roppongi.** Although far from downtown and not exactly in the most happening area, Roppongi's adventurous, creative menu and quality fish make it the best sushi place in Stockholm. This means it's almost always packed, so be ready to share the stripped-down space with other sushi lovers. The shrimp tempura rolls will leave you drooling for more, and the *tamaki* cones are plump and bursting with flavor. ⊠ *Hantverkarg. 76, Kungsholmen* ☎ *08/6501772* ▤ *MC, V* ⊗ *No lunch weekends.*

$ ⨯ **India Curry House.** The name pretty much says it all: you will find the best Indian food in Stockholm here, but if you are searching for more than that, don't come. The decor is a nondescript hodgepodge (more tacky-mess than shabby-chic). The waiters are not rude, but neither are they super friendly or efficient. But none of this matters if you have a hankering for great Indian food—you'll find searingly spicy vindaloo, mildly aromatic korma, and everything else in between. Delicious. ⊠ *Scheeleg. 6, Kungsholmen* ☎ *08/6502024* ▤ *MC, V* ⊗ *Closed weekends.*

¢–$ ⨯ **Il Forno.** You might not expect to find brick-oven pizza in Sweden, but Il Forno serves some of the best you'll find north of the Mediter-ranean. Choose from more than 25 combinations, all of which use only the freshest ingredients and a tasty, crunchy crust. The kitchen also churns out a number of pasta dishes and sells many varieties of Italian olives, olive oil, and other fine foods. As much Italian as Swedish is spoken here. Sit outside when possible—the interior can feel a bit stuffy. ⊠ *Atlasg. 9, Vasastan* ☎ *08/319049* ▤ *MC, V.*

Fodor'sChoice ★

Gamla Stan, Skeppsholmen & Södermalm

★ **$$$–$$$$** ✕ **Franska Matsalen.** This classic French restaurant in the Grand Hotel serves the best true French cuisine in the city—plus, you can enjoy an inspiring view of Gamla Stan and the Royal Palace across the inner harbor waters. The menu changes five times a year, but the emphasis is always on Swedish ingredients. Expect such dishes as pike perch with oxtail and truffles. The lofty measure of opulence here is commensurate with the bill. ✉ *Grand Hotel, Södra Blasieholmsh. 8, City* ☎ *08/6793584* ⟁ *Reservations essential* 🏛 *Jacket required* 🖃 *AE, DC, MC, V* ⊘ *Closed Sun. No lunch weekends.*

★ **$$$–$$$$** ✕ **Pontus in the Green House.** Pontus has long since cast off the shadow of his onetime mentor, Stockholm super chef Erik Lallerstedt, and become something of a culinary star himself, complete with requisite stable of restaurants. The Green House is his flagship, and a very worthy flagship it is. Green House oozes class: opulent but tasteful interiors, soft lighting, wood panels, and crisp table linen. The menu has both traditional Swedish and contemporary international cuisines. Everything is delicious, and expensive. For a calmer dining experience, choose a corner table upstairs; the ground floor always bustles. You'll be dining among Sweden's rich and famous. For a cheaper menu of traditional Swedish dishes, and slightly less fanfare, sit at the bar downstairs. ✉ *Österlångg. 17, Gamla Stan* ☎ *08/54521300* ⟁ *Reservations essential* 🖃 *AE, DC, MC, V* ⊘ *Closed Sun. No lunch Sat.*

$$$ ✕ **Den Gyldene Freden.** Sweden's most famous old tavern has been open for business since 1722. Every Thursday the Swedish Academy meets here in a private room on the second floor. The haunt of bards and barristers, artists and ad people, Freden could probably serve sawdust and still be popular, but the food and staff are worthy of the restaurant's hallowed reputation. The cuisine has a Swedish orientation, but Continental influences spice up the menu. Season permitting, try the oven-baked fillets of turbot served with chanterelles and crepes; the gray hen fried with spruce twigs and dried fruit is another good selection. ✉ *Österlångg. 51, Gamla Stan* ☎ *08/249760* 🖃 *AE, DC, MC, V* ⊘ *Closed Sun. No lunch.*

$$$ ✕ **Mistral.** Mistral's chief attraction seems to be that it is near impossible to get in; as with all things unobtainable, everyone wants it. If you do manage to get yourself one of the 18 "dinner only, no weekend" tables, you will quickly realize that Mistral has a great deal of bite to back up its considerable bark. The food here is nothing short of outstanding; since Mistral opened in 2003, it has garnered high praise from press and public. It also has managed to pick up one of Europe's highly prized Michelin stars. The food here is modern and creative, relaying heavily on very local ingredients; witness the smelt, line-caught from the waters just a few hundred feet from the restaurant's front door. Book a long, long time in advance. ✉ *Lilla Nyg. 21, Gamla Stan* ☎ *08/101224* ⟁ *Reservations essential* 🖃 *AE, DC, MC, V* ⊘ *Closed weekends, Mon., and July. No lunch.*

Fodor'sChoice ★

$$–$$$ ✕ **Eriks Bakficka.** A favorite among Östermalm locals, Eriks Bakficka is a block from the elegant waterside, a few steps down from street level.

Inside, the black-and-white tile floor, white-painted stone walls, wood tables strewn with candles, and green-glass lamps give the place a relaxed and approachable ambience. Owned by the well-known Swedish chef Erik Lallerstedt, the restaurant serves Swedish dishes, including a delicious baked pike fish with mussels and saffron. A lower-priced menu is served in the pub section. ⊠ *Fredrikshovsg. 4, Östermalm* ☎ *08/6601599* ▤ *AE, DC, MC, V* ⊙ *Closed July. No lunch weekends.*

$$–$$$ ✕ **Mårten Trotzig.** This contemporary functional space is both a dining room and a bar. The short menu demonstrates the chef's imagination, blending multicultural recipes in intriguing ways. Try the yellow- and red-tomato salad with arugula pesto, and then move on to the flounder fillet with artichoke hearts, asparagus, and a light grapefruit sauce. In a beautiful plant-lined courtyard, less-expensive lunch specials are served. The staff is young, the service professional. ⊠ *Västerlångg. 79, Gamla Stan* ☎ *08/4422530* ▤ *AE, DC, MC, V.*

★ **$–$$** ✕ **Koh Phangan.** Creative food is served until midnight at this lively Thai restaurant, where you'll be seated in individual "huts," each with a special name and style. The entire restaurant is decked out in colored lights, fake palm fronds, and trinkets from Thailand. Recorded jungle sounds play in the background. Sign up for a table on the chalkboard next to the bar when you arrive. Although you can expect at least an hour-long wait on weekends, the food is well worth it. Grilled fish and seafood with extravagant, spicy sauces are the specialty. ⊠ *Skåneg. 57, Södermalm* ☎ *08/6425040* ⊜ *Reservations not accepted* ▤ *AE, DC, MC, V.*

$–$$ ✕ **Grill Ruby.** This American-style barbecue joint (at least as American as it is possible to be in Gamla Stan) is just a cobblestone's throw away from the statue of St. George slaying the dragon. Next door to its French cousin, Bistro Ruby, Grill Ruby skips the escargots and instead focuses on grilled meats and fish. The steak with french fries and béarnaise sauce is delicious. On Sunday an American-style brunch is served, where you can enjoy huevos rancheros and a big Bloody Mary while blues and country music drift from the speakers. ⊠ *Österlångg. 14, Gamla Stan* ☎ *08/206015* ▤ *AE, DC, MC, V.*

$–$$ ✕ **Hannas Krog.** This bohemian neighborhood restaurant is almost always filled with locals. Although it may not be as super trendy as it was a decade ago, it remains a Södermalm hot spot. Diners are serenaded at 10 minutes to the hour by a mooing cow that emerges from the cuckoo clock just inside the door. The dishes—from Caribbean shrimp to Provençal lamb—are all flavorful. The crowds that gather here don't manage to slow down the consistent service. The bar in the basement is loud but pleasant. Local bands play there on occasion. ⊠ *Skåneg. 80, Södermalm* ☎ *08/6438225* ▤ *AE, DC, MC, V* ⊙ *No lunch weekends and July.*

$–$$ ✕ **Källaren Movitz.** At first glance Movitz looks like nothing more than a typical European pub, which is exactly what it is upstairs. But downstairs it's a restaurant serving Swedish cuisine with French and Italian influences. The refined table settings and abundant candlelight reflecting off the curves of the light yellow walls of what used to be a potato cellar in the 1600s make this an elegant place to dine. Dishes are sim-

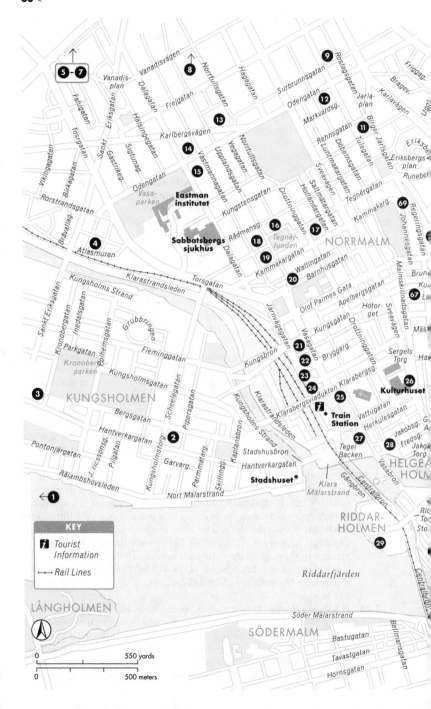

KEY

i Tourist Information

⊷ Rail Lines

Where to Stay & Eat in Northern Stockholm

73 74

TO LADUGÅRDSGÄRDET →

TO N. DJURGÅRDEN →

Humle-gården

Örekts-

ÖSTERMALM

Sturegatan

63

57

64

62

65

61

58

60

59

Norr Malmstorg

50

49

Kungsträdgårdsg.

XIIs rg

45

peran

ström-bron

Kungliga Slottet

48

47

46

Nybro-plan

51 52

53

Strandvägen

Ladugårds-landsviken

TO DJURGÅRDEN →

43 44

Skeppsholms-bron

SKEPPSHOLMEN

41 42

Svensksundsv. Långa Raden

Köpmang.

38 39 40

Österlångg.

AMLA TAN

i

34

Slussen

33 35

Skeppsbron

Strömmen

KASTELL-HOLMEN

Saltsjön

Stadsgården

Katarinavägen

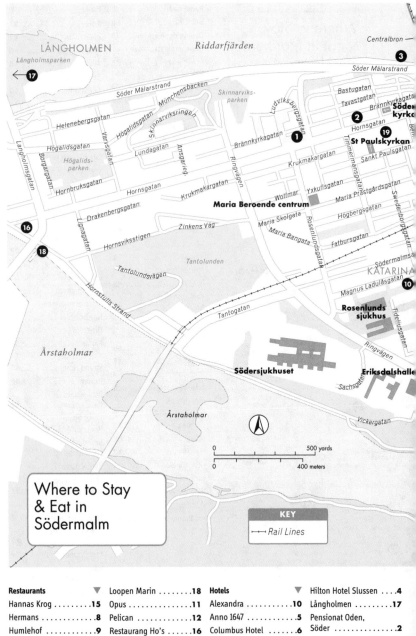

Where to Stay
& Eat in
Södermalm

KEY

⊢⟶ Rail Lines

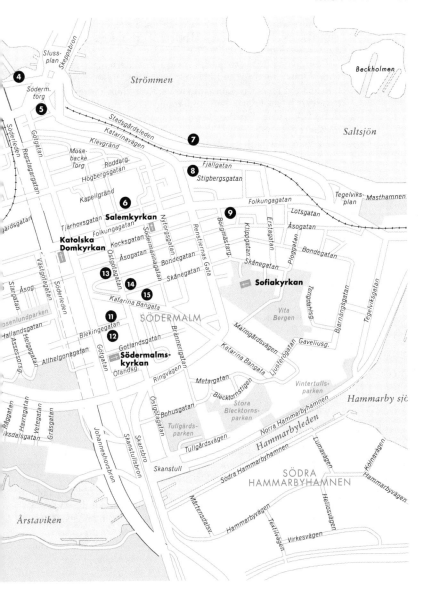

ple affairs with a real dinner-party-at-home feel; expect menu choices such as game, pasta, salmon, and plenty of rich sauces. ⊠ *Tyska Brinken 34, Gamla Stan* ☎ *08/209979* ▤ *AE, DC, MC, V* ⊘ *Closed Sun.*

$–$$ ✕ **Opus.** Don't let the stripped-down, albeit charming, small space fool you—Opus's food packs a big-time punch and has earned it a reputation as a top French restaurant in town. Everything is prepared with intense care by the French-born and -trained cook and is served attentively by his Polish wife. Together they own this popular little restaurant, where the sauces are unbeatable. Try the pork fillet with chanterelle sauce or the perch fillet with avocado sauce to find out for yourself. As the restaurant has only 10 tables, be sure to call ahead. ⊠ *Blekingeg. 63, Södermalm* ☎ *08/6446080* ⌂ *Reservations essential* ▤ *AE, DC, MC, V* ⊘ *Closed Sun. No dinner Mon.*

¢–$$ ✕ **Humlehof.** If you're feeling extra hungry and a bit tight on funds, go straight to this Bavarian restaurant serving traditional Swedish and eastern European dishes. Start by ordering an ice-cold Czech or Austrian draft beer, a bowl of what has to be the best goulash in Stockholm, and the *schweizer* (Swiss-style) schnitzel, which is as big as your face and served with salad and fried potatoes. If schnitzel's not your thing, try the panfried Haloumi cheese with sun-dried tomatoes, summer salad, and garlic bread. A TV in the corner above the bar means a sports-bar crowd gathers when a game is on, but it's never out of control and only adds to the restaurant's cheeriness. ⊠ *Folkungag. 128, Södermalm* ☎ *08/6410302* ▤ *MC, V.*

¢–$$ ✕ **Pelican.** Beer, beer, and more beer is the order of the day at Pelican, a
Fodor'sChoice traditional working-class drinking hall, a relic of the days when Söder-
★ malm was the dwelling place of the city's blue-collar brigade. Today's more bohemian residents find it just as enticing, with the unvarnished wood-paneled walls, faded murals, and glass globe lights fulfilling all their down-at-the-heel pretensions. The food here is some of the best traditional Swedish fare in the city. The herring, meatballs, and salted bacon with onion sauce are not to be missed. ⊠ *Blekingeg. 40, Södermalm* ☎ *08/ 55609090* ⌂ *Reservations not accepted* ▤ *MC, V* ⊘ *Closed Sun.*

$ ✕ **Loopen Marin.** Come and chill under the coconut palms (plastic ones, of course) at this relaxed and friendly yacht club and restaurant. Nonmembers are most certainly welcome, as are children. Cold beer and simple dishes such as quiche and lasagna are the order of the day here, to be enjoyed as you take in the blue water and passing boats. ⊠ *Hornstulls Strand 6, Södermalm* ☎ *08/844285* ▤ *No credit cards.*

$ ✕ **Restaurang Ho's.** Walk into this hidden gem of a Chinese restaurant and something about it just feels right. Nothing fancy—Ho's lets its authentic, intensely flavored food speak for itself. With more than 100 choices, the menu seems never-ending and includes Chinese takes on duck, squid, scallops, pork, chicken, beef, and tofu. The stir-fried squid with green and red peppers in black-bean sauce packs a serious punch. Finish with a classic fried banana and ice cream. ⊠ *Hornsg. 151, Södermalm* ☎ *08/844420* ▤ *MC, V* ⊘ *Closed Mon.*

¢–$ ✕ **Hermans.** Hermans is a haven for vegetarians out to get the most bang
Fodor'sChoice for their kronor. The glassed-in back deck and open garden both pro-
★ vide breathtaking vistas across the water of Stockholm harbor, Gamla

Stan, and the island of Djurgården. The food is always served buffet style and includes various vegetable and pasta salads, warm casseroles, and such entrées as Indonesian stew with peanut sauce and vegetarian lasagna. The fruit pies, chocolate cakes, and cookies are delicious. ⊠ *Fjällg. 23A, Södermalm* ☎ *08/6439480* 🖃 *MC, V.*

¢–$ ✕ **Indira.** This busy Indian restaurant about a block off Götgatan has an overwhelming 60 meal choices. The food is cheap and delicious and the service fast. Order as soon as you enter and find a seat at one of the mosaic-coated tables. There are a number of tables in the basement as well, so don't leave right away if it looks packed on the first floor. The chicken korma, with raisins and cashews, is fantastic, and the honey-saffron ice cream is a perfect end to a meal. ⊠ *Bondeg. 3B, Södermalm* ☎ *08/6414046* 🖃 *MC, V.*

¢ ✕ **Jerusalem Grill House.** Enter this wild grill and it may be hard to believe you're still in Stockholm. The men behind the counter sing along to music blaring from the sound system, and the menu is in both Swedish and Arabic. On the walls are surreal landscape paintings, odd sculptures, and loads of hookahs—in fact, there are five or six pipes that the regulars use to smoke their tobacco. Falafel, chicken kebabs, gyros, fried-vegetable plates, lamb fillets—they've got it all, as well as authentic Arabic tea and coffee. Late on weekend nights it's packed with hungry partygoers. ⊠ *Hornsg. 92, Södermalm* ☎ *08/6684131* 🖃 *No credit cards.*

WHERE TO STAY

Stockholm's hotels vary mostly according to location. For large, modern, international-style business hotels, the downtown and city areas are best. Gamla Stan is strong on slightly smaller hotels, just as luxurious, but with more of a homey feel. It is also the neighborhood for those with a nautical bent. Södermalm, Stockholm's bohemian side, is perfect if you're looking for the odd boutique hotels and plenty of quirky budget accommodations. All rooms in the hotels reviewed below are equipped with shower or bath unless otherwise noted. Unless otherwise stated, hotels do not have air-conditioning. Some hotels close during the winter holidays; call ahead if you expect to travel during that time.

Prices

Although Stockholm has a reputation for prohibitively expensive hotels, great deals can be found in summer, when prices are substantially lower and numerous discounts are available. More than 50 hotels offer the "Stockholm Package," which includes accommodations for one night, breakfast, and the Stockholmskortet, or Stockholm Card, which entitles the cardholder to free admission to museums and travel on public transport. Details are available from travel agents, tourist bureaus, and the **Stockholm Information Service** (🖃 Box 7542, 103 93 Stockholm ☎ 08/7892400 🖷 08/7892450). Also try **Hotellcentralen** (⊠ Centralstation, 111 20 Stockholm ☎ 08/7892425 🖷 08/7918666); the service is free if you go in person, but a fee applies if you call.

WHAT IT COSTS In Swedish Kronor				
$$$$	**$$$**	**$$**	**$**	**¢**
FOR 2 PEOPLE over 2,900	2,300–2,900	1,500–2,300	1,000–1,500	under 1,000

Prices are for two people in a standard double room in high season.

Downtown Stockholm & Beyond

$$$$ 🖼 **Sheraton Hotel and Towers.** Popular with business executives, the Sheraton is also an ideal hotel for the tourist on a generous budget looking for comfort and luxury. English is the main language at the restaurant and bar, which fill up at night once the piano player arrives. The lobby is a vast steel-and-glass affair with huge vases of fresh cut flowers, adding a dash of color. There's a gift shop selling Swedish crystal and international newspapers. Rooms have hardwood floors, leather chairs, thick rugs, and sturdy, cherrywood furniture. ⊠ *Tegelbacken 6, City, 101 23* ☎ *08/4123400* 🖷 *08/4123409* ⊕ *www.sheratonstockholm. com* 🛏 *462 rooms, 30 suites,* ⚴ *2 restaurants, room service, a/c, room TVs with movies, in-room broadband, in-room data ports, Wi-Fi, gym, sauna, piano bar, casino, convention center, parking (fee), no-smoking rooms* 🚭 *AE, DC, MC, V* ⵔ *BP.*

★ **$$$–$$$$** 🖼 **Berns Hotel.** This subtly ultramodern hotel was a hot spot when it opened its doors in the late 19th century, and it retains that status today. You can breakfast in the Red Room, immortalized by August Strindberg's novel of the same name; the hotel was one of his haunts. Rooms here have hardwood floors, white walls, feather-stuffed white quilts and fabrics in cobalt blue, chocolate brown, moss green, and stone—a lesson in comfortable modernism. All feature Berns's "recreation tower"— a rotating wooden tower containing TV, CD player, and minibar. The staff are always quietly on hand with a natural smile; just what you'd expect from a boutique hotel of this caliber. The restaurant/bar is a joint venture with restaurant entrepreneur and designer Terence Conran. Hotel rates include the use of a nearby fitness center with a pool. ⊠ *Näckströmsg. 8, City, 111 47* ☎ *08/56632000* 🖷 *08/56632201* ⊕ *www.berns.se* 🛏 *65 rooms, 3 suites* ⚴ *Restaurant, room service, a/c, minibars, in-room broadband, Wi-Fi, bar, meeting room, no-smoking rooms* 🚭 *AE, DC, MC, V* ⵔ *BP.*

$$$–$$$$ 🖼 **Nordic Hotel.** Next to the central station, this modern center for the business traveler is actually two hotels—Nordic Light and Nordic Sea— in one. Nordic Light focuses on simplicity, and, not surprisingly, light plays an important role, with responsive sound-and-movement systems in the lobby and multiple light settings, including light-therapy treatment, in the rooms. Rooms are a mix of dark wood, gray flannel, and black-and-white tile, with adjustable spotlights in the ceiling. Nordic Sea uses lighter wood with lots of blue fabric and mosaic tiles to create a Mediterranean touch. A huge aquarium in the lobby holds exotic fish, and you can chill out in Stockholm's only ice bar, where the temperature never rises above freezing. For something more classic, Nordic Light's all-white martini bar offers more than 200 takes on the cocktail of cocktails. ⊠ *Vasaplan, City, 101 37* ☎ *08/50563000* 🖷 *08/*

50563060 ⊕ *www.nordichotels.se* ⟿ *542 rooms, 28 suites* ⚬ *2 restaurants, room service, a/c, room TVs with movies, in-room broadband, in-room data ports, Wi-Fi, 2 bars, 2 lounges, meeting rooms, parking (fee), no-smoking rooms* ▭ *AE, DC, MC, V* ⟨⟩| *BP.*

$$$ 🖼 **Royal Viking (Radisson SAS).** For the weary traveler, the Royal Viking's location right next to the central station is a gift; fall off the airport train and into one of the comfortable beds. When you awake, enjoy the attractive natural textiles and artwork, sturdy writing desks, separate seating areas, and plush robes in the large bathrooms. Triple-glazed windows and plenty of insulation keep traffic noise to a minimum. The large, modern lobby, extensively renovated in 2002, takes the edge off what was previously another faceless international business hotel. At night the excellent bar can get extremely busy. ✉ *Vasag. 1, City, 101 24* ☏ *08/50654000* 🖷 *08/50654001* ⊕ *www.radissonsas.com* ⟿ *459 rooms, 21 suites* ⚬ *Restaurant, room service, a/c, minibars, room TVs with movies, in-room broadband, Wi-Fi, indoor pool, sauna, bar, convention center, no-smoking rooms* ▭ *AE, MC, V.*

$$$ 🖼 **Sergel Plaza.** The lobby in this stainless-steel-paneled hotel is welcoming, with cane chairs set up in a pleasant seating area below skylights. The bright rooms are practical but tend to lack the luxury that the price tag may lead you to expect. In fact, the run-of-the-mill furnishings and a tad too much gray make it a bit dull, save for the occasional alarming tangerine and mint-green striped chair. But its central location on the main pedestrian mall makes it a great base if you're not going to spend much time at the hotel. For breakfast there is an international buffet or a Japanese breakfast; the restaurant serves innovative Swedish and international dishes. At night the piano bar behind the lobby fills with guests. ✉ *Brunkebergstorg 9, City, 103 27* ☏ *08/51726300* 🖷 *08/51726311* ⊕ *www.scandic-hotels.se* ⟿ *405 rooms* ⚬ *Restaurant, room service, room TVs with movies, in-room broadband, in-room data ports, sauna, bar, casino, convention center, no-smoking rooms* ▭ *AE, DC, MC, V* ⟨⟩| *BP.*

$$$ 🖼 **Stallmästaregården.** Since 1645, restaurant Stallmästaregården has been wowing travelers with its culinary achievement. The adjoining hotel, a relative newcomer, opened in 2000, and it has done plenty to catch up with its older sibling's reputation. Romance is the loose theme at this hotel, with light-filled rooms stuffed with 18th-century Swedish antiques and Chinese artifacts. Despite the goods, rooms seem to retain an air of simplicity that befits a Scandinavian-designed hotel. Each room is different in design, but all share the pleasing trait of not really feeling like hotel rooms. Add to this the delightful parkland setting and it's not hard to imagine yourself as a welcome guest of 18th-century Swedish nobility. Seekers of 21st-century bustle are happy here, as well, with downtown Stockholm a mere 10 minutes away by car. ✉ *Nortull, Haga, 113 47* ☏ *08/6101300* 🖷 *08/6103140* ⊕ *www.stallmastaregarden.se* ⟿ *49 rooms, 4 suites* ⚬ *Restaurant, in-room broadband, bar, meeting rooms, free parking, no-smoking rooms* ▭ *AE, DC, MC, V* ⟨⟩| *BP.*

$$–$$$ 🖼 **Birger Jarl.** At this high-design hotel the lobby doubles as a modern-art gallery, with frequently changing exhibitions. Some rooms have been individually designed by several of the country's top designers: it

costs extra to stay in these. Most rooms are not large, but all are well furnished and have nice touches, such as heated towel racks in the bathrooms; all double rooms have bathtubs. Four family-style rooms have extra floor space and sofa beds. You can choose your breakfast from an extensive buffet just off the lobby, but room service is also available. ☒ *Tuleg. 8, Vasastan, 104 32* ☎ *08/6741800* 🖷 *08/6737366* ⊕ *www.birgerjarl.se* ⇱ *225 rooms* ⚴ *Coffee shop, room service, in-room broadband, in-room data ports, sauna, meeting room, no-smoking rooms* ▱ *AE, DC, MC, V* ⦿ *BP.*

$$–$$$ 🏨 **Crystal Plaza Hotel.** Housed in one of Stockholm's oldest hotel buildings (1895), the Crystal Plaza, with a circular tower and peach walls, is sure to catch the eye of anyone walking down Birger Jarlsgatan. Most rooms have a mix of birch-wood furniture, hardwood floors with small rugs, and the requisite hotel artwork on the walls. Rooms facing the inner courtyard can be a bit quieter than those on the street. If you want only the best, throw down a little extra money for one of the circular tower rooms, two of which have balconies. The hotel's location, close to the hip bars of Stureplan and downtown shopping, makes it an ideal place for folks looking to have quick access to a good time in the city. ☒ *Birger Jarlsg. 35, City, 111 45* ☎ *08/4068800* 🖷 *08/241511* ⊕ *www.crystalplazahotel.se* ⇱ *111 rooms, 1 suite* ⚴ *Restaurant, minibars, in-room broadband, bar, no-smoking rooms* ▱ *AE, DC, MC, V* ⦿ *BP.*

★ **$$–$$$** 🏨 **Lydmar Hotel.** Favored by black-clad music- and film-industry types, the Lydmar appeals to the more aesthetically conscious traveler. Only a 10-minute walk from the downtown hub of Sergels Torg and right on the doorstep of Stureplan, the epicenter of Stockholm's nightlife, the Lydmar is more than just a hotel—it's also one of the trendiest bars in town. Even if you don't stay here, be sure to take a ride in the elevator, in which you can choose from eight kinds of elevator music, all of (believe it or not) quality. The lobby lounge is alive on weekends with jazz and DJs spinning the latest club music. Rooms here are ultramodern with such features as sunken beds, wall-mounted light panels, polished concrete walls, plasma-screen TVs, Italian sofas, asymmetric coffee tables and super-soft bed quilts. The full-size bottles of bathroom products are a nice touch. ☒ *Stureg. 10, City, 114 36* ☎ *08/56611300* 🖷 *08/56611301* ⊕ *www.lydmar.se* ⇱ *61 rooms, 5 suites* ⚴ *Restaurant, room service, a/c, minibars, in-room DVD, in-room broadband, Wi-Fi, sauna, bar, meeting room, no-smoking rooms* ▱ *AE, DC, MC, V* ⦿ *BP.*

$$–$$$ 🏨 **Scandic Hotel Continental.** In the city center across from the train station, the Continental is a reliable option for those looking for a central hotel at a more affordable price. Rooms have a minibar, trouser press, and satellite television, as well as wood floors and rather cheery burgundy, turquoise, and pastel furnishings. Single travelers on a tight budget can opt for one of the windowless cabin rooms. An extravagant Scandinavian buffet is served in the breakfast room. ☒ *Klara Vattugränd 4, City, 101 22* ☎ *08/51734200* 🖷 *08/517342311* ⊕ *www.scandic-hotels.com* ⇱ *268 rooms* ⚴ *Restaurant, room service, minibars, room TVs with movies, in-room broadband, Wi-Fi, sauna, bar, meeting room, no-smoking rooms* ▱ *AE, DC, MC, V* ⦿ *BP.*

$$-$$$ ✕⊞ **Villa Källhagen.** The changing seasons are on display in this beau-
Fodor'sChoice tiful country hotel, reflected through the huge windows, glass walls, and
★ bedroom skylights. To what was originally an inn dating from 1810,
an extension was added in 1994, with natural light the main focus. Rooms
are spacious and furnished in light woods and beautifully colored fabrics. It's only a few minutes from the city center, but its woodland surroundings can put you a million miles away. The restaurant also relies
heavily on the seasons, serving a delicious blend of fresh Swedish ingredients cooked with a French influence. ⊠ *Djurgårdsbrunnsv. 10, N.
Djurgården, 115 27* ☎ *08/6650300* ⊟ *08/6650399* ⊕ *www.kallhagen.
se* ➟ *20 rooms* ⚒ *Restaurant, bar, meeting room, no-smoking rooms*
⊟ *AE, DC, MC, V* ⭤ *BP.*

$$ ⊞ **Adlon.** Although in a building dating from 1884, the Adlon consid-
ers itself a high-tech business hotel. In truth, though, what was high-
tech when Adlon introduced it is now mostly considered standard in
most hotels. Still, rooms here are light-filled and cleanly dressed in light
woods and orange and sky-blue fabrics; the fairly large desks come with
complimentary high-speed Internet access. Add all this to its central lo-
cation and a variety of business services, and Adlon can still boast its
business-friendly credentials. ⊠ *Vasag. 42, City, 111 20* ☎ *08/4026500*
⊟ *08/208610* ⊕ *www.adlon.se* ➟ *83 rooms* ⚒ *Bar, business services,
meeting rooms, no-smoking rooms* ⊟ *AE, DC, MC, V* ⭤ *BP.*

$$ ⊞ **Central Hotel.** Less than 300 yards from the central station, this practical hotel lives up to its name. The reception area is white, with a sky-
light, giving an immediate freshness and simplicity to the hotel. Rooms
follow suit, with only the burgundy curtains and chairs interrupting the
otherwise pleasing minimalism. Thanks to extra sound insulation, the
chaos of Vasagatan remains outside the room. Bathrooms have showers only. ⊠ *Vasag. 38, City, 101 20* ☎ *08/56620800* ⊟ *08/247573*
⊕ *www.centralhotel.se* ➟ *93 rooms, 1 suite* ⚒ *In-room broadband, in-
room data ports, meeting room, no-smoking rooms* ⊟ *AE, DC, MC,
V* ⭤ *BP.*

★ **$$** ✕⊞ **Claes på Hörnet.** This may be the most exclusive—and smallest—
hotel in town, with only 10 rooms in a former 1739 inn. The rooms,
comfortably furnished with period antiques, go quickly (book three or
so months in advance, especially around Christmas). The restaurant ($$)
is worth visiting even if you don't spend the night: its old-fashioned din-
ing room serves Swedish and Continental dishes such as outstanding
strömming (Baltic herring) and cloudberry mousse cake. Reservations
are essential. Note that the restaurant is closed in July. ⊠ *Surbrunnsg.
20, Vasastan, 113 48* ☎ *08/165130* ⊟ *08/6125315* ➟ *10 rooms*
⚒ *Restaurant* ⊟ *AE, DC, MC, V* ⭤ *BP.*

$$ ✕⊞ **Stockholm Plaza Hotel.** On one of Stockholm's foremost streets for
shopping and entertainment, and only a short walk from the city's
nightlife and business center, this hotel is ideal if you want to be in a
central location. The building was built in 1884, and the Elite hotel
chain took over in 1984. Rooms are furnished in an elegant, traditional
manner, and many include the original stuccowork on the ceilings.
⊠ *Birger Jarlsg. 29, Downtown, 103 95* ☎ *08/56622000* ⊟ *08/
56622020* ⊕ *www.elite.se* ➟ *151 rooms, 18 suites* ⚒ *Restaurant, room*

service, minibars, room TVs with movies, in room broadband, Wi-Fi, bar, meeting rooms, parking (fee), no-smoking rooms ⊟ *AE, DC, MC, V* ⊠ *BP.*

★ **$–$$** ⊞ **Tegnérlunden.** A quiet city park fronts this modern hotel, a 10-minute walk along shop-lined Sveavägen from the downtown hub of Sergels Torg. Rooms here are unusually stylish for a hotel in this price range and have the added appeal of not feeling at all like hotel rooms. The modern furniture, oak tables and desks, comfortable armchairs, and potted plants will all remind you of an urban apartment. The lobby is bright with marble, brass, and greenery, as is the sunny rooftop breakfast room. ⊠ *Tegnérlunden 8, Downtown, 113 59* ☎ *08/54545550* ⊟ *08/54545551* ⊕ *www.hoteltegnerlunden.se* ⊲ *102 rooms, 2 suites* ⚘ *Room TVs with movies, Wi-Fi, sauna, meeting room, no-smoking rooms* ⊟ *AE, DC, MC, V* ⊠ *BP.*

$ ⊞ **Arcadia.** On a hilltop near a large waterfront nature preserve, this converted dormitory is within 15 minutes of downtown by bus or subway or 30 minutes on foot along pleasant shopping streets. Rooms are furnished in a spare, neutral style, with plenty of natural light. The adjoining restaurant serves meals on the terrace in summer. To get here, take Bus 43 to Körsbärsvägen. ⊠ *Körsbärsv. 1, 114 89* ☎ *08/56621500* ⊟ *08/56621501* ⊕ *www.arcadia.elite.se* ⊲ *84 rooms* ⚘ *Restaurant* ⊟ *AE, DC, MC, V* ⊠ *BP.*

$ ⊞ **August Strindberg.** A narrow frescoed corridor leads from the street to the flagstone courtyard, into which the hotel's restaurant expands in summer. Rooms have carpeted floors, unusual in this part of the world, but are otherwise plainly furnished. Kitchenettes are available; some rooms can be combined into family apartments. The four floors have no elevator. ⊠ *Tegnérg. 38, Vasastan, 113 59* ☎ *08/325006* ⊟ *08/209085* ⊕ *www.hotellstrindberg.se* ⊲ *21 rooms* ⚘ *Restaurant, minibars, in-room broadband, some kitchenettes, no-smoking rooms* ⊟ *MC, V* ⊠ *BP.*

¢–$ ⊞ **Hotel Gustav Wasa.** The Gustav Wasa, named after the first king of Sweden, is right next to Odenplan Square. The hotel is in a 19th-century residential building and has fairly large, bright rooms with herringbone hardwood floors, original trim and details along the ceilings, and a funky blend of antiques and furniture that's more modern. Some rooms have wonderful original tiled fireplaces. Ask for a room with a window out to the street in order to get a direct view of the grand Gustav Wasa Church and the Odenplan. The other available view, of the inner courtyard, is much less exciting. The downtown location and lower prices make this an excellent place for budget travelers who prefer a friendly hotel. ⊠ *Västmannag. 61, Vasastan, 113 25* ☎ *08/343801* ⊟ *08/307372* ⊕ *www.gustavvasahotel.se* ⊲ *41 rooms* ⊟ *AE, DC, MC, V* ⊠ *BP.*

Fodor'sChoice
★

¢ ⊞ **Bema.** This small hotel is relatively central, on the ground floor of an apartment block near Tegnérlunden park. Rooms have a modern Swedish style, with beech-wood furniture. One four-bed family room is available. Breakfast is served in your room. Given the price, it's difficult to beat. ⊠ *Upplandsg. 13, Vasastan, 111 23* ☎ *08/232675* ⊟ *08/205338* ⊲ *12 rooms* ⊟ *MC, V.*

Gamla Stan & Skeppsholmen

$$$$ 🏨 **Grand Hotel.** At first glance the Grand seems like any other world-
Fodor'sChoice class international hotel, and in many ways it is. Its location is one of
★ the best in the city, on the quayside just across the water from the Royal
Palace; it boasts an impressive guest list of visiting political dignitaries,
royal families, Nobel Prize winners, and movie stars. The service is
slick, professional, and predicts your every need. The large rooms are
sumptuous and decadent, with robes so fluffy, beds so soft, and antiques
so lovely you may never want to leave. But the Grand offers something
else: a touch of the uniquely Scandinavian. You can feel it in the relaxed
atmosphere that pervades the hotel, you can smell it in the fresh, salt-
tinged air that wafts through the open windows, and you can see it in
the antique wood floors, pastel silks that drape the furniture, and the
purity of the light that penetrates all corners of the hotel. If there is a
more exquisite hotel anywhere in town, it is yet to be found. ⊠ *Södra
Blasieholmshamnen 8, Box 16424, City, 103 27* ☎ *08/6793500* 🖷 *08/
6118686* ⊕ *www.grandhotel.se* ⟳ *310 rooms, 21 suites* ⟰ *2 restaurants, room service, a/c, minibars, room TVs with movies, in-room
broadband, in-room data ports, Wi-Fi, gym, sauna, bar, shops, concierge,
meeting room, no-smoking rooms* ☰ *AE, DC, MC, V* ⦿*| BP.*

$$–$$$$ 🏨 **Radisson SAS Strand Hotel.** An art-nouveau monolith, built in 1912 for
the Stockholm Olympics, this hotel has been completely and tastefully
modernized. It's on the water across from the Royal Dramatic Theater,
directly in front of the quay, where many of the boats leave for the
archipelago. It's also only a short walk from the Old Town and the mu-
seums on Skeppsholmen. No two rooms are alike, but all are furnished
with simple and elegant furniture, offset by white woodwork and hues
of moss green and cocoa brown. The Strand restaurant has a sharp, urban
feel, with modern, straight-lined furniture and a cool color scheme of stone,
earth-brown, and natural greens. An SAS check-in counter for business-
class travelers adjoins the main reception area. ⊠ *Nybrokajen 9, Box
16396, City, 103 27* ☎*08/50664000* 🖷*08/6112436* ⊕*www.radissonsas.
com* ⟳*152 rooms* ⟰ *Restaurant, room service, a/c, minibars, room TVs
with movies, in-room broadband, in-room data ports, Wi-Fi, sauna,
meeting room, no-smoking rooms* ☰ *AE, DC, MC, V* ⦿*| BP.*

$$–$$$ 🏨 **Lady Hamilton.** As charming as its namesake, Lord Nelson's mistress,
the Lady Hamilton is a modern hotel inside a typical Gamla Stan rus-
set-red 15th-century building. Swedish antiques fill the guest rooms
and common areas, including such obscure objects as old spirit cabi-
nets, complete with original bottles. Romney's *Bacchae* portrait of Lady
Hamilton hangs in the foyer, where she also supports the ceiling in the
form of a large smiling figurehead from an old ship. The breakfast
room, furnished with captain's chairs, looks out onto the lively cobblestone
street, and the subterranean sauna rooms, in whitewashed stone, pro-
vide a secluded fireplace and a chance to take a dip in the building's
original, medieval well. ⊠*Storkyrkobrinken 5, Gamla Stan, 111 28* ☎*08/
50640100* 🖷 *08/50640110* ⊕ *www.lady-hamilton.se* ⟳ *34 rooms
*⟰ *Minibars, room TVs with movies, in-room broadband, sauna, bar,
meeting room, no-smoking rooms* ☰ *AE, DC, MC, V* ⦿*| BP.*

★ **$$–$$$** 🖵 **Reisen.** On the waterfront in Gamla Stan, this hotel opened in 1819. The rooms looking out over the water are fantastic, and for a small supplement you can get a room with a private sauna and Jacuzzi. A mix of nautical-inspired antiques and simple, modern furniture fill the rooms, many of which have original exposed brick and wood ceiling beams. There is a fine Italian restaurant with a grill, tea and coffee service in the library, and what is reputed to be the best piano bar in town. A small swimming pool, dominated by businessmen cooling off after the sauna, is built under the medieval arches of the foundations. ⊠ *Skeppsbron 12–14, Gamla Stan, 111 30* ☎ *08/223260* 🖷 *08/201559* ⊕ *www. firsthotels.com* 🛏 *144 rooms, 7 suites* ☖ *Restaurant, room service, in-room broadband, indoor pool, sauna, piano bar, meeting room, no-smoking floor* 🖃 *AE, DC, MC, V.*

$$ 🖵 **Lord Nelson.** Fans of all things nautical will love this hotel, a little sister to the nearby Lady Hamilton and Victory hotels. Your first high-seas encounter is with the enormous, carved-wood Nelson that stands rather sternly in the reception. Your deck (floor) and room will be each named for a type of ship. Inside is a model of the same ship and plenty of blue and white everywhere. Rooms are small, like cabins, but this just adds to the experience—minus the seasickness. Noise from traffic in the pedestrian street outside can be a problem in summer. ⊠ *Västerlångg. 22, Gamla Stan, 111 29* ☎ *08/50640120* 🖷 *08/50640130* ⊕ *www.lord-nelson.se* 🛏 *31 rooms* ☖ *Café, room TVs with movies, in-room broadband, sauna, meeting room, no-smoking room* 🖃 *AE, DC, MC, V.*

$$ 🖵 **Rica Hotel Gamla Stan.** The feel of historical Stockholm living is rarely more prevalent than in this quiet hotel tucked away on a narrow street in one of the Gamla Stan's 17th-century houses. All rooms are decorated in the Gustavian style, with hardwood floors, Oriental rugs, and antique furniture. A short walk from the Gamla Stan metro stop, it's a perfect home base for later exploring. ⊠ *Lilla Nyg. 25, Gamla Stan 111 28* ☎ *08/7237250* 🖷 *08/7237259* ⊕ *www.rica.se* 🛏 *51 rooms* ☖ *Minibars, meeting room, no-smoking floor* 🖃 *AE, DC, MC, V* ⦿ *BP.*

$$ 🖵 **Victory.** Slightly larger than its brother and sister hotels, the Lord Nelson and Lady Hamilton, this extremely atmospheric Gamla Stan building dates from 1640. History defines the Victory: in the cellar you can see part of a medieval fortress wall, and, in the 1930s construction workers stumbled across Sweden's biggest silver treasure ever found, just beneath the hotel. The theme is nautical, with artifacts from the HMS *Victory,* as well as Swedish antiques. Each room is named after a 19th-century sea captain. ⊠ *Lilla Nyg. 5, Gamla Stan, 111 28* ☎ *08/50640000* 🖷 *08/50640010* ⊕ *www.victory-hotel.se* 🛏 *48 rooms* ☖ *Restaurant, minibars, room TVs with movies, in-room broadband, Wi-Fi, 2 saunas, bar, meeting room, no-smoking floor* 🖃 *AE, DC, MC, V* ⦿ *BP.*

$–$$ 🖵 **Mälardrottningen.** One of the more unusual establishments in Stockholm, Mälardrottningen was once Barbara Hutton's yacht. Since 1982 it has been a hotel, with a crew as service conscious as any in Stockholm. Tied up on the freshwater side of Gamla Stan, it is minutes from everything. Not surprisingly, the theme here is nautical, with endless mahogany and polished brass, groups of maritime pictures on the walls, and rooms that are a riot of navy-blue, maroon, and white. Some of the below-deck cabins are a bit stuffy, but in summer you can take your meals out on deck. The ship's chief assets are novelty and absence of traffic noise. ✉ *Riddarholmen 4, Riddarholmen, 111 28* ☎ *08/54518780* 📠 *08/243676* 🌐 *www.malardrottningen.se* *59 cabins* *Restaurant, BBQ, in-room broadband, sauna, bar, meeting room, no-smoking rooms* 💳 *AE, DC, MC, V* *BP.*

Östermalm

$$$–$$$$ Fodor'sChoice ★ **Diplomat.** Within easy walking distance of Djurgården, this elegant hotel is less flashy than most in its price range, but oozes a certain European chic, evident in its subtle, tasteful designs and efficient staff. The building is a turn-of-the-20th-century town house that housed foreign embassies in the 1930s and was converted into a hotel in 1966. Rooms are all individual but have fresh colors, clean lines, and subtle hints of floral prints in common, and those in the front, facing the water, have magnificent views over Stockholm Harbor. The T-Bar, formerly a rather staid tearoom and restaurant, is now one of the trendiest bars among the city's upper crust. The second-floor bar is ideal for a break from sightseeing. ✉ *Strandv. 7C, Östermalm, 104 40* ☎ *08/4596800* 📠 *08/4596820* 🌐 *www.diplomathotel.com* *128 rooms* *Restaurant, room service, a/c, minibars, room TVs with movies, in-room broadband, in-room data ports, Wi-Fi, sauna, 2 bars, meeting room, no-smoking room* 💳 *AE, DC, MC, V* *BP.*

$$$ **Hotel Esplanade.** Right on the water and only a few buildings down from Stockholm's Royal Dramatic Theater, Hotel Esplanade is a beautiful hotel with a real touch of old Stockholm. Somewhere between a family home, a guesthouse, and a hotel, Esplanade is a resplendent work of art nouveau. From the confection of external architecture to the oiled-wood floors and classic period furnishings, this is a real museum piece of a hotel. The rooms with a view of the water are worth the little extra money. Be sure to call well ahead to book a room, since many regulars return every year. ✉ *Strandv. 7A, Östermalm, 114 56* ☎ *08/6630740* 📠 *08/6625992* 🌐 *www.hotelesplanade.se* *34 rooms* *In-room broadband, sauna, lobby lounge* 💳 *AE, DC, MC, V* *BP.*

$$–$$$ **Mornington.** Just off the main square of Östermalm, the Mornington is close to both the nightlife of Stureplan and the downtown business district. The lobby, bar, and restaurant area are hip places to hang out, and there's a lovely library of more than 4,000 books (mostly in Swedish) spread throughout the lobby; you can borrow them during your stay. All rooms are elegantly modern with cherrywood headboards and charcoal gray chairs and sofas setting an urban tone. ✉ *Nybrog. 53, Östermalm, 102 44* ☎ *08/50733000* 📠 *08/50733039* 🌐 *www.mornington.se* *140 rooms* *Restaurant, in-room DVD, in-room broadband, sauna, steam room, bar, meeting room, no-smoking rooms* 💳 *AE, DC, MC, V* *BP.*

$$ **Hotel Riddargatan.** On its way to being a fully fledged design hotel, the Riddargatan may not be truly cutting edge quite yet, but at these prices it's a great alternative for travelers who are conscious of style and budget in equal measure. The lobby pleases with its simplicity, the clean space broken only by the beech-wood wall panels and chocolate-brown leather sofas. The bedrooms are a calming blue, with pleasing curtains and accessories. Furnishings are modern and simple, making for a restful space away from the city. ⊠ *Riddarg. 14, Östermalm, 114 35* ☎ *08/55573000* 🖷 *08/55573011* ⊕ *www.profilhotels.se* 🖅 *58 rooms, 2 suites* ⚳ *In-room broadband, in-room data ports, Wi-Fi, bar, meeting room* 🖃 *AE, DC, MC, V* ⼌❙ *BP.*

★ **$$** 🖼 **Wellington.** From the outside the building resembles the Industrihuset (Industry House) across the street, but inside is a delightful hotel with polite, professional staff and quality service. In a quiet residential area in Östermalm near the Hedvig Eleonora Church and cemetery, the hotel is a calm home base from which to enjoy the city. Rooms have hardwood floors and a hint of Britishness about them in the tweeds, checks, and tartans used in chair covers, rugs, and bedspreads. Rooms facing the inner courtyard have balconies. Ask for a room on the top floor for a great view of the neighborhood's rooftops. The breakfast buffet is top-notch, serving all the Swedish classics, including pickled herring. ⊠ *Storg. 6, Östermalm, 114 51* ☎ *08/6670910* 🖷 *08/6671254* ⊕ *www.wellington.se* 🖅 *60 rooms* ⚳ *In-room data ports, sauna, bar, business services, meeting rooms, parking (fee)* 🖃 *AE, MC, V* ⼌❙ *BP.*

★ **$–$$** 🖼 **Örnsköld.** Right in the heart of the city, this hidden gem feels like an old private club, from its brass-and-leather lobby to the Victorian-style furniture in the moderately spacious, high-ceiling rooms. Rooms overlooking the courtyard are quieter, but those facing the street—not a particularly busy one—are sunnier. All the rooms are becoming a little faded, but somehow that seems to add to the charm. The hotel is frequented by actors appearing at the Royal Theater next door. ⊠ *Nybrog. 6, Östermalm, 114 34* ☎ *08/6670285* 🖷 *08/6676991* ⊕ *www. hotelornskold.se* 🖅 *33 rooms* 🖃 *AE, MC, V* ⼌❙ *BP.*

$ 🖼 **Pärlan.** The name of this hotel means the "Pearl" and that's exactly

Fodor'sChoice what it is. On the second floor of an early-19th-century building on a

★ quiet street, the Pärlan is a friendly alternative to the city's bigger hotels. Furniture throughout is a mix of fine antiques and flea-market bargains, making it quirky and homey. A balcony looking out over the inner courtyard is a perfect spot for eating breakfast, which is served buffet style in the kitchen every morning. Be sure to admire the ultra-Swedish tile oven in the corner of the dining room. If you want to get a feel for what it's like to really live in this neighborhood, this is your best bet. Book far in advance because the rooms are almost always full. ⊠ *Skepparg. 27, Östermalm, 114 52* ☎ *08/6635070* 🖷 *08/6677145* ⊕ *www. parlanhotell.com* 🖅 *9 rooms* 🖃 *AE, MC, V.*

Södermalm

$$$ 🖼 **Hilton Hotel Slussen.** Working with what appears to be a dubious location (atop a tunnel above a six-lane highway), the Hilton has pulled a rabbit out of a hat. Built on special noise- and shock-absorbing cushions, the hotel almost lets you forget about the highway. The intriguing labyrinth of levels, separate buildings, and corridors is filled with such unique details as a rounded stairway lighted from between the steps. The guest rooms are exquisitely designed and modern, with plenty of stainless steel and polished-wood inlay to accent the maroon color scheme. The Eken restaurant and bar serves food indoors and out. If you eat or drink too much, there's a gym with excellent facilities. The hotel is at Slussen, easily accessible from downtown. ⌂ *Guldgränd 8, Södermalm, 104 65* ☎ *08/51735300* 🖶 *08/51735311* ⊕ *www.hilton. com* ⚭ *264 rooms, 28 suites* ♧ *2 restaurants, room service, a/c, room TVs with movies, in-room broadband, Wi-Fi, indoor pool, gym, hair salon, sauna, piano bar, meeting room, no-smoking rooms* ▭ *AE, DC, MC, V* ⦿ *BP.*

$$$ ⊡ **Rival.** One of Stockholm's funkiest hotels burst onto the scene in 2003,
FodorśChoice causing as much of a stir among locals as its owner, pop group ABBA's
★ Benny Andersson, did when he broke into fame in the early 1970s. Rival is cool, but never to the point of being cold. Rooms here are full of delightful ideas—such as the glass bathroom walls that let you watch the bedroom television from the tub—and have a stylish comfort about them. Overstuffed duvets compete with plump armchairs for your attention, while modern art and photographs on the wall and stylish lamps and fixtures delight the eye. Cold minimalism is avoided by the use of wood paneling and dark green or red velvet curtains. If you can tear yourself away from your room, downstairs you'll find a very cool bar, a restaurant, a bakery, and a cinema. Rival is a magnificent place to call "home away from home" while visiting Stockholm. ⌂ *Mariatorget 3, Södermalm, 118 91* ☎ *08/54578900* 🖶 *08/54578924* ⊕ *www.rival.se* ⚭ *99 rooms, 2 suites* ♧ *Restaurant, room service, a/c, minibars, in-room DVD, in-room broadband, Wi-Fi, bar, cinema, meeting rooms, no-smoking rooms* ▭ *AE, DC, MC, V* ⦿ *BP.*

★ **$$** ⊡ **Anno 1647.** Named for the date the building was erected, this small, pleasant hotel is a piece of Stockholm history. Rooms vary in shape, but all have original, well-worn pine floors with 17th-century-style furniture. There's no elevator in this four-story building. The bar and café are a popular local hangout. The menu is international. Guest DJs control the sound waves. ⌂ *Mariagränd 3, Södermalm, 116 41* ☎ *08/ 4421680* 🖶 *08/4421647* ⊕ *www.anno1647.se* ⚭ *42 rooms, 2 suites* ♧ *Snack bar, some in-room broadband* ▭ *MC, V* ⦿ *BP.*

$–$$ ⊡ **Alexandra.** This economy hotel is a five-minute walk from the subway and only a few stops from the city center. Rooms are fairly big but have a definite late-1980s look, with pastels and floral prints. There are a number of cheaper rooms, adjacent to the parking garage and without windows. ⌂ *Magnus Ladulåsg. 42, Södermalm, 118 27* ☎ *08/ 4551300* 🖶 *08/4551350* ⊕ *www.alexandrahotel.se* ⚭ *68 rooms, 5 two-room suites* ♧ *Sauna, no-smoking rooms* ▭ *MC, V* ⦿ *BP.*

¢–$$ ⊡ **Columbus Hotel.** Just a few blocks from busy Götgatan, the Colum-
FodorśChoice bus is an oasis of calm in the busy urban streets of Södermalm. Built in
★ 1780, it was originally a brewery, then a jail, then a hospital, then a temporary housing area. Since 1976 the beautiful building, with its large, tranquil inner courtyard, has been a hotel. Rooms have wide beams, polished hardwood floors, antique furniture, and bright wallpaper and fabrics. Many look out over the courtyard, others on the nearby church. In summer breakfast is served outside. The peace and quiet this hotel provides, even though it's close to all the action, makes it ideal for a va-

cation. ✉ *Tjärhovsg. 11, Södermalm, 116 21* ☎ *08/50311200* 🖷 *08/50311201* ⊕ *www.columbus.se* ⇌ *64 rooms, 3 suites* ♿ *Café, bar, parking (fee)* ⊟ *AE, MC, V* ⦿ *BP.*

¢-$ 🎫 **Pensionat Oden, Söder.** Inexpensive and centrally located, this bed-and-breakfast is on the second floor of a 19th-century building. Hornsgatan, the street it's on, is busy and filled with pubs, restaurants, and shops. Rooms have hardwood floors, Oriental rugs, and an odd blend of new and old furniture. A kitchen is available for use. The hotel is popular with parents visiting their children in college, academics traveling on a budget, and backpackers. Book rooms well in advance, especially during the holidays. ✉ *Hornsg. 66B, Södermalm 111 60* ☎ *08/7969600* 🖷 *08/6124501* ⊕ *www.pensionat.nu* ⇌ *35 rooms, 8 with bath* ♿ *No-smoking rooms* ⊟ *MC, V.*

Youth Hostels

Don't be put off by the "youth" bit: there's actually no age limit. The standards of cleanliness, comfort, and facilities offered are usually extremely high.

¢-$ 🎫 **Den Röda Båten Mälaren** (The Red Boat). Built in 1914, the *Mälaren* originally traveled the waters of the Göta Canal under the name of *Sätra*. Today she has to settle for sitting still in Stockholm as a youth hostel. The hostel cabins are small but clean and have bunk beds. Many have fantastic views of the town hall across the water. There are also four "hotel" rooms, which have private baths and nicer furniture and details. In summer the restaurant offers great views of Stockholm along with basic, traditional Swedish food. Breakfast costs an additional Skr 55, but sheets are included in your rate. ✉ *Södermälarstrand kajplats 6, Södermalm 117 20* ☎ *08/6444385* 🖷 *08/6413733* ⊕ *www.theredboat. com* ⇌ *35 rooms, 4 with bath* ⊟ *MC, V.*

¢ 🎫 **af Chapman.** This circa-1888 sailing ship, permanently moored in Stockholm Harbor just across from the Royal Palace, is a landmark in its own right. Book early—the place is so popular in summer that finding a bed may prove difficult. Breakfast (SKr 45) is not included in the room rate; there are no kitchen facilities. ✉ *Flaggmansv. 8, Skeppsholmen, 111 49* ☎ *08/4632266* 🖷 *08/6117155* ⊕ *www.stfchapman. com* ⇌ *293 beds, 2- to 6-bed cabins* ♿ *Café* ⊟ *DC, MC, V* ⊘ *Closed mid-Dec.–mid-Jan.*

¢ 🎫 **Bosön.** Out of the way on the island of Lidingö, this hostel is part of the Bosön Sports Institute, a national training center pleasantly close to the water. You can rent canoes on the grounds and go out for a paddle. Breakfast is included in the room rate. There are laundry facilities and a kitchen you can use. All rooms are clean and fresh. ✉ *Bosön, 181 47 Lidingö* ☎ *08/6056600* 🖷 *08/7671644* ⇌ *70 beds* ♿ *Cafeteria, sauna, boating, laundry facilities* ⊟ *MC, V* ⦿ *BP.*

¢ 🎫 **City Backpackers.** You won't find cheaper accommodations closer to central station than City Backpackers, which has 65 beds. The 19th-century building typifies the European youth hostel, and this one is well run. Guests have access to a common kitchen, a lounge with cable TV, showers, and a courtyard. The seven-person apartment, with its own kitchen and bathroom, is ideal for a group of young backpackers or an adventurous large family. ✉ *Upplandsg. 2A, Vasastan* ☎ *08/206920* 🖷 *08/100464* ⊕ *www.citybackpackers.se* ↘ *15 rooms, one apartment* 🖃 *MC, V.*

¢ 🏨 **Gustaf af Klint.** A "hotel ship" moored at Stadsgården quay, near the Slussen subway station, the *Gustaf af Klint* harbors 120 beds in its two sections: a hotel and a hostel. The hostel section has 18 four-bunk cabins and 10 two-bunk cabins; a 14-bunk dormitory is also available from May through mid-September. The hotel section has 4 single-bunk and 3 two-bunk cabins with bedsheets and breakfast included. The hostel rates are SKr 120 per person in a 4-bunk room and SKr 140 per person in a 2-bunk room; these prices do not include bedsheets or breakfast, which are available at an extra charge. All guests share common bathrooms and showers. There are a cafeteria and a restaurant, and you can dine on deck in summer with stunning views across to Gamla Stan. ✉ *Stadsgårdskajen 153, Södermalm 116 45* ☎ *08/6404077* 🖷 *08/6406416* ⊕ *www.gustafafklint.se* ↘ *7 hotel cabins, 28 hostel cabins, 28 dormitory beds, all without bath* ⌂ *Restaurant, cafeteria* 🖃 *AE, MC, V.*

¢ 🏨 **Långholmen.** This former prison, built in 1724, was converted into a combined hotel and hostel in 1989. The hotel rooms are made available as additional hostel rooms in summer. Rooms are small, and windows are nearly nonexistent—you *are* in a prison, after all—but that hasn't stopped travelers from flocking here. Each room has two to five iron-frame beds, and all but 10 have bathrooms with shower. The hostel is on the island of Långholmen, which has popular bathing beaches and the Prison Museum. The Inn, next door, serves Swedish home cooking, the Jail Pub offers light snacks, and a garden restaurant operates in summer. ✉ *Långholmen, Box 9116, 102 72* ☎ *08/7208500* 🖷 *08/7208575* ⊕ *www.langholmen.com* ↘ *254 beds June–Sept., 26 beds Oct.–May (10 rooms do not have bath)* ⌂ *Restaurant, cafeteria, sauna, beach, laundry facilities* 🖃 *AE, DC, MC, V.*

¢ 🏨 **Skeppsholmen.** This former craftsman's workshop in a pleasant and quiet part of the island was converted into a hostel for the overflow from the *af Chapman,* another hostel an anchor's throw away. Breakfast costs an additional SKr 45. ✉ *Skeppsholmen, 111 49* ☎ *08/4632266* 🖷 *08/6117155* ↘ *155 beds, 2- to 6-bed rooms* ⌂ *Café, laundry facilities* 🖃 *DC, MC, V.*

Camping

You can camp in the Stockholm area for SKr 80–SKr 130 per night. **Bredäng Camping** (✉ 127 31 Skärholmen ☎ 08/977071) has camping and a youth hostel. Its facilities are excellent and include a restaurant and bar. At **Rösjöbaden Camping** (✉ 192 56 Sollentuna ☎ 08/962184), a short drive north of town, you can fish, swim, and play minigolf and volleyball. Fifteen kilometers (9 mi) from Stockholm, in Huddinge, is **Stockholm SweCamp Flottsbro** (✉ 141 25 Huddinge ☎ 08/4499580), where you can camp, play golf, rent canoes and bikes, and hang out on a beach.

NIGHTLIFE & THE ARTS

Stockholm's nightlife can be broken up into two general groups based on geography. First, there's Birger Jarlsgatan, Stureplan, and the city end of Kungsträdgården, which are more upscale and trendy, and thus more expensive. At the bars and clubs in this area it's not unusual to wait in line with people who look like they just stepped off the pages of a glossy magazine. To the south, in Södermalm, things are a bit looser and wilder, but that doesn't mean the bars are any less hip. At night Söder can get pretty crazy—it's louder and more bohemian, and partygoers often walk the streets.

In general, on weekends clubs and bars are often packed with tourists and locals, and you might have to wait in line. It's also sometimes hard to distinguish between a bar and nightclub, since many bars turn into clubs late at night. Many establishments will post and enforce a minimum age requirement, which could be anywhere from 18 to 30, depending on the clientele they wish to serve, and they may frown on jeans and sneakers. Your safest bet is to wear black clothes, Stockholm's shade of choice. Most places are open until around 3 AM. Wherever you end up, a night of bar-hopping in Stockholm has fresher air now, served with a tinge of desperation: in the summer of 2005 smoking was banned in all bars, clubs, and restaurants in the country.

The tourist guide *What's On* (⊕ www.stockholmtown.com) is available free of charge at most hotels, tourist centers, and some restaurants. It lists the month's events in both English and Swedish. The Thursday editions of the daily newspapers *Dagens Nyheter* (⊕ www.dn.se) and *Svenska Dagbladet* (⊕ www.svd.se) carry current listings of events, films, restaurants, and museums in Swedish. There's also a monthly guide called *Nöjesguiden* (the Entertainment Guide; ⊕ www.nojesguiden.se), which has listings and reviews in Swedish.

Nightlife

Bars & Nightclubs

Go to Stureplan (at one end of Birger Jarlsgatan) on any given weekend night, and you'll see crowds of people gathering around Svampen (the Mushroom), *the* meeting place for people getting ready to go out in this area.

★ **Berns Salonger** (⊠ Berns Hotel, Berzelii Park, City ☎ 08/56632000) has three bars—one in 19th-century style and two modern rooms—plus a huge veranda that's spectacular in summer. Music here gets so thumping you can hear it down the street. Glamour is on the menu at **Brasserie**
★ **Godot** (⊠ Grev Tureg. 36, Östermalm ☎ 08/6600614), a toned-down, chic bar and restaurant known for its excellent cocktail list and hip crowd. The red and gold interiors of nearby **Buddha Bar** (⊠ Biblioteksg. 9, Östermalm ☎ 08/54518500) are, not surprisingly, inspired by the lounges and opium dens of the Orient. No opium here, but an equally decadent night is guaranteed. **Folkhemmet** (⊠ Renstiernas Gata 30, Södermalm ☎ 08/6405595), marked by a blue F imitating the T for the

subway, is a longtime favorite of the artsy locals. It's friendly and inviting, but be prepared for a crowded bar. Don't let the name of **Hotellet** (⊠ Linneg. 18, Östermalm ☎ 08/4428900) fool you. Although originally designed as a hotel, it is now a very chic bar that has managed to retain that open lobby feel for its hot crowd. Close to the Mushroom is the casually hip **Lydmar Bar** (⊠ Stureg. 10, Östermalm ☎ 08/56611300), with black-leather couches and chairs and a small stage for bands and DJs. Many people who frequent the bar are in the music business. **Mosebacke Etablissement** (⊠ Mosebacke Torg 3, Södermalm ☎ 08/6419020) is a combined indoor theater, comedy club, and outdoor café with a spectacular view of the city. The crowd here leans toward over-30 hipsters. The **O-bar** (⊠ Stureplan 2, Östermalm ☎ 08/4405730), located upstairs through the restaurant Sturehof, is where the downtown crowd gathers for late-night drinks and music ranging from bass-heavy hiphop to hard rock. The **Sturehof** itself is a prime location for evening people-watching. The outdoor tables are smack dab in the middle of ★ Stureplan. Lovers of the late-night cocktail should head north to **Olssons Video** (⊠ Odeng. 14, Vasastan ☎ 08/6733800), where the darkened lounge caters to a slick clientele of cool urbanites thirsty for some of the best mixes in town. For what has to be Stockholm's biggest rum collection (more than 64 varieties), slide into **Sjögräs** (Sea Grass; ⊠ Timmermansg. 24, Södermalm ☎ 08/841200), where the drinks go down smoothly to the sounds of reggae. **Sophie's Bar** (⊠ Biblioteksg. 5, City ☎ 08/6118408) is one of Stockholm's major celebrity hangouts. It can be a bit elitist and uptight, probably the reason Madonna checked it out when she was in town. From Sophie's Bar it's a short walk to **Spy Bar** (⊠ Birger Jarlsg. 20, City ☎ 08/6118408), one of Stockholm's most exclusive clubs. It's often filled with local celebrities and lots of glitz and glamour. At Odenplan the basement bar of **Tranan** (⊠ Karlbergsv. 14, Vasastan ☎ 08/52728100) is a fun place to party in semidarkness to anything from ambient music to hard rock. Lots of candles, magazines, and art are inside. A trendy youngish crowd props up the long bar at **WC** (⊠ Skåneg. 51, Södermalm ☎ 08/7022963), with ladies' drink specials on Sunday. Luckily, the only things that'll remind you of the name (which stands for "water closet," or bathroom) are the holes in the middle of the bar stools.

Stockholm can also appease your need for pub-style intimacy. Guinness, ale, and cider enthusiasts rally in the tartan-clad **Bagpiper's Inn** (⊠ Rörstrandsg. 21, Vasastan ☎ 08/311855), where you can get a large selection of bar food. Those longing for a great whiskey travel a long way to the **Bishops Arms** (⊠ St. Eriksg. 115, Vasastan ☎ 08/56621788) where more than 150 are offered, not to mention more than 30 types of beer. **The Dubliner** (⊠ Smålandsg. 8, City ☎ 08/6797707), probably Stockholm's most popular Irish pub, serves up pub food, shows major sporting events on its big screen, and hosts live folk music on stage. It's ★ not unusual to see people dancing on the tables. The very British **Tudor Arms** (⊠ Grevg. 31, Östermalm ☎ 08/6602712) is just as popular as when it opened in 1969. Brits who are missing home cooking will be relieved when they see the menu. **Wirströms Pub** (⊠ Stora Nyg. 13, Gamla Stan ☎ 08/212874) is in labyrinthine 17th-century cellars. Expect live acoustic music, mostly anglophone patrons, and lots of beer. There are also 130 whiskeys available.

Cabaret

Börsen (⊠ Jakobsg. 6, City ☎ 08/7878500) offers high-quality international cabaret shows. Tucked behind the Radisson SAS near Nybroplan is **Wallmans Salonger** (⊠ Teaterg. 3, City ☎ 08/6116622), where singing and dancing waitstaff and talented stage performers entertain until midnight.

Casinos

Many hotels and bars have a roulette table and sometimes blackjack; games operate according to Swedish rules, which are designed to limit the amount you can lose. **Cosmopol Casino** (⊠ Kungsg. 65, City ☎ 08/7818800) is Stockholm's only international casino; it was opened in 2003 after a relaxation in Sweden's gambling laws. Glitz and glamour abound in the huge chandelier-strung former theater, where games are plentiful and winnings are unlimited—as are losses.

Dance Clubs

Blue Moon (⊠ Kungsg. 18, City ☎ 08/244700) is a multifloor club with a range of music and a restaurant for refueling between numbers. Music veers from dance and hip-hop to live rock and European easy listening, depending on the night you are there. **Café Opera** (⊠ Operahuset, City ☎ 08/6765807), at the waterfront end of Kungsträdgården, is a popular meeting place for young and old alike. It has the longest bar in town, fantastic 19th-century ceilings and details, plus dining and roulette, and major dancing after midnight. The kitchen offers a night menu until 2:30 AM. **Debaser** (⊠ Karl Johans torg 1, Södermalm ☎ 08/4629860) is the perfect place for those who like their dancing a bit wilder. The epicenter of Stockholm's rock music scene, this is where denim-clad legions come to shake their stuff. **Mälarsalen** (⊠ Torkel Knutssonsg. 2, Södermalm ☎ 08/6581300) caters to the nondrinking jitterbug and fox-trot crowd in Södermalm. Down on Stureplan is **Sturecompagniet** (⊠ Stureg. 4, Östermalm ☎ 08/6117800), a galleried, multifloor club where the crowd is young, the dance music is loud, and the lines are long.

Gay Bars

Hidden down behind the statue of St. George and the dragon on Gamla Stan, **Mandus Bar och Kök** (⊠ Österlångg. 7, Gamla Stan ☎ 08/206055) is a warm and friendly restaurant and bar perfect for drinking and talking late into the night. **Patricia** (⊠ Stadsgården, Berth 25, Södermalm ☎ 08/7430570) is a floating restaurant, disco, and bar right next to Slussen. And don't worry—the boat doesn't rock enough to make you sick. All are welcome at **TipTop** (⊠ Sveav. 57, Norrmalm ☎ 08/329800), but most of the clientele is gay. Men and women dance nightly to '70s disco and modern techno.

Jazz Clubs

The best and most popular jazz venue is **Fasching** (⊠ Kungsg. 63, City ☎ 08/53482964), where international and local bands play year-round. The classic club **Nalens** (⊠ Regeringsg. 74, City ☎ 08/50522200), which was popular back in the '50s and '60s, is back on the scene with

"SKÅL!"

MANY PEOPLE who have never seen Sweden have nonetheless conjured an often nearsighted image of what they think it is like: Nordic woodlands, crystalline-featured women, Greta Garbo, sexual freedom, and yet lives lived within rigid, formal constraints. There's some truth to the latter image of Swedish formality. So let's take a look at it.

Please take a seat as an invited guest at the dining table. It is set with a crisp white tablecloth, perfectly polished silver, a candelabra, napkins, and crystal glasses. The wine is chilled, and nothing is out of place. Your hostess is the shimmering image of Swedish household perfection.

Nowhere more than at the dining table will you encounter the unspoken truths of Swedish formality, especially in the toast. In Australia or New Zealand it is scarcely de rigueur and may be accompanied by a drawling "G'day, mate." In Britain it is all stiff upper lip and chivalry. In the United States the rules are as diverse as the cultures that populate it. But in Sweden there is only one way to toast, and its protocol is very specific and universally followed. So, do not touch your glass yet, even though it is full and you are nervous. Never touch the glass first; you must wait until one of the hosts, usually the man, lifts his glass to all. Do not drink. Everyone must reply to the proffered "skål" (meaning "cheers" and pronounced skohl) with a collective "skål." Then you will all tilt your glasses to the host and hostess. Delayed eye contact is imperative before, during, and after the measured sip of appreciation. Don't empty the glass. The meal has commenced.

From here on in during the dinner, toasting will still play a role, but the procedure is individualized and personal. Guests will toast each other. You are free to toast anyone but the hostess. She can toast anyone she pleases. This is a safeguard against hostess inebriation. The temptation, of course, is for everyone to intermittently toast her in thanks.

The roots of this alcohol-related tradition may lie with the Vikings. They always lived in peril, and no one could be trusted. The rule was to toast your "friend" with full eye contact and an arm behind the back to prevent a quick slitting of the throat. Later, state control would become big in Sweden; alcohol was once banned to stop the poor from brewing their potatoes into freedom-inducing alcohol. Even later alcohol was limited to stave off social and health problems. Today you can buy wine and spirits only in government-controlled liquor stores, called Systembolagett. Caution is part of the Swedish nature, and the alcohol rituals show it.

Back at the dinner table, most of the rules will be somewhat familiar to you, simply practiced in a more accentuated form.

We leave you with your Swedish hosts now. You can surely find your way from here. As a foreigner you will be granted some leeway in strictly adhering to the customs. But whatever you do, do not take the bottle as you leave. From that transgression there is certainly no way back.

major performances throughout the year; it has three stages. **Stampen** (⊠ Stora Nyg. 5, Gamla Stan ☎ 08/205793) is an overpriced but atmospheric club in Gamla Stan with traditional jazz nightly. Get there early for a seat.

Piano Bars

The **Anglais Bar** (⊠ Humlegårdsg. 23, City ☎ 08/51734000), at the Hotel Anglais, is popular on weekends. Most people there are English-speaking international travelers staying at the hotel. The **Clipper Club** (⊠ Skeppsbron 1214, Gamla Stan ☎ 08/223260), at the Hotel Reisen, is a pleasant, dark-wood, dimly lighted bar on Gamla Stan.

Rock Clubs

Pub Anchor (⊠ Sveav. 90, Norrmalm ☎ 08/152000), on Sveavägen's main drag, is the city's downtown hard-rock bar. **Krogen Tre Backar** (⊠ Tegnérg. 1214, Norrmalm ☎ 08/6734400) is as popular among hard-rock fans as Pub Anchor is. It's just off Sveavägen. International rock acts often play at **Klubben** (⊠ Hammarby Frabriksv. 13, Södermalm ☎ 08/4622200), a small bar and club in the Fryshuset community center south of town.

The Arts

Stockholm's theater and opera season runs from September through May. Both Dramaten (the National Theater) and Operan (the Royal Opera) shut down in the summer months. When it comes to popular music, big-name acts such as Neil Young, U2, Eminem, and even the Backstreet Boys frequently come to Stockholm in summer while on their European tours. Artists of this type always play at Globen sports arena. For a list of events pick up the free booklet *What's On,* available from hotels and tourist information offices. For tickets to theaters and shows try **Biljettdirekt** (☎ 0771/707070).

Classical Music

International orchestras perform at **Konserthuset** (⊠ Hötorget 8, City ☎ 08/102110), the main concert hall. The **Music at the Palace series** (☎ 08/102247) runs June through August. After Konserthuset, the best place for classical music is **Nybrokajen 11** (⊠ Nybrokajen 11, City ☎ 08/4071700), where top international musicians perform in relatively small halls. Off-season there are weekly concerts by Sweden's Radio Symphony Orchestra at **Berwaldhallen** (Berwald Concert Hall; ⊠ Strandv. 69, Östermalm ☎ 08/7845000).

Dance

When it comes to high-quality international dance in Stockholm, there's really only one place to go. **Dansenshus** (⊠ Barnhusg. 12–14, Vasastan ☎ 08/50899090) hosts the best Swedish and international acts, with shows ranging from traditional Japanese dance to street dance and modern ballet. You can also see ballet at the Royal Opera house.

Film

Stockholm has an abundance of cinemas, all listed in the *Yellow Pages* under "Biografer." Current billings are listed in evening papers, normally with Swedish titles; call ahead if you're unsure. Foreign movies are subtitled, not dubbed. Most, if not all, movie theaters take reservations over the phone: popular showings can sell out ahead of time. Cinemas are either part of the **SF** chain or of **Sandrew Metronome.** Listings for each can be found on the wall at the theater or in the back of the culture pages of the daily newspapers. **Biopalatset and Filmstaden Söder** (⊠ Medborgarplatsen, Södermalm ☎ 08/6443100 or 08/56260000) are on the south side of town and have many films from which to choose. **Filmstaden Sergel** (⊠ Hötorget, City ☎ 08/56260000) is a 14-screen complex at one end of Hötorget. If you are interested in smaller theaters with character, try the **Grand** (⊠ Sveav. 45, Norrmalm ☎ 08/4112400), a nice little theater with two small screens and not a bad seat in the house. **Röda Kvarn** (⊠ Biblioteksg. 5, City ☎ 08/7896073) is a beautiful old movie theater right near Stureplan. **Zita** (⊠ Birger Jarlsg. 37, Norrmalm ☎ 08/232020) is a one-screen theater that shows foreign films. A small restaurant is in the back.

Opera

It is said that Queen Lovisa Ulrika began introducing opera to her subjects in 1755. Since then Sweden has become an opera center of standing, a launchpad for such names as Jenny Lind, Jussi Björling, and
★ Birgit Nilsson. **Operan** (Royal Opera House; ⊠ Jakobs torg 2, City ☎ 08/7914300), dating from 1898, is now the de facto home of Sweden's operatic tradition. **Folkoperan** (⊠ Hornsg. 72, Södermalm ☎ 08/6160750) is a modern company with its headquarters in Södermalm. Casting traditional presentation and interpretation of the classics to the wind, the company stages productions that are refreshingly new.

Theater

Kungliga Dramatiska Teatern (Royal Dramatic Theater, called Dramaten; ⊠ Nybroplan, City ☎ 08/6670680) sometimes stages productions of international interest, in Swedish, of course. The exquisite **Drottningholms Slottsteater** (Drottningholm Court Theater; ⊠ Drottningholm, Drottningholm ☎ 08/6608225) presents opera, ballet, and orchestral music from May to early September; the original 18th-century stage machinery is still used in these productions. Drottningholm, the royal residence, is reached by subway and bus or by a special theater-bus (which leaves from the Grand Hotel or opposite the central train station). Boat tours run here in summer.

SPORTS & THE OUTDOORS

Like all Swedes, Stockholmers love the outdoors and spend a great deal of time enjoying outdoor sports and activities. Because the city is spread out on a number of islands, you are almost always close to the water. The many large parks, including Djurgården and Haga Park, allow people to quickly escape the hustle and bustle of downtown.

The most popular summertime activities in Stockholm are golf, biking, rollerblading, tennis, and sailing. In winter people like to ski and ice-skate.

Beaches

The best bathing places in central Stockholm are on the island of Långholmen and at Rålambshov, at the end of Norr Mälarstrand. Both are grassy or rocky lakeside hideaways. Topless sunbathing is virtually de rigueur.

Biking & Rollerblading

Stockholm is laced with bike paths, and bicycles can be taken on the commuter trains (except during peak traveling times) for excursions to the suburbs. The bike paths are also ideal for rollerblading. You can rent a bike for between SKr 160 and SKr 260 per day. Rollerblades cost between Skr 90 and SKr 120. Most places require a deposit of a couple thousand kronor. **Cykelfrämjandet** (⊠ Thuleg. 43, 113 53 ☎ 08/54591030 ⊕ www.cykelframjandet.a.se), a local bicyclists' association, publishes an English-language guide to cycling trips. City and mountain bikes can be rented from **Cykel & Mopeduthyrning** (⊠ Strandv. at Kajplats 24, City ☎ 08/6607959) for SKr 170.

Boating

Boating in Stockholm's archipelago is an exquisite summertime activity. From May to September sailboats large and small and gorgeous restored wooden boats cruise from island to island. Both types of boats are available for rental. Walk along the water on Strandvägen, where many large power yachts and sailboats (available for charter) are docked. Sea kayaking has also become increasingly popular and is a delightful way to explore the islands.

Contact **Svenska Seglarförbundet** (Swedish Sailing Association; ⊠ Af Pontins väg 6, Djurgården 115 21 ☎ 08/4590990 ⊕ www.ssf.se) for information on sailing. **Svenska Kanotförbundet** (Swedish Canoeing Association; ⊠ Rosvalla, Nyköping ☎ 0155/209080 ⊕ www.kanot.com) has information on canoeing and kayaking. **Capella Skärgårdscatering** (⊠ Flaxenviks Bryggv. 14, Åkersberga ☎ 08/54443390) has a large power yacht available for afternoon and overnight charters for groups of up to 40 people. At the end of Strandvägen, before the bridge to Djurgården, is **Tvillingarnas Båtuthyrning** (⊠ Strandvägskajen 27, City ☎ 08/6603714), which has large and small motorboats and small sailboats. **Point 65 N** (⊠ Styrmansg. 23, Östermalm ☎ 08/6630106), a short walk up from Strandvägen, has high-quality sea kayaks for rent. Its staff will help you get them down and back from the water if it's a two- or three-day rental.

Fitness Centers

Health and fitness is a Swedish obsession. The **S.A.T.S.** (⊠ Birger Jarlsg. 6C, City ☎ 08/54501460 ⊠ Odeng. 65, Vasastan ☎ 08/54542880) chain has women's and mixed-gym facilities for SKr 150 a day. For a relatively inexpensive massage, try the **Axelsons Gymnastiska Institut** (⊠ Gästrikeg. 10-12, Vasastan ☎ 08/54545900). **Friskis & Svettis** (⊠ St.

Eriksg. 54, Vasastan ☎ 08/4297000) is a local chain of indoor and, in summer, outdoor gyms specializing in aerobics; branches are scattered throughout the Stockholm area. Monday through Thursday at 6 PM, from the end of May into late August, it hosts free aerobic sessions in Rålambshovs Park.

Golf

There are numerous golf courses around Stockholm. Greens fees run from about SKr 450 to SKr 650, depending on the club. Contact **Sveriges Golfförbund** (⊠ Kevingestrand 20, Box 84, 182 11 Danderyd ☎ 08/6221500 ⊕ www.golf.se), which is just outside Stockholm, for information. **Stockholms Golfklubb**, which has a mid-level 18-hole course, is there as well. **Lidingö Golfklubb** (⊠ Kyttingev. 2, Lidingö ☎ 08/7317900) has an 18-hole forest-and-park course. It's about a 20-minute drive from the city center. **Ingarö Golfklubb** (⊠ Fogelvik, Ingarö ☎ 08/57028870), which has two 18-hole courses—one mid-level, one difficult—is also about 20 minutes away.

Running

Numerous parks with footpaths dot the central city area, among them **Haga Park** (which also has canoe rentals), **Djurgården,** and the wooded **Liljans Skogen.** A very pleasant public path follows the waterfront across from Djurgården, going east from Djurgårdsbron past some of Stockholm's finest old mansions and the wide-open spaces of Ladugårdsgärdet, a park that's great for a picnic or flying a kite.

Skiing

The **Excursion Shop** (⊠ Sweden Tourism, Kulturhuset, Sergels torg 3 ☎ 08/50828508) has information on skiing as well as other sport and leisure activities and will advise on necessary equipment. For a quick fix, Stockholmers take the 10-minute bus ride to the one-slope, one-lift Hammarbybacken (Hammarby Hill). Those with more time on their hands tend to go to Åre, Sweden's most popular ski resort.

Spectator Sports

The ultramodern, 281-foot **Globen** (⌂ Box 10055, Globentorget 2 121 27 ☎ 08/7251000), the world's tallest spherical building, hosts such sports as ice hockey and equestrian events. It has its own subway station. Inside the same sports complex as Globen is **Söderstadion** (⌂ Box 10055, 121 27 Globentorget 2 ☎ 08/7251000), the open-air stadium where the Hammarby soccer team plays professional soccer. North of the city is **Råsunda Stadion** (⌂ Box 1216, Solnav. 51, 171 23 Solna ☎ 08/7350900), Stockholm's largest soccer stadium and host to the biggest games between the city's teams.

Swimming

In the town center, **Centralbadet** (⊠ Drottningg. 88, City ☎ 08/54521315) has a lovely art-nouveau indoor pool, whirlpool, steam bath, and sauna.

Eriksdalsbadet (✉ Hammarby slussv. 20, Södermalm ☎ 08/50840250) is the city's largest swimming complex. At Stureplan the exclusive **Sturebadet** (✉ Sturegallerian, Östermalm ☎ 08/54501500) has a beautiful swimming pool, aquatic aerobics, and a sauna.

Tennis

With stars such as Björn Borg, Stefan Edberg, and Joachim "Pim Pim" Johansson, it's impossible for tennis not to be huge in Stockholm. Contact **Svenska Tennisförbundet** (✉ Lidingöv. 75, Box 27915, 115 94 Stockholm ☎ 08/4504310 ⊕ www.tennis.se) for information. Borg once played at **Kungliga Tennishallen** (Royal Tennis Hall; ✉ Lidingöv. 75, Norra Djurgården ☎ 08/4591500), which hosts the Stockholm Open every year. **Tennisstadion** (✉ Fiskartorpsv. 20, Norra Djurgården ☎ 08/54525254) has well-maintained courts.

SHOPPING

If you like to shop till you drop, then charge on down to any one of the three main department stores in the central city area, all of which carry top-name brands from Sweden and abroad for both men and women. For souvenirs and crafts peruse the boutiques and galleries in Västerlånggatan, the main street of Gamla Stan. For jewelry, crafts, and fine art, hit the shops that line the raised sidewalk at the start of Hornsgatan on Södermalm. Drottninggatan, Birger Jarlsgatan, Biblioteksgatan, Götgatan, and Hamngatan also offer some of the city's best shopping.

Department Stores & Malls

Fodor'sChoice ★ Sweden's leading department store is the unmissable **NK** (✉ Hamng. 18–20, across the street from Kungsträdgården, City ☎ 08/7628000); the initials, pronounced enn-*koh,* stand for Nordiska Kompaniet. You pay for the high quality here. **Åhléns City** (✉ Klarabergsg. 50, City ☎ 08/6766000) has a selection similar to NK, with slightly better prices. Before becoming a famous actress, Greta Garbo used to work at **PUB** (✉ Drottningg. 63 and Hötorget, City ☎ 08/4021611), which has 42 independent boutiques. Garbo fans will appreciate the small exhibit on level H2—a collection of photographs begins with her employee ID card.

★ **Bruno Galleria** (✉ Götg. 36, Södermalm ☎ 08/6412751) is a delightful glassed-in courtyard filled with cool clothing shops and interior-design stores; it's small, but perfectly appointed. **Gallerian** (✉ Hamng. 37, City ☎ 08/7912445), in the city center just down the road from Sergels Torg, is a large indoor mall closely resembling those found in the United States. It underwent a serious revamp in 2004, and is now the last word in designer-mall chic, with everything from toys to fashion, all in beautiful surroundings. **Sturegallerian** (✉ Grev Tureg. 9, Östermalm ☎ 08/6114606) is a midsize mall on super-posh Stureplan that mostly carries exclusive clothes, bags, and accessories; it's mostly populated by rich, beautiful young shoppers.

Markets

At **Hötorget** there's a lively outdoor market where you can buy fresh fruit and vegetables at prices well below those found in grocery stores. It's open daily from 9 to 6. For a good indoor market hit **Hötorgshallen** (⊠ Hötorget, City), directly under Filmstaden. The market is filled with butcher shops, coffee and tea shops, and fresh-fish markets. It's also open daily and closes at 6 PM. **Street** (⊠ Hornstulls Strand 1, Södermalm) is a waterside, weekend-only street market with stalls selling fashionable clothing, design, books, and other artsy and creative wares. If you're interested in high-quality Swedish food, try the classic European indoor market **Fodor'sChoice** **Östermalms Saluhall** (⊠ Östermalmstorg, Östermalm), where you can buy ★ superb fish, game, bread, vegetables, and other foodstuffs—or just have a glass of wine at one of the bars and watch the world go by.

Specialty Stores

Auction Houses

Perhaps the finest auction house in town is **Lilla Bukowski** (⊠ Strandv. 7, Östermalm ☎ 08/6140800), whose elegant quarters are on the waterfront. **Auktions Kompaniet** (⊠ Regeringsg. 47, City ☎ 08/235700) is downtown next to NK. **Stockholms Auktionsverk** (⊠ Jakobsg. 10, City ☎ 08/4536700) is under the Gallerian shopping center.

Books

Akademibokhandeln (⊠ Mäster Samuelsg. 28, City ☎ 08/6136100 ⊕ www.akademibokhandeln.se) has a large selection of books in English. If you don't find what you need at Akademibokhandeln, **Hedengrens** (⊠ Stureplan 4. Sturegallerian, Östermalm ☎ 08/6115128) is also well stocked, especially with fiction and poetry.

Gifts

Swedish pottery, jewelry, kitchen items, wooden toys, linens, and cookbooks from all over the country are available at **Svensk Hemslöjd** (⊠ Sveav. 44, City ☎08/232115). Though prices are high at **Iris Hantverk** (⊠ Kungsg. 55, City ☎ 08/214726), so is the quality of gift items and souvenirs.

Glass

Kosta Boda and Orrefors produce the most popular and well-regarded lines of glassware. The **Crystal Art Center** (⊠ Tegelbacken 4, City ☎ 08/217169), near the central station, has a great selection of smaller glass items. **Duka** (⊠ Sveav. 24–26, City ☎ 08/104530) specializes in crystal and porcelain at reasonable prices. **NK** carries a wide representative line of Swedish glasswork in its Swedish Shop, downstairs. **Nordiska Kristall** (⊠ Kungsg. 9, City ☎ 08/104372), near Sturegallerian, has a small gallery of one-of-a-kind art-glass sculptures as well as plates, vases, glasses, bowls, ashtrays, and decanters. **Svenskt Glas** (⊠ Birger Jarlsg. 8, City ☎ 08/7684024), near the Royal Dramatic Theater, carries a decent selection of quality Swedish glass, including bowls from Orrefors.

Interior Design

Sweden is recognized globally for its unique design sense and has contributed significantly to what is commonly referred to as Scandinavian design. All of this makes Stockholm one of the best cities in the world for shopping for furniture and home and office accessories.

On the corner of Östermalmstorg, in the same building as the marketplace, is **Bruka** (⌧ Humlegårdsg. 1, Östermalm ☎ 08/6601480), which has a wide selection of creative kitchen items as well as wicker baskets and chairs. Inside stylish mall Bruno Galleria, **David Design** (⌧ Gotg. 36, Södermalm ☎ 08/6947575) sells fine furniture, rugs, mirrors, and decorative items for the house. **DIS** (⌧ Humlegårdsg. 19, Östermalm ☎ 08/6112907) sells heavy dark-wood furniture that has an Asian flair. The rugs and pillowcases are also stunning.

For high-minded, trendy furniture that blends dark woods, stainless steel, and colorfully dyed wools, head to **House** (⌧ Humlegårdsg. 14, Östermalm ☎ 08/54585340). There's also a nice assortment of vases and glassware. For something little more classic, you can't do better than **Modernity** ★ (⌧ Sibylleg. 6, Östermalm ☎ 08/208025). This is *the* place for ultimate 20th-century Scandinavian design, with names like Arne Jacobsen, Alvar Aalto, and Poul Henningsen represented in full force. If you're after the *best* of Scandinavian design (and the most expensive), try **Nordiska Galleriet** (⌧ Nybrog. 11, Östermalm ☎ 08/4428360). It has everything from couches and chairs to tables and vases. Slightly out of the way, in the Fridhemsplan neighborhood in western Stockholm, ★ **R.O.O.M.** (⌧ Alströmerg. 20, Kungsholmen ☎ 08/6925000) has an impressive assortment of Swedish and international tables, chairs, rugs, pillows, beds—the list goes on. It also has a great book selection, lots of nice ceramic bowls and plates, and many decorations and utensils for the kitchen and bathroom. Not just a clever play on words, **Stockhome** (⌧ Kungsg. 25, City ☎ 08/4111300) has a great selection of things with which, well, to stock your home, including china, towels, glass, books, linen, even bicycles and patterned bandages. For elegant home furnishings, affluent Stockholmers tend to favor **Svenskt Tenn** (⌧ Strandv. 5A, Östermalm ☎ 08/6701600), best known for its selection of designer Josef Franck's furniture and fabrics.

Men's Clothing

Men in search of a little "street cred" can head for **Beneath** (⌧ Kronobergsg. 37, Kungsholmen ☎ 08/6431250), purveyor of ultrahip urban street wear and limited-edition labels. **Brothers** (⌧ Drottningg. 53, City ☎ 08/4111201) sells relatively inexpensive Swedish clothes that are often inspired by the more expensive international brands. For suits and evening suits for both sale and rental, **Hans Allde** (⌧ Birger Jarlsg. 58, City ☎ 08/207191) provides good old-fashioned service. **J. Lindeberg** (⌧ Grev Tureg. 9, Östermalm ☎ 08/6786165) has brightly colored and highly fashionable clothes in many styles. The golf line has been made famous by Swedish golfer Jesper Parnevik. Top men's fashions can be found on the second floor of **NK** (⌧ Hamng. 18–20, City ☎ 08/7628000), which stocks everything from outdoor gear and evening wear to swimsuits and workout clothes. The Swedish label **Tiger** (☎ 08/7628772), with a section inside NK, sells fine suits, shoes, and casual wear.

Paper Products

For unique Swedish stationery and office supplies in fun colors and styles, go to **Ordning & Reda** (⊠ NK, Hamng. 18–20, City ☎ 08/7282060).

Fodor'sChoice ★

Women's Clothing

Swedish designer **Anna Holtblad** (⊠ Grev Tureg. 13, Östermalm ☎ 08/54502220) sells her elegant designs at her own boutique. She specializes in knitted clothes. **Champaigne** (⊠ Biblioteksg. 2, City ☎ 08/6118803) has European and Swedish designs that are often discounted. **Filippa K** (⊠ Grev Tureg. 18, Östermalm ☎ 08/54588888) has quickly become one of Sweden's hottest designers. Her stores are filled with young women grabbing the latest fashions. **Hennes & Mauritz** (H&M; ⊠ Hamng. 22, City ☎ Drottningg. 53 and 56, City ☎ Sergelg. 1 and 22, City ☎ Sergels torg 12, City ☎ 08/7965500) is one of the few Swedish-owned clothing stores to have achieved international success. Here you can find updated designs at rock-bottom prices. The clothes at **Indiska** (⊠ Drottningg. 53 and elsewhere, City ☎ 08/109193) are inspired by the bright colors of India.

★

★

Kookai (⊠ Biblioteksg. 5, City ☎ 08/6119730) carries trendy, colorful European designs for young women. **Neu** (⊠ Nytorgsg. 36, Södermalm ☎ 08/6422004) is great for creations by up-and-coming designers that few have heard of, but, hopefully, many will know soon. One department store with almost every style and type of clothing and apparel is **NK** (⊠ Hamng. 18–20, City ☎ 08/7628000). **Polarn & Pyret** (⊠ Hamng. 10, Gallerian, Drottningg. 29, City ☎ 08/6709500) carries high-quality Swedish children's and women's clothing. For the modern rebel look, go to **Replay** (⊠ Kungsg. 6, City ☎ 08/231416), where the collection covers everything from jeans to underwear. For lingerie and fashionable clothing at a decent price, go to **Twilfit** (⊠ Nybrog. 11, Östermalm ☎ 08/6637505 ☎ Sturegallerian 16, Östermalm ☎ 08/6110455 ☎ Gamla Brog. 3638, Norrmalm ☎ 08/201954).

STOCKHOLM A TO Z

AIRPORTS & TRANSFERS

Initially opened in 1960 solely for international flights, Stockholm's Arlanda International Airport now also contains two domestic terminals. The airport is 42 km (26 mi) from the city center; a freeway links the city and airport. The airport is run by Luftfartsverket, a state-owned company.
🖪 **Arlanda International Airport** ⊠ 190 45 Stockholm-Arlanda ☎ 08/7976000 🖶 08/7978600 ⊕ www.arlanda.lfv.se.

AIRPORT Travel between Arlanda International Airport and Stockholm has been
TRANSFERS greatly improved with the completion of the Arlanda Express, a high-speed train service. The yellow-nose train leaves every 15 minutes (and every 10 minutes during peak hours), travels at a speed of 200 kph (125 mph), and completes the trip from the airport to Stockholm's central station in just 20 minutes; single tickets cost SKr 190.

Flygbussarna (airport buses) leave both the international and domestic terminals every 10–15 minutes from 6:30 AM to 11 PM, and make a number of stops on the way to their final destination at the Cityterminalen at Klarabergsviadukten, next to the central railway station. The trip costs SKr 89 and takes about 40 minutes.

A bus-taxi combination package is available. The bus lets you off by the taxi stand at Haga Forum, Järva Krog, or Cityterminalen and you present your receipt to the taxi driver, who takes you to your final destination. A trip will cost between SKr 190 and SKr 260, depending on your destination.

For taxis be sure to ask about a *fast pris* (fixed price) between Arlanda and the city. It should be between SKr 400 and SKr 450, depending on the final destination. The best bets for cabs are Taxi Stockholm, Taxi 020, and Taxi Kurir. All major taxi companies accept credit cards. Watch out for unregistered cabs, which charge high rates and won't provide the same service.

🚅 **Arlanda Express** ✉ Vasag. 11, Box 130, City ☎ 020/222224 or 08/58889000 ⊕ www.arlandaexpress.com. **Flygbussarna** ☎ 08/6001000 ⊕ www.flygbussarna.com. **Taxi 020** ☎ 020/202020. **Taxi Kurir** ☎ 08/300000. **Taxi Stockholm** ☎ 08/150000.

BIKE TRAVEL

One of the best ways to explore Stockholm is by bike. There are bike paths and special bike lanes throughout the city, making it safe and enjoyable. Bike rentals will be about SKr 120 per day. One of the best places to ride is on Djurgården. Cykel & Mopeduthyrning service that area.

🚅 **Cykel & Mopeduthyrning** (Bike and Moped Rentals) ✉ Standv. kajplats 24, City ☎ 08/6607959.

BOAT & FERRY TRAVEL

Waxholmsbolaget (Waxholm Ferries) offers the Båtluffarkortet (Inter Skerries Card), a discount pass for its extensive commuter network of archipelago boats; the price is SKr 300 for 5 days of unlimited travel. The Strömma Kanalbolaget operates a fleet of archipelago boats that provide excellent sightseeing tours and excursions.

🚅 **Strömma Kanalbolaget** ☎ 08/58714000 ⊕ www.strommakanalbolaget.com. **Waxholmsbolaget** ☎ 08/6795830 ⊕ www.waxholmsbolaget.se.

BUS TRAVEL TO & FROM STOCKHOLM

All the major bus services, including Flygbussarna, Swebus Express, Svenska Buss, and Interbus, arrive at Cityterminalen (City Terminal), next to the central railway station. Reservations to destinations all over Sweden can be made by calling Swebus.

🚅 **Cityterminalen** ✉ Karabergsviadukten 72, City ☎ 08/7625997. **Flygbussarna** ☎ 08/6001000 ⊕ www.flygbussarna.com. **Interbus** ☎ 08/7279000 ⊕ www.interbus.se. **Svenska Buss** ☎ 0771/676767 ⊕ www.svenskabuss.se. **Swebus Express** ☎ 0200/218218 ⊕ www.swebusexpress.se.

BUS TRAVEL WITHIN STOCKHOLM

Late-night bus service connects certain stations when trains stop running. The comprehensive bus network serves the entire city, including out-of-town points of interest, such as Vaxholm and Gustavsberg.

🚅 **Stockholms Lokaltrafik (SL)** ☎ 08/6001000 ⊕ www.sl.se.

CAR RENTAL

Rental cars are readily available in Sweden and are relatively inexpensive. Because of the availability and efficiency of public transport, there is little point in using a car within the city limits. If you are traveling elsewhere in Sweden, you'll find that roads are uncongested and well marked but that gasoline is expensive (about SKr 10 per liter, which is equivalent to SKr 40 per gallon). All major car-rental firms are represented, including Avis, Hertz, and Sixt. Statoil gas stations also rent out cars, as do local Swedish companies such as Berras and Auto, which can sometimes have better prices than the major companies.

▣ Major Agencies **Auto** ⊠ Östgötg. 75, Södermalm ☎ 08/6428040. **Avis** ⊠ Ringv. 90, Södermalm ☎ 08/6449980. **Berras** ⊠ Skepperg. 74, City ☎ 08/6611919. **Hertz** ⊠ Vasag. 26, City ☎ 08/240720. **Sixt** ⊠ Karlav. 2, City ☎ 08/4111522. **Statoil** ⊠ Vasag. 16, City ☎ 020/252525 throughout Sweden, 08/202064 ⊠ Birger Jarlsg. 68, Norrmalm ☎ 08/211593.

CAR TRAVEL

Approach the city by either the E20 or E18 highway from the west, or the E4 from the north or south. The roads are clearly marked and well sanded and plowed in winter. Signs for downtown read CENTRUM.

Driving in Stockholm is often deliberately frustrated by city planners, who have imposed many restrictions to keep traffic down. Keep an eye out for bus lanes, marked with BUSS on the pavement. Driving in that lane can result in a ticket. Get a good city map, called a Trafikkarta, available at most service stations for around SKr 75.

EMBASSIES

▣ Australia ⊠ Sergels torg 12, City ☎ 08/6132900 ⊕ www.austemb.se.
▣ Canada ⊠ Tegelbacken 4, City ☎ 08/4533000 ⊕ www.canadaemb.se.
▣ New Zealand Consulate-General ⊠ Stureplan 2, Östermalm ☎ 08/6112625.
▣ United Kingdom ⊠ Skarpög. 68, Östermalm ☎ 08/6713000 ⊕ www.britishembassy. se.
▣ United States ⊠ Strandv. 101, Östermalm ☎ 08/7835300 ⊕ www.usemb.se.

EMERGENCIES

Dial 112 for emergencies—this covers police, fire, ambulance, and medical help, as well as sea and air rescue services. Private care is available via CityAkuten. A hospital is called a *sjukhus,* which is Swedish for "sick house," and regular doctors' offices are called *Läkerhuset.* Dentists are listed under *tandläkare,* or *tandvård.* There is a 24-hour national health service via the emergency number listed below.

▣ Doctors & Dentists **Folktandvården** (national dental service) ☎ 020/6875500. **Läkerhuset Hötorgscity** ⊠ Sveav. 13–15, City ☎ 08/243800. **Läkerhuset Riddargatan 12** ⊠ Riddarg. 12, Östermalm ☎ 08/6797900.

▣ Emergency Services **CityAkuten** (Emergency Medical Care) ⊠ Apelbergsg. 48, City ☎ 08/4122960. **CityAkuten Tandvården** (Emergency Dental Care) ⊠ Olof Palmesg. 13A, Norrmalm ☎ 08/4122900.

▣ Hospitals **Ersta Sjukhus** ⊠ Fjällg. 44, Södermalm ☎ 08/7146100. **Karolinska Sjukhuset** ⊠ Solna (just north of Stockholm), Solna ☎ 08/51770000. **Södersjukhuset** ⊠ Ringv. 52, Södermalm ☎ 08/6161000. **St. Görans Sjukhus** ⊠ Sankt Göransplan 1, Kungsholmen ☎ 08/58701000.

🔳 Police **Polisen** (Stockholm Police Headquarters) ⊠ Norra Agneg. 33–37, Kungsholmen ☎ 08/4010000.

🔳 24-Hour Pharmacy **C. W. Scheele** ⊠ Klarabergsg. 64, City ☎ 08/4548130.

ENGLISH-LANGUAGE MEDIA

BOOKS Many bookshops stock English-language books. Akademibokhandeln has a wide selection of English books, with an emphasis on reference titles. Hedengren's has an extensive selection of English- and other foreign-language books, from fiction and nonfiction to photography and architecture. NK has a large bookstore with an extensive English-language section.

🔳 Bookstores **Akademibokhandeln** ⊠ Mäster Samuelsg. 28, near city center, City ☎ 08/6136100. **Hedengrens** ⊠ Stureplan 4, Sturegallerian shopping complex, Östermalm ☎ 08/6115132. **NK** ⊠ Hamng. 18–20, City ☎ 08/7628000.

RADIO There are two major radio stations with English-language programming in Stockholm. Radio Sweden, part of the state-owned radio company, has news about Sweden in English, daily and weekly English programs, as well as many shows from National Public Radio in the United States and from the BBC in the United Kingdom. You can pick up Radio Sweden at 89.6 FM.

SUBWAY TRAVEL

The subway system, known as T-banan (Tunnelbanan, with stations marked by a blue-on-white T), is the easiest and fastest way to get around. Servicing more than 100 stations and covering more than 96 km (60 mi) of track, trains run frequently between 5 AM and 3 AM.

TAXIS

Stockholm's taxi service is efficient but overpriced. If you call a cab, ask the dispatcher to quote you a *fast pris* (fixed price), which is usually lower than the metered fare. Reputable cab companies are Taxi 020, Taxi Stockholm, and Taxi Kurir. Taxi Stockholm has an immediate charge of SKr 25 whether you hail a cab or order one by telephone. A trip of 10 km (6 mi) should cost about SKr 97 between 6 AM and 7 PM, SKr 107 at night, and SKr 114 on weekends.

🔳 **Taxi 020** ☎ 020/202020. **Taxi Kurir** ☎ 08/300000. **Taxi Stockholm** ☎ 08/150000.

TOURS

BOAT TOURS Strömma Kanalbolaget runs sightseeing tours of Stockholm. Boats leave from the quays outside the Royal Dramatic Theater, Grand Hotel, and City Hall. Stockholm Sightseeing, which leaves from Skeppsbron in front of the Grand, has four tours, including the "Under the Bridges" and "Historical Canal" tours. Trips last from one to four hours and cost from SKr 100 to SKr 280.

🔳 **City Hall** late May–early Sept. ⊠ Hantverkarg. 1, Kungsholmen ☎ 08/50829000. **Stockholm Sightseeing** ⊠ Skeppsbron 22, Gamla Stan ☎ 08/57814000 ⊕ www. stockholmsightseeing.com. **Strömma Kanalbolaget** ⊠ Skeppsbron 22, Gamla Stan ☎ 08/58714000.

BUS TOURS   Comprehensive tours of much of Stockholm, taking in museums, Gamla
Stan, and City Hall, are available through City Sightseeing.
🚩 **City Sightseeing** ✉ Skeppsbron 11, Gamla Stan ☎ 08/58714000 ⊕ www.
citysightseeing.com.

PRIVATE GUIDES   You can hire your own guide from Guide Centralen. In summer be sure
to book guides well in advance.
🚩 **Guide Centralen** ✉ Sweden House, Hamng. 27, Box 7542, City ☎ 08/58714030.

WALKING TOURS   City Sightseeing runs several tours, including the "Romantic Stockholm" tour of the cathedral and City Hall; the "Royal Stockholm" tour,
which includes visits to the Royal Palace and the Treasury; and the "Old
Town Walkabout," which strolls through Gamla Stan in just over one
hour.
🚩 **City Sightseeing** ☎ 08/58714000 ⊕ www.citysightseeing.com.

TRAIN TRAVEL

Both long-distance and commuter trains arrive at the central station in
Stockholm on Vasagatan, a main boulevard in the heart of the city. For
train information and ticket reservations 6 AM–11 PM, call the SJ number below. There is a ticket and information office at the station where
you can make reservations. Automated ticket-vending machines are
also available.
🚩 **Citypendeln** (Commuter Train) ☎ 08/6001000 ⊕ www.citypendeln.se. **SJ** (State Railway Company) ✉ central station, City ☎ 0771/757575 ⊕ www.sj.se.

TRANSPORTATION AROUND STOCKHOLM

The cheapest way to travel around the city by public transport is to purchase the Stockholmskortet (Stockholm Card). In addition to unlimited
transportation on city subway, bus, and rail services, it offers free admission to more than 60 museums and several sightseeing trips. The card
costs SKr 220 for 24 hours, SKr 450 for two days, and SKr 640 for three
days; you can purchase the card from the tourist center at Sweden
House on Hamngatan, from the Hotellcentralen accommodations bureau at the central station, and from the tourist center at Kaknäs Tower.

Stockholm has an excellent bus system, which is operated by SL (Stockholm Local Traffic). In 2000 the subway system was bought from SL
by Connex, the same company that runs the subways in Paris and London. Tickets for Stockholm subways and buses are interchangeable. Maps
and timetables for all city transportation networks are available from
the SL information desks at Sergels Torg, the central station, Slussen,
and online.

Bus and subway fares are based on zones. All trips in downtown will
be SKr 30. As you travel farther out of downtown, zones are added to
the fare in increments of SKr 10. Each ticket is good for one hour on
both the bus system and the subway. Single tickets are available at station ticket counters and on buses, but it's cheaper to buy an SL Tourist
Card from one of the many Pressbyrån newsstands. There's also a pass
called a Rabattkupong, valid for both subway and buses; it costs SKr
80 and is good for 10 trips downtown (fewer if you travel in more zones)

within the greater Stockholm area. There is no time limit within which the 10 trips must be used. If you plan to travel within the greater Stockholm area extensively during a 24-hour period, you can purchase a 24-hour pass for SKr 95 and a 72-hour pass for SKr 180. The 24-hour pass includes transportation on the ferries between Djurgården, Nybroplan, and Slussen. The 72-hour pass also entitles you to admission to Skansen, Gröna Lund Tivoli, and Kaknäs Tower. Those under 18 or over 65 pay SKr 50 for a one-day pass and SKr 90 for a two-day pass.

Connex ☎ 08/6295000 ⊕ www.connex.nu. **SL** ☎ 08/6001000 ⊕ www.sl.se.

TRAVEL AGENCIES

For a complete listing of travel agencies, check in the *Yellow Pages* under "Resor-Resebyråer," or contact American Express. For air travel contact SAS. SJ, the state railway company, has its main ticket office at central station.

Local Agent Referrals **American Express** ✉ Magnus Ladulåsg. 5, Södermalm ☎ 08/4295400. **SAS** ✉ ☎ 0770/727727. **SJ** (Statens Järnvägar or State Railway Company) ✉ Vasag. 1, City ☎ 0771/757575 ⊕ www.sj.se.

VISITOR INFORMATION

Tourist Information **City Hall** ⊙ June–Aug. ✉ Hantverkarg. 1, Kungsholmen ☎ 08/50829000. **Fjäderholmarna** ☎ 08/7180100. **Kaknästornet** (Kaknäs TV Tower) ✉ Ladugårdsgärdet, Gädet ☎ 08/7892435 ⊕ www.stockholmtown.com. **Stockholm Central Station** ✉ Vasag., City ☎ 0771/757575. **Stockholm Information Service** Sweden House ✉ Hamng. 27, Box 7542, 103 93 Stockholm ☎ 08/50828508. **Swedish Travel and Tourism Council** ✉ Box 3030, Kungsg. 36, 103 61 Stockholm ☎ 08/7891000 🖷 08/7891038 ⊕ www.visit-sweden.com.

Side Trips from Stockholm

2

WORD OF MOUTH

"In Visby, my son and I raced up the stairs next to St. Maria Kyrka. At the top we turned back to look at the water and even my 8-year-old gasped at how beautiful the view was, with the sun setting over the ocean, the ruins, and the city. If you're going to Visby without kids, this is a great spot for a romantic sunset picnic."

—sprin2

"If you go to Uppsala, be sure to walk around the university's campus. At the start of the academic year, it's full of students and freshman initiations—fun stuff to watch."

—stardust

Updated by
Rob Hincks

STOCKHOLM IS A GREEN, LIVELY, AND PLEASANT CITY—that cannot be denied. But travel a little farther from town and you will see why even Stockholmers make a regular and even hurried exit from their city on summer weekends. Immediately outside of Stockholm is the archipelago, meaning paradise on earth to a Swede with a boat and some time to kill. You can get lost among the many thousands of islands and skerries. Fortunately, travelers without their own boat can also easily explore the archipelago, and can get there by bus, train, or car from the city. As you'll see, pleasures here are simple: sunbathing on a rock, dipping in the chilly Baltic, enjoying a simple meal in a local bistro, and lazily watching the sun sink below the horizon.

Farther afield (south of Stockholm, in the Baltic) is the island of Gotland, a settlement whose medieval walls whisper of pirates and hidden treasure. For most people, though, it is the warm climate, stunning nature reserves, and legendary nightlife that bring them here year after year. Fans of children's book author Astrid Lindgren's Pippi Longstocking head to these parts, too. The stories were set on Gotland, and later, when dramatized, were filmed here.

Uppsala, north of Stockholm, is one of Europe's oldest and most respected seats of learning. The town is full of medieval and Gothic buildings that are a testament to its long history and former position of power as capital of the country. The cathedral, castle, and university are no doubt highlights. But there's always the chance to let loose; this is a student town, after all. After a day of fine art and high culture, you can get your fill of fine dining and high jinks by heading out to enjoy the town's animated nightlife.

Where to Stay & Eat

Stockholm's immediate surroundings offer a wide variety of hotels and restaurants. Nothing beats a day of luxury at the classic Grand Hotel in the millionaires' seaside town of Saltsjöbaden, followed by a gourmet meal in its traditional French restaurant. Then again, how about resting your head in a welcoming bed-and-breakfast spot following a freshly caught, freshly grilled herring supper? It's a tough decision and one that is a pleasure to make. Perhaps it's best to go for two nights—or more—and try both options.

Whatever you do, it's always a good idea to remember that much of this area only opens for visitors between the months of June and September. If you are traveling outside these times, it is highly recommended that you call ahead.

WHAT IT COSTS In Swedish Kronor				
	$$$$	**$$$**	**$$**	**$**	**¢**
RESTAURANTS	over 420	250–420	150–250	100–150	under 100
HOTELS	over 2,900	2,300–2,900	1,500–2,300	1,000–1,500	under 1,000

Restaurant prices are for a main course at dinner. Hotel prices are for two people in a standard double room in high season.

Drottningholm

★ ❶ *1 km (½ mi) west of Stockholm.*

Fodor'sChoice
★

Occupying an island in Mälaren (Sweden's third-largest lake) some 45 minutes from Stockholm's center, **Drottningholms Slott** (Queen's Island Castle) is a miniature Versailles dating from the 17th century. The royal family once used this property only as a summer residence, but, tiring of the Royal Palace back in town, they moved permanently to one wing of Drottningholm in the 1980s. Designed and built by the same father-and-son team of architects who built Stockholm's Royal Palace, construction of the castle began in 1662 on the orders of King Karl X's widow, Eleonora. Today it remains one of the most delightful of European palaces, reflecting the sense of style practiced by mid-18th-century royalty. The interiors, dating from the 17th, 18th, and 19th centuries, are a rococo riot of decoration with much gilding and trompe l'oeil. Most sections are open to the public. ☎ *08/4026280* ⊕ *www.royalcourt.se* 🖃 *SKr 60* ⊙ *May–Aug., daily 10–4:30; Sept., daily noon–3:30; Oct.–Apr., weekends noon–3:30; guided tours in summer only.*

The lakeside gardens of Drottningholms Slott are its most beautiful asset, containing **Drottningholms Slottsteater,** the only complete theater to survive from the 18th century anywhere in the world. Built by Queen Lovisa Ulrika in 1766 as a wedding present for her son Gustav III, the Court Theater fell into disuse after his assassination at a masked ball in 1792 (dramatized in Verdi's opera *Un Ballo in Maschera*). In 1922 the theater was rediscovered; there is now a small theater museum here as well, where you can sign up for a backstage tour and see the original backdrops and stage machinery and some amazing 18th-century tools used to produce such special effects as wind and thunder. To get performance tickets, book well in advance at the box office; the season runs from late May to early September. A word of caution: the seats are extremely hard—take a cushion. ☎ *08/7590406, 08/6608225 box office* ⊕ *www.drottningholmsslottsteater.dtm.se* 🖃 *SKr 60* ⊙ *May, daily noon–4:30; June–Aug., daily 11–4:30; Sept., daily 1–3:30. Guided tours in English at 12:30, 1:30, 2:30, 3:30, and 4:30.*

Arriving & Departing

Boats bound for Drottningholms Slott leave from Klara Mälarstrand, a quay close to Stadshuset (City Hall). Call **Strömma Kanalbolaget** (✉ Skeppsbron 22, 111 30 ☎ 08/58714000 ⊕ www.strommakanalbolaget.com) for schedules and fares. Alternatively, you can take the T-bana (subway) to Brommaplan, and any of Buses 177, 301–323, or 336 from there. Call **Stockholms Lokal Trafik** (☎ 08/6001000) for details.

Mariefred

❷ *63 km (39 mi) southwest of Stockholm.*

The most delightful way to experience the true vastness of Mälaren is the trip to Mariefred—an idyllic little town of mostly timber houses—

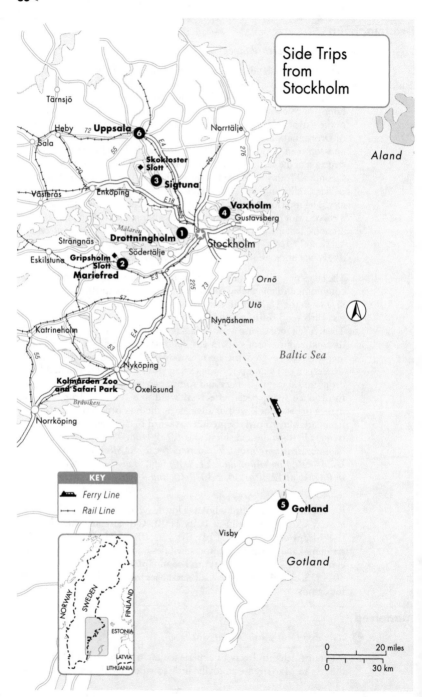

Side Trips from Stockholm

Tärnsjö

Heby 72 **Uppsala** ❻

Sala

Norrtälje

Åland

Skokloster Slott ❸ **Sigtuna**

Västerås Enköping

Vaxholm ❹ Gustavsberg

Mälaren

Strängnäs **Drottningholm** ❶ Stockholm

Eskilstuna **Gripsholm Slott** ❷ Södertälje

Mariefred

Ornö

Utö

Katrineholm Nynäshamn

Baltic Sea

Nyköping

Kolmården Zoo and Safari Park Öxelösund

Bråviken

Norrköping

KEY
Ferry Line
Rail Line

❺ **Gotland**

Visby

Gotland

NORWAY SWEDEN FINLAND

ESTONIA

LATVIA

LITHUANIA

0   20 miles
0   30 km

FOR SWEDISH ROYALS, CENTURIES OF BATTLES

THEY'RE YOUNG, THEY'RE BEAUTIFUL, and they've got blue blood running through their veins. What more could a tabloid wish for?

Swedish paparazzi, and their European colleagues, can't get enough of Sweden's Crown Princess Victoria (born 1977), Prince Carl Philip (born 1979), and Princess Madeleine (born 1982). The princesses, especially, are closely monitored, with reports on their workouts and diets, favorite designers, love affairs—even updates on the progress of Princess Madeleine's summer tan. Princess "Madde" was even voted the most beautiful woman in the world by Spanish gossip magazine Hola.

It seems like a charmed life, but such constant scrutiny can be too much, even for a princess trained for a life in the public eye. When the crown princess was 20, the royal court revealed that she suffered from bulimia, an illness that is said to have plagued many European princesses, from the late Princess Diana to Princess Mary of Denmark. The crown princess interrupted her studies in Stockholm and spent two years at Yale, where she could live in relative anonymity.

The royal family may be dealing with distinctly 21st-century struggles these days, but Swedish royal history is rife with battles. Viking kings battled for power over the land around Lake Mälaren in the first millennium. The first king to reign over a unified Sweden, Gustav Vasa, claimed the throne in 1523 after a bloody rebellion against Kristian II of Denmark. His sons then spent their lives battling each other: King Erik XIV, the snubbed suitor of Elizabeth I of England, created a scandal by marrying a commoner, then jailing his brother Johan, who he felt was getting dangerously popular. Johan and third brother Karl then joined forces to overthrow Erik, who died in jail, poisoned by arsenic-laced split-pea soup.

The glory days of Sweden's military began in 1611, when Gustav II Adolf became king. He led Sweden through the Thirty Years' War until his death at the Battle of Lützen in 1632. Swedish expansionism continued after his death; by 1718 all of Finland and Estonia, parts of Russia, and patches of the German coast were under Swedish rule.

The current royal family, the Bernadotte family, came from France in the 19th century. Then-king Karl XIII was old and had no heirs. Seeking to approach France and stave off Russia, Sweden invited one of Napoleon's marshals, Jean Baptiste Bernadotte, to become king of Sweden. He accepted and assumed the more Swedish-sounding name Karl XIV Johan.

Though debate has raged in Sweden for years whether to abolish the monarchy, it seems only a small percentage of the Swedish people would like to see the country without the royal family. Sweden's expansionist dreams have long been abandoned; Sweden hasn't been in a war for close to 200 years. And yet it seems the Swedish royal family is still looking for peace.

— Karin Palmquist

aboard the coal-fired steamer of the same name, built in 1903 and still going strong. The town's winding narrow streets, ancient squares, and wooded lakeside paths are all perfect for walking. The **Mariefred Tourist Office** has maps and information about tours.

Mariefred's principal attraction is **Gripsholm Slott.** Built in the 1530s by Bo Johansson Grip, the Swedish high chancellor, the castle contains fine Renaissance interiors, a superbly atmospheric theater commissioned in 1781 by the ill-fated Gustav III, and Sweden's royal portrait collection. ☎ *0159/10194* ⊕ *www.royalcourt.se* ✉ *SKr 60* ☉ *Mid-May–mid-Sept., daily 10–4. Mid-Sept.–mid-May, weekends noon–3; guided tours only.*

An old converted barn across from Gripsholm Slott (formerly the royal stables and a farm store) now houses **Grafikens Hus** (Graphic House), a center for contemporary graphic art and printmaking. Visitors can view exhibitions or take part in workshops covering all aspects of graphic art. The building is primarily used by working artists, giving visitors a genuine and interesting insight into printmaking as it happens. There are also a good coffee shop and a gift shop that sells artwork. ☎ *0159/ 23160* ⊕ *www.grafikenshus.se* ✉ *SKr 70* ☉ *May–Aug., daily 11–5; Sept.–Apr., Tues. 11–8, Wed.–Sun. 11–5.*

★ For more than 100 years the beautiful steamship **SS *Mariefred*** has slowly and regularly made her way from Stockholm to Mariefred and back—the same route, still with the original engines, making her unique in the world. The interior of the ship is museum-like, with many of the original fittings unchanged. Even the captain, Claes Insulander, although not original, has been at the helm for over a quarter century. SS *Mariefred* departs from Klara Mälarstrand, near Stadshuset, Stockholm's city hall. The journey takes 3½ hours each way, and there is a restaurant on board. ☎ *08/6698850* ✉ *SKr 180 round-trip* ☉ *Departures at 10: May, weekends; mid-June–late Aug., Tues.–Sun. Return trip departs from Mariefred at 4:30.*

You can also travel by narrow-gauge steam railway from Mariefred to a junction on the main line to Stockholm, returning to the capital by ordinary train. Contact the **Mariefred Tourist Office** for details.

Where to Stay & Eat

★ **$$** ✕▥ **Gripsholms Värdshus & Hotel.** At the oldest inn in the country, guests get a sense of the real Sweden. Lovingly restored and luxuriously appointed, this yellow-wood hotel stands on the site of an old monastery. Rooms are large and airy, with wooden floors and highlights of bright yellow and sky-blue. The whole hotel is full of art and artifacts, including some old Swedish-tile fireplaces and many of the original floral-painted ceilings. In an elegant wood-paneled dining room, the restaurant serves local dishes with an international twist, such as pike-perch with steamed scallops, bell pepper sauce, and olives or corn-fed chicken with hazelnuts, asparagus, and star anise. ✉ *Kykog. 1, 647 23* ☎ *0159/34750* 🖷 *0159/34777* ⊕ *www.gripsholms-vardshus.se* ⇆ *45 rooms, 10 suites* ⚵ *Restaurant, room service, in-room data ports, sauna, bar, meeting rooms, no-smoking rooms* ▭ *AE, DC, MC, V* ❙⬦❙ *BP.*

¢–$ ☐ **In My Garden.** This could possibly be one of the loveliest bed-and-
Fodor'sChoice breakfasts in Sweden. Housed in a turn-of-the-last-century villa with a
★ glassed-in veranda, this spot boasts stunning views across the lake.
There are only three rooms here, all of them with a delightfully personal
and tasteful touch, such as stuffed cushions, artwork, photographs,
and antiques. Relax in the evening on the porch, Stars-and-Stripes blan-
ket over your knees, and imagine, for a moment, that you are at your
dream summer home. ☒ *Strandv. 17, 647 30* ☎ *0159/13353* ⊕ *www.
inmygarden.se* 🛏 *3 rooms* ⚘ *Lounge* ☰ *MC, V* ⊙︎ *BP.*

Visitor Information
The **Mariefred Tourist Office** (☎ 0159/29799 ⊕ www.strangnas.se) is
open year-round.

Sigtuna

❸ *48 km (30 mi) northwest of Stockholm.*

An idyllic town on a northern arm of Lake Mälaren, Sigtuna was the
principal trading post of the Svea, the tribe that settled Sweden after
the last Ice Age; its Viking history is still apparent in the many runic
stones preserved all over town. Founded in 980, Sigtuna is Sweden's
oldest town, and as such it's not surprising that it has Sweden's oldest
street, Stora Gatan. After it was ransacked by Estonian pirates, its merchants went on to found Stockholm sometime in the 13th century. Little remains of Sigtuna's former glory, beyond parts of the principal church.
The town hall dates from the 18th century, and the main part of the
town dates from the early 1800s. There are two houses said to date
fromo the 15th century.

About 20 km (12 mi) northwest of Sigtuna and accessible by the same
ferryboat from Stockholm is **Skokloster Slott**, an exquisite baroque castle with equally exquisite grounds. Commissioned in 1654 by a celebrated
Swedish soldier, Field Marshal Carl Gustav Wrangel, the castle is furnished with the spoils of Wrangel's successful campaigns. Those with
more of an enthusiasm for old machines than for old houses can visit
the **Skokloster Motormuseum** on the castle grounds. The museum boasts
a very fine collection of old cars, planes, motorbikes, and engines. The
museum keeps the same hours as the castle and requires a SKr 50 entrance fee. ☒ *Bålsta* ☎ *018/386077* ⊕ *www.lsh.se/skokloster/info.htm*
🎟 *SKr 40* ⊙ *Daily 11–5.*

Where to Stay & Eat
$$–$$$ ✕☐ **Sigtuna Stadshotell.** Near the lakeshore, this beautiful hotel was built
Fodor'sChoice in 1909, and soon after became a central gathering place among locals—
★ despite at the time being considered one of the ugliest buildings in all
of Sigtuna. In its early days the hotel had Sigtuna's first cinema, and in
the cellar the state liquor store operated an inn. Today it has been carefully restored and tastefully furnished. The emphasis is on a clean and
natural interior, where oak, sandstone, and white cotton are the focus.
The restaurant is a fine-dining treat, serving up modern Swedish food
and great views of the lake. ☒ *Stora Nyg. 3, 193 30* ☎ *08/59250100*

🕮 *08/59251587* ⊕ *www.sigtunastadshotell.se* 🗲 *24 rooms* ♿ *Restaurant, room service, minibars, cable TV, in-room broadband, in-room data ports, Wi-Fi, sauna, spa, meeting rooms, no-smoking rooms* 🖃 *AE, DC, MC, V* ⦿ *BP.*

Arriving & Departing

Sigtuna can be reached by driving on E4 North to 263 or by taking a commuter train from Stockholm's central station to Märsta, where you change to Bus 570 or 575.

Vaxholm & the Archipelago

❹ *32 km (20 mi) northeast of Stockholm.*

Skärgården (the archipelago) is Stockholm's greatest natural asset: more than 25,000 islands and skerries, many uninhabited, spread across an almost tideless sea of clean, clear water. The islands closer to Stockholm are larger and more lush, with pine tree–covered rock faces and forests. There are also more year-round residents on these islands. As you move away from the mainland, the islands become smaller and more remote, turning into rugged, rocky islets. To sail lazily among these islands aboard an old steamboat on a summer's night is a timeless delight, and throughout the warmer months Swedes flee the chaos of the city for quiet weekends on the waters.

For the tourist with limited time, one of the simplest ways to get a taste of the archipelago is the one-hour ferry trip to Vaxholm, an extremely pleasant, though sometimes crowded, mainland seaside town of small, red-painted wooden houses. Guarding what was formerly the main sea route into Stockholm, Vaxholm's fortress now houses the small **Vaxholms Fästnings Museum** (Vaxholm Fortress Museum), which documents the defense of Stockholm over the centuries. The museum contains military memorabilia and tells how the imposing stone castle helped defend against the Danes and Russians in the 17th and 18th centuries. You can reach the fortress by taking a small boat from the town landing, which is in front of the tourist office; a discounted combination ticket includes the boat fare and entrance to the museum. 🕿 *08/ 54172157* 🎫 *SKr 40* ⊙ *Mid-May–Aug., daily noon–4. Group admission at other times by appointment.*

An even quicker trip into the archipelago is the 20-minute ferry ride to Ⓢ **Fjäderholmarna** (the Feather Islands), a group of four secluded islands. In the 19th-century the islands were the last chance for a refreshment stop for archipelago residents rowing into Stockholm to sell their produce. After 50 years as a military zone, the islands were opened to the public in the early 1980s. Today they are crammed with arts-and-crafts studios, shops, an aquarium, a small petting farm, a boat museum, a large cafeteria, an ingenious "shipwreck" playground, and even a smoked-fish shop.

Although it's on the mainland, **Saltsjöbaden** is far enough out into the wilds to be considered the archipelago. Construction of the seaside town started in 1891. Designed from the beginning to be a community for the affluent, Saltsjöbaden was based partly on the suburban communities springing up at the same time in the United States. By 1893 the railway had been extended to Saltsjöbaden, and the town was one of the first in Sweden to have electric streetlights. The town has some of Europe's grandest 19th-century residences, which were designed by the leading architects of the time. The best way to reach the town is by train. SJ runs a regular service from central Stockholm.

If you are interested in a longer voyage out into the islands, there are several possibilities. Contact the Sweden House and ask for the "Destination Stockholm Archipelago" catalog, which lists more than 350 holiday homes for rent. For booking accommodations, contact **Hotellcentralen** (☎ 08/7892425) in Stockholm's central station.

One of the most popular excursions is to **Sandhamn,** the main town on the island of Sandön, which is home to about 100 permanent residents. The journey takes about three hours by steamship, but there are faster boats available. The Royal Swedish Yacht Club was founded here at the turn of the 20th century, and sailing continues to be a popular sport. Its fine-sand beaches also make it an ideal spot for swimming. Another option is to try scuba diving—introductory lessons are available; ask at the Sweden House for details. Explore the village of Sandhamn and its narrow alleys and wooden houses, or stroll out to the graveyard outside the village, where tombstones bear the names of sailors from around the world.

The island of **Utö,** which contains Sweden's oldest iron mine (circa AD 1100–1200), is another popular spot. A number of the miners' homes from the 18th century have been restored. About 200 people live year-round on the island, which has cafés, camping sites, and swimming areas. You can also rent bicycles from a shop near the ferry landing. The boat trip to the island takes about three hours. Utö is particularly known for its bread. *Utö limpa,* a slightly sweetened and spiced sandwich bread, is to be found only on the island and is considered a high delicacy. Many of the thousands of people who go sailing in the archipelago every year make a special detour to stock up on the bread, partly because of its exquisite taste and partly because of its long-keeping properties.

A little closer to Stockholm is the island of **Grinda,** long a popular recreation spot among Stockholmers. Rental cabins from the '40s have been restored to their original condition; there are about 30 of these available through **Grinda Stugby** (☎ 08/54249072). The **Grinda Wärdshus** (☎ 08/54249491), a still-functioning inn from the turn of the 20th century, is one of the largest stone buildings in the archipelago. Since a number of walking paths cut through the woods and open fields, it takes just 15 minutes to walk from one end of Grinda to the other, and exploring is easy. The trip to the island takes about two hours.

At the far southern tip of Stockholm's archipelago lies **Trosa,** a town full of wooden houses that's right on the Baltic Sea. The tiny river that runs through the middle of the town is flanked by beautiful villas painted white, red, yellow, and mint green—a reflection of Trosa's heritage as a seaside retreat for stressed, wealthy Stockholmers. Around the small, cobbled town square are arts-and-crafts shops and market stalls selling fish, fruit, and vegetables.

★ Five kilometers (3 mi) to the north of Trosa is the impressive **Tullgarns Slott**. Built in the early 1700s, the palace was turned into a playful summer retreat in 1772 by King Gustaf's younger brother, Fredrik Adolf. The grounds include sculptured parks and gardens, an orangery, and a theater. The palace's interiors are full of ornate plasterwork, paintings of royals and landscapes, and many of the original French-influenced furnishings. ⊠ *Trosa* ☎ *08/55172011* ⊕ *www.royalcourt.se* ⊠ *SKr 50* ☉ *May–Sept., daily 11–4.*

off the beaten path

Fodor's Choice
★

Thirty kilometers (20 mi) northwest of Trosa, on the little island of Oaxen (accessible by bridge), is something of a culinary happening. **OAXEN SKÄRGÅRDSKROG** – (⊹ Drive E4 south from Stockholm for about 40 minutes; take the Hölö/Mörkö exit and follow signs to the restaurant ☎ 08/54249072 ⊕ www.oaxenkrog.se) can be described, almost without argument, as the very best restaurant in Sweden—an accolade confirmed for three years running in *White Guide,* Sweden's leading independent restaurant guide, as well as by numerous critics and magazines. Set in an old wooden waterside manor house, Oaxen's interior is sleek and modern, with stunning Danish furniture, dark brown walls, crisp white linens, and oiled oak floors. The pricey-but-worth-it food is a breathtaking collection of modern-European-inspired culinary works of art; the wine list and views across the water make the experience even more riveting. In short, if possible, don't miss eating at this restaurant.

If you'd prefer to stay on board a boat and simply cruise around the islands, seek out the **Blidösund**. A coal-fired steamboat built in 1911 that has remained in almost continuous service, the *Blidösund* is now run by a small group of enthusiasts who take parties of around 250 on evening music-and-dinner cruises. The cruises depart from a berth close to the Royal Palace in Stockholm. ⊠ *Skeppsbron 11, Stockholm* ☎ *08/4117113* ⊠ *SKr 160* ☉ *Departures early May–late Sept., Mon.–Thurs. 6:30 PM (returns at 10:15 PM).*

Among the finest of the archipelago steamboats is the **Saltsjön**, which leaves from Nybrokajen, close to the Strand Hotel. You can take a jazz-and-dinner cruise for SKr 150 from late June to mid-August. Call for details. To go to Utö, the attractive island known for its bike paths, bakery, and restaurant, will cost you SKr 190. In December there are three daily Julbord cruises, all of which serve a Christmas smorgasbord. ⊠ *Strömma Kanalbolaget, Skeppsbron 22, Stockholm* ☎ *08/58714000* ☉ *Departures July–mid-Aug. and Dec.*

Where to Eat

$$$ ✕ **Sandhamns Värdshus.** Built in 1672 as a guesthouse and restaurant for tired sailors, the bright-yellow Sandhamn Inn is a delightful place to stop for meal. A terrace provides a view over the colorful seaside town below, and in summer there's outdoor seating on a large veranda. The menu is rooted in Swedish traditions with a focus on local seafood. Try

the seafood stew spiced with saffron and served with freshly baked bread and aioli. ⊠ *Sandhamn* ☎ *08/57153051* ▤ *AE, DC, MC, V.*

★ **$$–$$$** ✕ **Fjäderholmarnas Krog.** A crackling fire on the hearth in the bar area welcomes the sailors who frequent this laid-back restaurant. In case you don't travel with your own sailboat, you can time your dinner to end before the last ferry returns to the mainland. The food here is self-consciously Swedish: fresh, light, and beautifully presented. The service is professional; it's a great choice for a special night out. ⊠ *Fjäderholmarna* ☎ *08/7183355* ▤ *AE, DC, MC, V* ☉ *Closed Oct.–Apr.*

$$ ✕ **Dykarbaren.** The idea for this old wooden harborside restaurant came from similar cafés in Brittany, France. Simple local dishes, mostly of fish, are served up in an informal wooden-table dining area. Originally just catering to local divers, Dykarbaren now serves everyone. ⊠ *Strandpromenaden, Sandhamn* ☎ *08/57153554* ▤ *AE, DC, MC, V.*

¢–$ ✕ **Café Lena Linderholm.** Lena is the wife of folk singer and cookbook writer Gösta Linderholm. She runs a very pleasant interior-design shop on the first floor of this old town house and a café on the second floor. Those with a passion for great coffee, overstuffed sandwiches, and delicious Swedish vanilla buns should make a beeline for this charming spot. ⊠ *Rådhusg. 19, Vaxholm* ☎ *08/54132165* ▤ *No credit cards.*

¢ ✕ **Tre Små Rum.** The old mint-green, red-roof house that contains "Three
Fodor'sChoice Small Rooms" is a fitting place for simple light lunches. The sandwiches
★ (made from freshly baked bread) are delicious at this lunch-only café. There are also delicious cakes and pastries—at least 40 types daily. If you don't want to sit inside in one of the rooms, there is a small outside seating area. ⊠ *Östra Långg., Trosa* ☎ *0156/12151* ▤ *MC, V* ☉ *No dinner.*

Where to Stay

Lodging options in the archipelago vary from island to island. The larger, more inhabited islands often have at least one decent hotel, if not a few, whereas some of the smaller, more deserted islands have only an inn or two or camping facilities. Hostels are available at low cost on some islands, and some private homes rent out rooms and offer B&B accommodations. It's also possible to rent small cabins. Details are available from the Sweden House. Wherever you stay, one of the joys of a night in this part of the world is to find yourself a rock somewhere to call your own and watch the sun fade to dusk and the summer moon dance on the Baltic waters.

$$$ ✕▥ **Grand Hotel Saltsjöbaden.** Many say that this is the only reason to
Fodor'sChoice come to the beautiful but quiet town of Saltsjöbaden. Next to the sea
★ and the surrounding countryside, the hotel is one of the most breathtaking in the whole archipelago. Built in 1893, it's a castlelike concoction of white stone, arched windows, and towers. The huge rooms are filled with colorful period furniture that is set off perfectly against the plain stone fireplaces and pastel walls. The restaurant ($$$) is a grand gilt, pillared, and mirrored affair with crisp linens, fine crystal, and a classic French menu. ⊠ *113 83 Saltsjöbaden* ☎ *08/50617000* 🖷 *08/50617025* ⊕ *www.grandsaltsjobaden.se* ➟ *121 rooms, 10 suites* ♨ *Restaurant, room service, minibars, cable TV, in-room broadband, Wi-Fi, miniature golf, 2 tennis courts, saltwater pool, sauna, spa, ice-skating, bar, no-smoking rooms* ▤ *AE, DC, MC, V* ⋈ *BP.*

$$ 🏨 **Sandhamn Hotel and Conference.** Built in the "archipelago" style, the Sandhamn overlooks the local harbor. Rooms have light-wood accents with pale white-and-blue furnishings. The curtains are linen. The recreational area has an indoor and outdoor pool as well as a gym. Live music is often played on the grounds in summer. The hotel adjoins the Seglarrestaurangen, also looking out over the water, which serves traditional Swedish cuisine with a French influence. ⊠ *130 30 Sandhamn* ☎ *08/57450400* 🖷 *08/57450450* ⊕ *www.sandhamn.com* ⇨ *81 rooms, 3 suites* ⌂ *Restaurant, in-room data ports, indoor-outdoor pool, gym, sauna, bar, meeting room* 🖃 *AE, DC, MC, V* ⎟◉⎟ *BP.*

$-$$ 🏨 **Waxholms Hotell.** Perched directly on Vaxholm's harbor, Waxholms is a stone's throw from where the ferries land. Rooms in this excellent little hotel are bright and elegant, and most have a view of the water and the fortress that sits in the harbor. The restaurant and bar are the best in town, and the wraparound dining room provides great views of the boats on the water. The varied menu concentrates on local fish and Swedish specialties. ⊠ *Hamng. 2, 185 21* ☎ *08/54130150* 🖷 *08/54131376* ⊕ *www.waxholmshotell.se* ⇨ *32 rooms, 2 suites* ⌂ *Restaurant, in-room broadband, Wi-Fi, bar, meeting room, no-smoking rooms* 🖃 *AE, DC, MC, V* ⎟◉⎟ *BP.*

★ $ 🏨 **Bomans.** Right on the water and brimming with history, this family-run hotel dates from the early 20th century. The bedrooms are stuffed with floral patterns, iron bedsteads, feather quilts, lace, and linen. Downstairs there is a small bar. Lace tablecloths, chandeliers, and tangerine linens and fabrics help create a warm mood in the very good restaurant (**$$**), where you can also dine outside in summer. The menu is unashamedly Swedish, with high-quality versions of such classic dishes as meatballs, salmon, and elk with lingonberries. ⊠ *Hamnen, 619 30 Trosa* ☎ *0156/52500* 🖷 *0156/52510* ⊕ *www.bomans.se* ⇨ *32 rooms, 2 suites* ⌂ *Restaurant, in-room data ports, sauna, spa, bar, meeting rooms, no-smoking rooms* 🖃 *AE, DC, MC, V* ⎟◉⎟ *BP.*

$ 🏨 **Grinda Wärdshus.** Housed in one of the archipelago's largest stone buildings, this 19th-century villa has homey rooms and bright, comfortable public areas. Since the hotel is right on the water, you may wish to take a refreshing dip in the sea before tackling the sumptuous breakfast buffet of Scandinavian classics. ⊠ *Södra Bryggan, 100 05 Grinda* ☎ *08/54249491* 🖷 *08/54249497* ⊕ *www.grindawardshus.se* ⇨ *28 rooms, 2 suites* ⌂ *Restaurant* 🖃 *AE, DC, MC, V* ⎟◉⎟ *BP.*

¢-$$ 🏨 **Utö Värdshus.** The rooms are large and well laid out here, with traditional furniture resembling that found in a Swedish farmhouse—lots of old pine and comfy, plump cushioning. Choose between a room in the sprawling white main hotel or one of the 30 that are in a cabin on the grounds. The restaurant (**$$**) has a grand wooden ceiling lighted with chandeliers. The food is eclectic, ranging from salmon with dill to Cajun chicken. ⊠ *Gruvbryggan, 130 56 Utö* ☎ *08/50420300* 🖷 *08/50420301* ⊕ *www.uto-vardshus.se* ⇨ *34 rooms* ⌂ *Restaurant, sauna, bar, no-smoking rooms* 🖃 *AE, DC, MC, V* ⎟◉⎟ *BP.*

★ ¢ 🏨 **Rum i Backen.** This pretty, early-20th-century wooden house on Vaxholm's main street is a charming B&B. It's run by a family that is more than happy to help you with anything you need. There's just one room, but as it's in an annex to the house, it's a sort of self-contained apartment, with a shower, kitchen, and small veranda. The breakfast, which you make yourself, is included. ⊠ *Kungsg. 14, 185 34 Vaxholm* ☎ *08/ 314021* ⊡ *08/54133315* ◄⬝ *1 room* ⊟ *No credit cards* ⑩ *CP.*

Sports & the Outdoors

A visit to the islands is one of the best opportunities you'll get in Sweden to take a bracing swim in the fresh, clean waters of the Baltic Sea. Sometimes surprisingly warm, mostly heart-racingly chilly, but always memorable, a quick dip in these waters will set you up for the day. There are literally thousands of great swimming spots, but Sandhamn and Utö have the sandy beaches and rocky outcrops that keep them among the best.

Vaxholm & the Archipelago A to Z

BOAT & FERRY TRAVEL

Regular ferry services to the archipelago depart from Strömkajen, the quayside in front of Stockholm's Grand Hotel. Boat cruises leave from the harbor in front of the Royal Palace or from Nybrokajen, across the street from the Royal Dramatic Theater. Ferries to the Feather Islands run almost constantly all day long in summer (April 29–September 17), from Slussen, Strömkajen, and Nybroplan. Contact Strömma Kanalbolaget, Waxholmsbolaget, or Fjäderholmarna.

An excellent way to see the archipelago is to purchase an **Inter Skerries Card,** which costs SKr 300 and allows unlimited boat travel throughout the islands for five days. Use the card for day trips from Stockholm, or go out for longer excursions and bounce around from island to island. The card is available at the Stockholm Tourist Center. 🚩 **Fjäderholmarna** ☎ 08/7180100. **Stockholm Tourist Center** ⊠ Sweden House, Hamng. 27, Box 7542, 103 93 Stockholm ☎ 08/50828508. **Strömma Kanalbolaget** ☎ 08/58714000. **Waxholmsbolaget** ☎ 08/6795830.

TOURS

A great way to discover the remote, less-visited parts of the archipelago is to go out with Sandhamnsguiderna, a tour group that operates out of Sandhamn. Experienced guides will take you on tailor-made excursions, in small or large groups, to explore the outer reaches of the deserted archipelago. A tour price depends on how many people go and for how long. 🚩 **Sandhamnsguiderna** ☎ 08/6408040 ⊕ www.sandhamnsguiderna.com.

TRAIN TRAVEL

There are regular train services to Saltsjöbaden from Stockholm's Slussen station, on Södermalm and operated by SL (Stockholm Local Traffic). The journey takes about 20 minutes. To get to Trosa, take a one-hour train ride from Stockholm to Vagnhärad, where there is a bus waiting to take the 10-minute trip to Trosa. 🚩 **SJ** ☎ 0771/757575 ⊕ www.sj.se. **SL** ☎ 08/6001000 ⊕ www.sl.se.

VISITOR INFORMATION

The Vaxholms Turistbyrå (Vaxholm Tourist Office) is in a large kiosk at the bus terminal, adjacent to the marina and ferry landing. Hours are daily 10–5. The Utö Turistbyrå (Utö Tourist Bureau) is near the ferry landing. More information on Grinda is available from the Stockholm Tourist Center at Sweden House.

🚩 **Sweden House** ⊠ Hamng. 27, Box 7542, 103 93 Stockholm ☎ 08/50828508. **Trosa Turistbyrå** ☎ 0156/52222 ⊕ www.trosa.com. **Utö Turistbyrå** ☎ 08/50157410. **Vaxholms Turistbyrå** ⊠ Söderhamnen, 185 83 Vaxholm ☎ 08/54131480 ⊕ www.visitvaxholm.se.

Gotland

❺ *85 km (53 mi) south of Stockholm.*

Gotland is Sweden's main holiday island, a place of ancient history, a relaxed summer-party vibe, wide sandy beaches, and wild cliff formations called *raukar*. Measuring 125 km (78 mi) long and 52 km (32 mi) at its widest point, Gotland is where Swedish sheep farming has its home. In its charming glades, 35 varieties of wild orchids thrive, attracting botanists from all over the world.

The first record of people living on Gotland dates from around 5000 BC. By the Iron Age it had become a leading Baltic trading center. When German marauders arrived in the 13th century, they built most of its churches and established close trading ties with the Hanseatic League in Lübeck. They were followed by the Danes, and Gotland finally became part of Sweden in 1645.

Gotland's capital, **Visby,** is a delightful hilly town of about 20,000 people. Medieval houses, ruined fortifications, churches, and cottage-lined cobbled lanes make Visby look like a fairy-tale place. Thanks to a very gentle climate, the roses that grow along many of the town's facades bloom even in November.

In its heyday Visby was protected by a wall, of which 3 km (2 mi) survive today, along with 44 towers and numerous gateways. It is considered the best-preserved medieval city wall in Europe after that of Carcassonne, in southern France. Take a stroll to the north gate for an unsurpassed view of the wall.

Visby's cathedral, **St. Maria Kyrka,** is the only one of the town's 13 medieval churches that is still intact and in use. Built between 1190 and 1225 as a place of worship for the town's German parishioners, the church has few of its original fittings because of the extensive and sometimes clumsy restoration work done over the years. That said, the sandstone font and the unusually ugly angels decorating the pulpit are both original features worth a look.

Burmeisterska Huset, the home of the *Burmeister*—or principal German merchant—organizes exhibitions displaying the works of artists from the island and the rest of Sweden. Call the tourist office in Visby to arrange for viewing. ⊠ *Strandg. 9* ☎ *No phone, Visby tourist office 0498/201700* ☜ *Free.*

The **Länsmuseet på Gotland,** Gotland's county museum, contains examples of medieval artwork, prehistoric gravestones and skeletons, and silver hoards from Viking times. Be sure to also check out the ornate "picture stones" from AD 400–600, which depict ships, people, houses, and animals. ⊠ *Strandg. 14* ☎ *0498/292700* ⊕ *www.lansmuseetgotland. se* ⊠ *SKr 40* ⊙ *Mid-May–Sept., daily 11–5; Oct.–mid-May, Tues.–Sun. noon–4.*

The **Visby Art Museum** has some innovative exhibitions of contemporary painting and sculpture. On the first floor is the permanent display, which is mostly uninspiring, save for a beautiful 1917 watercolor by local artist Axel Lindman showing Visby from the beach in all its splendid medieval glory. ⊠ *St. Hansg. 21* ☎ *0498/292775* ⊠ *SKr 40* ⊙ *May–Sept., daily 10–5.*

Ⓒ Medieval activities are re-created at **Kapitelhusgården.** Families can watch and take part in metal- and woodworking, coin making, dressmaking, archery, and hunting. ⊠ *Drottensg. 8* ☎ *0498/247637* ⊠ *Free* ⊙ *June–Aug., daily noon–6.*

The 4 km (2½ mi) of stalactite caves at **Lummelunda,** about 18 km (11 mi) north of Visby on the coastal road, are unique in this part of the world and are worth visiting. The largest was discovered in 1950 by three boys out playing. ⊠ *Lummelunds Bruk* ☎ *0498/273050* ⊕ *www. lummelundagrottan.se* ⊠ *SKr 70* ⊙ *May–Sept., daily 9–5.*

A pleasant stop along the way to Lummelunda is the **Krusmyntagården** (☎ *0498/296900*), a garden with more than 200 herbs, 8 km (5 mi) north of Visby.

The island has about 100 old churches dating from Gotland's great commercial era still in use. **Barlingbo,** from the 13th century, has vaulted paintings, stained-glass windows, and a remarkable 12th-century font. The exquisite **Dalhem** was constructed about 1200. **Gothem,** built during the 13th century, has a notable series of paintings of that period. **Grötlingbo** is a 14th-century church with stone sculptures and stained glass (note the 12th-century reliefs on the facade). **Öja,** a medieval church decorated with paintings, houses a famous holy rood from the late 13th century. The massive ruins of a Cistercian monastery founded in 1164 are now called the **Roma Kloster Kyrka** (Roma Cloister Church). **Tingstäde** is a mix of six buildings dating from 1169 to 1300.

Curious rock formations dot the coasts of Gotland, remnants of reefs formed more than 400 million years ago, and two **bird sanctuaries, Stora** and **Lilla Karlsö,** stand off the coast south of Visby. The bird population consists mainly of guillemots, which look like penguins. Visits to these sanctuaries are permitted only in the company of a recognized guide. ☎ *0498/240500 for Stora, 0498/485248 for Lilla* ⊠ *SKr 225 for Stora, SKr 200 for Lilla.* ⊙ *May–Aug., daily.*

Where to Eat

★ **$$** ✕ **Donners Brunn.** In a beautiful orange-brick house on a small square in Visby, the chef proprietor of this restaurant, Bo Nilsson, was once chef at the renowned Operakällaren in Stockholm. The menu uses excellent local ingredients to make French-influenced dishes that are reasonably priced, given their quality. The house specialty of Gotland lamb with fresh asparagus and hollandaise sauce is delicious. ⊠ *Donners Plats 3* ☎ *0498/271090* ⚠ *Reservations essential* ☰ *AE, DC, MC, V.*

$$ ✕ **Gutekällaren.** Despite the name, the Gotlander *Cellar* is above ground in a 12th-century building. The dining here is a sociable affair with tightly packed wooden tables in a cozy room comfortably lighted by candles. The food is a cross between Mediterranean and Asian-inspired cuisine. For a real treat, try the delicious lamb dish. ⊠ *Stora Torget 3* ☎ *0498/ 210043* ☰ *DC, MC.*

$–$$ ✕ **Clematis.** This campy restaurant is one of the most popular in Visby— guests are thrown back a few centuries to the Middle Ages for an authentic night of food, song, and dance. You get a flat slab of bread instead of a plate, and your only utensil is a knife. The staff dons period attire and is known to break into a tune while delivering food to tables. Traditional Swedish fare is served, with a focus on meats and island ingredients. Drinks are served in stone goblets. ⊠ *Strandg. 20* ☎ *0498/ 292727* ☰ *AE, DC, MC, V* ☉ *No lunch.*

$–$$ ✕ **Krusmyntagården.** This marvelous little garden-café opened in the late '70s and has been passed down through several owners. The garden now has more than 200 organic herbs and plants, many of which are used in the evening BBQ feasts. ⊠ *Brissund* ☎ *0498/296900* ☰ *AE, DC, MC, V.*

¢–$$ ✕ **Konstnärsgården.** Hans and Birgitta Belin run a wonderful establishment in the tiny village of Ala. He is an artist, she a chef. As you eat your lovingly prepared food in this old manor-house restaurant, you can view and buy works by Hans and other artists. The venison that's often on the menu comes from deer raised on the premises, and in the summer months whole lambs are spit-roasted outdoors in the orchard gardens. ⊠ *30 km (19 mi) southeast of Visby, Ala* ☎ *0498/55055* ☰ *MC, V.*

¢–$ ✕ **Björklunda Värdshuset.** This small restaurant in an old stone farmhouse is run by a husband-and-wife team. You can have an aperitif in the apple orchard before tucking into the menu of local salmon, lamb, and pork dishes, all of which come in ample proportions. ⊠ *Björklunda, Burgsvik* ☎ *0498/497190* ☰ *AE, DC, MC, V.*

Where to Stay

$–$$ ▦ **Strand Hotel.** An environmentally friendly hotel with efficient heating and cooling systems, the Strand may ease your conscience with its approach. In any case, the lap pool, sauna, and bright, comfortable rooms will ease your spirit. The clubby, relaxing bar has large leather sofas in an adjoining library. ⊠ *Strandg. 34, 621 56* ☎ *0498/258800* ☎ *0498/ 258811* ⊕ *www.strandhotel.net* ⏎ *110 rooms, 6 suites* ⚲ *Restaurant, indoor pool, sauna, bar, no-smoking rooms* ☰ *AE, DC, MC, V* ¶○¶ *BP.*

$–$$ ▦ **Wisby Hotell.** The tall, thin building that's now the Wisby dates from the 1200s and is at the junction of two narrow streets. A hotel since 1855, the ocher-color walls, light floral-patterned fabrics, dark wood, and vaulted ceilings give it old European grandeur. There are two excellent bars in the hotel, one a glassed-in courtyard that serves cocktails and the other a cozy pub with a good beer selection. ⊠ *Strandg. 6, 621 24* ☎ *0498/257500* ☎ *0498/257550* ⊕ *www.wisbyhotell.se* ⏎ *134 rooms, 94 with bath; 10 suites* ⚲ *Restaurant, in-room broadband, Wi-Fi, 2 bars, no-smoking rooms* ☰ *AE, DC, MC, V* ¶○¶ *BP.*

$ 🏨 **Hotell Solhem.** A hotel that resembles a beach house, the Solhem offers wonderful views of Visby Harbor and the sea beyond. The rooms and public areas are small, but the hotel is very bright and simply furnished, making up for the lack of space. ⊠ *Solhemsg. 3, 621 58* 🕿 *0498/ 259000* 🖷 *0498/259011* ⊕ *www.hotellsolhem.se* ➽ *94 rooms, 1 with bath* ⚭ *Sauna, bar* ▭ *AE, DC, MC, V* ⑩ *BP.*

¢–$ 🏨 **Toftagården.** Near the Gotland coast about 20 km (12 mi) from Visby, the placid verdant grounds here are ideal for strolling, lazing about, and reading in the shade. The long sandy beach in Tofta is also nearby, as is the Kronholmen Golf Course. Most of the brightly furnished rooms, all on the ground floor, have their own terrace. There are also a number of cottages with kitchens—a two-night minimum stay is required for these. If the seawater at the beach is too cold, take a dip in the heated outdoor pool. The restaurant serves very good regional fare. ⊠ *Toftagården, 621 98* 🕿 *0498/297000* 🖷 *0498/265666* ⊕ *www. toftagarden.se* ➽ *50 rooms, 15 cottages* ⚭ *Restaurant, some kitchenettes, pool, sauna* ▭ *AE, DC, MC, V* ⑩ *BP.*

¢ 🏨 **Hotel St. Clemens.** Four buildings make up the St. Clemens, in Visby's Old Town. They range in age from a relatively young sixtysomething years to about four centuries, dating from the 1600s. Rooms are simple and a little clumsily furnished with mismatched materials, but they are comfortable, most with an armchair or sofa; some have small kitchens. There are two gardens on the property, one of which is shared with St. Clemens Church, one of Visby's oldest. ⊠ *Smedjeg. 3, 621 55* 🕿 *0498/219000* 🖷 *0498/279443* ⊕ *www.clemenshotell.se* ➽ *32 rooms* ⚭ *Some kitchenettes, cable TV, sauna, free parking* ▭ *AE, DC, MC, V* ⑩ *CP.*

¢ 🏨 **Kronholmens Gård.** This charming little complex has its own small beach a short walk from Kronholmen's acclaimed 27-hole golf course. There are two cabins. One has four rooms, each with five small beds. Inside the other is a common kitchen and living room that all cabin guests share. For families hoping to save a little money and who enjoy cooking for themselves, this is a great spot on the island. Weekly discounts are available. ⊠ *Västergarn, 620 20 Klintehamn* 🕿 *0498/245004* 🖷 *0498/ 245023* ➽ *1 four-bedroom cabin* ⚭ *Sauna* ▭ *AE, DC, MC, V.*

★ ¢ 🏨 **Villa Alskog.** A short drive from the sandy beaches in the south of Gotland, Villa Alskog is a delightful inn surrounded by beautiful open spaces, stone fences, and small groves of trees. The building dates from 1840 and was originally a residence for the local priest. Its 10 guest rooms are bright and simply furnished, with hardwood floors. Most have a private bath; when you reserve a room, verify that it's one that has its own bath. The location is ideal for swimming, hiking, and horseback riding. ⊠ *620 16 Alskog* 🕿 *0498/491188* 🖷 *0498/491120* ⊕ *www.villa-alskog.se* ➽ *15 rooms* ⚭ *Restaurant, café, hot tub, sauna, meeting room* ▭ *AE, DC, MC, V* ⑩ *BP.*

Nightlife & the Arts

Medeltidsveckan (Medieval Week), celebrated in early August, is a city-wide festival marking the invasion of the prosperous island by Danish king Valdemar on July 22, 1361. Celebrations begin with Valdemar's grand entrance parade and continue with jousts, an open-air market on Strandgatan, and street-theater performances re-creating the period.

In the ruins of **St. Nicolai,** the old dilapidated church in Visby, regular concerts are held throughout the summer months. Everything from folk to rock to classical is available. The tourist office has details.

There are many bars and drinking establishments on Gotland, but the best are in Visby. The town comes alive on summer nights; the best way to experience it is simply to wander the streets, follow the loudest noise, and go with the flow. If you do want to preplan your evening, try **Hamnplan** (⊠ Strandv. ☎ 0498/210710) (formerly called Skeppet), a lively place with both live music and DJs. Come prepared for a frantic, young crowd.

Gutekällaren (⊠ Stora Torget 3 ☎ 0498/210043) is a huge nightclub and a separate restaurant that share the same name. For a lively and varied evening, you'll find three floors, three dance areas, and 10, count them, 10 bars.

Sports & the Outdoors

Bicycles, tents, and camping equipment can be rented from **Gotlands Cykeluthyrning** (⊠ Skeppsbron 2 ☎ 0498/214133 ⊕ www. gotlandscykeluthyrning.com). **Gotlandsleden** is a 200-km (120-mi) bicycle route around the island; contact the tourist office for details.

For an aquatic adventure, **Gotlands Upplevelser** (⊠ Visby ☎ 0730/751678) will rent you a canoe and a life jacket or windsurfing equipment. They also offer rock-climbing courses. Call for prices and locations.

If you do nothing else on Gotland, go for a swim. The island has miles and miles of beautiful golden beaches and unusually warm water for this part of the world. The best and least-crowded beaches are at Fårö and Själsö in the north of the island.

Shopping

Barbro Sandell (⊠ Kustv. 146, Norrlanda ☎ 0498/39075) is a bright shop with one of the island's best selections of fabrics, textiles, and paper printed with patterns inspired by original designs from the 1700s.

G.A.D (Good Art and Design; ⊠ Södra Kyrkog. 16 ☎ 0498/249410) sells stunningly simple modern furniture that has been designed and made on Gotland. Just as at its shop in Stockholm, the firm sells high-end pieces with a cosmopolitan flair.

Gotland A to Z

BOAT & FERRY TRAVEL

Regular and high-speed car ferries sail from Nynäshamn, a small port on the Baltic an hour by car or rail from Stockholm; commuter trains leave regularly from Stockholm's central station for Nynäshamn. Timetables change frequently, so it is best to consult the operating company, Gotland City Travel, before departure. The regular ferry takes about 5 hours; the fast ferry takes 2½ hours. Boats also leave from Oskarshamn, farther down the Swedish coast and closer to Gotland by about an hour. Call Gotland City Travel for more information.

🚢 **Gotland City Travel** ⊠ Kungsg. 57 ☎ 08/4061500 ⊕ www.destinationgotland.se.

CAR RENTAL
🚗 **Biltjänst** ✉ Endrev. 45, Visby ☎ 0498/218790. **MABI Rental Cars** ✉ Visby ☎ 0498/279396.

EMERGENCIES
🚗 **Visby Hospital** ☎ 0498/269000.

TOURS
Guided tours of the island and Visby are available in English by arrangement with the tourist office.

VISITOR INFORMATION
The main tourist office is Gotlands Turistförening (Gotland Tourist Association) in Visby. You can also contact Gotland City Travel in Stockholm for lodging or ferry reservations.
🚗 **Gotland City Travel** ☎ 08/4061500. **Gotlands Turistförening & Visby Turistbyrå** ✉ Hamng. 4, Visby ☎ 0498/201700 ⊕ www.gotland.info. **Gotlands Turistservice** ✉ Österv. 3A, Visby ☎ 0498/203300 ⊕ www.gotlandsturistservice.com.

Uppsala

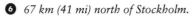 *67 km (41 mi) north of Stockholm.*

For the title of "Sweden's principal university town," Uppsala has only one rival: Lund, to the south. August Strindberg, the nation's leading dramatist, studied here—and by all accounts hated the place. Ingmar Bergman, his modern heir, was born in town. It is also a historic site where pagan (and extremely gory) Viking ceremonies persisted into the 11th century. Uppsala University, one of the oldest institutions in Europe, was established in 1477 by Archbishop Jakob Ulfson. As late as the 16th century, nationwide *tings* (early parliaments) were convened here. Today it is a quiet home for about 170,000 people. Built along the banks of the Fyris River, the town has a pleasant jumble of old buildings that is dominated by its cathedral, which dates from the early 13th century.

In recent years Uppsala has shaken off the shadow of nearby Stockholm and is emerging as a destination in its own right. The town has established itself as something of a center for medical research and pharmaceuticals. Add to the mix the student population, and Uppsala has become a thriving place, with housing and office developments springing up in equal numbers to restaurants, bars, cultural venues, and shops.

The last day of April never fails to make the town become one big carnival—the Feast of Valborg. To celebrate the arrival of spring (and the end of the school year), students of the university don sailorlike hats and charge down the hill from the university library (try not to get in their way). The university chorus then sings traditional spring songs on the steps of the main building. And finally the whole town slips into mayhem. Thousands descend on the city as the streets are awash in champagne and celebrations. It's an age-old custom worth seeing, but it's not for the fainthearted.

Ideally you should start your visit with a trip to **Gamla Uppsala** (Old Uppsala), 5 km (3 mi) north of the town. Here under three huge mounds lie the graves of the first Swedish kings—Aun, Egil, and Adils—of the 6th-century Ynglinga dynasty. Close by in pagan times was a sacred grove containing a legendary oak from whose branches animal and human sacrifices were hung. By the 10th century Christianity had eliminated such practices. A small church, which was the seat of Sweden's first archbishop, was built on the site of a former pagan temple.

Today the archbishopric is in Uppsala itself, and **Gamla Uppsala Kyrka**, the former seat, is largely kept up for the benefit of tourists. The whitewashed walls and simple rows of enclosed wooden pews make the church plain but calming. The tomb of Anders Celsius, the inventor of the temperature scale that bears his name, and some faded panels depicting the life of St. Erik, Sweden's patron saint, are about the only other things to look at inside.

need a break?

To sample a mead brewed from a 14th-century recipe, stop at the **Odinsborg Restaurant** (☎ 018/323525), near the Gamla Uppsala burial mounds. The building has been a restaurant and meeting place of sorts for more than 500 years, and is full of antiques, Viking objects, and ancient wall and ceiling paintings. It makes a beautiful and historic spot to grab a drink.

The **Gamla Uppsala Museum** contains exhibits and archaeological findings from the Viking burial mounds that dominate the local area. The museum distinguishes between the myth and legends about the area and what is actually known about its history. Next to Gamla Uppsala Church, the ultramodern building made of wood and copper will change color as it ages. Its aggressive design inspires either admiration or dislike among Uppsala's populace. ☎ 018/239300 ⚲ SKr 50 ☉ May–Aug., daily 11–5; Sept.–Apr., Wed. and weekends noon–3.

★ Back in Uppsala, your first visit should be to **Uppsala Domkyrka** (Uppsala Cathedral). Its 362-foot twin towers—whose height equals the length of the nave—dominate the city. Work on the cathedral began in the early 13th century; it was consecrated in 1435 and restored between 1885 and 1893. Still the seat of Sweden's archbishop, the cathedral is also the site of the tomb of Gustav Vasa, the king who established Sweden's independence in the 16th century. Inside is a silver casket containing the relics of St. Erik. ☎ 018/187177 ⊕ www.uppsalacathedral.com ⚲ Free ☉ Daily 8–6.

The **Domkyrka Museet**, in the north tower, has arts and crafts, church vestments, and church vessels on display. ☎ 018/187177 ⚲ SKr 30 ☉ May–Aug., daily 9–5; Sept.–Apr., Sun. 12:30–3.

Gustav Vasa began work on **Uppsala Slott** (Uppsala Castle) in the 1540s. He intended the building to symbolize the dominance of the monarchy over the church. It was completed under Queen Christina nearly a century later. Students gather here every April 30 to celebrate the Feast of Valborg and optimistically greet the arrival of spring. Call the tourist center for more information. ✉ Ingång C, 753 10 Uppsala ⚲ Castle SKr 60 ☉ English guided tours of castle mid-Apr.–Sept., daily at 1 and 3; Oct.–mid-Apr., weekdays at 11 and 2, weekends at 10, 11, 2, and 3.

In the excavated Uppsala Slott ruins, the **Vasa Vignettes,** scenes from the 16th century, are portrayed with effigies, costumes, and light and sound effects. ☒ *SKr 40* ⊙ *Mid-Apr.–Aug., daily 11–4; Sept., weekends 10–5.*

One of Uppsala's most famous sons, Carl von Linné, also known as Linnaeus, was a professor of botany at the university during the 1740s. He created the Latin nomenclature system for plants and animals. The **Linné Museum** is dedicated to his life and works. (⊠ *Svartbäcksg. 27* ☎ *018/136540* ☒ *SKr 25* ⊙ *Late May and early Sept., weekends noon–4; June–Aug., Tues.–Sun. 1–4.*).The botanical treasures of Linnaeus's old garden have been re-created and are now on view in **Linnéträdgården.** The garden's orangery houses a pleasant cafeteria and is used for concerts and cultural events. ⊠ *Svartbäcksg. 27* ☎ *018/4712576* ⊕ *www.linnaeus.uu.se* ☒ *SKr 30* ⊙ *May–Aug., daily 9–9; Sept.–Apr., daily 9–7.*

Uppsala Universitetet (Uppsala University; ☎ 018/4710000 ⊕ www.uu. se), founded in 1477, is known for the **Carolina Rediviva** university library, which contains a copy of every book published in Sweden, in addition to a large collection of foreign works. Two of its most interesting exhibits are the *Codex Argentus,* a Bible written in the 6th century, and Mozart's original manuscript for his 1791 opera *The Magic Flute.*

Completed in 1625, the **Gustavianum,** which served as the university's main building for two centuries, is easy to spot by its remarkable copper cupola, now green with age. The building houses the ancient anatomical theater—one of only seven in the world to function on natural light—where human anatomy lectures and public dissections took place. The Victoria Museum of Egyptian Antiquities is in the same building. ⊠ *Akademig. 3* ☎ *018/4717571* ⊕ *www.gustavianum.uu.se* ☒ *SKr 40* ⊙ *June–Aug., daily 11–3; Anatomical Theater June–Aug., daily 10–4; Sept.–May, weekends 11–4.*

Where to Stay & Eat

★ **$$–$$$** ✕ **Guldkanten.** When Uppsala's grand old food hall burned down in 2002, Guldkanten burned with it. Now it's back with chef Anders Ericsson at the stoves, producing ambitious, modern, and delicious food inspired by Swedish ingredients and flavors from the Mediterranean and eastern Europe. Delightful dishes, such as tortellini of crab with fennel puree or pigeon with blinis, cabbage, and figs, are deftly presented and full of flavor. The restaurant is fronted by a sweeping semicircular window overlooking the river, and the interior is a subtle blend of dark wood and cream furnishings. ⊠ *St. Eriks torg 8* ☎ *018/150151* ⚐ *Reservations essential* ☰ *AE, DC, MC, V.*

$–$$$ ✕ **Hambergs Fisk.** The black-and-white floor tiles give a feeling of a fish shop to Hambergs, and that is exactly what it is. Here you can feast on delicious concoctions from traditional seafood platters to more adventurous creations. During the day you can stop at the deli counter on the way out and pick up fresh fish, fish paté, or other goodies. Fish-phobes need not apply. ⊠ *Fyris torg 8* ☎ *018/710050* ☰ *AE, DC, MC, V.*

$–$$$ ✕ **Wermlandskällaren.** A beautiful vaulted cellar is the venue for this tightly packed and welcoming little restaurant. The look—exposed brick walls,

CloseUp

VALBORG EVE

THE STREETS OF THE ANCIENT UNIVERSITY TOWN OF UPPSALA are awash with humanity. Across the urban landscapes the people stream, apparently without aim. There is joy in the air and beer on the doorsteps. It is April 30, the day of Valborg Eve. The warmer months are coming. This is a contemporary interpretation of the traditional mass in honor of St. Valborg, the daughter of an Anglo-Saxon king and a nun who lived from 710 to 799; she was considered a spirit of God on earth.

Such noble origins are far from the minds of the masses today. Revelry is the theme. The day begins early with champagne breakfasts, and by midday the park outside one of Europe's oldest universities, founded in 1477, is crowded with picnickers. Most are adorned in their (high school) graduation caps, and all are full of whiskey and song. The chancellor gives his speech. The choirs sing. Like a shotgun spray, the people disperse to the parks. Everything feels possible today.

Although Valborg has religious roots, its meaning has evolved over the centuries. From something that centered on the village church, it has developed into an event with an agrarian theme. In these harsh climes the farmers and their families would shrug their cares away and feel the release from the long winter. The sun shone, the animals were out of their barns, and the fields were being planted. The cycle of nature had begun again. It is a moment very closely linked to the seasons, to which the Swedes, not surprisingly, are very sensitive, given their trying winters.

One of the great rituals of Valborg Eve is the night bonfire. It owes its origins not to God, but to paganism, and stems from the terrible otherworldly fears that people then held, surely metaphoric tales that encoded the tribulations of the human condition.

The bonfire was believed to deliver protection from the spiritual realm. It was said to haunt the evil spirits themselves and chase away dangerous animals. Today it is, in a sense, a time in which people destroy the results of their spring cleaning. All the collected rubbish and pruned trees are used to build the pile, which is then torched.

Those who have shown great stamina or restraint during the day will be present at the huge bonfire that lights the night. It is a big social occasion, accompanied by traditional herring and schnapps. Here you, too, can fly like a bird on the wings of collective elation and unshackled human release. And did we mention the champagne, whiskey, and schnapps?

well-worn stone floors, dark-wood furniture, flickering candles—suggests that traditional food is on offer here. Think again. Salim Chowdhury works hard on his menu, presenting artistic and delicious contemporary food, gathering flavors from across the globe. Dishes such as smoked ostrich with Parmesan, nuts, and dates, or langoustines with spiced Swedish cheese and vanilla champagne sauce defy classification and wow the palate. ⊠ *Nedre Slottsg. 2* ☎ *018/132200* ⊟ *AE, DC, MC, V.*

$ ✕ **Hyllan.** Suspended on a half floor above the rebuilt food hall, Hyllan is a dim, cozy place—some would even say it's romantic. Dark woods and cream and red sofas and chairs set the mood in the bar; the dining area follows suit. The food here consists of well-prepared bistro staples. Think steaks, salads, mussels, cod with horseradish, and the like. It's a busy, friendly place, especially at the bar, and makes for a great one-stop night out. ⊠ *St. Eriks torg 8* ☎ *018/150150* ⊟ *AE, DC, MC, V.*

¢–$ ✕ **Günthers.** This classic old café has stood by the river for more than 100 years. On the wall as you enter is proof of royal appointment as cake makers to the king—still valid today. Inside, the dark-wood paneling, the thick carpet, and the solid wooden chairs and tables look as though they just might outlast the royal warrant. One side of the main room is taken up by huge glass cabinets containing exquisite cakes, delicate pastries, crusty well-filled sandwiches, and hot dishes like lasagna. Lunch here, ending with a few pieces of cake, should see you through until breakfast. ⊠ *Östra Åg. 31* ☎ *018/130757* ⊟ *MC, V* ☉ *No dinner.*

$–$$$ ⊞ **Gillet.** Operated by the Radisson SAS group, Uppsala's largest hotel first opened in 1971. Rooms are bright and large, with pleasant watercolors, soft furnishings, and hardwood floors. The hotel is only a short walk from Uppsala's most famous buildings. The public areas are a little bland and standardized, but very comfortable. ⊠ *Dragarbrunnsg. 23, 751 42* ☎ *018/681800* ⊟ *018/681818* ⊕ *www.radissonsas.com* ⇨ *160 rooms, 1 suite* ♨ *2 restaurants, room service, minibars, room TVs with movies, in-room broadband, in-room data ports, Wi-Fi, pool, gym, sauna, meeting rooms, parking (fee), no-smoking rooms* ⊟ *AE, DC, MC, V* ◎ *BP.*

$–$$ ⊞ **Grand Hotel Hörnan.** A mansionlike creation from 1906, the Hörnan's city-center location means that it's near the train station and has views of both the castle and the cathedral. The rooms are spacious and have antique furnishings and soft lighting. Once the grandest hotel in town, Hörnan has faded a bit these days, but still keeps its head up, retaining a noble air of its former self. ⊠ *Bandgårdsg. 1, 753 20* ☎ *018/139380* ⊟ *018/120311* ⊕ *www.grandhotellhornan.com* ⇨ *37 rooms* ♨ *Bar, meeting rooms* ⊟ *AE, DC, MC, V* ◎ *BP.*

$ ⊞ **Scandic Uplandia.** This branch of the giant Nordic chain has the usual modern comforts and high-tech amenities expected of an international business hotel. There's also the pleasing design that's found in the best Scandinavian hotels. Blond wood accented with moss-green and aquamarine fabrics gives the decor a sophisticated edge. ⊠ *Dragarbrunnsg. 32, 751 40* ☎ *018/4952600* ⊟ *018/4952611* ⊕ *www.scandic-hotels. se* ⇨ *133 rooms, 2 suites* ♨ *Restaurant, room service, room TVs with movies, in-room broadband, in-room data ports, Wi-Fi, sauna, bar, meeting rooms, no-smoking rooms* ⊟ *AE, DC, MC, V* ◎ *BP.*

¢ 🖼 **First Hotel Linné.** The namesake of this white-stone town-house hotel with lush gardens is the botanist Linnaeus (Carl von Linné). The hotel's interior is in harmony with the gardens outside: soft floral prints and warm colors dominate. In winter, enjoy the huge open fireplace. Rooms are done in a bright, modern Scandinavian design, with earth and red tones. Most of the floors and furniture are made of wood. On a sunny July morning the garden is one of the nicest places in town to have breakfast. ⊠ *Skolg. 45, 750 02* ☎ *018/102000* 🖶 *018/137597* ⊕ *www.firsthotels.com* ➾ *116 rooms, 6 suites* ⚙ *Restaurant, minibars, in-room broadband, Wi-Fi, sauna, bar, no-smoking rooms* ▤ *AE, DC, MC, V* ¶◎¶ *BP.*

Nightlife & the Arts

Bowlaget (⊠ Skolg. 6 ☎ 018/553310) is Uppsala's newest and coolest meeting spot. In this huge venue you can move between a modern bar and restaurant, a neon-blue bowling alley, a sports bar with plasma-screen TVs, and a very loud, very bumpin' nightclub. Enter for dinner, leave at dawn. For a relaxed evening, head to **Katalin** (⊠ Östra Station ☎ 018/140680), a former goods shed behind the railway station, now a funky bar and restaurant. The emphasis here is on the music, with live jazz, rock, and Swedish pop making most people forget about dinner. **Uppsala Stadsteater** (Town Theater; ⊠ Kungsg. 53 ☎ 018/160300) is a local theater known for its high-quality productions, many directly from Stockholm and a fair number in English.

Sports & the Outdoors

🕲 Building on the foreign concept of a petting zoo, **4H-gård** (4H farm; ⊠ N. Gränbyv. 20 ☎ 018/261270) is proving very popular with children as well as adults across Sweden. The farm offers children an opportunity to see and sometimes pet animals such as horses, rabbits, cows, goats, sheep, hens, and pigs. There's plenty of open space here, on the outer reaches of town, so even if animals aren't your thing, you can come for a pleasant walk. The best ways to get there are driving by car or taking bus number 3 from the center of town (Stora Torget).

Shopping

Jaber (⊠ Fyris torg 6 ☎ 018/135050) is something of a draw for the area's wealthy elite. It is a family-run clothes shop with a line of gorgeous international designs, matched only by the personal service it provides. **Trolltyg** (⊠ Östra Åg. 25 ☎ 018/146304) has an exclusive selection of the sort of clean-line clothes and household furnishings for which Scandinavian design is known. The shop is wonderfully laid out and is a joy to explore, especially the fabrics section. **Öster om Ån** (⊠ Svartbäcksg. 18 ☎ 018/711545) is a handicraft cooperative that was formed many years ago. The co-op is still hugely popular today, offering a unique and beautiful range of ceramics, knitted goods, woodwork, and jewelry.

Uppsala A to Z

SIGHTSEEING TOURS

You can explore Uppsala easily on your own, but English-language guided group tours can be arranged through the Uppsala Guide Service. 🛈 **Uppsala Guide Service** ☎ 018/7274818.

TRAIN TRAVEL

Trains between Stockholm and Uppsala run twice hourly throughout the day year-round. The cost of a one-way trip is SKr 75. For timetables and train information, contact SJ.

🚈 SJ ☎ 0771/757575 ⊕ www.sj.se.

VISITOR INFORMATION

The main tourist office run by the Uppsala Convention and Visitors Bureau is in the town center; in summer a small tourist information office is also open at Uppsala Castle.

🚈 **Main Tourist Office** ✉ Fyris torg 8 ☎ 018/7274800 ⊕ www.uppland.nu.

The Bothnian Coast

3

WORD OF MOUTH

"It was gorgeous seeing the country [by car]. Sweden is unbelievably beautiful. Pristine, really. Even the tiniest roadside cafe served food and snacks on real plates with real cutlery and glasses. [My kids] swam their way through the country, in lakes, the Baltic Sea on Sweden's southeast coast, and the Atlantic on its western coast. The coasts and lakes everywhere are really underdeveloped. No beachside condos and very few lakefront houses. It really was lovely."

—kflodin

Updated by
Rob Hincks

INDENTED WITH SHIMMERING FJORDS, peppered with pine-clad islands, and lined with sheer cliffs, the Bothnian Coast is a dramatic sliver of land on Sweden's east coast.

Its history and prosperity come from the sea and the forest. This is as true of the grand 19th-century stone houses built from the profits of international sea trading and the paper industry as it is of the ancient fishing villages, which are now used mainly as holiday homes for urban Swedes. The Bothnian Coast has both kinds of dwellings in abundance. In the north of the region you can see traces of the religious fervor that took hold in past centuries, evident in the small religious communities and the many ancient, well-preserved churches and artifacts in towns such as Umeå and Skellefteå.

Many of the original wood cottages that dotted this coastline have been destroyed by fires over the years. The worst damage, caused by Russia's many incursions through the area in the 18th century, prompted towns along the coast to rebuild themselves in grand styles more befitting a capital than a local fishing town. Aided by the burgeoning shipping trade in the 1800s, port towns such as Gävle, Sundsvall, and Umeå created cities of wide boulevards, huge central squares, and monumental stone buildings partly to discourage future fires from spreading.

Exploring the Bothnian Coast

Traveling up the Bothnian Coast is a simple task, mostly involving a single road or railway track. All the major towns are on the coast and are relatively evenly spread, making it easier for you to plan your rests. The coastline is rocky and rugged in places and is bordered by the beautiful forests and lakes of Hälsingland. By car, the E4 highway quickly eats up the miles, and takes in all the major sights. By train, the coastal line that links Stockholm to the north of Sweden does the same.

About the Hotels & Restaurants

You have to pick and chose your restaurants carefully along the Bothnian Coast. Much of the remoteness that makes the area attractive has also created some rather mediocre dining spots. The region's past riches, fueled by fishing and forestry, have left many grand-looking restaurants with a much vaunted past. But looks can be deceiving, and it is always a good idea to check out the menu and any independent reviews before you sit down to dinner.

Food along the Bothnian Coast is, not surprisingly, heavy on fish. Deliciously fresh and oily herrings and piquant smoked fish are a particular specialty. If you are looking for some interesting international flavors, stick to the big cities. The delight of an area such as this is the chance to sample some good local flavor. Restaurants are rarely busy along the Bothnian Coast, and most can be booked the day before or even on the day of your visit.

The rules for restaurants along Sweden's east coast can equally be applied to hotels. The many stone monoliths that dot the landscape, often

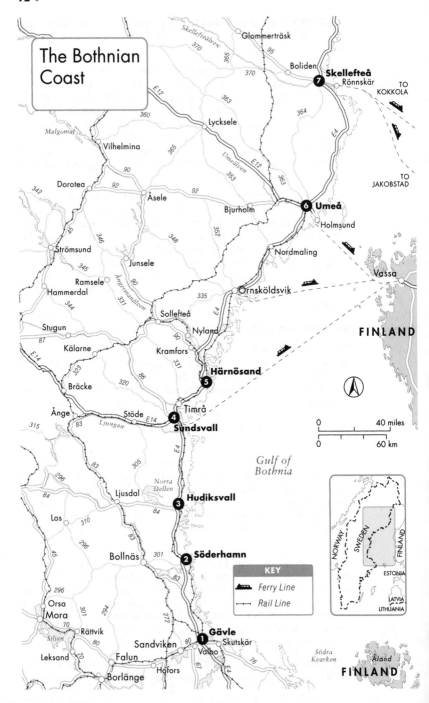

christened with grand names, can all too often be just relics of the past; this often means faded grandeur offset by tired furnishings. It is usually best to stick to the big chain hotels or the small, privately run guesthouses and bed-and-breakfasts.

Outside the major towns many of the hotels run on a skeleton staff, so don't always expect room service or even a hotel restaurant. It is always a good idea to call ahead to check first.

WHAT IT COSTS In Swedish Kronor				
$$$$	**$$$**	**$$**	**$**	**¢**
RESTAURANTS over 420	250–420	150–250	100–150	under 100
HOTELS over 2,900	2,300–2,900	1,500–2,300	1,000–1,500	under 1,000

Restaurant prices are for a main course at dinner. Hotel prices are for two people in a standard double room in high season.

Timing

Like much of coastal Sweden, the Bothnian Coast is a harsh place to be in the winter months. This leaves the high season of mid-May to mid-September as the best time to visit. This is the time of year when most of the attractions in the region are open and when the Baltic Sea becomes approachable for boat traffic. Many museums close on Monday and some of the shops in smaller towns have half-day closing on Saturday.

Gävle

❶ *180 km (111 mi) north of Stockholm (via E4).*

Gävle, the capital of the county (*landskap* in Swedish) Gästrikland, is considered by many Swedes a gateway to the northern wildernesses. The town was granted its charter in 1446. That great age is not evident in the mix of grand 19th-century boulevards and parks and modern, bland shopping centers that make up much of the small downtown area. The original town was destroyed in a great fire in the mid-1800s, and the only part that survives today is the small enclave that lay south of the river, a watery barrier that kept the flames at bay. The grand architectural style of much of the town reflects the wealth it once enjoyed as a major trading port. Today it is better known as home of Gevalia, Sweden's largest coffee producer, which is quite evident on the days the town is filled with the delicious aroma of roasting beans drifting from the factory chimneys.

The **Joe Hill Museet,** dedicated to the Swedish emigrant who went on to become America's first well-known protest singer and union organizer, is in Hill's former home in the oldest section of Gävle. Once a poor working-class district, this is now the most highly sought-after residential part of town, with art studios and crafts workshops nearby. The museum—furnished in the same style as when Hill lived there—contains very few of his possessions but does display his prison letters. The house itself bears witness to the poor conditions that forced so many Swedes to emigrate to the United States (estimated to be between

850,000 and 1 million between 1840 and 1900). Hill, who was born Joel Hägglund, was a founder of the International Workers of the World and was executed for the murder of a Salt Lake City grocer in 1914. He maintained his innocence, an opinion shared by many, right up to the end. ✉ *Nedre Bergsg. 28* ☎ *026/613425* 🎫 *Free* ⏲ *June–Aug., daily 9–4.*

For a glimpse of Gävle's past, go to the **Länsmuseet** (County Museum). Inside this impressive redbrick building is a museum celebrating the history of the town and area. On the ground floor are changing exhibits on local artists and photographers. Upstairs there are old farm implements, clothes, and re-creations of local house interiors that extend from the 12th century to the 1930s. The largest part of the museum is dedicated to the town's maritime history, and includes model ships as well as trinkets and treasures brought back from sea voyages long ago. ✉ *Strandg. 20* ☎ *026/655635* 🌐 *www.lansmuseetgavleborg.se.* 🎫 *SKr 40* ⏲ *Weekdays 10–4, weekends noon–4.*

If uniqueness is what you seek, head straight to **Mackmyra**, Sweden's only whiskey distillery, a 10-minute car journey from town. Mackmyra is a relatively new dram, and the first production of it is still in barrel, due to be released around 2008. But take heart: visitors can still tour the distillery and taste what will soon become a fully fledged Swedish whiskey, straight out of the cask. And early indications are good. Conditions at Mackmyra (soil, climate, water supply) are very similar to those in Scotland, and local critics have already given the whiskey a big thumbs up. Opening hours at the moment are sporadic, but it's definitely worth checking the Web site to book a tour if your timing is right. ✉ *Bruksg. 4, Valbo* ☎ *026/541880* 🌐 *www.mackmyra.se* 🎫 *SKr 250 for tour and 2 tastings* ⏲ *Check Web site for hrs.*

Housed in what used to be the local train storage shed, the **Sveriges Järnvägsmuseum** (Swedish Railway Museum) has many different engines and coach cars on display. The royal hunting car from 1859 is thought to be the world's oldest. ✉ *Rälsg. 1* ☎ *026/106448* 🌐 *www.banverket.se* 🎫 *SKr 40* ⏲ *Tues.–Sun. 10–4.*

Where to Stay & Eat

$–$$ ✕ **Helt Enkelt Bar & Kök.** Roughly translated, the name means "quite simple," a good description of the sleek, stylish interior of this modern restaurant that leans more than a little on the perennially popular flavors of the Mediterranean to spice up its innovative cooking. Located right in the center of town, this place pulls in a good evening crowd, so be sure to make reservations. Eat early and be on your way or hang around after dinner when the local scenesters arrive. ✉ *Norra Kungsg. 3* ☎ *026/120604* 💳 *AE, DC, MC, V* ⏲ *No lunch Mon.–Sat.*

$–$$ ✕ **Söderhjelmska Gården.** This classic Swedish wooden house dates from 1773, and stands out from the rest of mostly modern Gävle. The interior, furnished in traditional white wood and blue linen, is split into the same small rooms that existed when it was still a residence. In summer you can also eat in the tree-lined garden. The traditional Swedish menu emphasizes fish. Reservations recommended. ⊠ *S. Kungsg. 23* ☎ *026/613393* ☰ *AE, DC, MC, V.*

⟳ **$** ✕ **Cafe Artist.** The smell of the home-baked bread (a staple in Sweden) is what hits you first when you walk through the door here. It's never a mistake to drop by for dinner, where there is always an excellent buffet on offer, as well as very good tapas and excellent marinated herring. And while you munch away, any kids you have in tow can play to their hearts' content in the in-house playroom. ⊠ *Norra Slottsg. 9* ☎ *026/647033* ☰ *AE, DC, MC, V* ⊙ *No lunch.*

$–$$ ▦ **Scandic Hotel Gävle Väst.** Located just outside town on the E4 highway, the Scandic greets guests with a surprisingly peaceful atmosphere. With airy rooms decorated in traditional Scandinavian style and a large pine forest as a backdrop, this hotel is a lovely place to stay or to relax for an afternoon. ⊠ *Johanneslötsv. 6, 806 28* ☎ *026/4958100* 🖷 *026/4958111* ⊕ *www.scandic.se* ⇲ *200 rooms, 15 suites* ⌂ *Restaurant, room TVs with movies, in-room broadband, Wi-Fi, indoor pool, gym, sauna, bar, laundry service, concierge, meeting rooms, free parking* ☰ *AE, DC, MC, V.*

$ ▦ **Hotel Park Inn.** Design-conscious budget hotel chain Park Inn is on a rapid march through Europe, bringing affordable style to previously ailing hotels. This former, slightly dowdy business hotel has been given a face-lift: rooms are decorated with fresh, bright colors and a simplistic design. ⊠ *Norra Slottsg. 9, 801 38* ☎ *026/647000* 🖷 *026/647009* ⇲ *200 rooms, 6 suites* ⌂ *Restaurant, room service, minibars, in-room broadband, in-room data ports, Wi-Fi, indoor pool, sauna, bar, laundry service, concierge, meeting rooms, parking (fee), no-smoking rooms* ☰ *AE, DC, MC, V.*

Nightlife & the Arts

In the small park between Norra Rådmansgatan and Norra Kungsgatan is the grand stone building that contains **Gävle Teatren** (Gävle Theater; ⊠ Norra Råmansg. 23 ☎ 026/129200). Its beautiful gilded auditorium was built in the late 1800s. Many of the plays it stages are in English. For a fun night out, head to **Brända Bocken** (⊠ Stortorget ☎ 026/124545), a restaurant that features a very popular bar in the evening. Friday and Saturday nights the place becomes a disco and the most popular nightspot in town. **Heartbreak Hotel** (⊠ Norra Strandg. 15 ☎ 026/&183020) is a bar and nightclub with a 1950s American rock-and-roll theme. Memorabilia of Elvis and others are plastered on the walls. If you're lucky, you may catch one of the many Elvis impersonators who perform periodically.

Shopping

★ The beautiful furniture, clothes, and kitchenware at the **Gefle Design Forum** (⊠ Drottningg. 25 ☎ 026/188008) come from Stockholm Design House, the capital's well-known design group. It's also a good place to pick up fun gift items. For a more general shop, head to **Gallerian Nian** (⊠ Drotningg. 9) a modern mall-style building with several branded stores and a few good lunch cafés, for when the bags get too heavy.

CloseUp

THE SWEDISH BALANCING ACT

WHEN THE WORLD THINKS OF **SWEDEN** and the Swedes, blond-haired beauties are never far from mind. The truth is, if you plotted a map of global sales of blond hair dye, there would be a lot of pins in Sweden. When Swedish women talk about their roots, it's not only their Viking ancestors they refer to.

It's almost impossible to say what constitutes being a typical Swede today. Long ago the nation realized that it had become a mix of people and influences from across the globe, and that the country is even better for it. That's not to say that there isn't a national identity, because there is—a strong one. Those searching for clues to this identity should simply examine the Swedish State.

The State plays a very important role in Swedish life. It controls and sells all alcohol, owns and runs every drugstore in the land, and keeps an eagle eye on levels of decadence, taxing accordingly.

Living in a fairly controlled, clean, well-operating environment may consequently lead to the relaxation and comfort that is source of Sweden's famed liberal attitude. People here live in clean towns and cities with excellent infrastructures; everyone has access to public transportation and affordable sports facilities; and families have unbeatable parental-leave benefits and subsidized day care.

The delicate balance of old and new; of fierce tradition and enterprising modernity; of booming capitalism and an extensive welfare system; of swimming nude whenever possible while maintaining a stiff and formal attitude; and of freedom and control is a uniquely Swedish phenomenon—and an interesting one to experience firsthand.

— Rob Hincks

Söderhamn

❷ *75 km (47 mi) north of Gävle (via E4).*

Söderhamn is a town with a lot of space. Besides the extensive open countryside that borders the town, the center is awash with parks, gardens, and wide boulevards. In summer Swedes come from all over to enjoy the pretty public spaces. The many trees help to remove air pollution, making sitting in an open-air café here exceptionally pleasing. The town's architecture is a mix of monumental 18th-century buildings, erected with fortunes made by fishing, and modern shopping precincts built to replace areas devastated by numerous fires. This coastal town is also close to one of the finest archipelagos in the region: more than 500 islands, islets, and skerries are near.

For stunning panoramic views of the town and the surrounding forest and sea, climb **Oscarborg**, a 75-foot tower at the edge of town. Built in 1895, the white tower and attached building resemble a Disney-esque fairy-tale castle.

Dating to the 1600s, **Smedjan** (Blacksmiths) is a living, working museum where you can watch craftsmen use traditional methods to make horseshoes and other items. ⊠ *Kungsgården* ☎ *0270/35031* ☒ *Free* ☉ *July, Mon. 2–4, Thurs. 6–8. All other times by appointment.*

Where to Stay & Eat

$–$$$ ✕ **Restaurang Albertina.** This converted red wooden barn is on the water's edge, just north of Söderhamn, in the old fishing village of Skärså. Inside, scrubbed wooden walls and beamed ceilings blend with the crisp, white table linens. Fish is the specialty here. The locally caught salmon that they serve here is among the best in the region. ⊠ *Skärså* ☎ *0270/732010* ☱ *AE, DC, MC, V.*

¢–$ ✕ **Rådhus Konditoriet.** Inside an uninspiring building is a restaurant that doubles as one of the few photography galleries in the north of Sweden. The gallery and the excellent selection of sandwiches, specialty teas, and light meals make it worth the trip. ⊠ *Kykog. 10* ☎ *0270/12457* ☱ *AE, MC, V* ☉ *Closed Sun.*

$–$$ ☷ **First Hotell Statt.** The oldest hotel in town is also the most luxurious. All the rooms are individually furnished and have wooden floors and a comfortable mix of blond wood and pastel furnishings. The public areas have their original chandeliers, stuccowork ceilings, and large open fireplaces, giving the hotel a feel of old luxury. ⊠ *Oxtorgsg. 17, 826 22* ☎ *0270/73570* 🖷 *0270/13524* ⊕ *www.firsthotels.se* ☞ *78 rooms, 1 suite* ♧ *Restaurant, in-room broadband, Wi-Fi, sauna, bar, nightclub, convention center* ☱ *AE, DC, MC, V.*

¢ ☷ **Centralhotellet.** As the name suggests, it's the central location that makes this hotel worth the stay. The rooms were all refurbished in 2004, and are much improved, featuring simple spaces and plenty of light wood. ⊠ *Rådhustorget, 826 32* ☎ *0270/70000* 🖷 *0270/16060* ⊕ *www. centralhotellet.se* ☞ *27 rooms* ♧ *Restaurant, in-room broadband, bar, nightclub, free parking, no-smoking rooms* ☱ *AE, DC, MC, V.*

Nightlife & the Arts

Söderhamn's First Hotell Statt opens an enclosed garden in summer, billing it as **Innergården** (⊠ Oxtorgsg. 17 ☎ 0270/73570), the Swedish word for "courtyard." Crowds of locals gather for drinks, music, and wonderful Swedish summer evenings in what is essentially the town's only decent evening alternative.

The Outdoors

For an energetic inland-water adventure, there are myriad lakes and rivers around Söderhamn that are perfect for canoeing. For more information contact **Fritidskontoret** (leisure office; ☎ 0270/60000).

Shopping

For something special check out **Kungsboden City** (⊠ Köpmang. 8 ☎ 0270/18117), a store with a good selection of clothes and interesting jewelry.

Hudiksvall

❸ *60 km (37 mi) north of Söderhamn (via E4).*

Granted its town charter in 1582, Hudiksvall's history is bound up with the sea. Having been partially destroyed by fire 10 times, Hudiksvall is now an interesting mix of architectural styles. The small section of the old town that remains is built around a central harbor and contains some fine examples of flower-strewn courtyards and traditional wood-panel buildings built along narrow, cobbled streets.

The **Fiskarstan** (Fishertown; ☎ 0650/19100 tourist office) neighborhood is tightly packed with striking streets of fishermen's huts and houses and boardwalks of wooden fish stores that hang precariously over the water. Lilla Kyrkogatan, the oldest street in town, leads to Hudiksvall's Church, which is still marked by cannonballs from a Russian invasion in 1721. Guided tours, maps, and information can be arranged through the town's tourist office.

Inside a former bank building in the middle of town, the **Hälsinglands Museum** offers insight into the development of Hudiksvall and the surrounding region. Furniture, house reconstructions, religious artifacts, local textiles, and art are all organized and displayed thoughtfully. It's a revealing picture of life in the area. ☒ Storg. 31 ☎ 0650/19600 ☒ Free ☉ Mon. noon–4, Tues.–Thurs. 9–4, Sat. 11–3.

Where to Stay & Eat

¢–$$ ✕ **Gretas Krog.** Built right by the fishing docks, this restaurant is rarely empty and seldom disappoints. The interior trades predictably on fishing history through sepia photographs of weather-beaten fishermen and old nets strung from the ceiling, but there is something undeniably cozy about it all. The menu is packed with good local specialties and traditional Swedish cuisine. ☒ Västra Tväkajen ☎ 0650/96600 ☒ AE, DC, MC, V ⚓ Reservations essential ☉ No lunch.

¢–$ ✕ **Jambo Cafe.** This is a lunch-only hot spot where Hudiksvall's young couples come to pass the summer days. On offer are a huge and varied hot-sandwich selection, fresh salads, and classic Swedish café dishes. ☒ Svallertorget ☎ 0650/13025 ☒ MC, V.

¢–$$ ▦ **First Hotell Statt.** The grand 19th-century yellow-stone facade of this hotel, with its pillars and arches, looks like that of a typical Swedish town hall. Once you've gone inside, the more familiar marble floor and pastel shades confirm that you have arrived at your hotel. Rooms here are nothing special; most are in need of redecoration. All the bathrooms were refurbished in 2005, so the hotel has started working on it. ☒ Storg. 36, SE-824 22 ☎ 0650/15060 ☒ 0650/96095 ⊕ www.firsthotels.se ⇗ 106 rooms, 8 suites ⚭ Restaurant, pool, gym, sauna, pub, nightclub, convention center ☒ AE, DC, MC, V ⧗ BP.

Nightlife & the Arts

Inside the Folkets Hus (People's House), a 1950s building built for town gatherings, **Café August** (☒ Rådhusparken ☎ 0650/38450) is a lively nightspot. Although the building isn't glamorous, the interior has original paintings on the walls and a pleasingly quiet color scheme throughout. As night falls, the place comes alive with two floors of modern dance music, live bands, and an outdoor bar area for cooling off. **Pub Tre Bockar** (☒ Bankgränd 1 ☎ 0650/99994) is a traditional English pub. The dark-wood interior is jammed with people on weekend evenings. They all want to sample the jazz and good beer.

Sports & the Outdoors

Hudiksvall's archipelago is centered around the peninsula of **Hornslandet,** just north of the town. As well as the usual fishing, swimming, and boating, the peninsula has Europe's second-largest system of mountain caves, which can be explored by experts and beginners alike. Call **Alf Siden** (☎ 0650/70492), who arranges and conducts official tours of the caves. His English is almost nonexistent, but his knowledge of the caves is quite the opposite, so bear with him.

Shopping

Slöjd i Sjöboden (✉ Möljen ☎ 0650/12041) is a series of old fishing huts now housing stalls where 15 local craftspeople sell their wares. Locally inspired textiles, jewelry, ceramics, and glassware can all be bought at very good prices.

Sundsvall

4 *80 km (50 mi) north of Hudiksvall (via E4).*

Sundsvall also goes by the name of Stenstan (Stone Town), and rightly so. When the town was razed by fire in 1888, it was rebuilt entirely out of stone, which is atypical for this part of Sweden. The reconstruction added more parks and widened roads to prevent later fires from spreading. Add to these Sundsvall's impressive limestone and brick buildings, and it begins to resemble Sweden's largest cities, Stockholm and Göteborg.

Gustav Adolfs kyrka, at the far end of Storgatan, is Sundsvall's main church. In keeping with much of the city, it's a grand 19th-century affair that's built of red brick. There is a pleasing order about the interior, its vaults and pillars all constructed from smooth square stones that look like children's building blocks.

The best place to get a feel for the city and its history is at the **Kulturmagasinet** (Culture Warehouse), a series of four 19th-century waterfront warehouses that now include a museum, library, archives, a children's culture center, art exhibitions, and street music. The museum, which traces the town's history, is built over an old street, where tram tracks and cobblestones are still in place. It gives a good sense of what Sundsvall was like when it was still a busy trading port. ✉ *Packhusg. 4* ☎ *060/191000* 🖼 *June–Aug. SKr 20, Sept.–May free* ☉ *Mon.–Thurs. 10–7, Fri. 10–6, Sat. 11–4.*

Sundsvall is a good city to walk around in, as most of the points of interest are woven into the streets, boulevards, and squares of **Storgatan and Stora Torget.** History comes to life here with churches, the town hall, and grand porticoed stone buildings all flexing their architectural muscles. Guided tours and maps can be arranged through the **tourist office** (☎ 060/610450).

Where to Stay & Eat

★ **$$–$$$** ✕ **Restaurang Grankotten.** The food here, described as modern Swedish with a French influence, has won praise from all over. Dishes such as veal with truffles and anything that uses the delicious local elk are worth traveling for. The views of Sundsvall from the turn-of-the-19th-century building are stunning, especially if you dine outside in summer. ⊠ *Norra Stadsberget* ☎ *060/614222* ♨ *Reservations essential* 🖃 *AE, DC, MC, V* ☺ *Closed Sun.*

$–$$ ✕ **Skeppsbrokällaren.** Classic Swedish design and furnishings and good Scandinavian cuisine are the main attractions at this quiet basement restaurant on the site of the original boat entrance to the city. For a more calming dining experience book a table in the Röda Rummet (Red Room), a smaller, darkened dining area at the back of the restaurant. ⊠ *Sjög. 4* ☎ *060/173660* ♨ *Reservations essential* 🖃 *AE, DC, MC, V.*

★ **$–$$** 🏨 **Elite Hotel Knaust.** The Knaust family opened this art nouveau hotel in 1860, and it has lost none of its original glory. The sweeping marble staircase and black-and-white-tile lobby is extraordinary and worth a look even if you are not staying. Comfort and luxury are watchwords in the rooms, which have warm, lush fabrics and artwork. The hotel is downtown, conveniently near Sundsvall's shops and other attractions. ⊠ *Storg. 13, 851 05* ☎ *060/6080000* 🖷 *060/6080010* ⊕ *www.elite.se* ⇨ *94 rooms, 9 suites* ♨ *Restaurant, minibars, cable TV, room TVs with movies, in-room broadband, in-room data ports, Wi-Fi, gym, sauna, bar, business services, convention center* 🖃 *AE, DC, MC, V* ❘O❘ *BP.*

$ 🏨 **Comfort Hotel Sundsvall.** Grand stone arches and portals give an impression of stately luxury to this central hotel. The interior doesn't quite live up to the grand facade, but the rooms are large, comfortable, and individually furnished in earth and red tones and have wooden floors. ⊠ *Sjög. 11, 852 34* ☎ *060/150720* 🖷 *060/123456* ⊕ *www.choicehotels.se* ⇨ *52 rooms* ♨ *Restaurant, cable TV, in-room broadband, in-room data ports, Wi-Fi, pool, sauna, bar, free parking* 🖃 *AE, DC, MC, V.*

Nightlife & the Arts

Bars and pubs provide the best source of evening entertainment in Sundsvall. **Cafe le fil du rasoir** (⊠ Nybrog. 10 ☎ 060/6080008), was less of a mouthful previously when it was named Spegelbaren, but it's still a great place to hang out, with its large mirrors, glass ceilings, and 19th-century paintings. If you have spare vacation money to use up, then head for **Casino Cosmopol** (⊠ Casino Parken 1 ☎ 060/141100). Housed in the old railway station, built in 1875, it is Sweden's oldest international-style casino. The **Kulturmagasinet** (⊠ Packhusg. 4 ☎ 060/191000) is a museum with art exhibitions (mostly of Swedish artists); a children's theater; and live music, readings, and debates.

Sports & the Outdoors

The nearby Ljungan Riveris an excellent spot for rafting. Tours include one hour of white-water rafting, beautiful scenery, and lunch on a small island. Contact the tourist office (☎ 060/610450) for more information.

Shopping

Northern Sweden's largest shopping mall, **Ikano Huset,** is 8 km (5 mi) north of Sundsvall, along Route E4. All the major Swedish shopping brands are here, like IKEA for home furnishings and H&M for clothes, plus many, many others. **Handelsgården** (⊠ Norra Stadsberget ☎ 060/154000) is the place for local handicrafts made from iron and wood, as well as jams and other homemade goodies.

Härnösand

⑤ *40 km (25 mi) north of Sundsvall (via E4).*

Dating from 1585, Härnösand is a town rich in history. Narrow ancient streets lined with wood-panel houses contrast with 18th- and 19th-century boulevards and squares. The town has a long history as an administrative center for local government, a history hinted at in its orderly layout and infrastructure as well as in the grandeur of its buildings. In the center of town is Sweden's smallest—and only—white cathedral.

With works by both Chagall and Matisse on display, **Härnösands Konsthall** is an art museum of considerable note. The museum has works by many of Sweden's prominent painters and sculptors and puts on around 20 exhibitions per year. ⊠ *Stora Torget 2* ☎ *0611/348142* ≊ *Free* ⊙ *Tues.–Fri. 11–3, Sat. noon–3.*

Länsmuseet Västernorrland is an excellent, well-thought-out history museum that covers Härnösand and the surrounding area. The museum also has one of the country's largest collections of weapons. ⊠ *Murberget* ☎ *0611/88600* ⊕ *www.ylm.se* ≊ *Free* ⊙ *Tues.–Sun. 11–5.*

Where to Stay & Eat

$–$$ ✕ **Spjutegåden.** Stark-white walls are broken up by small local paintings at this very traditional restaurant in a building from the early 1800s. The floor and ceiling are both made of white wood, and a huge, open fireplace makes the room cozy. The menu consists of very good traditional Swedish food with international touches. As in most Swedish restaurants, the fish dishes are delicious. ⊠ *Murberget* ☎ *0611/511090* ⚘ *Reservations essential* ▤ *MC, V.*

¢–$$ ✕ **Highlander.** At this Celtic-theme pub all the requisite details are in place—even a staff dressed in kilts. There are Irish beers and a good selection of wines. The food is hearty and filling, with lots of beef and other meat dishes on the menu. ⊠ *Nybrog. 5* ☎ *0611/511170* ▤ *AE, MC, V* ⊙ *Closed Sun.*

$–$$ ▥ **First Hotel.** Of the three hotels in Härnösand, this is the best choice. Large, functional rooms decorated in blues and dark wood, all with wood floors, armchairs, a desk, and generally very good views of the harbor and the sea beyond. ⊠ *Skeppsbron 9, 871 30* ☎ *0611/554440* ⎙ *0611/554447* ⊕ *www.firsthotels.se* ⇱ *95 rooms, 2 suites* ⚘ *Restaurant, cable TV, gym, sauna, bar, pub, meeting room, no-smoking rooms* ▤ *AE, DC, MC, V.*

Nightlife & the Arts

The place to be seen in Härnösand is **Apothequet** (⊠ Nybrog. 3 ☎ 0611/511717), a nightclub and bar popular with those in their late twenties and thirties. Modern hits are mixed with classics in this darkened lounge. When you can dance no more, the bar does great cocktails.

Shopping

Ångermanlands Hemslöjd (⊠ Storg. 25 ☎ 0611/511327) is perfect for picking up a few local handicrafts. Most of the goods are handmade from materials such as wool, iron, wood, glass, and ceramics, and are typical of this area of Sweden.

Umeå

❻ *225 km (140 mi) north of Härnösand (via E4).*

Built on the River Ume, Umeå is the largest city in northern Sweden. Because it's a university town with an active student population, there are many bars, restaurants, festivals, and cultural events.

Aside from taking a walk around the city's open squares and wide boulevards, the best way to get to know Umeå is by visiting **Gammlia**, a series of museums that focus on the city and surrounding area. The open-air museum has a living village made up of farmhouses and working buildings. Actors in period costumes demonstrate how people lived hundreds of years ago. You can wander around amid farm animals of all kinds and learn about baking bread, preserving meat, and harvesting grain. There are also a church and historic gardens. The indoor museums, which have exhibitions on Umeå's history, consist of the fishing and maritime museum, the Swedish ski museum, and a modern art museum that shows works from major Swedish and international artists. A sort of intellectual theme park, it can take the better part of a day to see everything in Gammlia. ⊠ *Gammliav.* ☎ *090/171800* ⊕ *www.vasterbottensmuseum.se* 🖙 *Free* ☉ *Daily 10–5.*

off the beaten path

NORRBYSKÄR – Around 1800 this island had Europe's largest sawmill, and an ambitious group of Swedes attempted to set up a utopian commune around this industry. The attempt at good living didn't work, and the commune broke up around 1830. Today you can visit the island and trace the commune's ill-fated journey in the small museum. There is also a children's minitown, guided tours of the community's building remains, a small hotel, a restaurant, and a café. The island is also perfect for picnics, fishing, swimming, and safaris to view the local seal population. Norrbyskär is a 15-minute boat trip from Umeå. For details and prices contact the **Umeå tourist office** (☎ 090/161616).

Where to Stay & Eat

$$–$$$ ✕ **Viktor.** Viktor is a restaurant outside the three big cities of Stockholm,
Fodor'sChoice Göteborg, and Malmö that can easily compete with the best they have
★ to offer. The dining room here is simple and elegant, with touches of old Swedish (such as antique brass candlesticks) mixed with 1950s Scandinavian design. The food is best described as new Scandinavian, using uniquely Nordic ingredients spiced with flavors from around the globe. ⊠ *Vasag. 11* ☎ *090/711115* 🖃 *AE, DC, MC, V.*

$–$$ ✕ **Lottas Krog.** On the site of a former Italian bistro, this Swedish eating house has kept some of its Mediterranean feel. The food, though, is unashamedly local, with Swedish classics filling the menu, especially at lunchtime. ⊠ *Nyg. 22* ☎ *090/129551* 🖃 *AE, DC, MC, V.*

$–$$ 🏨 **Scandic Hotel Plaza.** A clean, modern glass-and-brick structure that dominates the city skyline, the Scandic is one of the most stylish hotels in the region. The huge open lobby has a staircase of marble and steel, copper-tone pillars, and tile floors. A lounge, restaurant, bistro, and bar all lead off from the lobby. At the very top of the hotel is a luxury health suite and spa, which has exceptional views of the city. Rooms are large, well equipped, and decorated in pastel shades. ⊠ *Storg. 40, 903 04* ☎ *090/ 2056300* 🖷 *090/2056311* ⊕ *www.scandic-hotels.se* ⇨ *196 rooms, 1 suite* ⌂ *2 restaurants, minibars, room TVs with movies, in-room broadband, Wi-Fi, sauna, bar, lounge, convention center, no-smoking rooms* ⊟ *AE, DC, MC, V.*

$ ▥ **Hotel Winn.** The beautiful powder-blue clapboard exterior of this hotel encloses a modern, officelike reception area, but one that is comfortable and welcoming nonetheless. Rooms are very stylishly furnished with paintings and lots of dark wood and asymmetrical fittings. The Mucky Duck, a classic English-style pub on the premises, serves roughly 40 types of beer and is always busy in the evening. ⊠ *Vasaplan, 901 06* ☎ *090/ 711100* 🖷 *090/711150* ⊕ *www.winnhotel.se* ⇨ *87 rooms, 4 suites* ⌂ *Restaurant, in-room broadband, Wi-Fi, sauna, bar, pub, meeting rooms, no-smoking rooms* ⊟ *AE, DC, MC, V.*

¢–$ ▥ **Royal Hotel.** The entrance to this hotel hints at its former life as a cinema, but the exterior is otherwise unremarkable. Inside, though, the Royal is very comfortable, if a little basic. They say good things come in threes, and this hotel has three that make the stay here worthwhile: 24-hour room service (rare in these parts); an excellent in-house restaurant called Gretas ($$; specialty is grilled meat); and, in a nod to its past, a small cinema showing three films nightly. ⊠ *Skolg. 62, 903 29* ☎ *090/100730* 🖷 *090/100739* ⊕ *www.rica.se* ⇨ *68 rooms, 2 suites* ⌂ *Restaurant, minibars, room TVs with movies, in-room broadband, Wi-Fi, sauna, bar, cinema, meeting rooms, no-smoking rooms* ⊟ *AE, DC, MC, V.*

Nightlife & the Arts

Being a student town, Umeå is never short of a good night out. The nightlife scene here, as in many Swedish towns, revolves around bars and pubs. The **Bishops Arms** (⊠ Renmarkstorget 8 ☎ 090/100990) is a classic English-style pub. The owners even contracted English builders to ensure authenticity. There are 25 beers of tap, more by the bottle, and a staggering 240 different whiskeys. For an informal night out try **Rex** (⊠ Rådhustorget ☎ 090/126050), a friendly and popular haunt that attracts a young crowd. For those who prefer something a little more sedate and traditional, **Äpplet** (⊠ Vasaplan ☎ 090/156200) puts on fox-trot, cha-cha, and tango for all comers. It also serves good food.

Shopping

Inredarna (⊠ Rådhusesplanaden 10 ☎ 090/141228) sells the latest in Scandinavian and European interior design, from furniture to little plastic coat hooks.

Skellefteå

❼ *140 km (87 mi) north of Umeå (via E4).*

In 1324 King Magnus Eriksson invited anyone who believed in Jesus Christ, or anyone who wanted to convert to Christianity, to settle a town near the River Skellefte. Thus was Skellefteå born, and for hundreds of years it was a devout Christian township. Today the town makes a living from the electronics and computer industries and from nearby gold and silver mining.

Fodor'sChoice
★

The focus of the town's religious beliefs still stands today, in the form of **Skellefteå Landskyrka.** Inside the area known as Bonnstan—a 400-room "village" built to house traveling churchgoers in the 17th century when attendance was compulsory—the striking neoclassical Skellefteå County Church has a dome roof. It has some exquisite medieval sculptures, including an 800-year-old walnut wood carving of the Virgin Mary, one of only a handful of Romanesque Madonna carvings left anywhere in the world.

One of the very few art museums in the world dedicated to female artists, **Anna Nordlander Museum** displays about 80 of this Swedish painter's portraits and landscapes. Born in 1843, Nordlander found that success came quickly and increased steadily until her death from tuberculosis at the age of 36. ⊠ *Nyg. 56* ☎ *0910/735080* 🖼 *Free* ☉ *Mon.–Thurs. noon–4.*

Where to Stay & Eat

$–$$ ✕ **Balzac.** This is a superb local restaurant with an excellent choice of international dishes. Sit down with the locals and fill up on couscous, Caesar salad, grilled goat cheese, and much more. ⊠ *Tjärhovsg. 14* ☎ *0910/15605* ▤ *MC, V.*

$–$$ ✕ **NordanåGården.** In the heart of a small recreational area called Nordanå, you will find this very classic, very authentic old-style Swedish restaurant. Home-style choices fill the menu; check out the delicious lunch specials. ⊠ *Nordanå* ☎ *0910/53350* ⌂ *Reservations essential for dinner* ▤ *MC, V.*

$–$$ 🏨 **Scandic Hotel.** This modern building is shaped like an upturned boat, half of which is made of glass. This huge glassed portion is the Winter Garden, which houses the lobby, lounges, restaurants, and an extraordinary collection of huge trees, tropical palms, and flowers. The large rooms are furnished in blond wood and come with all the modern additions you would expect of an international hotel. ⊠ *Kanalg. 75, 931 78* ☎ *0910/752400* ☎ *0910/752411* ⊕ *www.scandic-hotels.se* 🛏 *111 rooms, 4 suites* ⌂ *2 restaurants, room TVs with movies, in-room broadband, Wi-Fi, indoor pool, gym, sauna, bar, convention center, free parking, no-smoking rooms* ▤ *AE, DC, MC, V.*

$ 🏨 **Best Western Malmia Hotel.** Each room is individually furnished in this modern hotel. The building's low light, candles, and dark furnishings make for a restful stay. ⊠ *Torget 2, 931 31* ☎ *0910/732500* ☎ *0910/732529* ⊕ *www.malmia.se* 🛏 *98 rooms, 1 suite* ⌂ *Restaurant, in-room broadband, in-room data ports, Wi-Fi, hot tub, sauna, bar, parking (fee), no-smoking rooms* ▤ *AE, DC, MC, V.*

Nightlife & the Arts

Locally sponsored and managed **Pinkerton** (⊠ Magasingränd 3 ☎ 091085060) has the promotion of Skellefteå music very much on its mind. The dark, cool club serves up cold beer, snacks, and lots of local pop, blues, jazz, and rock bands.

Shopping

The market stalls arranged under the large roof of the **Handelsgården** (⌂ Storg. 46 ☎ 09/10779924) mean that the place offers one-stop shopping for ceramics, glass, jewelry, woodwork, textiles, prints and artwork, and delicatessen foods.

The Bothnian Coast A to Z

AIR TRAVEL

CARRIERS The only carrier to Sundsvall Airport is SAS, which operates seven flights a day from Stockholm. To Umeå from Stockholm, there are eight flights a day with SAS, five with Malmö Aviation, and three with Fly Nordic. To Skellefteå from Stockholm, SAS operates five flights daily and Skyways offers three.

🛈 **Fly Nordic** ☎ 08/52806820 ⊕ www.flynordic.com. **Malmö Aviation** ☎ 0771/550010 ⊕ www.malmoaviation.com. **SAS** ☎ 0770/727727 ⊕ www.scandinavian.net. **Skyways** ☎ 0771/959500 ⊕ www.skyways.se.

AIRPORTS

Sundsvall Airport (20 km [12 mi] west of Sundsvall) is the area's main airport. A bus service to Sundsvall and Härnösand runs in connection with arriving and departing SAS flights and costs SKr 65 to Sundsvall and SKr 90 to Härnösand. A taxi will cost SKr 225 and up.

Umeå airport (4 km [2½ mi] from town) has regular connecting flights from Stockholm. A bus service into the city center runs every 10 minutes and costs SKr 35. A taxi will cost SKr 120 and up.

Skellefteå (20 km [12 mi] from Skellefteå center) is well served by flights from Stockholm. A bus service into the city center runs in connection with all arriving and departing flights and costs SKr 65. A taxi will cost about SKr 265.

🛈 **Sundsvall Airport** ☎ 060/197600. **Taxi Sundsvall** ☎ 060/199000.
🛈 **Umeå Airport** ☎ 090/716190. **Flygtaxi** ☎ 020/979797.
🛈 **Skellefteå Airport** ☎ 0910/57600. **Flygtaxi** ☎ 020/979797.

BUS TRAVEL

Swebus operates a twice-daily service from Stockholm to Gävle. Y-Buss operates daily from Stockholm to Hudiksvall, Sundsvall, Härnösand, and Umeå.

🛈 **Swebus Express** ☎ 0200/218218 ⊕ www.swebusexpress.se. **Y-Buss** ☎ 0771/334444 ⊕ www.ybuss.se.

CAR RENTAL

Avis and Hertz have offices in Gävle, Sundsvall, and Umeå. Europcar has offices in Gävle, Skellefteå, and Sundsvall.

🛈 **Avis** ✉ Gävle ☎ 026/186880 ✉ Sundsvall ☎ 060/570210 ✉ Umeå ☎ 090/131111. **Europcar** ✉ Gävle ☎ 026/621095 ✉ Skellefteå ☎ 0910/17333 ✉ Sundsvall ☎ 060/570120. **Hertz** ✉ Gävle ☎ 026/644938 ✉ Sundsvall ☎ 060/669080 ✉ Umeå ☎ 090/177140.

CAR TRAVEL

From Stockholm take E4 directly north 180 km (111 mi) to Gävle. From Göteborg take E20 284 km (177 mi) to Örebro, Route 60 north 164 km (102 mi) to Borlänge, and Route 80 west 70 km (43 mi) to Gävle. From Gävle the E4 runs the entire length of the Bothnian Coast through every major town north to Skellefteå.

EMERGENCIES

For emergencies dial 112. There are several hospitals in the area and emergency dental care is available at Sundsvall and Umeå. There are late-night pharmacies in Sundsvall and Umeå.

🖪 **Gävle Hospital** ☎ 026/154000. **Hudiksvall Hospital** ☎ 065/092000. **Skellefteå Hospital** ☎ 0910/771000. **Söderhamn Hospital** ☎ 0270/77000. **Sundsvall Hospital** ☎ 060/181000. **Umeå Hospital** ☎ 090/7850000.

🖪 Dental Care ✉ Sundsvall ☎ 060/613135 ✉ Umeå ☎ 070/3992480.

🖪 Late-Night Pharmacies ✉ Sundsvall and Umeå ☎ 0771/450450.

TOURS

The Bothnian Coast covers many miles, and tours of the entire area are not available. Individual towns and cities usually offer their own tours, either of the town or of points of interest in the surrounding area. The Umeleden Way is a waterside cycling path with many stops, including Europe's largest hydroelectric power station. Details of tours can be obtained from an individual town's tourist information offices.

🖪 **Gävle City Tour** ☎ 026/147430. **Hudiksvall Town Walk** ☎ 0650/19100. **Skellefteå Countryside Tours** ☎ 0910/736020. **Umeleden Way** ☎ 090/161616.

TRAIN TRAVEL

SJ operates seven train services daily from Stockholm to Gävle, Söderhamn, Hudiksvall, and Sundsvall. Tågkompaniet operates a night train from Stockholm to Umeå, with connections to Skellefteå.

🖪 **SJ** ☎ 0771/757575. **Tågkompaniet** ☎ 0771/444111.

VISITOR INFORMATION

🖪 **Gävle** ✉ Drottningg. 37 ☎ 026/147430. **Härnösand** ✉ Järnvägsg. 2 ☎ 0611/188140 ⊕ www.turism.harnosand.se. **Hudiksvall** ✉ Storg. 33 ☎ 0650/19100 ⊕ www.hudiksvall. se. **Skellefteå** ✉ Trädgårdsg. 7 ☎ 0910/736020 ⊕ turistinfo.skelleftea.se. **Söderhamn** ✉ Resecentrum ☎ 0270/75353 ⊕ www.turism.soderhamn.se. **Sundsvall** ✉ Stora Torget ☎ 060/610450 ⊕ www.sundsvallturism.com. **Umeå** ✉ Renmarkstorget 15 ☎ 090/161616 ⊕ www.umea.se.

Göteborg (Gothenburg)

4

WORD OF MOUTH

"I really enjoyed the view from the Utkiken tower. One good view of Göteborg! I also enjoyed a boat tour on the Göta Canal. I really enjoyed this city on foot as well. It has a very friendly feel. Enjoy!"

—annikany

"If you have only a short time in the city I would include a boat trip around the canals and harbour, a walk around the Haga area, and include going up to Skansen Kronan for the views."

—Where2Travel

"Consider getting a Göteborg Pass—lots of attractions, public transit, and parking are free with it."

—WillTravel

Updated by
Rob Hincks

DON'T TELL THE RESIDENTS OF GÖTEBORG that they live in Sweden's "second city," but not because they will get upset. People here are known for their amiability and good humor. They just may not understand what you are talking about. People who call Göteborg (pronounced YOO-teh-bor; most visitors stick with the simpler "Gothenburg") home seem to forget that the city is diminutive in size and status compared to Stockholm.

Spend a couple of days here and you'll forget, too. You'll find it's easier to ask what Göteborg hasn't got to offer rather than what it has. With an active port situated at the mouth of Göta Älv (Göta River), the city of almost 500,000 inhabitants has plenty to offer. Culturally it is superb, boasting a fine opera house and theater, one of the country's best art museums, as well as a fantastic applied-arts museum. There's plenty of history to soak up, from the ancient port that gave the city its start to the 19th-century factory buildings and workers' houses that helped put it on the commercial map. For those looking for nature, the wild west coast and tame green fields are both within striking distance. And don't forget the food. From 1995 to 2005, eight of the 10 "Swedish Chef of the Year" winners were cooking in Göteborg, using the world-class local fish to give them an edge, no doubt.

Home to Scandinavia's largest port and largest corporation (Volvo Cars), the city is a thriving commercial success. Historically, Göteborg owes its existence to the sea. Tenth-century Vikings sailed from its shores, and a settlement was founded here in the 11th century. Not until 1621, however, did King Gustav II Adolf grant Göteborg a charter to establish a free-trade port modeled off others already thriving on the Continent. The west-coast harbor would also allow Swedish ships to avoid Danish tolls exacted for passing through Öresund, the stretch of water separating the two countries. Foreigners were recruited to realize these visions: the Dutch were its builders—hence the canals that thread the city—and many Scotsmen worked and settled here, though they have left little trace.

Today Göteborg resists its second-city status by being a leader in attractions and civic structures. The Scandinavium, with a capacity of 14,000 people, is one of Europe's largest indoor arenas; the Ullevi Stadium stages some of the Nordic area's most important concerts and sporting events; Nordstan is one of Europe's biggest indoor shopping malls; and Liseberg Nöjespark, Scandinavia's largest amusement park, attracts more than 3 million visitors a year, all eager to see what the fuss is about.

EXPLORING GÖTEBORG

Göteborg begs to be explored by foot. A small, neat package of a city, it can be divided up into three main areas, all of which are closely interlinked. If your feet need a rest, though, there is an excellent streetcar network that runs to all parts of town—and in summer you can feel the wind in your hair, as some streetcars go roofless. The main artery of Göteborg is Kungsportsavenyn (more commonly referred to as Avenyn, "the Avenue"), a 60-foot-wide tree-lined boulevard that bisects the city along a northwest–southeast axis. Avenyn starts at Göteborg's cultural heart, Götaplatsen, home to the city's oldest cultural institutions, where ornate carved-stone buildings keep watch over shady boulevards lined with exclusive restaurants and bars. Follow Avenyn north and you'll find the main commercial area, now dominated by the modern Nordstan shopping center. Beyond is the waterfront, busy with all the traffic of the port, as well as some of Göteborg's newer cultural developments, in particular its magnificent opera house.

To the west of the city are the Haga and Linné districts. Once home to the city's dockyard, shipping, and factory workers, these areas are now chic, bohemian enclaves alive with arts-and-crafts galleries, antiques shops, boutiques selling clothes and household goods, and street cafés and restaurants. Most of these shops are inside the original wood-and-brick cottages that line the narrow streets.

Cultural Göteborg

A pleasant stroll will take you from Götaplatsen's 1930s architecture along Avenyn—the boulevard Kungsportsavenyn lined with elegant shops, cafés, and restaurants—to finish at Kungsportsplats. At the square the street becomes Östra Hamngatan and slopes gently up from the canal.

a good walk

Start your tour in **Götaplatsen** ❶ ▶, a square dominated by a fountain statue of Poseidon; behind him is the **Konstmuseet** ❷. Stroll downhill past the cafés and restaurants along Avenyn to the intersection with Vasagatan. A short way to the left down Vasagatan, at the junction with Teatergatan, you can visit the **Röhsska Museet** ❸, one of the few museums dedicated to Swedish design.

Continue down Vasagatan. If the weather's good, take a look at the Vasa Parken (Vasa Park). Then turn right to go north on Viktoriagatan, cross the canal, and make an immediate left to visit one of the city's most peculiar attractions, **Feskekörkan** ❹, whose name is an archaic spelling of *Fisk Kyrkan,* the Fish Church. It resembles a place of worship but is actually an indoor fish market.

You may now feel inspired to visit the city's principal place of worship, **Domkyrkan** ❺. Follow the canal eastward from Feskekörkan and turn left onto Västra Hamngatan; walk about four blocks to the church. Continue northward on Västra Hamngatan and cross the canal to get to Norra Hamngatan, where you'll find the **Stadsmuseet** ❻, housed in the 18th-century Swedish East India Company.

TIMING   Depending on how much time you want to spend in each museum, this walk may take anywhere from a couple of hours to the better part of a day. Note that many sites close Monday off-season.

What to See

❺ **Domkyrkan** (Göteborg Cathedral). The cathedral, in neoclassic yellow brick, dates from 1802, the two previous cathedrals on this spot having been destroyed by fire. Though disappointingly plain on the out-

Göteborg
(Gothenburg)

side, the interior is impressive. Two glassed-in verandas originally used for the bishop's private conversations run the length of each side of the cathedral. The altar is impressively ornate and gilt. Next to it stands a post-Resurrection cross, bare of the figure of Jesus and surrounded by his gilded burial garments strewn on the floor. ⊠ *Kyrkog. 28, Centrum* ☎ *031/7316130* ☎ *Free* ☉ *Weekdays 8–6, Sat. 9–4, Sun. 10–3.*

need a break?
On the old square dominated by the city's food hall, tucked away discreetly at the side, is a wonderful piece of social history. The perfectly preserved **Ölhallen** (⊠ Kungstorget 7 ☎ 031/136079) is a historic beer hall and a great place to stop for a refreshing afternoon drink. The tiled floor, dark wood paneling, and corner counter of the bar are all original. Pictures on the wall depict old scenes of the city. A relic of the days when beer halls attracted only the working class, today all sorts come to its dark corners to gossip or just pass the afternoon with a newspaper.

❹ **Feskekörkan** (Fish Church). Built in 1872, this fish market gets its nickname from its Gothic-style architectural details. The beautiful arched and vaulted wooden ceiling covers rows and rows of stalls, each offering silvery, slippery goods to the shoppers who congregate in this vast hall. ⊠ *Fisktorget, Rosenlundsg, Centrum.*

off the beaten path
FISKHAMNEN (Fish Docks) – An excellent view of **Älvsborgsbron** (Älvsborg Bridge), the longest suspension bridge in Sweden, is available from Fiskhamnen, west of Stigbergstorget. Built in 1967, the bridge stretches 3,060 feet across the river and was built high enough for ocean liners to pass beneath. Also look toward the sea to the large container harbors—Skarvikshamnen, Skandiahamnen, and Torshamnen—which today welcome most of the city's cargo.

▶ ❶ **Götaplatsen** (Göta Place). This square was built in 1923 in celebration
FodorśChoice of the city's 300th anniversary. In the center is the Swedish-American
★ sculptor Carl Milles's fountain statue of Poseidon choking a codfish. Behind the statue stands the Konstmuseet, flanked by the **Konserthuset** (Concert Hall) and the **Stadsteatern** (Municipal Theater), contemporary buildings in which the city celebrates its important contribution to Swedish cultural life. The **Stadsbiblioteket** (Municipal Library) maintains a collection of more than half a million books, many in English.

❷ **Konstmuseet** (Art Museum). This impressive collection of the works of leading Scandinavian painters and sculptors encapsulates some of the moody introspection of the artistic community in this part of the world. The museum's Hasselblad Center devotes itself to showing the progress in the art of photography. The Konstmuseet's holdings include works by Swedes such as Carl Milles, Johan Tobias Sergel, impressionist Anders Zorn, Victorian idealist Carl Larsson, and Prince Eugen. The 19th- and 20th-century French art collection is the best in Sweden, and there's also a small collection of old masters. ⊠ *Götaplatsen* ☎ *031/612980* ☎ *SKr 40* ☉ *Tues. and Thurs. 11–6, Wed. 11–9, Fri.–Sun. 11–5.*

off the beaten path

LISEBERG NÖJESPARK – Göteborg proudly claims Scandinavia's largest amusement park. The city's pride is well earned: Liseberg is one of the best-run, most efficient parks in the world. In addition to a wide selection of carnival rides, Liseberg also has numerous restaurants and theaters, all set amid beautifully tended gardens. Nostalgics will love the huge wooden roller coaster here. Built in 2004, it's the largest in Scandinavia and, just to add to the thrill, it creaks throughout the ride. It's about a 30-minute walk east from the city center or a 10-minute ride by bus or tram; in summer a vintage open streetcar makes frequent runs to Liseberg from Brunnsparken, in the middle of town. See www.liseberg.se for deviations to schedule around holidays. ⊠ *Örgrytev. 5, Liseberg* ☎ *031/400100* ⊕ *www. liseberg.se* 🖼 *SKr 60* ☉ *Mid-Apr.–mid-May, Sat. noon–9, Sun. noon–8; mid-May–July, weekdays 3–10, Sat. noon–11, Sun. noon–8; Aug., Mon.-Thurs. and Sun. 11–11, Fri. and Sat. 11 AM–midnight; Sept., Thurs. and Fri. 4 PM–10 PM, Sat. noon–10, Sun. noon–8.*

❸ **Röhsska Museet** (Museum of Arts and Crafts). This museum's fine collections of furniture, books and manuscripts, tapestries, and pottery are on view. Artifacts date back as far as 1,000 years, but it's the 20th-century gallery, with its collection of many familiar household objects, that seems to provide the most enjoyment. ⊠ *Vasag. 37–39, Vasastan* ☎ *031/ 613850* ⊕ *www.designmuseum.se* 🖼 *SKr 40* ☉ *Tues. noon–8, Wed.–Fri. noon–5, weekends 10–5.*

❻ **Stadsmuseet** (City Museum). Once the warehouse and auction rooms of the Swedish East India Company, a major trading firm founded in 1731, this palatial structure dates from 1750. Today it contains exhibits on the Swedish west coast, with a focus on Göteborg's nautical and trading past. One interesting exhibit deals with the East India Company and its ship the *Göteborg*. On its 1745 return from China, she sank just outside the city, while crowds there to greet the returning ship watched from shore in horror. ⊠ *Norra Hamng. 12, Centrum* ☎ *031/612770* 🖼 *SKr 40* ☉ *Daily 10–5.*

need a break?

Hidden on a modern, pedestrianized shopping block is the wonderful café **Mauritz** (⊠ Fredsg. 2, Centrum ☎ 031/806971), which does a very welcome, very good cup of coffee. Inside the small café it's standing room only, but the smell of the bean-roasting machine in the back is enough to make you want to stay put. Try one of their homemade rye rolls with spiced cheese and orange jelly.

off the beaten path

VÄRLDSKULTURMUSEET – Next door to the amusement park Liseberg, Göteborg's newest museum deals with more serious issues. Housed in a beautiful modern glass and concrete building, the World Culture Museum addresses the many issues facing various global cultures. By using art and photography exhibitions and by running workshops, discussion forums, and lectures, the museum manages to alert the conscience and keep visitors interested at the same time. ⊠ *Söderv. 54, Liseberg* ☎ *031/632730* ⊕ *www.varldskulturmuseet. se* 🖼 *Free* ☉ *Tues. noon–5, Wed.–Fri. noon–9, weekends noon–5.*

Commercial Göteborg

Explore Göteborg's port-side character, both historic and modern, at the waterfront development near the town center, where the markets and boutiques can keep you busy for hours.

a good walk

Begin at the harborside square known as Lilla Bommen Torg, where the **Utkiken ❼** ⌐ offers a bird's-eye view of the city and harbor. The waterfront development here includes the ship-turned-restaurant *Viking*, the **Maritima Centrum ❽**, and the **Göteborgs Operan (Opera House) ❾**.

From Lilla Bommen Torg take the pedestrian bridge across the highway to Nordstan, Sweden's largest indoor shopping mall. Leave the mall at the opposite end, which puts you at Brunnsparken, the hub of the city's streetcar network. Turn right and cross the street to Gustav Adolfs Torg, the city's official center, dominated by **Rådhuset ❿**. On the north side of the square is **Börshuset ⓫**, built in 1849.

Head north from the square along Östra Hamngatan and turn left onto Postgatan to visit **Kronhuset ⓬**, the city's oldest secular building, dating from 1643. Surrounding the entrance to Kronhuset are the **Kronhusbodarna**, carefully restored turn-of-the-20th-century shops and arts-and-crafts boutiques.

Return to Gustav Adolfs Torg and follow Östra Hamngatan south over the Stora Hamnkanal to Kungsportsplats, where the Saluhall (Market Hall) has stood since 1888. A number of pedestrians-only shopping streets branch out through this neighborhood on either side of Östra Hamngatan. Crossing the bridge over Vallgraven from Kungsportsplats brings you onto Kungsportsavenyn and the entrance to **Trädgårdsföreningens Park ⓭**.

TIMING   The walk itself will take about two hours; allow extra time to explore the sites and to shop. Note that the Kronhusbodarna is closed Sunday.

What to See

⓫ **Börshuset** (Stock Exchange). Completed in 1849, the former Stock Exchange building houses city administrative offices as well as facilities for large banquets. The fabric of the large, opulent banqueting halls and blue-stucco anterooms is under considerable strain through age. The building is not open to the public, but if you can get in, you won't be disappointed. ⊠ *Gustav Adolfs torg 5, Nordstan.*

★ ❾ **Göteborgs Operan** (Gothenburg's Opera). A statement in steel and glass, the opera house opened in 1994, immediately dominating this section of the waterfront with its bold lines and shape. Set against a backdrop of the old docks, it makes for a striking image. The productions here are world-class and well worth seeing if you get the chance. ⊠ *Christina Nilssonsg., Nordstan* ☎ *031/108000 for bookings.*

Kronhusbodarna (Historical Shopping Center). Glassblowing and watch-making are among the arts and crafts offered in this area of shops that adjoin the Kronhuset. There is also a nice, old-fashioned café. ⊠ *Kronhusg. 1D, Nordstan* ☉ *Closed Sun.*

⑫ Kronhuset (Crown House). Göteborg's oldest secular building, dating from 1643, was originally the city's armory. In 1660 Sweden's Parliament met here to arrange the succession for King Karl X Gustav, who died suddenly while visiting the city. The building is now used for classical concerts and the City Museum's annual Christmas market. ✉ *Postg. 68, Nordstan* ☎ *031/710832.*

❽ Maritima Centrum (Marine Center). In the world's largest floating maritime museum you'll find modern naval vessels, including a destroyer, submarines, lightship, cargo vessel, and various tugboats, providing insight into Göteborg's historic role as a major port. The main attraction is a huge naval destroyer, complete with a medical room in which a leg amputation operation is graphically re-created, with mannequins standing in for medical personnel. ✉ *Packhuskajen 8, Nordstan* ☎ *031/105950* 💰 *SKr 60* ⊙ *May–July, daily 10–6; Aug.–Apr., daily 10–4.*

❿ Rådhuset. Though the town hall dates from 1672, when it was designed by Nicodemus Tessin the Elder, its controversial modern extension by Swedish architect Gunnar Asplund is from 1937. The building therefore offers two architectural extremes. One section has the original grand chandeliers and trompe-l'oeil ceilings; the other has glass elevators, mussel-shape drinking fountains, and vast expanses of laminated aspen wood. Together they make a fascinating mix. ✉ *Gustav Adolfs torg 1, Nordstan.*

⑬ Trädgårdsföreningens Park (Horticultural Society Park). Beautiful open green spaces, manicured gardens, and tree-lined paths are the perfect place to escape for some peace and rest. Rose fanciers can head for the magnificent rose garden with 5,000 roses of 2,500 varieties. Also worth a visit is the Palm House, whose late-19th-century design echoes that of London's Crystal Palace. ✉ *Just off Kungsportsavenyn, Centrum* ☎ *031/3655858* 💰 *Park SKr 15, Palm House SKr 20* ⊙ *Park May–Aug., daily 7 AM–9 PM; Sept.–Apr., daily 7 AM–7:30 PM. Palm House May–Aug., daily 10–5; Sept.–Apr., daily 10–4.*

FodorsChoice ★

▶ **❼ Utkiken** (Lookout Tower). This red-and-white-stripe skyscraper towers 282 feet above the waterfront, offering an unparalleled view of the city, its green spaces, and the contrasting industrial landscape of the port—so don't miss out on a visit to the viewing platform at the top. ✉ *Lilla Bommen 1, Lilla Bommen* ☎ *031/3655858.*

off the beaten path

GULLBERGSKAJEN – For an interesting tour of the docks, head northeast from Lilla Bommen about 1½ km (1 mi) along the riverside to the Gullbergskajen, just off Gullbergsstrandgatan. Today this is the headquarters of a local boating association, its brightly colored pleasure craft contrasting with the old-fashioned working barges either anchored or being repaired at Ringön, just across the river.

NYA ELFSBORGS FÄSTNING – Boats leave regularly from Lilla Bommen to the Elfsborg Fortress, built in 1670 on a harbor island to protect the city from attack. ☎ *031/609660* 💰 *SKr 85* ⊙ *Early May–Aug., 7 departures daily; Sept., weekends.*

 ☃ **SJÖFARTSMUSEET & AKVARIET** – This museum combines maritime history with an aquarium. The museum has model ships, cannons, a ship's medical room, and a collection of figureheads. The adjacent aquarium contains a good selection of Nordic marine life and a more exotic section with, among other animals, two alligators and some piranhas. ⊠ *Karl Johansg. 1–3, 2 km (1 mi) west of city center, Majorna* ☎ *031/612900* ☑ *SKr 40* ☺ *Sept.–Apr., Tues., Thurs., and Fri. 10–4, Wed. 10–9, weekends 11–5; May–Aug., daily 10–5.*

VIKING – This four-masted schooner built in 1907 was among the last of Sweden's sailing cargo ships. The ship is now used as a hotel and restaurant, with cabins for two without bath starting at SKr 650. The restaurant serves up traditional Swedish fare starting at SKr 79. ⊠ *Gullbergskajen, Lilla Bommen, Hamnen* ☎ *031/635800.*

Haga & Linné Districts

Just west of the main city, the Haga and Linné districts are at the forefront of the new cosmopolitan Göteborg. These areas once housed the city's poor, and were so run-down that they were scheduled for demolition. They now make up some of the city's most attractive areas. The older of the two neighborhoods, the Haga district, is full of cozy cafés, secondhand stores, and artists' shops along cobbled streets. The Linné district is the trendiest neighborhood in Göteborg, and real-estate prices have shot up accordingly. Corner restaurants, expensive boutiques, and stylish cafés cater to neighborhood residents and to Göteborg's wealthy young elite, there to see and be seen.

a good walk

Set off from the east end of **Haga Nygatan** ⑭ ▶ and stroll west past the busy cafés and boutiques selling art-deco light fixtures and antique kitchenware. Turn left onto Landsvägsgatan and walk up to join Linnégatan, the Dutch-inspired street that's now considered Göteborg's "Second Avenyn." There is an air of quiet sophistication about Linnégatan, with small antiques and jewelry shops competing for attention against secluded street cafés and high-end design and crafts shops.

Walk south along Linnégatan for five minutes to get to **Slottsskogen** ⑮. If relaxing is your thing, you can spend some time lounging in this huge, tranquil expanse of parkland. Alternatively, you can visit the **Naturhistorika Museet** ⑯, Göteborg's oldest museum, or the **Botaniska Trädgården** ⑰, on the south side of the park.

Leave the park the same way you came in, and wind your way north up Nordenhemsgatan. At the end of this street turn right onto Första Långgatan and then onto Södra Allégatan. Here you can find the beautiful and tranquil oasis of the **Hagabadet** ⑱, a superbly renovated bathhouse.

TIMING At a gentle pace the walk alone will take about one hour. If you allow yourself to be tempted by the great shopping, superb cafés, and both museums, you could spend almost a whole day in this part of the city.

What to See

⑰ Botaniska Trädgården (Botanical Gardens). With 1,200 plant species, this is Sweden's largest botanical garden. Herb gardens, bamboo groves, a Japanese valley, forest plants, and tropical greenhouses are all on display. Once you've captured some inspiration, you can pick up all you need to create your own botanical garden from the on-site shop. ☒ *Carl Skottsbergsg. 22A, Slottsskogen* ☎ *031/7411101* ☒ *Greenhouses SKr 20, park free* ☉ *Park daily 9–sunset; greenhouses May–Aug., daily 10–5; Sept.–Apr., daily 10–4.*

⑱ Hagabadet. This stunning bathhouse was built at the end of the 19th

Fodor'sChoice century by the Swedish philanthropist Sven Renström. Originally used
★ by local dock- and factory workers, it now plays host to Göteborg's leisure-hungry elite. It's well worth a visit. The pretty pool is art nouveau, with wall paintings, an arched ceiling, and lamps with a diving-lady motif. The Roman baths and the massage and spa area all exude relaxation, but the architecture alone is worth a visit, even if you don't intend to take the plunge. ☒ *Södra Allég. 3, Haga* ☎ *031/600600* ☒ *SKr 360 for a 1-day pass to use facilities; otherwise free* ☉ *Mon.–Thurs. 7 AM–9:30 PM, Fri. 7 AM–8:30 PM, Sat. 9–6, Sun. 10–6.*

➤ ⑲ Haga Nygatan. The redbrick buildings that line this street were originally poorhouses donated by the Dickson family, the city's British industrialist forefathers. ROBERT DICKSON can still be seen carved into the facades of these buildings. Like most buildings in Haga, the buildings' ground floors were made of stone in order to prevent the spread of fire (the upper floors are wood). The Dickson family's impact on the architecture of the west of Sweden can also be seen in the impressive, fanciful mansion that belonged to Robert's grandson James, in Tjolöholm, to the south of Göteborg. ☒ *Haga Nyg. Haga.*

need a break? Half the fun of Haga is to do what the locals do: just relax. **Jacobs** (☒ Haga Nyg. 10 ☎ 031/7118044), a cool little café, is the perfect place to do this. If you're lucky you can secure one of the outdoor tables that are lined up in a narrow strip along the café's street front. This is the ideal spot to watch folks from the neighborhood. Inside there are wonderful art-nouveau globe lamps to illuminate the delicious cakes and frothy lattes.

⑯ Naturhistorika Museet. Although the Natural History Museum has a collection containing more than 10 million preserved animals, you may be disappointed to discover that the majority are tiny insects that sit unnoticed in rows of drawers. It's worth a visit to see the world's only stuffed blue whale, harpooned in 1865. ☒ *Slottsskogen* ☎ *031/7752400* ⊕ *www.gnm.se* ☒ *SKr 60* ☉ *Sept.–Apr., Tues.–Fri. 9–4, weekends 11–5; May–Aug., daily 11–5.*

off the beaten path SKANSEN KRONAN – To the south of Haga is one of Göteborg's two surviving 17th-century fortress towers. Built on a raised mound of land, the tower houses the military museum, containing displays of weapons dating from the Middle Ages and Swedish uniforms from the 19th and 20th centuries. The museum's presentations can be a

SWEDISH INGENUITY

PERHAPS IT WAS ALFRED NOBEL'S **DOING.** His 1867 invention of dynamite was hardly the sort of thing one expected from a nation so committed to peace. Since that momentous invention, it seems Swedish inventors have been intent on helping the world.

The theme of light drove Swedish inventors, with the safety match, the paraffin stove, the gas-powered lighthouse, and the blowtorch all patented before the 20th century. Sweden's contributions have continued into the modern age, with inventions of astounding everyday value, such as the ball bearing, the adjustable wrench, an improved zipper, the Celsius thermometer (named for Anders Celsius), the Tetra Pak, the screw propeller, the three-point retractable car safety-belt, the heart pacemaker, the three-phase electricity system, and the computer mouse.

It seems a logical next step that various Swedish brands have become the symbols of our everyday lives. If you're not sitting on a piece of IKEA furniture right now, you're probably within arm's reach of one. In large cities across the world, you'll find young crowds in H&M stores, whose affordable cutting-edge fashion is hard to resist. And finally, if one car in the world speaks of everyday values and represents this country, it surely is the Volvo.

If all this Swedishness is too much for you, perhaps you need a drink—something American, maybe. But wait, that classic Coca-Cola bottle you're about to reach for? That's right, designed by a Swede.

— Rob Hincks

little dry at times, and are probably only for the true enthusiast of military history. But the view northward across the city makes the journey worthwhile.

🐣 ⑮ **Slottsskogen.** Spend some time in this stunning area of parkland containing cafés, farm animals, a seal pond, Sweden's oldest children's zoo, and many birds—in summer even pink flamingos. Slottsskogen is one of the best parts of the city for relaxing. ✉ *South of Linnég., Slottsskogen* ⊙ *Daily dawn–dusk.*

off the beaten path

VOLVO MUSEUM – In Arendal, 8 km (5 mi) west of the city center, the Volvo Museum pays homage to the car company that in one way or another helps support 25% of Göteborg's population. Not surprisingly, exhibits include most of Volvo's cars over the years as well as some prototypes, the first electric car, and an early jet engine, the first one used by the Swedish Air Force. A 20-minute film helps to put the whole history into perspective at this well-put-together museum. ✉ *Avd. 1670 ARU (off Rd. 155 toward Öckerö/Torslanda), Arendal* ☎ *031/ 664814* ⊕ *www.volvo.com* ✉ *SKr 40* ⊙ *June–Aug., Tues.–Fri. 10–5, weekends 11–4; Sept.–May, Tues.–Fri. noon–5, weekends 11–4.*

WHERE TO EAT

Göteborg is filled with people who love to eat and cook, so you've come to the right place if you're interested in food. The fish and seafood here are some of the best in the world, owing to the clean, cold waters off Sweden's west coast. And Göteborg's chefs are some of the best in Sweden, as a glance at the list of recent "Swedish Chef of the Year" winners will confirm. Call ahead to be sure restaurants are open, as many close for a month in summer.

	WHAT IT COSTS	In Swedish Kronor			
	$$$$	**$$$**	**$$**	**$**	**¢**
AT DINNER	over 420	250–420	150–250	100–150	under 100

Prices are for a main course at dinner.

$$$–$$$$ ✕ **Sjömagasinet.** Since 1994 Leif Mannerström has headed up what is
Fodor'sChoice probably the best seafood restaurant in Sweden. Mannerström, a gray-
★ bearded kitchen maestro, is something of a godfather on the Göteborg
food scene and has for many years been the leading champion of west-
coast fish. In the delightful oak-beamed dining room (a 200-year-old ren-
ovated shipping warehouse), you can eat carefully presented, delicious
fish dishes with a classical French touch. An outdoor terrace opens up
in summer, complete with authentic sea air. ⊠ *Klippans Kulturreservat,
Kiel-terminalen* ☎ *031/7755920* ⌲ *Reservations essential* ▤ *AE, DC,
MC, V.*

★ **$$$** ✕ **28+.** Step down from the street into this former wine-and-cheese cel-
lar to find an elegant restaurant owned by two of the best chefs in Göte-
borg. Finely set tables, flickering candles, and country-style artwork evoke
the mood of a rustic French bistro. Italian and American flavors blend
their way into the impeccable French dishes; choose a five- or seven-
course meal, or take your pick à la carte. Note that one of the best wine
cellars in Sweden is at your disposal, and that the cheese selection here
is unsurpassed. ⊠ *Götabergsg. 28, Centrum* ☎ *031/202161* ⌲ *Reservations essential* ▤ *AE, DC, MC, V* ☺ *Closed Sun.*

$$$ ✕ **Linnéa.** Chef Bengt Sjöström is an artist. His food is so beautifully pre-
sented it seems a shame to eat it. He works with Swedish glass and ce-
ramic companies who design unique plates and glasses for him to show
off his food to full effect. A lobster dish comes with a tiny glass of cham-
pagne on the side, the cheese on a stylish miniature wooden cutting board.
But eat it you must, because Sjöström's culinary art is equally accom-
plished, using local seafood and classic European cooking techniques.
⊠ *Södrav. 32, Vasastan* ☎ *031/161183* ⌲ *Reservations essential* ▤ *AE,
DC, MC, V* ☺ *Closed Sun.*

$$$ ✕ **Magnus & Magnus.** Though the dining room is tiny and perhaps a lit-
tle tightly packed, somehow that seems to add to the experience. Mag-
nus & Magnus feels like a friendly meeting place: it's always packed
and always loud. The food is contemporary and very well prepared, re-
lying on both Swedish ingredients and international flavors. In summer
there is a secluded backyard where dinner and drinks are served and,

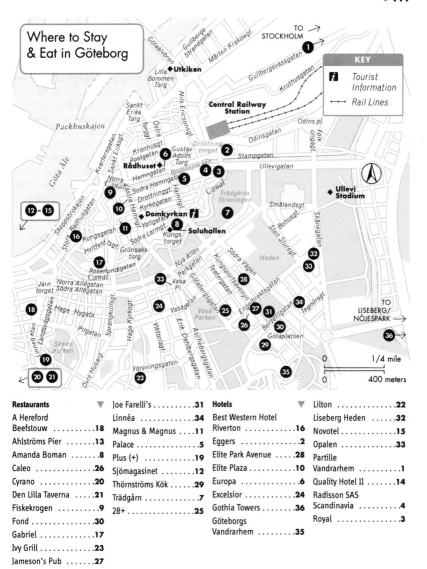

Where to Stay & Eat in Göteborg

KEY

🛈 Tourist Information

↤→ Rail Lines

Restaurants ▼

A Hereford Beefstouw	.........**18**
Ahlströms Pier	.......**13**
Amanda Boman	.......**8**
Caleo	............**26**
Cyrano	............**20**
Den Lilla Taverna	.....**21**
Fiskekrogen	..........**9**
Fond	..............**30**
Gabriel	.............**17**
Ivy Grill	............**23**
Jameson's Pub	.......**27**
Joe Farelli's	.........**31**
Linnéa	.............**34**
Magnus & Magnus	....**11**
Palace	.............**5**
Plus (+)	.............**19**
Sjömagasinet	.......**12**
Thörnströms Kök	.....**29**
Trädgårn	............**7**
28+	................**25**

Hotels ▼

Best Western Hotel Riverton	............**16**
Eggers	..............**2**
Elite Park Avenue	....**28**
Elite Plaza	..........**10**
Europa	..............**6**
Excelsior	............**24**
Gothia Towers	.......**36**
Göteborgs Vandrarhem	........**35**
Lilton	..............**22**
Liseberg Heden	......**32**
Novotel	.............**15**
Opalen	.............**33**
Partille Vandrarhem	........**1**
Quality Hotel 11	.......**14**
Radisson SAS Scandinavia	.........**4**
Royal	..............**3**

as the sun goes down, DJs spin disks. ✉ *Magasing. 8, Centrum* ☏ *031/133000* ♨ *Reservations essential* ▤ *AE, DC, MC, V.*

★ **$$$** ✕ **Thörnströms Kök.** The steep climb up the street to Thörnströms is perfect for working up a thirst. Why not start then with a choice from the excellent wine list, on which every wine is available by the glass. Take your table in one of the three small and elegant dining rooms, and enjoy a series of small dishes of modern European food using the finest local ingredients. Staff here are friendly and very knowledgeable about the wines and the menu. ✉ *Teknologg. 3, Vasastan* ☏ *031/182066* ♨ *Reservations essential* ▤ *AE, DC, MC, V* ☺ *No lunch.*

$$$ ✕ **Trädgårn.** Spicy, Asian-influenced cuisine stands out against linen tablecloths in this earth-tone restaurant; the vegetarian menu is extensive. A wall of glass in the two-story dining hall affords a beautiful view; another wall is covered in blond-wood paneling, a contrast to the black-slate floor. ✉ *Nya Allén, Centrum* ☏ *031/102080* ▤ *AE, DC, MC, V* ☺ *Closed Sun. No lunch fall–spring.*

$$–$$$ ✕ **A Hereford Beefstouw.** At this, an American steak house in Sweden, the chefs grill beef selections in the center of the three dining rooms. The restaurant is popular in a town otherwise dominated by fish restaurants. Thick wooden tables, pine floors, and landscape paintings give the place a rustic touch. ✉ *Linnég. 5, Linnéstaden* ☏ *031/7750441* ▤ *AE, DC, MC, V* ☺ *No lunch weekends and July.*

$$–$$$ ✕ **Ahlströms Pier.** Across the river from central Göteborg lies Eriksberg, where former dockyards mix with modern buildings. Perched at the end of a pier that juts out into the harbor, this restaurant has a main dining hall in an elegant triangular room on the second floor and a less-expensive brasserie on the first floor; contemporary French-inspired Swedish fare is on the menu at both. In summer, food is served on an outdoor patio. Finding the pier by car can prove difficult; consider taking a ferry from the city side of the river. ✉ *Dockepiren, Eriksberg* ☏ *031/519555* ♨ *Reservations essential* ▤ *AE, DC, MC, V* ☺ *Main dining hall closed Sun.*

$$–$$$ ✕ **Fiskekrogen.** The Fish Inn has more than 30 fish and seafood dishes from which you can choose. Lunches are particularly good value, and ideal if you're coming from the Stadsmuseet across the canal. ✉ *Lilla Torget 1, Centrum* ☏ *031/101005* ▤ *AE, DC, MC, V* ☺ *Closed Sun.*

★ **$$–$$$** ✕ **Fond.** Stefan Karlsson's fantastic restaurant can boast one of the best locations in Göteborg, right on the beautiful Götaplatsen. Karlsson, chef of the year in 1995, continues to produce top-quality gourmet delights with a real emphasis on local and seasonal ingredients. All his herbs and vegetables are grown by a farmer just 5 km (3 mi) from town. Karlsson loves to travel; the flavors he has picked up as a globe-trotter spice up his modern Swedish menu. From the semicircular dining room, diners looks out on the square through glass windows, while one wall in the restaurant is part of the original city wall. Almost-bare wooden tables and primary-color linens make an interesting informal contrast to the haute cuisine that emerges from the kitchen. ✉ *Götaplatsen, Vasastan* ☏ *031/812580* ▤ *AE, DC, MC, V* ☺ *Closed Sun.*

$$–$$$ ✕ **Palace.** In the center of Brunnsparken, the Palace is one of Göteborg's most popular summer spots for eating, dancing, and drinking. Live bands and DJs play the '70s and '80s favorites of the well-dressed fortysome-things who frequent the restaurant and nightclub. The extensive single-malt whiskey collection is known around town: call ahead to arrange a tasting. The menu of mostly traditional Swedish cuisine is extensive. ✉ *Brunnsparken* ☎ *031/807550* ▤ *AE, DC, MC, V* ☺ *Closed Sun.*

$$ ✕ **Ivy Grill.** Stepping inside the Ivy is like stepping into a traditional Ivy League university clubhouse. The elegant stone town house is filled with American university pennants, Latin inscriptions on the walls, shelves full of tomes, chocolate-brown leather chairs, and lots of dark wood. The menu, though, is anything but traditional, with dishes like deep-fried scallops with sweet-and-sour salad and wasabi yogurt—such delicacies appear amusingly at odds with their surroundings. In summer you'll find a tented terrace bar, perfect for predinner drinks. ✉ *Vasaplatsen 2, Vasastan* ☎ *031/7114404* ▤ *AE, DC, MC, V* ☺ *Closed Sun.*

$–$$ ✕ **Plus** (+). This atmospheric and relaxing restaurant recalls the Sweden of the past. It's inside a beautiful early-1900s ramshackle wooden house whose foundations are attached to the original rock on which the city was built. (As you travel through town, you may see some of this rock poking up through the modern sidewalks and streets.) Eat well-prepared fish and meat dishes with a varied international flavor at polished wood tables, all the while sitting beneath antique chandeliers. There's a superb selection of malt whiskeys and grappas here, the perfect way to end the evening. ✉ *Linnég. 32, Linnéstaden* ☎ *031/240890* ▤ *AE, DC, MC, V.*

$–$$ ✕ **Caleo.** The name means *to be warmed* in Latin; certainly a suitable moniker for this place. The natural shades throughout the restaurant and the ever-smiling staff are enough to thaw even the most frozen of spirits. And the food, with all the warming, delicious flavors of the Mediterranean, is enough to make you want to get up and dance—something you won't be able to do in the slightly cramped dining room. ✉ *Engelbrektsg. 39, Vasastan* ☎ *031/7089340* ▤ *AE, DC, MC, V.*

$–$$ ✕ **Cyrano.** A little piece of southern France in Sweden, this superb, authentically Provençal bistro is an absolute must. Inside, the tables are crammed close together, art hangs on the walls, and French touches extend throughout. Highlights include a sumptuously creamy fish soup, sardines with garlic, and grass-fed lamb with tomatoes and sweet peppers. Laid back and friendly, with helpful service, Cyrano continues to draw in the trendier citizens of Göteborg. ✉ *Prinsg. 7, Linnéstaden* ☎ *031/143110* ▤ *AE, DC, MC, V.*

Fodor'sChoice ★

¢–$$ ✕ **Joe Farelli's.** Dimly lighted, with booths along the walls and black-and-white photographs of the Big Apple, Joe Farelli's is as close to a New York restaurant as you'll get in Göteborg. Very central, on Avenyn, it's a good place to stop for a dish of pasta or a burger in between sights. ✉ *Kungsportsavenyn 12, Centrum* ☎ *031/105826* ▤ *AE, MC, V.*

¢–$$ ✕ **Jameson's Pub.** On Tuesday night this English pub on Avenyn comes alive to the beat of live blues, R&B, and rock music. There's live en-

tertainment on the weekends as well; check in to find out who's performing. The food, affordable and surprisingly good, is an eclectic mix
of traditional Swedish and international favorites. ⊠ *Kungsportsavenyn
32, Centrum* ☎ *031/187770* ⊟ *AE, MC, V.*

$ ✕ **Den Lilla Taverna.** A very good, lively, and popular place, this Greek
restaurant has paper tablecloths and Greek mythological scenes painted
on the walls. Live bouzouki music on Wednesday and Saturday evenings
gives the place an authentic feel. ⊠ *Oliver Dahlsg. 17, Linnéstaden* ☎ *031/
128805* ⊟ *AE, MC, V.*

$ ✕ **Gabriel.** A buffet of fresh shellfish and the fish dish of the day draw
crowds to this restaurant on a balcony above the fish hall. You can watch
all the trading as you eat lunch. The butter-fried herring with mashed
potatoes is highly recommended. ⊠ *Feskekörkan, Centrum* ☎ *031/
139051* ⊟ *AE, DC, MC, V* ☉ *Closed Sun. and Mon. No dinner.*

★ **¢–$** ✕ **Amanda Boman.** This little restaurant in one corner of the market hall
at Kungsportsplats keeps early hours, so unless you eat an afternoon
dinner, plan on lunch instead. The cuisine is primarily Swedish and is
simply presented. A big white-china bowl of fish soup and a glass of
white wine here is hard to beat, and you can watch the bustling market activity through the rising steam from your bowl. ⊠ *Saluhallen, Centrum* ☎ *031/137676* ⊟ *AE, MC, V* ☉ *Closed Sun. No dinner.*

WHERE TO STAY

Some hotels close during the winter holidays; call ahead if you expect to
travel during that time. All rooms in the hotels reviewed below are
equipped with shower or bath unless otherwise noted. Göteborg also has
some fine camping sites if you want an alternative to staying in a hotel.

WHAT IT COSTS In Swedish Kronor				
$$$$	**$$$**	**$$**	**$**	**¢**
FOR 2 PEOPLE over 2,900	2,300–2,900	1,500–2,300	1,000–1,500	under 1,000

Prices are for two people in a standard double room in high season.

$$$ 🏨 **Elite Plaza.** A five-minute walk from the central station, the Plaza is
FodorśChoice   one of the smartest hotels in the city. The palatial building, an archi-
★   tectural attraction itself, dates from 1889, and has been modernized with
care to give it an air of grandeur, quality, and restfulness. All original
features have been retained, from the stucco ceilings to the English mo-
saic floors, and are tastefully matched with modern art and up-to-date
guest facilities. Rooms are comfortable and luxurious, with earth tones,
dark-wood furnishings, and beautiful marble-and-tile bathrooms. The
only complaint is that they can be a little on the small side. The hotel
restaurant, Swea Hoff, serves delicious international cuisine, Swedish
specialties, and seafood, and there is a very well-chosen wine list. The
dark, leather-chair-filled bar serves some of the best martinis in the city.
⊠ *Västra Hamng. 3, Box 110 65, Centrum, 404 22* ☎ *031/7204000*
🖷 *031/7204010* 🛏 *143 rooms, 5 suites* ♺ *Restaurant, room service,
a/c, in-room safes, minibars, in-room broadband, in-room data ports,*

Wi-Fi, gym, sauna, bar, pub, convention center, no-smoking rooms ⊟ *AE, DC, MC, V* ⦿ *BP.*

★ $$$ ⌂ **Gothia Towers.** A striking modern hotel with more than 700 rooms in two 23-story glass towers, this is the place to stay for great views over Göteborg, especially from the top-floor sky bar. Rooms here are sleek and urban with clean lines, dark wood, natural stone, and shades of brown and cream. The huge, bright lobby is a great place to watch the world go by. ⊠ *Mässansg. 24, Liseberg, 402 26* ☎ *031/7508800* 🖷 *031/ 7508882* ⦿ *www.gothiatowers.com* ⇘ *704 rooms, 8 suites* ⚘ *3 restaurants, room service, a/c, minibars, room TVs with movies, in-room broadband, Wi-Fi, 2 bars, convention center, meeting rooms, parking (fee), no-smoking rooms* ⊟ *AE, DC, MC, V* ⦿ *BP.*

$$$ ⌂ **Radisson SAS Scandinavia.** Across Drottningtorget from the central train station, the Radisson SAS is a modern and spectacular international hotel. The attractive atrium lobby has two restaurants: Frascati, which serves international cuisine, and the Atrium piano bar, with a lighter menu. Rooms are large and luxurious and decorated in pastel shades. Hotel guests receive a discount at the health club on the premises. ⊠ *Södra Hamng. 5965, Centrum, 401 24* ☎ *031/7585000* 🖷 *031/7585001* ⦿ *www. radisson.com* ⇘ *349 rooms* ⚘ *Restaurant, room service, a/c, minibars, cable TV, room TVs with movies, in-room broadband, in-room data ports, indoor pool, health club, hair salon, piano bar, casino, shops, convention center, travel services, no-smoking rooms* ⊟ *AE, DC, MC, V* ⦿ *BP.*

$$-$$$ ⌂ **Elite Park Avenue.** Now part of the ever-expanding Elite chain of hotels, Elite Park Avenue, a Göteborg institution, has had a thorough upgrade. It still has all the character of a hotel that has played host to everyone from the Beatles and Michael Jackson to George Bush (as confirmed by the brass plaque in the reception), but now it has a more up-to-date quality to brag about. The rooms have a pure, modern simplicity about them, with light fabrics and stylish Scandinavian furniture. ⊠ *Kungsportsavenyn 3638, Box 53233, Götaplatsen, 400 16* ☎ *031/7271000* 🖷 *031/7271010* ⦿ *www.elite.se* ⇘ *318 rooms, 10 suites* ⚘ *2 restaurants, room service, a/c, minibars, cable TV, room TVs with movies, in-room broadband, in-room data ports, gym, bar, meeting room, no-smoking floors* ⊟ *AE, DC, MC, V* ⦿ *BP.*

$$ ⌂ **Best Western Hotel Riverton.** Convenient for people arriving in the city by ferry, this hotel is close to the European terminals and overlooks the harbor. Built in 1985, it has a glossy marble floor and reflective ceiling in the lobby. Rooms are decorated with abstract-pattern textiles and whimsical prints. ⊠ *Stora Badhusg. 26, Kungshöjd, 411 21* ☎ *031/7501000* 🖷 *031/7501001* ⦿ *www.bestwestern.com* ⇘ *191 rooms* ⚘ *Restaurant, room service, in-room broadband, hot tub, sauna, bar, meeting room, free parking, no-smoking rooms* ⊟ *AE, DC, MC, V* ⦿ *BP.*

★ $$ ⌂ **Eggers.** Dating from 1859, Best Western's Eggers may have more character and charm than any other hotel in the city. It is a minute's walk from the train station and was probably the last port of call in Sweden for many emigrants to the United States. Rooms vary in size, and all are beautifully decorated, often with antiques. A complimentary buffet breakfast is the only meal served. ⊠ *Drottningtorget, Box 323, Centrum, 401 25* ☎ *031/806070* 🖷 *031/154243* ⦿ *www.bestwestern.com*

➫ *65 rooms* ♨ *Cable TV, meeting room, no-smoking rooms* ⊟ *AE, DC, MC, V* ✹ *BP.*

$$ 🔳 **Europa.** This large hotel is part of the Nordstan mall complex, very close to the central train station. The rooms are modern, airy, and colorful, if a little standardized. Some rooms have data ports; ask for one of these if it's a consideration. Service throughout is efficient and friendly. ✉ *Köpmansg. 38, Nordstan, 411 06* ☎ *031/7516500* 🖷 *031/7516511* ⊕ *www.scandic-hotels.com* ➫ *450 rooms, 5 suites* ♨ *Restaurant, cable TV, indoor pool, sauna, some in-room data ports, convention center, parking (fee), no-smoking floor* ⊟ *AE, DC, MC, V* ✹ *BP.*

$$ 🔳 **Novotel.** The redbrick industrial-age architecture of this old brewery belies a mishmash of architectural styles inside. As it is situated just west of the city on the Göta Älv, the top floors afford spectacular views of Göteborg. Rooms are plain with deep-red curtains and wood floors. There's a large central atrium, complete with obligatory fake foliage, with a restaurant, Carnegie Kay, attached. ✉ *Klippan 1, Majorna, 414 51* ☎ *031/149000* 🖷 *031/422232* ⊕ *www.novotel.se* ➫ *148 rooms, 5 suites* ♨ *Restaurant, cable TV, in-room data ports, sauna, bar, free parking, no-smoking rooms* ⊟ *AE, DC, MC, V* ✹ *BP.*

$$ 🔳 **Opalen.** If you are attending an event at the Scandinavium, or if you have children and are heading for the Liseberg amusement park, this hotel is ideally located. Rooms are bright and modern, with wood floors and pastel fabrics. ✉ *Engelbrektsg. 73, Box 5106, Liseberg, 402 23* ☎ *031/7515300* 🖷 *031/7515311* ⊕ *www.scandic-hotels.com* ➫ *242 rooms, 8 suites* ♨ *Restaurant, room service, minibars, room TVs with movies, in-room broadband, Wi-Fi, sauna, bar, parking (fee), no-smoking floors* ⊟ *AE, DC, MC, V* ✹ *BP.*

$$ 🔳 **Quality Hotel 11.** On the water's edge in Eriksberg, Hotel 11 combines the warehouse style of the old waterfront with a modern interior of multitier terraces. Commonly used by large companies for business conferences, the hotel also welcomes families that want to stay across the harbor from downtown Göteborg. The rooms are clean, bright, and modern; some offer panoramic views of the harbor. Next door is Eriksbergshallen, a theater and conference hall that hosts international performances. ✉ *Masking. 11, 417 64 Eriksberg, (from city follow signs to Norra Älvstranden)* ☎ *031/7791111* 🖷 *031/7791110* ⊕ *www. hotel11.se* ➫ *184 rooms, 8 suites* ♨ *Restaurant, in-room data ports, Wi-Fi, sauna, bar, meeting room, no-smoking rooms* ⊟ *AE, DC, MC, V* ✹ *BP.*

$ 🔳 **Liseberg Heden.** Not far from the famous Liseberg amusement park, Liseberg Heden is a popular family hotel in the Rica Hotels chain. Each of the modern rooms has light-color walls, a satellite television, a minibar, and a large desk; most rooms also have wood floors and primary-color geometric wall hangings. Perks include a sauna and a very good restaurant. ✉ *Sten Stureg., Liseberg, 411 38* ☎ *031/7506900* 🖷 *031/ 7506930* ⊕ *www.rica.se* ➫ *184 rooms* ♨ *Restaurant, minibars, cable TV, in-room broadband, sauna, meeting room, no-smoking rooms* ⊟ *AE, DC, MC, V* ✹ *BP.*

$ 🔳 **Excelsior.** Although a little worn around the edges, this stylish 1880 building on a street of classic Göteborg houses is the place to stay to get some character and history. The Excelsior has been in operation since 1930, and its guest rooms are full of homey comfort and faded grandeur. They tend to a be little dark, though, not helped by the heavy, dark fabrics that pervade throughout. Greta Garbo and Ingrid Bergman both stayed here, and, more recently, so did musician Sheryl Crow. Classic suites—Garbo's was number 535—with splendid 19th-century style cost no more than ordinary rooms. ⊠ *Karl Gustavsg. 7, Vasastan, 411 25* ☎ *031/175435* 🖷 *031/175439* ⊕ *www.hotelexcelsior.nu* 🛏 *64 rooms, 3 suites* 🍴 *Restaurant, cable TV, bar, no-smoking room* ☰ *AE, DC, MC, V* 🍴 *BP.*

★ $ 🖼 **Royal.** Göteborg's oldest hotel, built in 1852, is small, family owned, and traditional. Make a stop in the entrance hall to admire the intricate, original ceiling paintings. Rooms, most with parquet floors and their original stuccowork, are individually decorated with reproductions of elegant Swedish traditional furniture. The Royal is in the city center a few blocks from the central train station. ⊠ *Drottningg. 67, Centrum, 411 07* ☎ *031/7001170* 🖷 *031/7001179* ⊕ *www.hotel-royal.com* 🛏 *84 rooms* 🍴 *Cable TV, no-smoking floor* ☰ *AE, DC, MC, V* 🍴 *BP.*

¢ 🖼 **Göteborgs Vandrarhem.** This hostel is 5 km (3 mi) from the train station in a modern apartment block. Rooms are very basic, with Swedish-designed furnishings. Breakfast (SKr 55) is not included in the rates, which are per person in a shared apartment. ⊠ *Mölndalsv. 23, Liseberg, 412 63* ☎ *031/401050* 🖷 *031/401151* ⊕ *www.goteborgsvandrarhem.se* 🛏 *150 beds, 4- to 6-bed apartments* ☰ *MC, V.*

¢ 🖼 **Lilton.** This unobtrusive bed-and-breakfast-style hotel is inside a small, ivy-covered brick building. Rooms are simple and comfortable, the service friendly and unfussy. ⊠ *Föreningsg. 9, Vasastan, 411 27* ☎ *031/828808* 🖷 *031/822184* ⊕ *www.lilton.se* 🛏 *14 rooms* 🍴 *No room TVs, no smoking* ☰ *AE, MC, V* 🍴 *CP.*

¢ 🖼 **Partille Vandrarhem.** This hostel is in a pleasant old house 15 km (9 mi) outside the city, next to a lake for swimming. Rooms here are very basic, with simple plastic-mat flooring and a bed to call your own. Still, it's the location that counts. You can order meals or prepare them yourself in the guest kitchen. Room rates are per person based on two or more people sharing a room. ⊠ *Landvetterv., 433 24 Partille* ☎ *031/446501* 🖷 *031/446163* 🛏 *120 beds, 2- to 4-bed rooms* 🍴 *Free parking* ☰ *No credit cards.*

NIGHTLIFE & THE ARTS

Music, Opera & Theater

Home of the highly acclaimed Göteborg Symphony Orchestra, **Konserthuset** (⊠ Götaplatsen ☎ 031/7265300) has a mural by Sweden's Prince Eugen in the lobby, original decor, and Swedish-designed furniture from 1935. **Operan** (⊠ Christina Nilssons gata, Packhuskajen ☎ 031/108000), where Göteborg's opera company performs, incorporates a 1,250-seat auditorium with a glassed-in dining area overlooking the harbor. **Stadsteatern** (⊠ Johannebergsg. 1, Götaplatsen ☎ 031/615050 tickets, 031/615100 information) puts on high-quality productions of classics by

Shakespeare, Molière, Ibsen, and other playwrights. Most of its plays are performed in Swedish.

Nightlife

Bars

Hipsters should head to **Barsiden** (⌂ Kungsportsavenyn 5, Centrum ☎ 031/7111541), a painfully chic, minimalist bar where the city's beautiful ones pull up designer stools. Go to **Bitter** (⌂ Linnëg. 59, Linnë ☎ 031/249120) and you will leave with a taste that is anything but. The cocktails in this mirror-lined, darkened bar are superb. Big spenders can splash on the whiskey cocktail Bigg Mamma, a bargain at SKr 600. As its name implies, **The Dubliner** (⌂ Östra Hamng. 50, Inom Vallgraven ☎ 031/139020) is a brave attempt at re-creating what the locals imagine to be old Irish charm. It's the perfect place for a relaxed pint and a chat with the locals. **Napoleon** (⌂ Vasag. 11, Vasastan ☎ 031/137550) is a dark, mellow hangout crowded with oddities. Even the exterior walls are covered in paintings. If you're looking for an urbane bar, try **Nivå** (⌂ Kungsportsavenyn 9, Centrum ☎ 031/7018090), a popular bar with a stylish tile interior and a crowd to match. **Uppåt Framåt** (⌂ Magasingatan 3, Centrum ☎ 031/138755) has no pretensions to be anything other than a stylish, welcoming, super-friendly bar serving excellent cocktails in a cushion-filled lounge—something it achieves very well.

Discos & Cabaret

The **Cabaret Lorensberg** (⌂ Elite Park Avenue Hotel, Kungsportsavenyn 36, Centrum ☎ 031/206058) plays traditional and contemporary music and has song and dance performances by gifted artists. **Deep** (⌂ Kungsportsavenyn 15, Centrum ☎ No phone) is a hot and bustling club packed with thirtysomethings. The roof bar offers an often-welcome fresh-air break. At **Rondo** (⌂ Örgrytev. 5, Liseberg ☎ 031/400200) you can dance the night away on Sweden's largest dance floor while surrounded by people of all ages. The crowd is always friendly, and there's a live band. One of the city's liveliest haunts is **Trädgårn** (⌂ Nya Allén, Centrum ☎ 031/102080), a complex of five bars, a disco, and show bands housed in a strange building resembling a half-built sauna.

Jazz Clubs

Performers at **Jazzhuset** (⌂ Eric Dahlbergsg. 3, Vasastan ☎ 031/133544) tend to play traditional, swing, and Dixieland jazz. Modern jazz enthusiasts usually head for **Nefertiti** (⌂ Hvitfeldtsplatsen 6, Centrum ☎ 031/7111533), the trendy, shadowy club where the line to get in is always long.

Film

Like all Swedish cinemas, the ones in Göteborg show mostly English-language films. The films are subtitled, never dubbed. The strangest movie theater in town is **Bio Palatset** (⌂ Kungstorget, Centrum ☎ 031/174500), a converted meat market turned into a 10-screen cinema. The walls are in various clashing fruit colors, and the floodlighted foyer has sections scooped out to reveal Göteborg's natural rock. **Hagabion** (⌂ Linnég. 21,

Linnéstaden ☎ 031/428810) is a good art-house cinema housed in an old ivy-covered school.

SPORTS & THE OUTDOORS

Beaches

There are several excellent local beaches. The two most popular—though they're rarely crowded—are Askim and Näset. To reach Askim, take the Express Blå bus from the central station bus terminal. It's a 10-km (6-mi) journey south of the city center. For Näset, catch Bus 19 from Brunnsparken for the 11-km (7-mi) journey southwest of Göteborg.

Diving

The water on the west coast of Sweden, although colder than that on the east coast, is a lot clearer: it's great for diving around rocks and wrecks. Wrap up for a dive and bring your diving certificate. Among the many companies offering diving is **Aqua Divers** (⊠ G. Turev. 20 ☎ 031/220030).

Fishing

Mackerel fishing is popular here. The **MS *Daisy*** (☎ 031/963018), which leaves from Hjuvik on the Hisingen side of the Göta River, takes expeditions into the archipelago. If you are in town from the first Monday after the third Sunday in September through to May, you are there during lobster season. The *Daisy* also runs lobster fishing trips; this is your chance to catch the sweetest-tasting lobster in the world. With plenty of salmon, perch, and pike, the rivers and lakes in the area have much to offer. For details call Göteborg's **Sportfiskarnas Fishing Information Line** (☎ 031/7730700).

Golf

Chalmers Golfklubb (⊠ Härrydav. 50, Landvetter ☎ 031/918430) was initially a golf club for Göteborg's Technical University, but is now open to the public. It has an 18-hole course, one of the area's best. All players are welcome, but as with all Swedish courses, you must have a handicap certificate to play. Among the many golf courses surrounding Göteborg, **Göteborgs Golfklubb** (⊠ Golfbanev. 17, Hovås ☎ 031/282444) is Sweden's oldest golf club. It has an 18-hole course.

Indoor Swimming

Hagabadet (⊠ Södra Allég. 3, Haga ☎ 031/600600) is a calming sanctuary with a stunning art-nouveau pool, as well as a relaxing sauna and steam area. For something a little more lively, **Vatten Palatset** (⊠ Häradsv. 3, Lerum ☎ 0302/17020) is a decent indoor pool. As well as regular swimming, this huge complex offers indoor and outdoor adventure pools, waterslides, water jets, wave pools, bubble pools, and saunas.

Running

Many running tracks wind their way around Göteborg, but to reach the most beautiful one, hop on Tram 8 at Gamelstadstorget and take it to Angered Centrum. Here the **Angered and Lärjeåns Dalgång** winds its way through 8 km (5 mi) of leafy forests and undulating pastures.

SHOPPING

Department Stores

Åhléns (☎ 031/3334000), a national chain of mid-priced department stores, is in the Nordstan mall. For something much more upmarket (and more expensive), try the local branch of **NK** (✉ Östra Hamng. 42, Centrum ☎ 031/7101000) for men's and women's fashions and excellent household goods.

Specialty Stores

Antiques

Antikhallarna (Antiques Halls; ✉ Västra Hamng. 6, Centrum ☎ 031/7741525) has one of Scandinavia's largest antiques selections. Sweden's leading auction house, **Bukowskis** (✉ Kungsportsavenyn 43, Centrum ☎ 031/200360), is on Avenyn. For a memorable antiques-buying experience, check out **Göteborgs Auktionsverk** (✉ Tredje Långg. 9, Linnéstaden ☎ 031/7047700). There's a large amount of very good silver, porcelain, and jewelry hidden among the more trashy items. Viewings on Friday 10–2, Saturday 10–noon, and Sunday 11–noon precede the auctions on Saturday and Sunday starting at noon.

Crafts

Excellent examples of local arts and crafts can be bought at **Bohusslöjden** (✉ Kungsportsavenyn 25, Centrum ☎ 031/160072). If you are looking to buy Swedish arts and crafts and glassware, visit the various shops in **Kronhusbodarna** (✉ Kronhusg. 1D, Nordstan ☎ 031/7110832). They have been selling traditional, handcrafted quality goods, including silver and gold jewelry, watches, and handblown glass, since the 18th century.

Interior Design

★ If you love the cool, sleek Scandinavian interiors you see on your travels, head to **Room** (✉ Magasing. 3, Centrum ☎ 031/606630), whose rooms are tastefully stuffed with furniture, fabrics, soft furnishings, ornaments, and kitchen gadgets—all of it divine.

Men's Clothing

STUK (✉ Södra Larmg. 16, Centrum ☎ 031/130842) sells what they describe as tailored denim, which means jeans, jackets, and trousers in denim and cotton for the semiformal but fashion-conscious shopper. **Ströms** (✉ Kungsg. 2729, Centrum ☎ 031/177100) has occupied its street-corner location for two generations, offering clothing of high quality and good taste.

Women's Clothing

H & M (Hennes & Mauritz; ✉ Kungsg. 5557, Centrum ☎ 031/3399555) sells clothes roughly comparable to the choices at flashier Old Navy or Marks & Spencer. **Moms** (✉ Vasag. 15, Vasastan ☎ 031/7113280) is a must for trendy street wear, with an excellent range of Nudie Jeans, the cool label born in Göteborg. **Ströms** (✉ Kungsg. 27–29, Centrum ☎ 031/177100) offers clothing of high quality and mildly conservative style.

Food Markets

There are several large food markets in the city area, but the most impressive is **Saluhallen** (✉ Kungsgtorget, Centrum ☎ 031/7117878). Built in 1889, the barrel-roof, wrought-iron, glass, and brick building stands like a monument to industrial architecture. Everything is available here, from fish, meat, and bakery products to deli foods, herbs and spices, coffee, cheese, and even just people-watching.

GÖTEBORG A TO Z

AIR TRAVEL TO & FROM GÖTEBORG

CARRIERS Among the airlines operating to and from Göteborg are Air France, British Airways, City Airline, Finnair, Fly Nordic, KLM, Malmö Aviation, SAS, and SN Brussels Airlines.

🛈 **Air France** ☎ 08/51999990. **British Airways** ☎ 0770/110020. **City Airline** ☎ 0200/250500. **Finnair** ☎ 0771/781100. **Fly Nordic** ☎ 08/52806820 **KLM** ☎ 08/58799757. **Malmö Aviation** ☎ 020/550010. **SAS** ☎ 0770/727727. **SN Brussels Airlines** ☎ 08/58536547.

AIRPORTS & TRANSFERS

Landvetter Airport is approximately 26 km (16 mi) from the city.

🛈 **Landvetter Airport** ☎ 031/941100 🌐 www.lfv.se.

AIRPORT TRANSFERS Landvetter is linked to Göteborg by freeway. Buses leave Landvetter every 15–30 minutes and arrive 30 minutes later at Nils Ericsonsplatsen by the central train station, with stops at Lisebergsstationen, Korsvägen, the Elite Park Avenue, and Kungsportsplatsen; weekend schedules include some nonstop departures. The price of the trip is SKr 70. For more information, call Flygbussarna.

The taxi ride to the city center should cost no more than SKr 325.

🛈 **Flygbussarna** ☎ 0771/414300. **Scandinavian Limousine** ☎ 031/7942424. **Taxi Göteborg** ☎ 031/650000.

BOAT & FERRY TRAVEL

Traveling the entire length of the Göta Canal by passenger boat to Stockholm takes between four and six days. For details contact the Göta Kanalbolaget or Rederi AB Göta Kanal.

🛈 **AB Göta Kanalbolaget** ☎ 0141/202050 🌐 www.gotakanal.se. **Rederi AB Göta Kanal** ✉ Pusterviksg. 13, 413 01 ☎ 031/806315 🌐 www.gotacanal.se.

BUS TRAVEL TO & FROM GÖTEBORG

All buses arrive in the central city area, in the bus station next to the central train station. The principal bus company is Swebus, the national company based in Stockholm.

🚍 **Swebus Express** ☎ 0200/218218 ⊕ www.swebusexpress.se.

CAR RENTAL

Avis, Hertz, and Europcar have offices at the airport and the central railway station.

🚍 **Avis** ☎ 031/946030 at airport, 031/805780 at central railway station. **Europcar** ☎ 031/947100. **Hertz** ☎ 031/946020.

CAR TRAVEL

Göteborg is reached by car either via the E20 or the E4 highway from Stockholm (495 km [307 mi]) from the east, or on the E6/E20 coastal highway from the south (Malmö is 290 km [180 mi] away). Markings are excellent, and roads are well sanded and plowed in winter.

CONSULATES

🚍 United Kingdom ✉ S. Hamng. 23, Centrum ☎ 031/3393300.

EMERGENCIES

Dial 112 for emergencies anywhere in the country, or dial the emergency services number listed below day or night for information on medical services. Emergencies are handled by the Mölndalssjukhuset, Östra Sjukhuset, and Sahlgrenska hospitals. There is a private medical service at CityAkuten weekdays 8–6. There is a 24-hour children's emergency service at Östra Sjukhuset as well.

The national dental-service emergency number and the private dental-service number are listed below. The national service is available 8–8 on weekdays, and the private service weekdays between 8 and 5; for after-hours emergencies contact a hospital.

🚍 **Folktandvården Dental-Service Emergencies** ☎ 031/807800. **Tandakuten Private Dental Services** ☎ 031/800500.

🚍 **Medical Services Information (SOS Alarm)** ☎ 031/7031500.

🚍 **After-hours emergencies** ☎ 08/4073000. **CityAkuten** ✉ Drottningg. 45, Centrum ☎ 031/101010. **Mölndalssjukhuset** ☎ 031/3431000. **Östra Sjukhuset** ☎ 031/3434000. **Sahlgrenska Hospital** ☎ 031/3421000.

🚍 24-Hour Pharmacy **Vasen** ✉ Götg. 12, in Nordstan shopping mall, Nordstan ☎ 0771/450450.

ENGLISH-LANGUAGE MEDIA

BOOKS Nearly all bookshops stock English-language books. The broadest selection is at Akademibokhandeln.

🚍 Bookstores **Akademibokhandeln** ✉ Postg. 26-32, Nordstan ☎ 031/150284 ✉ Norra Hamng. 26, Nordstan ☎ 031/617030.

LODGING

CAMPING Göteborg has several fine camping sites.

🚍 **Askim** ☎ 031/286261 Askim Strand 🏕 031/681335. **Göteborg** ☎ 031/840200 Kärralund 🏕 031/840500. **Uddevalla** ☎ 0522/644117 Hafstens Camping.

TAXIS
Taxi Göteborg is the main local taxi company.
🔟 **Taxi Göteborg** ☎ 031/650000.

TOURS
BOAT TOURS   For a view of the city from the water and an expert commentary on its
sights and history in English and German, take one of the Paddan sightseeing boats. *Paddan* is Swedish for "toad," an apt commentary on the
vessels' squat appearance. The boats pass under 20 bridges and take in
both the canals and part of the Göta River.
🔟 **Paddan** ✉ Kungsportsplatsen, Centrum ☎ 031/609670 ⌧ SKr 95.

BUS TOURS   A 90-minute bus tour and a two-hour combination boat-and-bus tour
of the chief points of interest leave from outside the main tourist office
at Kungsportsplatsen every day from mid-May through August and on
Saturday in April, September, and October. Call the tourist office for
schedules.

TRAIN TRAVEL
There is regular service from Stockholm to Göteborg, which takes a little over 4½ hours, as well as frequent high-speed (X2000) train service,
which takes about 3 hours. All trains arrive at the central train station
in Drottningtorget, downtown Göteborg. For schedules call SJ, the
Swedish national rail company. Streetcars and buses leave from here for
the suburbs, but the hub for all streetcar traffic is a block down Norra
Hamngatan, at Brunnsparken.
🔟 **SJ** ☎ 0771/757575 ⊕ www.sj.se.

TRANSPORTATION AROUND GÖTEBORG
Stadstrafiken is the name of Göteborg's excellent transit service. Transit brochures, which are available in English, explain the various discount passes and procedures; you can pick one up at a TidPunkten office.

The best bet for the tourist is the Göteborg Pass, which covers free use
of public transport, various sightseeing trips, and admission to Liseberg
and local museums, among other benefits. The card costs SKr 175 for
one day and SKr 295 for two days; there are lower rates for children
younger than 18. You can buy the Göteborg Pass as well as regular tram
and bus passes at Pressbyrån shops, camping sites, and the tourist information offices.
🔟 **TidPunkten** ✉ Drottningtorget, Brunnsparken, and Nils Ericsonsplatsen, Centrum
☎ 0771/414300.

TRAVEL AGENCIES
See the *Yellow Pages* under "Resor-Resebyråer."
🔟 Local Agent Referrals **Carlson Wagonlit Travel** ✉ Kronhusg. 7, Nordstan ☎ 031/
7563700 **Ticket Travel Agency** ✉ Östra Hamng. 35, Centrum ☎ 031/176860.

VISITOR INFORMATION
The main tourist office is Göteborg's Turistbyrå in Kungsportsplatsen.
There are also offices at the Nordstan shopping center and in front of
the central train station at Drottningtorget.

A free English-language newspaper with listings called *Metro* is available in summer; you can pick it up at tourist offices, shopping centers, and some restaurants, as well as on streetcars.

The Friday edition of the principal morning newspaper, *Göteborgs Posten,* includes a weekend supplement with entertainment listings—it's in Swedish but is reasonably easy to decipher.

Göteborg's Turistbyrå's Web site has a good events calendar.

The Göteborg Pass, available from the Göteborg tourist office, and on their Web site, offers discounts and savings for sights, restaurants, hotels, and other services around the city.

Göteborg's Turistbyrå ✉ Kungsportsplatsen 2, 411 10 ☎ 031/612500 🖷 031/612501 ⊕ www.goteborg.com. **Nordstan shopping center** ✉ Nordstadstorget, 411 05 ☎ 031/612500.

Side Trips from Göteborg

5

WORD OF MOUTH

"In Varmland, a breathtaking province known for its forests and lakes, my 10-year-old would get out of the car to run on large stretches of empty roads, which were surrounded by rolling hills blanketed in wild flowers."

—kflodin

"The coast between Göteborg and the Norwegian border is very beautiful. It has a lot in common with the coast of Maine—lots of granite rocks and lobster fishing. Don't miss the towns of Fjällbacka and Grebbestad"

—Daniel

BOHUSLÄN

Updated by
Rob Hincks

IT WAS FROM THE ROCKY, RUGGED SHORES of Bohuslän that the 9th- and 10th-century Vikings sailed southward on their epic voyages. This coastal region north of Göteborg provides a foretaste of Norway's fjords farther north. Small towns and lovely fishing villages nestle among the distinctively rounded granite rocks and the thousands of skerries (rocky isles or reefs) and larger islands that form Sweden's western archipelago. The ideal way to explore the area is by drifting slowly north of Göteborg, taking full advantage of the uncluttered beaches and small rustic fishing villages. Painters and sailors haunt the region in summer.

Kungälv

❶ *15 km (9 mi) north of Göteborg.*

Though today it is something of a bedroom community for Göteborg, Kungälv was an important battleground in ancient times, strategically placed at the confluence of the two arms of the Göta River. The town's several historic sights include a white wooden church, dating from 1679, with an unusual baroque interior. Narrow cobbled streets are full of ancient, leaning wooden houses.

The trip from Göteborg takes you first along the Göta Älv, a wide waterway that 10,000 years ago, when the ice cap melted, was a great fjord. Some 30 minutes into the voyage the boat passes below a rocky escarpment, topped by the remains of **Bohus Fästning** (Bohus Castle), distinguished by two round towers known as Father's Hat and Mother's Bonnet. It dates from the 14th century and was once the mightiest fortress in western Scandinavia, commanding the confluence of the Göta Älv and Nordre Älv rivers. It was strengthened and enlarged in the 16th century and successfully survived 14 sieges. From 1678 onward, the castle began to lose its strategic and military importance; it fell into decay until 1838, when King Karl XIV passed by on a river journey, admired the old fortress, and ordered its preservation.

For a sense of Kungälv's military past, first visit the ruins of **Bohus Fästning** (Bohus Castle). ☎ *030/15662* ⌨ *SKr 35* ☉ *Apr., weekends 11–5; May–Aug., daily 10–7; Sept., daily 11–5.*

Just north of Kungälv along the Trollhätte Canal stretch is the quiet village of **Lödöse,** once a major trading settlement and a predecessor of Göteborg. From here, the countryside becomes wilder, with pines and oaks clustered thickly on either bank between cliffs of lichen-covered granite.

Sports & the Outdoors

The tiny village of Rönang, on the island of Tjörn, offers excellent **deep-sea fishing;** mackerel and cod are among the prized catches. There are several companies that can take you out, usually in a boat that holds 12 people. One of the best outfitters is **Havsfiske med Hajen** (⊠ Hamnen, Marstrand ☎ 0304/672447). Most boats leave twice daily. To get to Tjörn, drive over the road bridge from Stenungsund, just north of Kungälv on the E6.

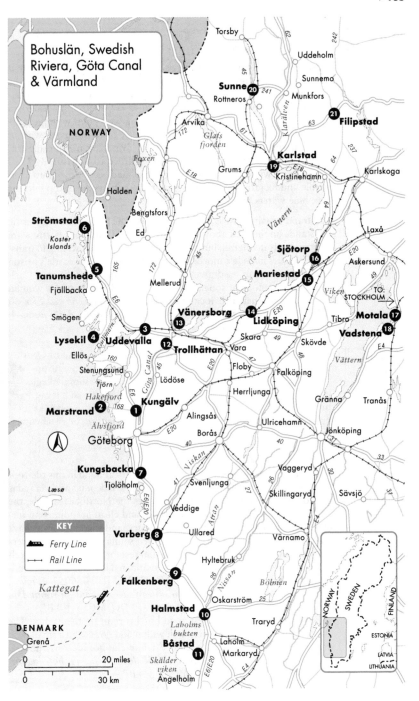

Bohuslän, Swedish Riviera, Göta Canal & Värmland

NORWAY

Torsby
Uddeholm
Sunnemo
Munkfors
Sunne ⓴
Rottneros
241
Arvika
Glafs fjorden
Foxen
Grums
Karlstad ⓳
Kristinehamn
Filipstad ㉑
Karlskoga
Halden
Bengtsfors
Strömstad ⑥
Koster Islands
Ed
Vänern
Laxå
Sjötorp ⑯
Askersund
Tanumshede ⑤
Fjällbacka
Mellerud
Mariestad ⑮
Viken
TO: STOCKHOLM
Smögen
Vänersborg ⑬
Lidköping ⑭
Tibro
Motala ⑰
Lysekil ④ Uddevalla ③
Skara
Skövde
Vadstena ⑱
Ellös
Stenungsund
Trollhättan ⑫
Vara
Floby
Falköping
Vättern
Tjörn
Lödöse
Herrljunga
Gränna
Tranås
Hakefjord
Kungälv ①
Marstrand ②
Alingsås
Ulricehamn
Jönköping
Älvsfjord
Göteborg
Borås
Kungsbacka ⑦
Tjolöholm
Vaggeryd
Svenljunga
Skillingaryd
Sävsjö
Læsø
Veddige
Ullared
Värnamo
Varberg ⑧
Hyltebruk
Bölmen
Falkenberg ⑨
Oskarström
Kattegat
Halmstad ⑩
Traryd
DENMARK
Laholms bukten
Grenå
Båstad ⑪
Laholm
Markaryd
Ängelholm

KEY
⚓ Ferry Line
├─┼─┤ Rail Line

0 ___ 20 miles
0 ___ 30 km

NORWAY SWEDEN FINLAND
ESTONIA
LATVIA
LITHUANIA

Marstrand

❷ *17 km (11 mi) west of Kungälv (via Rte. 168).*

Unusually high stocks of herring used to swim in the waters around Marstrand, which is on an island of the same name. The fish made the town extremely rich. But after the money came greed and corruption: in the 16th century Marstrand became known as the most immoral town in Scandinavia, a reputation that reached its lowest point with the murder of a town cleric in 1586. Soon after this the town burned down and the fish disappeared. As Göteborg and Kungälv became major trade centers, in the early 19th century Marstrand turned to tourism. By 1820 all the town's wooden herring-salting houses had been turned into fashionable and lucrative bathhouses, and people still come to dip into the clear, blue waters and swim, sail, and fish.

Marstrand's main draw is **Carlstens Fästning,** the huge stone-wall castle that stands on the rock above the town. Tours of Carlstens Fortress are not completely in English, but most guides are more than willing to translate. The tours include a morbidly fascinating look at the castle's prison cells, where you can see drawings done in blood and hear tales of Carlstens's most famous prisoner, Lasse-Maja—he dressed up as a woman to seduce and then rob local farmers. ☎ *0303/60265* 🗐 *SKr 60* ☉ *June–mid-Aug., daily 11–6; mid-Aug.–end of Aug., daily noon–4; Sept.–May, weekends 11–4.*

off the beaten path

GULLHOLMEN – A frequent ferry from Ellös, on the island of Orust, will take you on the short ride to the windswept, rugged clifftops of the small island of Gullholmen. In its 13th-century fishing village, tiny, red-painted wooden houses huddle together around a large church. The rest of Gullholmen is set aside as a nature reserve that supports bird life of all kinds. The island of Orust can be reached via Route 160 off E6.

Where to Stay & Eat

$$ ✕🏨 **Grand Hotell Marstrand.** History and luxury abound in this tile-roof hotel, which resembles a French château. Large balconies and verandas open onto a small park, beyond which lies the North Sea. Inside, the hotel is stylishly simple, with bold colors and clean Scandinavian furniture. The rooms are equally light and airy, and the bathrooms have white tiles and brass fittings. A windowed sauna in one of the towers looks out over the harbor. The traditional restaurant ($$) serves excellent local seafood specialties: the garlic-marinated langoustine is a standout. ✉ *Rådhusg. 2, 440 30* ☎ *0303/60322* 🖴 *0303/60053* ⊕ *www. grandmarstrand.se* 🛏 *22 rooms, 6 suites* ⚒ *Restaurant, in-room data ports, sauna, bar, convention center* ▤ *AE, DC, MC, V* ⦿ *BP.*

$ 🏨 **Hotell Nautic.** This basic but good hotel is right on the harbor. The rooms are quite plain but functional, with wood floors and a small desk and chair. The building is a classic white-clapboard construction. ✉ *Långg. 6, 440 35* ☎ *0303/61030* 🖴 *0303/61200* ⊕ *www.hotellnautic. com* 🛏 *29 rooms* ▤ *AE, DC, MC, V* ⦿ *BP.*

Nightlife

Among the usual peppering of provincial drinking places, **Marstrands Värd-shus** (✉ Hamng. 23 ☎ 0303/60369) stands out as one of the best. The large outdoor veranda is the perfect place to soak up some late-evening summer rays while you enjoy the glitzy crowd around you.

Sports & the Outdoors

The coastline around Marstrand looks most beautiful from the water. **Franckes Marina** (✉ Södra Strandg. ☎ 0303/61584 ⊕ www.franckes.se) will rent you a boat, complete with captain, for cocktails, sightseeing, and fishing. It costs about SKr 1,500 for a two-hour excursion and SKr 650 for each additional hour. Fishing equipment is available for SKr 75 per person.

Shopping

The center of Marstrand is full of ancient cobbled streets, pastel-painted wooden houses, and arts-and-crafts shops selling locally inspired paint-ings, handicrafts, and ceramics. Else Langkilde of **Konstnärsateljé Langk-ilde** (✉ Myren 71 ☎ 0703/965131) paints intriguingly with vivid colors. Worth a visit is **Mary Carlsson** (✉ Kungsg. 2–4 ☎ 0303/60507), who does a fine line of ceramics and gift items.

Uddevalla

❸ *64 km (40 mi) north of Kungälv, 79 km (49 mi) north of Göteborg.*

A former shipbuilding town located at the head of a fjord, Uddevalla is best known for a 1657 battle between the Danes and the Swedes. Heavy rains doused the musketeers' tinderboxes, effectively ending hostilities.

The history of the entire Bohuslän region can be seen at the **Bohusläns Museum.** Exhibitions reflect the local culture, countryside, and indus-tries, including, of course, fishing. The museum also traces the history of local inhabitants over the 10,000 years since people first settled this part of Sweden. ✉ *Museeg. 1* ☎ *0522/656500* ⊕ *www.bohusmus.se* 🎟 *Free* 🕐 *Mon.–Thurs. 10–8, Fri.–Sun. 10–4.*

off the beaten path

GUSTAFSBERG – Adjoining Uddevalla to the west, Gustafberg lays claim to being Sweden's oldest seaside resort, having been mentioned by the botanist Linnaeus in a book he wrote in 1746. There is little left to see of the resort now, save the richly ornamented wooden Society House and a few 18th-century villas, but there is a beautiful little park that leads down to the water's edge, a perfect place for a refreshing swim.

Ten thousand years ago, receding land ice formed the unique shell banks, the world's largest, just outside Uddevalla. When the 1-km-thick (½-mi-thick) ice melted, huge masses of water mixed with saltwater from the sea and left behind fossils from more than 100 species. **Skalbanksmuseet,** the Shell Bank Museum, organizes guided walks in the shell banks every Monday. ✉ *Kurödsv. 1* ☎ *0522/13891* 🎟 *Museum free, guided tours SKr 30* 🕐 *Apr. and May, weekends 11–5; June–Aug., daily 11–5; Sept., weekends 11–5. Mon. tour time varies.*

Where to Stay

$ 🏨 **Bohusgården.** From its cliff-top location, this modern concrete-block hotel has stunning views of the sea. But even though the rooms are comfortable, they're not that inspiring. The plain, cold, and basic furnishings make them livable but not very welcoming. It is the spa that attracts guests. Pampering treatments include facials, mineral-water baths, massages, and more opulent services. ⊠ *Nordens väg 6, 451 43* ☎ *0522/36420* 🖷 *0522/34472* ⊕ *www.bohusgarden.se* 🛏 *133 rooms* ♨ *Restaurant, pool, spa, bar, meeting rooms, free parking, no-smoking rooms* 🞸 *AE, DC, MC, V* ⎹⊚⎸ *BP.*

$ 🏨 **Carlia.** A hotel by this name has been in Uddevalla for more than 100 years in one form or another. In its latest guise it has large comfortable rooms with furnishings and fabrics that are a touch on the floral side; a homey bar; and a well-equipped reading area with books, newspapers, and periodicals. All the suites have whirlpool tubs. ⊠ *N. Drottningg. 26, 451 31* ☎ *0522/14140* 🖷 *0522/17081* ⊕ *www.carlia.com* 🛏 *114 rooms, 7 suites* ♨ *In-room broadband, in-room data ports, sauna, bar, library, meeting rooms, free parking* 🞸 *AE, DC, MC, V* ⎹⊚⎸ *BP.*

Lysekil

❹ *30 km (19 mi) west of Uddevalla via E6 and Rte. 161.*

Perched on a peninsula at the head of Gullmarn Fjord, Lysekil has been one of Sweden's most popular summer resorts since the 19th century, when the wealthiest citizens of Sweden would come to take the therapeutic waters. Back then, the small resort was made up mainly of fancy villas painted mustard and brown. Today you can still see the original houses, but among them now are amusement arcades and cotton-candy stalls.

The surrounding coastline has great, rugged walking trails. These trails offer stunning views of the undulating skerries and islets that dot the water below. Guided botanical and marine walks can be organized by the **tourist office** (☎ 0523/13050).

Havets Hus (House of the Sea) concentrates on the fish and other sea life found in local waters. The giant aquariums contain everything from near-microscopic life-forms to giant cod and even a small but menacing shark. The tour ends with a walk with a stunning view of the fish through a 26-foot glass tunnel. The in-house café has a hole in the floor that looks down into the water above the tunnel. As you sip your coffee, you can watch with amusement as slightly befuddled people wander below you and parents try to stop their children from throwing their cakes in to feed the fish. ⊠ *Strandv.* ☎ *0523/19671* ⊕ *www.havetshus. lysekil.se* 🖭 *SKr 75* ⊙ *Daily 10–4 (mid-June–mid-Aug., daily 10–6).*

Take any of the many flights of steps that start from Lysekil's main seafront road to get to **Lysekils Kyrka** (Lysekil Church). Probably the town's most impressive landmark, Lysekil Church was carved from the pink granite of the area and has beaten-copper doors. Its windows were painted by Albert Eldh, the early-20th-century artist. ⊠ *Stora Kyrkog.*

Twenty minutes north of Lysekil on Route 162 is **Nordens Ark**. A cut above the usual safari parks, Nordens Ark is a sanctuary for endangered animals. This haven of tranquillity is home to red pandas, lynxes, snow leopards, and arctic foxes. The best way to see the elusive wild animals is to follow the small truck that delivers their food at feeding times. ✉ *Åby Säteri, Hunnebostrand* ☎ *0523/79590* ⊕ *www.nordensark.se* 🖃 *SKr 120* ☉ *Mar.–mid-June, daily 10–5; mid-June–mid-Aug., daily 10–7; mid-Aug.–Oct., daily 10–5; Nov.–Feb., daily 10–4.*

off the beaten path

SMÖGEN – At the very tip of a westerly outcrop of land, Smögen is an ideal point for a quick stopover. To get here, head north on Route 162 and then west on Route 171 until it stops. The small village's red fishing huts, crystal-blue water, and pretty scrubbed boardwalks appear on many postcards of Bohuslän. Down on the main boardwalk, a stop at the **Skäret** (✉ Hamnen 1 ☎ 0523/32317) is a must. As well as having a great ocean view from the upstairs veranda, this small café/bar makes exquisite cakes and bread.

FJÄLLBACKA – Twenty-seven kilometers (16 mi) north of Lysekil, directly along the coast route, is this village with pastel wooden houses nestled in the rock. Fjällbacka, part of an archipelago, was where actress Ingrid Bergman had a summer house. In the square named after her, you can see her statue peering out over the water where her ashes were scattered, to the distant island Dannholmen. Behind the square is a dramatic ravine known as Kungskliftan (King's Cliff), where, among many others added since, you can find King Oscar II's name, which he scratched into the rock in 1887.

Where to Stay & Eat

$-$$ ✕ **Brygghuset.** A short boat ride and a walk through a breathtaking hilltop fishing village on the island of Fiskebäckskil will bring you to this lovely little restaurant. The interior is rustic, with wooden beams and plain wooden tables. Watch the chefs in the open kitchen as they prepare excellent local fish dishes. In summer there is outdoor eating, or you can just choose a glass of wine from the excellent wine list and watch the boats sail by. The ferry *Carl Wilhelmsson* leaves from outside the tourist office in Lysekil every half hour, bringing you to the restaurant 20 minutes later. ✉ *Lyckans Slip, Fiskebäckskil* ☎ *0523/22222* ⌁ *Reservations essential* 🖃 *AE, DC, MC, V.*

FodorsChoice
★

$-$$ ✕ **Pråmen.** This modern-looking restaurant has large windows and is propped on legs that allow it to jut out over the water. The view is great; with the windows open you can smell the sea. You can feast on good portions of simply cooked local fish and wash it down with cold beer. ✉ *Södra Hamng.* ☎ *0523/13452* 🖃 *AE, DC, MC, V.*

¢-$ 🏨 **Lysekil Havshotell.** This tall, narrow hotel has great views from atop a cliff. Stripped-wood floors and a miscellany of furnishings and fabrics create relaxed surroundings. Many rooms have sofas and provide bathrobes. Only breakfast is served, and there's a stocked bar (done on the honor system) in each room. For the best view across the water, reserve Room 18, which costs SKr 200 extra. ⊠ *Turistg. 13, 453 30* ☎ *0523/79750* 🖶 *0523/14204* ⊕ *www.strandflickorna.se* ⤴ *15 rooms, 2 suites* ⚍ *In-room broadband, in-room data ports, meeting room* ⊟ *AE, MC, V* ⦿*| BP.*

¢ 🏨 **Strand Vandrarhem.** This hostel on the seafront offers simple, friendly accommodations. Unless you stipulate otherwise and pay an additional fee, you may find yourself sharing the room with another guest (the rooms are outfitted with bunk beds). The welcome here is warm, and the breakfast (SKr 50 extra) is excellent. ⊠ *Strandv. 1, 453 30* ☎ *0523/79751* 🖶 *0523/12202* ⊕ *www.strandflickorna.se* ⤴ *20 rooms* ⊟ *MC, V.*

Nightlife & the Arts

In July Lysekil comes alive to the sounds of the annual **Lysekil Jazz Festival.** Big-name Swedish, and some international, jazz musicians play in open-air concerts and in bars and restaurants. Contact **Lysekils Turistbyrå** (tourist office; ☎ 0523/13050) for details of events.

Sports & the Outdoors

For a taste of the sea air and a great look at some local nature, take one of the regular seal safaris. Boat trips to view these fascinating, wallowing, slippery mammals leave from the main harbor three times daily between June and August, cost SKr 130, and take about two hours. Details and times are available from **Lysekils Turistbyrå** (☎ 0523/13050).

Tanumshede

❺ *45 km (28 mi) north of Lysekil (via Rtes. 161 and E6).*

From roughly 4000 BC to 3000 BC, Tanumshede was a coastal settlement. Now it's 5 km (3 mi) from the sea, since sea level is now 50 feet lower than it was then. Although the town itself is not extraordinary, it does hold the largest single collection of **Bronze Age rock carvings** (*hällristningar*) in Europe. People from all over the world flock to this UNESCO World Heritage Site to see the rudimentary scrapings that depict battles, hunting, and fishing.

Most of the carvings are within a short distance of the road, etched onto the weather-worn rocks that were picked up and deposited around the countryside by retreating Ice Age glaciers; the ones that are farther out, carved onto the largest rocks, are best reached by bicycle. Bikes can be rented from **Tanum Strand** (⊠ Tanums Strand, Grebbestad ☎ 0525/19000), for SKr 50 per hour or Skr 200 per day.

Heralded for its fantastic architecture, the **Vitlycke Museet** tells the story of the area's famous rock carvings and conveys what life was like between 1500 and 500 BC. It also makes some amusing and seemingly random attempts at decoding the messages held in the stones. ⊠ *Vitlycke 2* ☎ *0525/20950* ⊕ *www.vitlyckemuseum.se* ▣ *SKr 50* ☉ *Apr.–Sept., daily 10–6; Oct.–Mar., by appointment only.*

Strömstad

6 *90 km (56 mi) northwest of Uddevalla, 169 km (105 mi) north of Göteborg.*

This popular Swedish resort claims to have more summer sunshine than any other town north of the Alps. Formerly Norwegian, it has been the site of many battles between warring Danes, Norwegians, and Swedes. A short trip over the Norwegian border takes you to Halden, where Sweden's warrior king, Karl XII, died in 1718.

Although it is of no particular historical importance, **Strömstads Kyrka** is well worth a visit just to marvel at its interior design. The Strömstad Church's seemingly free-form decoration policy throws together wonderfully detailed, crowded frescoes; overly ornate gilt chandeliers; brass lamps from the 1970s; and model ships hanging from the roof. In the graveyard you can find the stone of Adolf Fritiof Cavalli-Holmgren, the eccentric jeweler's son who went on to become a financier and Sweden's richest man for a brief period around 1900. He was responsible for the design of the grand, copper-roof town hall in the middle of Strömstad. He never actually got to see it or to live in its specially created penthouse apartment, since he fell out with the local council over the design. ⌧ *S. Kyrkog. 10* ☎ *0526/10029.*

The **Strömstad Museum,** housed in a beautiful 18th-century redbrick mansion, has thoughtful, informative displays on the town's history and the importance of fishing as a local industry. Attached to the museum is a good town archive that includes old pictures showing how life was lived here. ⌧ *Södra Hamng. 26* ☎ *0526/10275* 🔳 *SKr 20* ☉ *Weekdays 11–4, Sat. 11–2.*

> **off the beaten path**
>
> **KOSTER ISLANDS –** There are regular ferryboats from Strömstad to the Koster Islands, Sweden's two most westerly inhabited islands. With no motorized vehicles allowed, the two islands are a perfect place for tranquil bike riding. Bikes can be rented for SKr 50 where you disembark from the boat. Most of the island is a sanctuary for wildlife, so the only sounds you'll hear through the meadows are birdcalls. Small, red wooden houses occasionally hold a café or coffee shop. The prawn sandwiches are always superb.

Where to Stay & Eat

$–$$$ ✕ **Göstases.** Somewhat resembling the interior of a wooden boat, this restaurant on the quayside specializes in locally caught fish and seafood. Knots, ropes, life preservers, stuffed fish, and similar paraphernalia abound. But it all pales when you see the low prices for fresh lobster, crab, prawns, and fish, all of which can be washed down with equally affordable cold beer. Sit outside in summer and watch the fishing boats bring in your catch and the pleasure boats float by. ⌧ *Strandpromenaden* ☎ *0526/10812* 🔳 *MC, V.*

$ ✕🏨 **Laholmen.** This huge, sprawling hotel and restaurant offers good-quality food and excellent accommodations on a grand scale. The

CloseUp

AQUAVIT: A LOVE STORY

THE ORIGINS OF SWEDISH AQUAVIT (akvavit) are as muddled as the drink is crystal-clear. Most historians have it down as a drink of the common people, distilled in backyards and backwoods, using homegrown potatoes or grain. For many hundreds of years, it served as a useful elixir for keeping winter's perpetual cold at bay. Many a dark Swedish night was illuminated with a little spiced, home-distilled aquavit: mother danced to father's accordion, and grandfather's tales were as spicy as the herbal spirits.

This is a romantic image and one with a certain amount of truth in it. The full truth, though, is a lot harsher. By the late 1800s, Sweden's love affair with the home-distilled spirit reached epidemic proportions, particularly in poor rural areas—drunkenness and ill health combined to incapacitate a good percentage of the population.

The State stepped in, taking control of the production, sale, and import of all alcohol, a practice that still stands today. As with gin in England, only when production was controlled did aquavit become a more quality, drinkable spirit.

Fine spirits with an alcohol content of 40 to 50 percent, and with complex flavors of dill, caraway, aniseed, coriander, fennel, and saffron, became the norm. The restriction of availability and increased price, along with a vast improvement in quality, saw aquavit promoted from a daily sustenance to a toasting beverage for festivals and special occasions.

Aquavit is taken when tradition dictates. Not until midsummer's crayfish table, Christmas, or perhaps a wedding, will the sweet and bitter tones of ice-cold aquavit pass through Swedish lips. When it does, though, it is with such ferocity that you wonder why the Swedes don't drink it more often, such is their love for it.

Despite the growing global fascination for all things Swedish—think Absolut vodka, H&M, and IKEA—you would be hard pressed to find a hip, urban Swede propping up a bar with an aquavit. Unlike other global cities, where aquavit is becoming the order of the day, metropolitan Swedes still look to whiskey, vodka, or tequila as their weekend accessory.

A Swedish party with aquavit is guaranteed to exude many songs, far too many toasts for its own good, and a general collective promise the next morning never to drink again. Whether drinking in memory of ancestors or simply to enjoy a Swedish tradition, when Swedes bring on the aquavit, very little gets done the following day.

— Rob Hincks

rooms are a bit garish, with overly vivid color schemes, but they are large and well equipped. The restaurant ($) has a good buffet and an interesting menu of local dishes, including exquisite prawn sandwiches at lunch. The restaurant as well as most guest rooms have views across the pretty harbor and the water beyond, which is scattered with skerries. ⊠ *Laholmen, 452 30* ☎ *0526/19700* 🖷 *0526/10036* ⊕ *www. laholmen.se* ⇆ *152 rooms, 4 suites* ⚓ *Restaurant, sauna, bar, lounge, convention center* ⊟ *AE, DC, MC, V* ⊙ *BP.*

Bohuslän A to Z

BUS TRAVEL

Buses to the region leave from behind the central train station in Göteborg; the main bus company is Västtrafik. The trip to Strömstad takes between two and three hours.

🚌 **Västtrafik** ☎ 0771/414300.

CAR TRAVEL

The best way to explore Bohuslän is by car. The E6 highway runs the length of the coast from Göteborg north to Strömstad, close to the Norwegian border, and for campers there are numerous well-equipped and uncluttered camping sites along the coast's entire length.

TRAIN TRAVEL

Regular service along the coast connects all the major towns of Bohuslän. The trip from Göteborg to Strömstad takes about two hours, and there are several trains each day. For schedules call SJ.

🚆 **SJ** ⊠ Göteborg ☎ 0771/757575.

VISITOR INFORMATION

🚉 **Göteborg Turistbyrå** ⊠ Kungsportsplatsen 2, 411 10 Göteborg ☎ 031/612500 🖷 031/ 612501 ⊕ www.goteborg.com. **Kungälv** ⊠ Fästningsholmen ☎ 0303/239200 ⊕ www. kungalv.se/turism. **Kungshamn** ⊠ Hamng. 6 ☎ 0523/665550 ⊕ www.kungshamn.com. **Lysekil** ⊠ Södra Hamng. 6 ☎ 0523/13050. **Marstrand** ⊠ Hamng. ☎ 0303/60087. **Strömstad** ⊠ Torget, Norra Hamnen ☎ 0526/62330 ⊕ www.stromstadtourist.se. **Tanumshede** ⊠ Bygdegårdsplan ☎ 0525/18380. **Uddevalla** ⊠ Kungstorget 4 ☎ 0522/99720 ⊕ www.uddevallaforum.se.

SWEDISH RIVIERA

The coastal region south of Göteborg, Halland—locally dubbed the Swedish Riviera—is the closest that mainland Sweden comes to having a resort area. Fine beaches abound, and there are plenty of sporting activities. But Halland's history is dark, since it was the front line in the fighting between Swedes and Danes. Evidence of such conflicts can be found in its many medieval villages and fortifications. The region stretches down to Båstad, in the country's southernmost province, Skåne.

Kungsbacka

❼ *25 km (15 mi) south of Göteborg.*

This bedroom community for Göteborg holds a market for all sorts of goods on the first Thursday of every month—a 600-year-old tradition.

A break in a high ridge to the west, the **Fjärås Crack,** offers a fine view of the coast. Formed by melting ice 13,000 years ago, the ridge made a perfect transport route for nomadic tribes of 10,000 years ago, who used it to track the retreating ice northward to settle their new communities. Some important archaeological discoveries have been made here, and much of the information learned is on display on signs dotted along the ridge. The signs act as a sort of self-guided outdoor museum, dealing with the geological and anthropological history of the ridge.

At Tjolöholm, 12 km (7 mi) down the E6/E20 highway from Kungsbacka, is **Tjolöholms Slott** (Tjolöholm Castle), a manor house built by James Dickson, a Scottish merchant and horse breeder. (He was also the grandson of Robert Dickson, the philanthropist and founder of the Swedish East India Trade Company.) The English Tudor–style house, constructed at the beginning of the 20th century, contains many fascinating elements. By and large, they have become a tribute to Dickson's passion for all things modern, including an early version of a pressurized shower and a horse-drawn vacuum cleaner with a very long hose to reach up through the house windows. Dickson died of lead poisoning before the house was completed—he cut his finger while opening a bottle of champagne and wrapped the lead-foil wrapper around the cut. The house he left behind offers much insight into one man's dream. ✉ *Fjärås* ☎ *0300/544200* 🖅 *SKr 60* ☉ *Apr.–mid-June, weekends 11–4; mid-June–Aug., daily 11–4; Sept., weekends 11–4; Oct., Sun. 11–4.*

Fodor'sChoice
★

Near Tjolöholm is the tiny 18th-century village of Äskhult, the site of an open-air museum, the **Äskhults 1700-tals by** (Äskhult's 18th-Century Village). When land reforms forced farmers to combine patches of land into large estates, the four farmers living in Äskhult refused and kept their land separate. This refusal left the village unable to expand while both of the neighboring areas became towns. And so it stayed that way, until the last inhabitants moved away in the mid-19th century. Today you can wander through the houses and farm buildings to get a glimpse of what life was like for 18th-century peasant farmers. ☎ *0300/542159* 🖅 *SKr 25* ☉ *May–Aug., daily 10–6; Sept., weekends 10–6.*

en route
Forty kilometers (25 mi) southeast of Kungsbacka (on E6 and Route 153) is the shopping mecca of **Ullared,** once a single discount store, now a whole town of huge outlet stores and malls visited by 3 million Swedes each year. It's overwhelming, but even the most resolute nonshoppers may find it difficult to resist the selection and the prices.

Varberg

❽ *40 km (25 mi) south of Kungsbacka, 65 km (40 mi) south of Göteborg.*

Varberg is a busy port with connections to Grenå, in Denmark. Although the town has some good beaches, it's best known for a suit of medieval clothing preserved in the museum inside the 13th-century **Varbergs Fästning** (Varberg Fortress). The suit belonged to a man who was murdered and thrown into a peat bog. The peat preserved his body, and his clothes are the only known suit of ordinary medieval clothing. The museum also contains a silver bullet said to be the one that killed Karl XII. ☎ *0340/82830* 🖃 *SKr 50* ☉ *Fortress open yr-round; guided fortress tours June 15–Aug. 9, daily 11–4 every hr on the hr. Museum mid-June–mid-Aug., daily 10–6; mid-Aug.–mid-June, weekdays 10–4, weekends noon–4.*

Where to Stay & Eat

$–$$ ✕ **Societen.** Housed in the cream-and-green carved-wood confection that is the 19th-century Society House, this restaurant presents dining on a grand scale. Two huge, high-windowed dining rooms offer French-influenced dishes such as mussels with eggplant and garlic. There's fox-trot dancing on Friday and live bands and DJs on Saturday. Two separate lively bar areas are on hand if you need to increase your intake of courage before taking to the dance floor. 🖂 *Societetsparken* ☎ *0340/676500* 🖢 *Reservations essential* 🖃 *AE, DC, MC, V.*

$$ 🏨 **Varbergs Kurort Hotell & Spa.** A former sanatorium on the beachfront, this grandiose hotel stuffs curly pieces of art-nouveau furniture into every room. Guest rooms are a little small but comfortable. There is a large and well-equipped spa and sauna area with hot tubs, a heated seawater pool, a regular pool, and a Turkish steam bath. Experienced instructors offer spinning, aerobics, and yoga classes. 🖂 *Nils Kreugers väg 5, 432 24* ☎ *0340/629800* 🖷 *0340/629850* 🖎 *106 rooms, 38 suites* 🖢 *Restaurant, 2 indoor pools, health club, sauna, spa, bar* 🖃 *AE, DC, MC, V* 🍴 *BP.*

Falkenberg

❾ *30 km (20 mi) south of Varberg, 100 km (60 mi) south of Göteborg.*

With its attractive beaches and the plentiful salmon that swim in the Ätran River, Falkenberg is one of Sweden's most attractive resorts. Its Gamla Stan (Old Town) is full of narrow cobblestone streets and quaint, old wooden houses.

When the weather gets hot, what better way to quench that raging thirst than a stroll around a cool brewery, followed by a glass of ice cold beer? At the **Brewery in Falkenberg** groups can do just that. The beer Falcon has been brewed on the premises since 1869, and a tour of the facility takes in both old brewing traditions and modern beer-making technology. The tour ends with dinner and refreshing glasses of the house brew. 🖂 *Åstadv.* ☎ *0346/721255* 🖎 *4-hr tour, including dinner and beer tasting, SKr 350 per person in groups of minimum 15.*

Doktorspromenaden, on the south side of the river in the town center, is a beautiful walk set against a backdrop of heathland and shade trees. The walk was set up in 1861 by a local doctor in an effort to encourage the townsfolk to get more fresh air. ⊠ *Doktorspromenaden.*

Although it does have the usual archaeological and historical artifacts depicting its town's growth and development, the **Falkenberg Museum** also has an unusual and refreshing obsession with the 1950s. The curator here thinks that is the most interesting period of history, and you can make up your own mind once you've learned about the local dance-band scene, visited the interior of a shoe-repair shop, and seen a collection of old jukeboxes. ⊠ *Skepparesträtet 2* ☎ *0346/886125* ⌨ *Free* ☾ *June–Aug., Tues.–Sun. noon–4; Sept.–May, Tues.–Fri. and Sun. noon–4.*

Falkenberg's first movie theater is now home to **Fotomuseum Olympia,** a fascinating display of cameras, camera equipment, and photographs dating back to the 1840s. ⊠ *Sandg. 13* ☎ *0346/87928* ⌨ *SKr 35* ☾ *Mid-June–Aug., Tues.–Thurs. 1–7, Sun. 1–6; Sept.–May, Tues.–Thurs. 5–7, Sun. 2–6.*

In the middle of Gamla Stan stands the 12th-century **St. Laurentii Kyrka** (St. Laurentii Church). After the construction of a new church at the end of the 19th century, St. Laurentii was deconsecrated and used as a shooting range, a cinema, and a gymnasium, among other things. It was reconsecrated in the 1920s and is now fully restored with its 16th-century font and silver, as well as some awe-inspiring 17th- and 18th-century wall paintings.

Where to Stay & Eat

$–$$ ✕ **Restaurant Hertigen.** This beautiful white villa sits on wooded grounds on an island just outside the center of town. Dining takes place on a large veranda and garden in summer. The classic French dishes are prepared with a nod in the direction of local cooking styles. ⊠ *Hertings Gård* ☎ *0346/10018* ⌨ *Reservations essential* ▤ *AE, DC, MC, V.*

$–$$ ▥ **Elite Hotel Strandbaden.** A sprawling, white wood-and-glass building, Elite Hotel Strandbaden sits right on the beach at the south end of town. The rooms here are quite small but well equipped, with amenities and modern, comfortable furnishings. Most have a view of the sea. There is a state-of-the-art spa and health club in the hotel, and a very good restaurant decked out in startling blue and orange. ⊠ *Havsbadsallén, 311 42* ☎ *0346/714900* 🖷 *0346/16111* ⊕ *www.elite.se* ↪ *135 rooms, 5 suites* ♢ *Restaurant, minibars, cable TV, in-room data ports, health club, sauna, bar* ▤ *AE, DC, MC, V* ⦿❘ *BP.*

$ ▥ **Grand Hotel Falkenberg.** Not as imposing as the name suggests, this pretty, yellow, 19th-century hotel is comfortable and friendly, with very large rooms. The interior is a jumble of furnishings from the last 30 years, with the odd antique thrown in for good measure. Cherrywood and rich fabrics are used throughout. ⊠ *Hotellg. 1, 311 31* ☎ *0346/14450* 🖷 *0346/14459* ⊕ *www.grandhotelfalkenberg.se* ↪ *70 rooms, 3 suites* ♢ *2 restaurants, sauna, 2 bars, lounge* ▤ *AE, DC, MC, V* ⦿❘ *BP.*

Sports & the Outdoors

BEACHES A 15-minute walk south from the town center is **Skrea Strand,** a 3-km (2-mi) stretch of sandy beach. At the northern end of the beach is the huge swimming complex **Klitterbadet** (✉ Klitterv. ☎ 0346/886330 🖾 SKr 35 ⏰ June–Aug., Sun. and Mon. 9–4, Tues. and Thurs. 6 AM–7 PM, Wed. and Fri. 9–7, Sat. 9–5; Sept.–May, Mon. 4 PM–8 PM, Tues. and Thurs. 6 AM–8 AM and noon–8, Wed. noon–8, Fri. noon–7, Sat. 9–5, Sun. 9–3), with pools (including one just for children), waterslides, a sauna, a whirlpool, a 50-meter-long pool with heated seawater, and steam rooms. Farther south the beach opens out onto some secluded coves and grasslands.

FISHING In the 1800s Falkenberg had some of the best fly-fishing in Europe. This prompted a frenzy of fishermen, including many English aristocrats, to plunder its waters. But despite the overfishing, the Ätran is one of few remaining rivers in Europe inhabited by wild salmon. Fishing permits and rod rentals can be arranged through the local **tourist office** (☎ 0346/886100).

Shopping

Törngrens (✉ Krukmakareg. 4 ☎ 0346/10354 ⏰ Weekdays 9–5) is probably the oldest pottery shop in Scandinavia, and is now owned by the seventh generation of the founding family. Call ahead to make sure the shop is open.

Halmstad

❿ *40 km (25 mi) south of Falkenberg, 143 km (89 mi) south of Göteborg.*

With a population of 55,000, Halmstad is the largest seaside resort on the west coast. The Norre Port town gate, all that remains of the town's original fortifications, dates from 1605. The modern town hall has interior decorations by the so-called Halmstad Group of painters, which formed here in 1929.

Most of Halmstad's architectural highlights are in and around **Stora Torget,** the large town square. In the middle is the fountain *Europa and the Bull,* by the sculptor Carl Milles. Around the square are many buildings and merchants' houses dating from Halmstad's more prosperous days in the last half of the 19th century.

At the top of Stora Torget is the grand **St. Nikolai Kyrka,** a huge church from the 14th century containing fragments of medieval murals and a 17th-century pulpit.

No Swedish town would be complete without its local museum, and the **Länsmuseet Halmstad** is more accomplished than most. Everything from archaeological finds to musical instruments to dollhouses is on display. There's also a haunting display of large figureheads taken from ships that sank off the local coastline. ✉ *Tollsg.* ☎ *035/162300* ⊕ *www.hallmus.se* 🖾 *SKr 40* ⏰ *Tues., Thurs., and Sun. noon–4, Wed. noon–9.*

★ The bizarre **Martin Luther Kyrka** is unique among churches. Built entirely out of steel in the 1970s, its exterior resembles that of a shiny tin can. The interior is just as striking, as the gleaming outside gives way to rust-orange steel and art-deco furnishings that contrast with the outside. To some, Martin Luther Church may seem more like a temple to design, not deity. ⊠ *Långg.* ☎ *035/151961* ⊙ *Weekdays 9–3, Sun. services at 10.*

In the 1930s the Halmstad Group, made up of six local artists, caused some consternation with their surrealist and cubist painting styles, influenced strongly by such artists as René Magritte and Salvador Dalí. The **Mjellby Konstgård** (Mjellby Arts Center) contains some of the most important works created over the group's 50-year alliance. ⊠ *Mjellby, (4 km [2½ mi] from Halmstad)* ☎ *035/137195* ⬚ *SKr 50* ⊙ *Mar.–Oct., daily 1–5; July, daily 11–5.*

🐾 The **Tropik Centre,** just a few minutes' walk from the center of Halmstad, holds flora and fauna that come from outside Sweden. Tropical plants, birds, snakes, monkeys, spiders, and crocodiles are all safely tucked away behind glass, ready both to amuse and to, perhaps, horrify you. ⊠ *Tullhuset, Strandg.* ☎ *035/123333* ⊕ *www.tropikcenter.se* ⬚ *SKr 70* ⊙ *July, daily 10–6; Aug.–June, daily 10–4.*

Where to Stay & Eat

$$–$$$ ✕ **Pio & Co.** Half informal bar and half bistro, this restaurant offers something for all. It's a bright and airy place with good service and excellent Swedish classics on the menu—the steak and mashed potatoes is wonderful. The list of drinks is extensive. ⊠ *Storg. 37* ☎ *035/210669* ⊟ *AE, DC, MC, V.*

$$ 🏨 **Scandic Hallandia.** A shiny white-tile floor, white ceiling tiles, and a circular podlike lobby create a strange first impression. But don't be alarmed. Rooms here come with all the space, comfort, modernity, and up-to-date technology you would expect from a Scandinavian hotel. ⊠ *Rådhusg. 4, 302 43* ☎ *035/2958600* 🖷 *035/2958611* ⊕ *www. scandic-hotels.se* ⇆ *130 rooms, 1 suite* ♿ *Restaurant, in-room data ports, sauna, spa, bar, convention center* ⊟ *AE, DC, MC, V* ⏐⊙⏐ *BP.*

$ 🏨 **Hotel Continental.** Built in 1904 in the national romantic style, the interior of this hotel has been nicely preserved. The sophisticated design includes exposed-brick walls, subtle spotlighting, and light wood fittings. The rooms are bright, modern, and spacious. Five rooms have whirlpool baths. ⊠ *Kungsg. 5, 302 45* ☎ *035/176300* 🖷 *035/128604* ⊕ *www.continental-halmstad.se* ⇆ *46 rooms, 3 suites* ♿ *In-room broadband, in-room data ports, sauna, spa, bar, meeting rooms, parking (fee)* ⊟ *AE, DC, MC, V* ⏐⊙⏐ *BP.*

Nightlife & the Arts

The nightlife in Halmstad centers around the bars in Storgatan, the main street that runs into Stora Torget. **Harry's** (☎ *035/105595*) is worth a visit, if only to see its bizarre English phone box with a life-size model of Charlie Chaplin inside. **Pio & Co.** (☎ *035/210669*) has a cozy "cognac corner" in the lounge area of the restaurant.

Sports & the Outdoors

There are many good beaches around Halmstad. **Tjuvahålan,** extending west of Halmstad, has an interesting old smugglers' cove that provides pleasant walking. For details, contact the **tourist office** (☎ 035/132320).

Båstad

⓫ *35 km (22 mi) south of Halmstad, 178 km (111 mi) south of Göteborg.*

In the southernmost province of Skåne, Båstad is regarded by locals as Sweden's most fashionable resort, where ambassadors and local captains of industry have their summer houses. Aside from this, it is best known for its tennis. In addition to the **Båstad Open,** a grand prix tournament in late summer, there is the annual **Donald Duck Cup** in July, for children from ages 11 to 15; it was the very first trophy won by Björn Borg, who later took the Wimbledon men's singles title an unprecedented five times in a row. Spurred on by Borg and other Swedish champions, such as Stefan Edberg and Mats Wilander, thousands of youngsters take part in the Donald Duck Cup each year. For details, contact the **Svenska Tennisförbundet** (Swedish Tennis Association; ⊠ Lidingöv. 75, Stockholm ☎ 08/4504310).

The low-rise shuttered buildings in the center of Båstad give it an almost French provincial feel. In the main square is **St. Maria Kyrka** (St. Maria's Church), which looks much more solidly Swedish. Dating from the 15th century, the plain exterior hides a haven of tranquillity within the cool thick walls. The unusual altar painting depicts Christ on the cross with human skulls and bones strewn beneath him.

Norrviken Gardens, 3 km (2 mi) northwest of Båstad, are beautifully laid out in different styles, including a Japanese garden and a lovely walkway lined with rhododendrons. The creator of the gardens, Rudolf Abelin, is buried on the grounds. A restaurant, shop, and pottery studio are also on the premises. ☎ *0431/369040* ⊕ *www.norrvikenstradgardar.net* ⊠ *May–Aug. SKr 90; Sept.–Apr. free* ⊙ *May–Sept., daily 10–5 (July–mid-Aug., daily 10–8); Oct.–Apr., daily dawn–dusk.*

Where to Stay & Eat

$$ ✕ **Swenson's Krog.** Well worth the 3-km (2-mi) journey out of Båstad, this harbor-front restaurant was originally a fisherman's hut and has been converted into a magnificent dining room with cornflower-blue walls, wooden floors, and a glass roof. The menu is full of Swedish classics such as white asparagus with lemon-butter sauce and delicious homemade meatballs. The service is friendly, with the family atmosphere really shining through. ⊠ *Pål Romaresg. 2, Torekov* ☎ *0431/364590* ⌕ *Reservations essential* ⊟ *AE, DC, MC, V.*

¢ ✕ **Wooden Hut.** Actually, this restaurant has no name: it's just a wooden hut on the harbor side. It has no tables either. It has no wine list, no waiters, no interior design, no telephone, and it doesn't accept credit cards. What this restaurant does have is simple and delicious smoked mackerel with potato salad, which will magically take you away from all the pomp and wealth that sometimes bogs Båstad down. Walk past all the hotels and restaurants, smell the fresh sea air, and get ready for a great meal. ⊠ *Strandpromenaden* ☎ *No phone* ⌘ *Reservations not accepted* ▤ *No credit cards.*

$$ ✕⌦ **Hotel Skansen.** Set in a century-old bathhouse, Skansen's interior reflects the best of modern design. Wonderfully simple earth, cream, and moss-green tones create a sense of comfort, simplicity, and relaxation. The lovely rooms, many with a glass roof or wall, are all decorated with furniture from Stockholm's cool interior shop R.O.O.M. Restaurant Sand ($–$$), with a sea view, serves stylish and well-prepared Swedish fare, with fish as a specialty. The bar is well stocked, but the nightclub is nothing special. ⊠ *Kyrkog. 2, 269 21* ☎ *0431/558100* ⎙ *0431/558110* ⊕ *www.hotelskansen.se* ⇆ *138 rooms, 1 suite* ⌂ *Restaurant, in-room data ports, sauna, spa, steam room, bar, nightclub* ▤ *AE, DC, MC, V* ¶⊙︎ *BP.*

¢–$ ⌦ **Hjortens Pensionat.** A classic summer resort hotel, Hjortens Pensionat is Båstad's oldest inn. The antiques-filled rooms are light and the common areas are comfortably cluttered with ornaments and deep armchairs. Right in the center of Båstad, the hotel is close to shops, beaches, and tennis courts. ⊠ *Roxmansv. 23, 269 36* ☎ *0431/70109* ⎙ *0431/70180* ⊕ *www.hjorten.net* ⇆ *42 rooms, 37 with bath* ⌂ *Restaurant, bar* ▤ *DC, MC, V* ¶⊙︎ *BP.*

Swedish Riviera A to Z

BUS TRAVEL
Buses to Kungsbacka, Varberg, Falkenberg, Halmstad, and Båstad leave from behind Göteborg's central train station.
🚌 **Hallandstrafiken** ☎ 0771/331030. **Västtrafik** ☎ 0771/414300.

CAR TRAVEL
Simply follow the E6/E20 highway south from Göteborg toward Malmö. The highway runs parallel to the coast.

TRAIN TRAVEL
Regular train services connect Göteborg's central station with Kungsbacka, Varberg, Falkenberg, Halmstad, and Båstad.
🚆 **SJ** ⊠ Göteborg ☎ 0771/757575.

VISITOR INFORMATION
🛈 **Båstad** ⊠ Stortorget 1 ☎ 0431/75045. **Falkenberg** ⊠ Holgersg. 9 ☎ 0346/886100. **Halmstad** ⊠ Halmstad Slott ☎ 035/132320. **Kungsbacka** ⊠ Storg. 41 ☎ 0300/834595. **Laholm** ⊠ Rådhuset ☎ 0430/15450. **Varberg** ⊠ Brunnsparken ☎ 0340/86800.

GÖTA CANAL

Stretching 614 km (382 mi) between Stockholm and Göteborg, the Göta Canal is actually a series of interconnected canals, rivers, lakes, and even a stretch of sea. Bishop Hans Brask of Linköping in the 16th century was the first to suggest linking the bodies of water; in 1718 King Karl XII ordered the canal to be built, but work was abandoned when he was killed in battle the same year. Not until 1810 was the idea again taken up in earnest. The driving force was a Swedish nobleman, Count Baltzar Bogislaus von Platen (1766–1829), and his motive was commercial. Von Platen saw the canal as a way of beating Danish tolls on ships that passed through the Öresund. He also sought to enhance Göteborg's standing by linking the port with Stockholm, on the east coast. At a time when Swedish fortunes were at a low ebb, the canal was also viewed as a way to reestablish faith in the future and boost national morale.

The building of the canal took 22 years and involved 58,000 men. Linking the various stretches of water required 87 km (54 mi) of man-made cuts through soil and rock and building 58 locks, 47 bridges, 27 culverts, and three dry docks. Unfortunately, the canal never achieved the financial success that von Platen sought. By 1857 the Danes had removed shipping tolls, and in the following decade the linking of Göteborg with Stockholm by rail effectively ended the canal's commercial potential. The canal has nevertheless come into its own as a modern-day tourist attraction.

You may have trouble conceiving of the canal's industrial origins as your boat drifts lazily down this lovely series of waterways; across the enormous lakes, Vänern and Vättern; and through a microcosm of all that is best about Sweden: abundant fresh air; clear, clean water; pristine nature; and well-tended farmland. A bicycle path runs parallel to the canal, offering another means of touring the country. You can bike faster than the boats travel, so it's easy to jump off and on as you please.

Trollhättan

⑫ *70 km (43 mi) north of Göteborg.*

In this pleasant industrial town of about 53,000 inhabitants, a spectacular waterfall was rechanneled in 1906 to become Sweden's first hydroelectric plant. On specific days in summer the waters are allowed to follow their natural course, a fall of 106 feet in six torrents. This sight is well worth seeing. The other main point of interest is the 82-km-long (51-mi-long) Trollhätte Canal, of which a 10-km (6-mi) stretch runs through the city. The canal's six locks date from 1916. Along the canal are also disused locks from 1800 and 1844, beautiful walking trails, and the King's Cave, a rock formation on which visiting monarchs have carved their names since 1754. Trollhättan also has a fine, wide marketplace and waterside parks. The city has become somewhat of a center of the Swedish film industry, earning it the nickname "Trollywood." Lukas Moodyson (*Show Me Love, Together,* and *Lilja 4-Ever*) is just one of the directors who have chosen Trollhättan production studios.

In the summer months the **Trollhättans Turistbyrå** (Tourist Office; ✉ Åkerssjöv. 10 ☎ 0520/488472 ⊕ www.visittrollhattan.se) offers the Sommarkort (Summer Pass), with free entrance to the Innovatum, the Innovatum Cableway, Saab Bilmuseum, and the Canal Museum. It costs SKr 100 per day, and accompanying children under 16 are free.

The best way to see the town's spectacular waterfalls and locks is on the **walking trail** that winds its way through the massive system. The walk takes in the hydroelectric power station and the canal museum. Part of the walk is atop wooded cliffs that overlook the spectacular cascades of water. The falls flow freely in May and June, weekends at 3, and July and August, Wednesday and weekends at 3. In July the falls are also illuminated at 11 PM on Wednesday, Saturday, and Sunday. Details and directions can be found at the tourist office, which will also tell you the best places to watch the waterfall when the waters are allowed to follow their natural course.

Culture abounds at **Folkets Hus** (People's House), in the pedestrianized downtown area. Part of the building is given over to dramatic, ever-changing displays of contemporary art and art installations. ⊠ *Kungsg. 25* ☎ *0520/422500* ▨ *Free* ☉ *Kulturhallen (Culture Hall) at Folkets Hus, Sun. and Mon. noon–4, Tues.–Thurs. noon–7, Sat. 11–2.*

The **Innovatum Cableway** will take you 1,312 feet across the canal at a height of nearly 98 feet, with spectacular views of the canal, the town, and the waterfall area. ⊠ *Åkerssjöv. 10* ☎ *0520/488480* ▨ *SKr 40* ☉ *June–Aug., daily 10–6.*

ⓒ Kids visiting the **Innovatum–Kunskapens Hus** (Innovatum–Technology Center) get to touch, examine, and poke at objects illustrating technology, energy, media, design, and industrial history. In the film studio you can edit yourself into contemporary Swedish movies. A big hit are the two robots, Max and Gerda, that spend their days vacuum-cleaning their futuristic apartment. As a reward for their hard work, the staff at Innovatum feeds the robots trash at set times. ⊠ *Åkerssjöv. 10* ☎ *0520/488480* ⊕ *www.innovatum.se* ▨ *SKr 60* ☉ *Tues.–Sun. 10–6.*

The canal and the locks gave Trollhättan its life, and a visit to the **Kanalmuseet** (Canal Museum) tells as full a history of this as you can find. Housed in a redbrick 1893 waterside building, the museum covers the history of the canal and the locks and displays model ships, old tools, and fishing gear. ⊠ *Åkersbergsv., Övre Slussen* ☎ *0520/472206* ▨ *SKr 15* ☉ *May, weekends noon–5; June–Aug., daily 10–7.*

The **Saab Bilmuseum** (Saab Car Museum) surveys Saab's automotive output from 1946 to the present. Since the exhibition consists primarily of row upon row of cars, fenced off by rope, there's little here for any but true car enthusiasts. ⊠ *Åkerssjöv. 10* ☎ *0520/84344* ⊕ *www.saab. com* ▨ *SKr 50* ☉ *Tues.–Fri. 11–4.*

Where to Stay & Eat

¢–$ ✕ **Shangri La.** The large, elegant dining room is decorated in deep brown and gold shades to go along with the restaurant's mixed Asian theme. In summer you can sup on the outdoor terrace against a backdrop of humming waterfalls. ⊠ *Storg. 36* ☎ *0520/10222* ▤ *AE, MC, V.*

¢–$ ✕ **Strandgatan.** This popular, relaxed café is in an 1867 building that once housed canal workers. There's always a good crowd, especially in summer. Locals come to while away the hours over coffee, bagels, home-cooked international cuisine, and beer and wine. ⊠ *Föerningsg. 1* ☎ *0520/83717* ▤ *AE, DC, MC, V.*

$ 🏨 **Scandic Swania.** Stunning views over the waterfalls and locks to the hills above town are what distinguish this comfortable hotel near Trollhättan's center. Ask for a top-floor room at the front of the hotel and enjoy the sights. If you're up for a party, one of Trollhättan's few clubs is in the basement. ⊠ *Storg. 49, 461 23* ☎ *0520/89000* 🖷 *0520/89001* ⊕ *www.scandic-hotels.se* ⟿ *196 rooms, 13 suites* ⸖ *Restaurant, in-room broadband, in-room data ports, bar, lounge, nightclub, no-smoking rooms* ▤ *AE, DC, MC, V* 🍽 *BP.*

Nightlife

Trollhättan's twenty-five- to fiftysomethings make up an age range as diverse as the music at **Butlers** (⊠ Spannmålsg. 11 ☎ 0520/481880), which consists of anything from live Euro easy-listening bands to the latest dance tunes spun by DJs. This is considered a very hip place in these parts.

The Outdoors

Daily boat trips from the center of town take you right into the heart of the lock system and waterfalls. The **MS *Strömkarlen*** (☎ 0520/32100 🖃 SKr 180) leaves two times daily (at 10 and 1:30) June 29–August 10.

Vänersborg

⑬ *15 km (9 mi) north of Trollhättan, 85 km (53 mi) north of Göteborg.*

Eventually, the canal enters **Vänern,** Sweden's largest and Europe's third-largest lake: 3,424 square km (1,322 square mi) of water, 145 km (90 mi) long and 81 km (50 mi) wide at one point.

At the southern tip of the lake is Vänersborg, a town of about 30,000 inhabitants that was founded in the mid-17th century. The church and the governor's residence date from the 18th century, but the rest of the town was destroyed by fire in 1834. Vänersborg is distinguished by its fine lakeside park, the trees of which act as a windbreak for the gusts that sweep in from Vänern.

Fans of the esoteric may find the **Vänersborgs Museum** worth a visit. The oldest museum in Sweden outside Stockholm, it has been restored to its 1888 appearance, and as such it has become an unintentional museum of museums. A gloomy apartment in which the museum's janitor once lived is now part of an exhibit—one that preserves the space in all its 1950s glory. The museum's most eccentric collection is one of birds from southwestern Africa—Namibia, Botswana, and Angola. This collection is the most extensive in the world and is the base of an exchange between the museum and the National Museum of Namibia. ⊠ *Östra Plantaget* ☎ *0521/264100* ⊕ *www.alvlanmus.se* 🖃 *SKr 20* ⊙ *June–Aug., Tues.–Thurs. and weekends, noon–4; Sept.–May, Tues., Thurs., and weekends, noon–4.*

A few minutes' walk from the center of town, **Skracklan Park** is a good place to relax. Take a break in the 1930s coffeehouse after walking along the park's promenade. A lake, parkland, and trees are set around the park's centerpiece, a statue of Frida, the muse of a famous local poet named Birger Sjöberg (1885–1929). Frida always has fresh flowers stuffed into her bronze hand.

off the
beaten
path

HALLEBERG AND HUNNEBERG – Five kilometers (3 mi) east of Vänersborg are the twin plateaus of Halleberg and Hunneberg. Thought to be 500 million years old, these geological wonders are the site of early Viking forts and the resting place of early humans. But they are best known for their stunning natural beauty and the fauna they support: the county's biggest herd of elk. As tradition dictates, the king of Sweden still comes here every October for the royal hunt. To see the animals yourself, head for the walking trail that winds around Halleberg. At dawn or dusk the leggy, long-faced giant elk, inquisitive by nature, will be more than comfortable eating apples from your hand. Whether you'll be so comfortable, once you see the size of them, is another matter. Those less daring can hide behind a guide from the **Älgens Berg & Kungajaktsmuseum** (Elk Mountain & Royal Hunt Museum). ⊠ *Vargön* ☎ *0521/277991* 🏛 *Museum SKr 60; private guide 1 hr SKr 795, 30 mins SKr 530* ⊙ *May–Aug., daily 10–6; Sept.–Apr., Tues.–Sun. 11–4.*

Where to Stay & Eat

¢–$ ✕ **Pizzeria Roma.** Directly across the road from the hotel Ronnums Herrgård, this small restaurant is perfect for informal meals. The very good and very cheap pizza and pasta served here are worth suffering the somewhat stark and brightly lighted interior. ⊠ *Stora Gårdsv. 2* ☎ *0521/221070* 🚪 *MC, V.*

$ 🏨 **Park Inn.** A mile outside town, this old manor house has been converted into a hotel of some local repute. Some rooms are a little shabby, so try to get one in the main building. What you do get here is peace, natural beauty, and a very good hotel restaurant—not to mention a good story, too: Nicole Kidman stayed here for two months while filming in nearby Trollhättan. The breakfast offered with the room is worthy of a king. ⊠ *Parkv., Vargön, 468 30* ☎ *0521/260000* 🖨 *0521/260009* ⊕ *www.ronnums-herrgard.parkinn.se* 🛏 *60 rooms, 10 suites* ⚿ *Restaurant, bar, free parking, no-smoking rooms* 🚪 *AE, DC, MC, V* ⚏ *BP.*

¢ 🏨 **Hotell Strand.** Lodging choices are limited in Vänersborg, but the Hotell Strand's welcoming staff make it the best in town. ⊠ *Hamng. 7, 462 33* ☎ *0521/13850* 🖨 *0521/15900* ⊕ *www.strandhotell.com* 🛏 *28 rooms* ⚿ *Free parking, no-smoking rooms* 🚪 *AE, DC, MC, V* ⚏ *BP.*

Nightlife

Nightlife is limited here, but at **Club Roccad** (⊠Kungsg. 23 ☎0521/61200) there's always good, modern dance music, and the cool, dark interior attracts a young, good-looking crowd that's serious about dancing.

Lidköping

⑭ *55 km (34 mi) east of Vänersborg, 140 km (87 mi) northeast of Göteborg.*

On an inlet at the southernmost point of Vänern's eastern arm lies the town of Lidköping, which received its charter in 1446 and is said to have the largest town square in Sweden. **Nya Stadens Torg** (New Town Square) is dominated by the old courthouse building, a replica of the original that burned down in 1960. Lidköping had been razed by fire several times before that, leaving a lot of the old town gone. However, the 17th-century houses around the square Limtorget survived, and are still worth seeing today.

A pleasant enough town, Lidköping's villagelike layout comes from an old rule forbidding buildings from being taller than the streets they stand on are wide. The only exception seems to be the ugly industrial park on the northern edge of town, which obscures an otherwise perfect view of Lake Vänern.

The **Rörstrands Museum** has on display a wealth of pieces that trace the history of china. Rörstrands, Europe's second-oldest porcelain company, also offers tours of its adjoining factory. The factory shop carries a large range of beautiful china at very reasonable prices. ⊠ *Fabriksg. 4* ☎ *0510/82348* ⊕ *www.rorstrandsmuseum.se* ⊠ *Free* ☉ *Weekdays 10–6, Sat. 10–2, Sun. noon–4. Factory tours Thurs. and Fri. for groups; call for details.*

Vänermuseet is dedicated to Lake Vänern's history, the life it supports, and the ways in which it has helped the surrounding area develop. What could be a slightly dull subject is vividly brought to life in this well-planned, modern museum, which has exhibits of meteorites and fossils as well as model ships and maritime photographs. ⊠ *Framnäsv. 2* ☎ *0510/770065* ⊕ *www.vanermuseet.se* ⊠ *SKr 40* ☉ *Tues.–Fri. 10–5, Thurs. 10–7, weekends noon–5.*

off the beaten path

HUSABY HYRKA – This church, 15 km (9 mi) east of Lidköping, is a site of great religious and historical significance. The church itself, dating from the 12th century, houses some fine 13th-century furniture, 15th-century murals, and carved floor stones. But the biggest draw is outside the church, at St. Sigfrid's Well. Here, in 1008, King Olof Skötkonung converted to Christianity—the first Swedish king to do so—and was baptized by the English missionary Sigfrid. Since that time many Swedish kings have come to carve their names in the rock. Most signatures can still be clearly read today.

LÄCKÖ SLOTT – One of Sweden's finest 17th-century Renaissance palaces is 24 km (15 mi) to the north of Lidköping. It's on a peninsula off the site where the eastern arm of Vänern divides from the western. Läckö Castle's 250 rooms were once the home of Magnus Gabriel de la Gardie, a great favorite of Queen Christina. Only the Royal Palace in Stockholm is larger. In 1681 Karl XI confiscated it to curtail the power of the nobility, and in 1830 all its furnishings were auctioned off. Many have since been restored to the palace. ⊠ *Kållandsö* ☎ *0510/484660* ⊠ *May–Sept. SKr 70* ☉ *May–Sept., daily 10–6.*

en route

On a peninsula 20 km (12½ mi) to the east of Lidköping, the landscape is dominated by the great hill of **Kinnekulle**, towering 900 feet above Lake Vänern. The hill is rich in colorful vegetation and wildlife and was a favorite hike for the botanist Linnaeus. A Swedish summer morning was never greeted better than from its summit, the mist-strewn lake stretched out below.

Where to Stay & Eat

$–$$ ✕ **Götes Festvåning.** Anything with pike (*gädda*) is particularly worth trying at this typical Swedish dining room serving good regional specialties. ⊠ *Östra Hamnen 5* ☎ *0510/21700* 🖃 *DC, MC, V.*

$ ⌂ **Stadtshotellet.** Like most town-hotels in Sweden, the Stadtshotel offers a faded grandeur with a lot of character. Rooms are a little on the small side but comfortable and bright, most with a white-and-blue color scheme. The best ones overlook the river and the main town square. ⊠ *Gamla Stadens torg 1, 531 02* ☎ *0510/22085* 🖃 *0510/21532* ⊕ *www.stadtlidkoping.se* 🛏 *67 rooms, 2 suites* ᶜ *Restaurant, bar, no-smoking rooms* 🖃 *AE, DC, MC, V* ⧛ *BP.*

¢   ⌂ **Hotell Rådhuset.** This basic hotel is somewhat oddly located inside a former office building. The rooms are large and have cable TV. There are several computers on which you can access the Internet. ⊠*Nya Stadens torg 8, 531 31* ☎ *0510/22236* 🖃 *0510/22214* 🛏 *24 rooms* ᶜ *Cable TV, in-room broadband, sauna* 🖃 *AE, DC, MC, V* ⧛ *BP.*

Mariestad

⑮ *40 km (25 mi) northeast of Lidköping.*

This town on the eastern shore of Lake Vänern is an architectural gem and an excellent base for some aquatic exploring. The town's center has a fine medieval quarter, a pretty harbor, and houses built in styles ranging from Gustavian (a baroque style named after King Gustav Vasa of the 1500s) to art nouveau. Others resemble Swiss chalets.

Domkyrkan, the late-Gothic cathedral on the edge of the old part of town, stands as a monument to one man's competitiveness. Commissioned at the end of the 16th century by Duke Karl—who named the town after his wife, Maria—it was built to resemble and rival Klara Kyrka in Stockholm, the church of his brother King Johan III, of whom he was insanely jealous. Karl made sure the church was endowed with some wonderfully excessive features, which can still be seen today. The stained-glass windows have real insects (bees, dragonflies, etc.) sandwiched within them, and the silver-and-gold cherubs are especially roly-poly and cute.

Vadsbo Museum is a museum of the local area's industry, which centers not surprisingly around the lake. The museum is just off the old town, on a small island in the River Tidan, which flows off Vänern. Named after the old jurisdiction of Vadsbo, the museum—housed in the medieval judge's residence—has displays on the region from the prehistoric age to the 20th century. ⊠ *Residensö, Marieholmn* ☎ *0501/755831* 🎫 *SKr 25* ⊙ *June–Aug., Tues.–Sun. 1–4, Wed. 1–7; Sept.–May, weekends 1–3.*

off the beaten path

GULLSPÅNG – Forty kilometers (25 mi) north of Mariestad, this town is the starting place for 20 km (12 mi) of railway track, originally built to improve Sweden's rail links in the 1960s but now used for leisure purposes. The tracks run through some beautiful countryside and along the Gullspångälv (Gullspång River), which has great swimming. You get to travel the tracks in handcars, which aren't often seen outside cartoons and cowboy movies. The small cars are operated by having two people push a lever up and down. If you've got the energy, it's a great trip.

Where to Stay & Eat

$–$$ ✕ **St. Michel.** The outdoor patio of this old-style restaurant shoots out into Lake Vänern on stilts. Both the indoor and outdoor seating options offer beautiful views of the lake. The traditional Swedish dishes are heavily meat-based, and most come with a side of *rösti* (hash potatoes mixed with grated cheese and chopped onions and shaped to a pancake). ✉ *Kungsg. 1* ☎ *0501/19900* ▤ *MC, V* ☉ *Closed Sun. No lunch Sat.*

$ ▥ **Stadtshotellet.** This is the best choice in a town full of below-average hotels. The building is unobtrusive, but the rooms are comfortable, if a little bland in their furnishings. ✉ *Nyg. 10, 542 30* ☎ *0501/13800* ⎙ *0501/77640* ⊕ *www.stadtshotelletmariestad.com* ⤴ *29 rooms* ⟁ *Restaurant, in-room broadband, in-room data ports, bar, no-smoking rooms* ▤ *AE, MC, V* ⫛ *BP.*

Nightlife & the Arts

Evenings can be fairly quiet and relaxing in Mariestad, but the bar at **Restaurang Björnes Magasin** (✉ Karlag. 2 ☎ 0501/18050) can be a lively spot for the young adults in town.

The Outdoors

The nearby island of **Torsö** is perfect for fishing and lying out on the beach. It's reachable by a 1-km-long (½-mi-long) bridge that makes for a good jog or bike ride. For information on hiring equipment for fishing, contact the **tourist office** (✉ Hamnplan ☎ 0501/10001).

Sjötorp

⑯ *27 km (17 mi) northeast of Mariestad, 207 km (129 mi) northeast of Göteborg.*

At the lakeside port of Sjötorp, the Göta Canal proper begins. A series of locks raises steamers to the village of Lanthöjden—at 304 feet above sea level it's the highest point on the canal. The boats next enter the narrow, twisting lakes of Viken and Bottensjön and continue to Forsvik through the canal's oldest lock, built in 1813. Boats then sail out into **Vättern,** Sweden's second-largest lake, nearly 129 km (80 mi) from north to south and 31 km (19 mi) across at its widest point. Its waters are so clear that in some parts the bottom is visible at a depth of 50 feet. The lake is subject to sudden storms that can whip its normally placid waters into choppy waves.

Motala

⑰ *13 km (8 mi) north of Vadstena, 262 km (163 mi) northeast of Göteborg.*

Before reaching Stockholm, the canal passes through Motala, where Baltzar von Platen is buried. He had hoped that four new towns would be established along the waterway, but only Motala rose according to plan. He designed the town himself, and his statue is in the main square. Motala itself is not an essential sight. Instead, it's the activities along the canal and lake, along with a few very good museums, that make Motala worth a stop.

★ Stop at the **Motala Motormuseum** even if you are not in the slightest bit interested in cars. All the cars and motorcycles on display—from 1920s Rolls-Royces to 1950s Cadillacs and modern racing cars—are presented in their appropriate context, with music of the day playing on contemporary radios; mannequins dressed in fashions of the time; and newspapers, magazines, televisions, and everyday household objects all helping to set the stage. More a museum of 20th-century technology and life than one solely of cars, it makes for a fascinating look back at the last century. ⊠ *Hamnen* ☎ *0141/58888* ⊕ *www.motala-motormuseum. se* 🎫 *SKr 50* ⊙ *June–Aug., daily 10–8; May and Sept., daily 10–6; Oct.–Apr., weekdays 8–5, weekends 11–5.*

Europe's most powerful radio transmitter was built in Motala in 1927. In later years radio became an important industry for this little town. The **Rundradiomuseet** uses interactive displays to present the history of radio's birth as well as a glimpse into its future. ⊠ *Radiov.* ☎ *0141/ 52202* 🎫 *SKr 40* ⊙ *May, daily noon–4; June–mid-Aug., daily 10–6; mid-Aug.–Oct., weekends noon–4.*

Where to Stay

$ 🏨 **Ramada Palace Hotel.** Ship models decorate the lobby windows of this hotel with a nautical theme. The rooms are designed to look like cabins, though fortunately larger and more comfortable. Paintings of sea motifs and round windows in the bathrooms add to the charm. Just a five-minute walk from the train station, this hotel is close to most of Motala's sights. ⊠ *Kungsg. 1, 591 30* ☎ *0141/216660* 🖷 *0141/57221* ⊕ *www.ramadapalace.se* 🛏 *55 rooms, 1 suite* ♨ *Sauna, bar, free parking* ☰ *AE, MC, V* ⏹ *BP.*

---

en route   At Borenshult a series of locks takes the boat down to **Boren,** a lake in the province of Östergötland. On the southern shore of the next lake, Roxen, lies the city of **Linköping,** capital of the province and home of Saab, the aircraft and automotive company. Once out of the lake, you follow a different stretch of canal past the sleepy town of **Söderköping.** A few miles east, at the hamlet of Mem, the canal's last lock lowers the boat into Slätbaken, a Baltic fjord presided over by the **Stegeborg Slottsruin,** the ancient ruins of the Stegeborg Fortress. The boat then steams north along the coastline until it enters **Mälaren** through the Södertälje Canal and finally anchors in the capital at Riddarholmen.

Vadstena

🔞 *249 km (155 mi) northeast of Göteborg (via Jönköping).*

This little-known gem of a town grew up around the monastery founded by St. Birgitta, or Bridget (1303–73), who wrote in her *Revelations* that she had a vision of Christ in which he revealed the rules of the religious order she went on to establish. These rules seem to have been a precursor for the Swedish ideal of sexual equality, with both nuns and monks sharing a common church. Her order spread rapidly after her death, and at one time there were 80 Bridgetine monasteries in Europe. Little remains of the Vadstena monastery; in 1545 King Gustav Vasa ordered its demolition, and its stones were used to build **Vadstena Slott** (Vadstena Castle), a huge fortress created to defend against Danish attack. It was later refurbished and used as a home for Gustav's mentally ill son. Many of the original decorations were lost in a fire in the early 1600s. Unable to afford replacement decorations, the royal family had decorations and fittings painted with three-dimensional effect directly onto the walls. Many of the "curtains" that can be seen today come from this period. Swedish royalty held court at Vadstena Slott until 1715. It then fell into decay and was used as a granary. Recent efforts have returned the castle to something approaching its former glory. Today it houses part of the National Archives, the tourist bureau, and is also the site of an annual summer opera festival. ☎ *0143/31570* ✉ *SKr 50 (in winter SKr 30)* ⊗ *Mid-May–end of May, daily 11–4; June and Aug., daily 10–6; July, daily 10–7; Sept. 1–Sept. 15, daily 10–4; Sept. 16–mid-May, daily 11–2; guided tours on the hr June–Aug.*

The triptych altarpiece on the south wall of the **Vadstena Kyrka** (Vadstena Church) shows St. Birgitta presenting her book of revelations to a group of kneeling cardinals. In a cherub-covered tomb are the remains of Gustav Vasa's son. St. Birgitta's bones are here as well, but less grandly stored in a red-velvet box inside a glass case.

Housed in what was once Sweden's oldest mental hospital, the **Hospital Museet** is a fascinating, moving reminder of centuries of misguided treatments and "cures" for the mentally ill. Devices on display include a chair into which patients were strapped and spun until they were sick and a bath in which unruly patients were scalded. Perhaps the most moving display includes photographs of inmates from the 19th century and the drawings they made of the tortures inflicted upon them. The tour also includes **Mårten Skinnares Hus,** a very well-preserved private medieval residence once inhabited by the hospital priest. ✉ *Lastköpingsg.* ☎ *0143/31570* ✉ *SKr 50* ⊗ *June and Aug., daily 2–3; July, daily 1–3; 1 guided tour in June and Aug. (2 PM) and 2 in July (1 PM and 2 PM).*

A donation of a private doll collection was the start of the **Leksaksmuseet** (Toy Museum). Private donations have now expanded the museum's holdings into one of the largest in Sweden. The museum also has an interesting collection of clocks from the 17th century on. ✉ *Lilla Hamnarmen* ☎ *0143/29275* ✉ *SKr 45* ⊗ *May and Sept., daily 8–6; June–Aug., 8–8; Oct.–Apr., 8–4.*

off the beaten path

The little town of **GRÄNNA, –** 30 km (18 mi) southwest of Vadstena, is a perfect place for a quick overnight stop. The town is famous for two things: a popular pink-and-white peppermint candy and being the birthplace of late adventurer and polar balloonist Salomon August Andrée. The museum dedicated to Andrée is called the **Grenna Museum & Polar Center** (✉ Braheg. 38 ☎ 0390/41015). Regardless of candy and adventurers, Gränna is a lovely place for exploring and wandering, with narrow streets and beautiful, many-color weatherboard houses. When you are ready, retire to **Gyllene Uttern** (✉ Gränna ☎ 0390/10800 ⊕ www.gylleneuttern.se), a gorgeous hotel and restaurant with superb lake views well worth the trip alone.

FodorśChoice
★

Where to Stay

$–$$ 🏨 **Vadstena Klosterhotel.** Sweden's oldest secular building, parts of which date from the 13th century, is now a hotel. Rooms are modern and well appointed, and there are three comfortable lounges. You can choose a view of either Lake Vättern or the hotel's courtyard. The former is infinitely more preferable and only SKr 100 extra. ✉ *Klosterområdet off Lasarettsg., 592 24* ☎ *0143/31530* 🖷 *0143/13648* ⊕ *www.klosterhotel. se* ➪ *65 rooms, 3 suites* ⚘ *Restaurant, lounge, meeting room, no-smoking rooms* ⊟ *AE, DC, MC, V* ⍓ *BP.*

$ 🏨 **Starby Kungsgård.** This functional guesthouse, reached via Route 50, is next to a renovated manor house and restaurant. The rooms use light wood throughout and have earth-tone carpets and green, blue, and brown color schemes. The complex is surrounded by a park on the outskirts of town. ✉ *Ödeshögsv., 592 21* ☎ *0143/75100* 🖷 *0143/75170* ➪ *61 rooms* ⚘ *Restaurant, indoor pool, hot tub, sauna, spa, meeting room, free parking* ⊟ *AE, DC, MC, V* ⍓ *CP.*

Göta Canal A to Z

BIKE TOURS
For two-day bike tours along the canal from Sjötorp to Tåtorp and back, contact Resespecialisten utmed Göta Kanal. The price is SKr 1,000 for adults and SKr 500 for children under 13. The price includes lodging in a youth hostel in Töreboda, a breakfast, lunch, and dinner, as well as a bike rental for an adult. The same company also has four-day combined bike and boat tours along the canal for SKr 2,500 (all inclusive) for adults.

🖪 **Resespecialisten utmed Göta Kanal** ✉ Kungsg. 10, 545 30 Töreboda ☎ 0506/12500 ⊕ www.gotakanalturer.com.

CAR TRAVEL
From Stockholm follow E20 west; from Göteborg take Route 45 north to E20. For much of the route the canal is actually Lake Vänern, Sweden's largest lake, which cuts the canal in two. From Trollhättan to Sjötorp, you hug the lake shore. The canal proper is mostly surrounded by meadows, so gas-driven waterside transport is out of the question.

CRUISE TRAVEL
Rederi Göta Canal has cruises along the canal from one to six days, originating in Göteborg (with bus service to the canal). Prices vary. For more details about cruises along the Göta Canal, *see* "Boat & Ferry Travel" *in* Göteborg A to Z.

🖪 **Rederi Göta Canal** ✉ Pusterviksg. 13, Göteborg ☎ 031/806315 ⊕ www.stromma.se.

TRAIN TRAVEL

Call SJ for information about service. All towns along the canal are either on a main rail line, or have good bus connections to the nearest train stop.

🚆 SJ ✉ Göteborg ☎ 0771/757575.

VISITOR INFORMATION

🏠 **Karlsborg** ✉ Ankarv. 2 ☎ 0505/17350. **Lidköping** Götene-Lidköping Turistbyrå ✉ Bang. 3 ☎ 0510/20020. **Mariestad** ✉ Hamnplan ☎ 0501/10001 ⊕ www.turism. mariestad.se. **Motala** ✉ Göta Kanalbolagsmuseet, Hamnen ☎ 0141/225254. **Skövde** ✉ Sandtorget ☎ 0500/446688. **Uddevalla** ✉ Kungstorget 4 ☎ 0522/99720 ⊕ www. uddevallaforum.se. **Vadstena** ✉ Slottet ☎ 0143/31570. **Vänersborg** Vänersborgs Turist ✉ Järnvägsstationen ☎ 0521/271400 ⊕ www.vanersborg.se/turist.

VÄRMLAND

Close to the Norwegian border on the north shores of Vänern, the province of Värmland is rich in folklore. It was also the home of Alfred Nobel and the birthplace of other famous Swedes, among them Nobel Prize–winning novelist Selma Lagerlöf, poet Gustaf Fröding, former prime minister Tage Erlander, and present-day opera star Håkan Hagegård. Värmland's forested, lake-dotted landscape attracts artists seeking refuge and Swedes on holiday.

Karlstad

🔟 *255 km (158 mi) northeast of Göteborg.*

Värmland's principal city (population 80,000) is on Klarälven (Klara River) at the point where it empties into Vänern. Karlstad received its charter in 1684, and the city, then known as Tingvalla, changed its name to Karlstad, meaning Karl's Town, to honor King Karl IX who had extended the charter. In **Residenstorget,** the square in front of the county governor's residence, there is a statue of Karl IX by the local sculptor Christian Eriksson.

Only 11 buildings survived a devastating fire in 1865, but miraculously, the fire did not claim a single life. The tourist office organizes free guided walks, in English upon request, during the summer months. The city makes bicycles available for free at Stora Torget, the main square, in the summertime.

Northeast of Stora Torget is **Östra Bron** (East Bridge). Completed in 1811, it is Sweden's longest arched stone bridge, its 12 arches spanning 510 feet across the water. Anders Jacobsson, the bridge's builder, carved his name on a stone in the bridge's center.

One of the buildings that survived the 1865 fire, the **Biskopsgården** (Bishop's Residence) is a beautiful, two-story, cream-color wooden building with red window trims that was built in 1781. The row of huge elm trees that surrounds the building acted as a natural firebreak and saved it from the flames. The building is now a private home.

Karlstad is the site of the **Emigrantregistret** (Emigrant Registry), which maintains detailed records of the Swedes' emigration to America. Those of Swedish extraction can trace their ancestors at the center's research facility. ⊠ *Hööksg. 2* ☎ *054/617720* 🖥 *Free* ☉ *June–Aug., daily 8:30–3; Sept.–May, Mon. 8:30–8, Tues.–Fri. 8:30–4.*

Consecrated in 1730, **Karlstads Katedral** (Karlstad's Cathedral; ⊠ Kungsg.) fared fairly well in the great fire of 1865. Only one tower was destroyed, and a new, pointier tower was subsequently added. Particular features worth looking for are the angels by the altar, made by sculptor Tobias Sergel, and the altar itself, made of limestone and with a crystal cross, and the font, also made of crystal.

☉ In 1920, ten farm buildings were moved to **Marieberg Skogspark** (Marieberg Forest Park) to create an open-air museum. A delight for the whole family, the park has nature trails, a minizoo, a beach, walking trails, minigolf, restaurants, and an outdoor theater. In the middle of the forest there is a "nature room," giving a glimpse of Värmland's flora and fauna. ☎ *054/296990* ☉ *Dawn–dusk.*

The original building of the **Värmlands Museum** has been connected by a glass walkway to a red, seven-pointed wing by architect Carl Nyrén. Värmland's history and local notables like sculptor Christian Eriksson and poet Gustaf Fröding are the subjects of the exhibits. ⊠ *Sandgrun* ☎ *054/143100* 🖥 *SKr 40* ☉ *Tues.–Fri. 10–5, weekends 11–5.*

Where to Stay & Eat

$$–$$$ ✕ **Restaurang Munken.** Walking down the steps into this cellar restaurant is like stepping into a *Three Musketeers* set. Low, arched stone ceilings, long wooden benches, and dim candlelight make this a cozy, informal spot. The food is warming, filling Swedish fare with a heavy Continental hand. Anything with veal is worth trying here. ⊠ *Västra Torgg. 17* ☎ *054/185150* ☰ *AE, DC, MC, V* ☉ *Closed Sun.*

$$–$$$ ✕ **Värdshuset Alstern.** Overlooking Lake Alstern, this elegant restaurant offers Swedish and Continental cuisine, with fish dishes the specialty. ⊠ *Morgonv. 4* ☎ *054/834900* ☰ *AE, MC, V.*

¢–$$ ✕ **Ristorante Alfie.** The three dining rooms are dimly lighted, and the dark-wood tables are close together, making Alfie a very sociable dining experience. The menu includes pizzas and pasta and a huge and varied steak menu. The entrecôte steaks, served extremely rare with béarnaise sauce, are some of the best around. ⊠ *Västra Torgg. 19* ☎ *054/216262* ☰ *AE, DC, MC, V.*

$$ ⌂ **Radisson SAS Plaza Hotel.** The very large rooms here are in soothing neutral tones and come with excellent amenities. There is a sauna and relaxation area on the top floor, which offers great views across the city. ⊠ *Västra Torgg. 2, 652 25* ☎ *054/100200* 🖷 *054/100224* 💬 *131 rooms, 5 suites* ⌂ *Restaurant, room service, minibars, room TVs with movies, in-room broadband, in-room data ports, Wi-Fi, bar, lounge, dance club* ☰ *AE, DC, MC, V* ⑩ *BP.*

$ ⌂ **Comfort Hotel Bilan.** Security will be the least of your worries here since the hotel is in a converted old county jail. Not surprisingly, the outside is a little imposing and uninviting, but once inside, public areas and rooms all have cheery furnishings and fabrics. In the basement there is a museum where you can look at the original cells and see letters and some of the objects—including a hacksaw—once sent to prisoners. ⊠ *Karlbergsg. 3, 652 24* ☎ *054/100300* 🖶 *054/219214* 🛏 *68 rooms* ♿ *Restaurant, indoor pool, sauna, meeting room, no-smoking rooms* ▤ *AE, DC, MC, V* ⦿ *BP.*

$ 🖼 **Elite Stadtshotellet.** On the bank of the Klarälven, this hotel from 1870 is steeped in tradition. All the rooms are decorated differently, some in modern Swedish style, others in ways that evoke their original look. You can dine at the fancy Matsalen or in the more casual atmosphere of the Bishop's Arms, an English pub offering 50 types of beer. ⊠ *Kungsg. 22, 651 08* ☎ *054/293000* 🖶 *054/293031* 🛏 *139 rooms* ♿ *Restaurant, room service, room TVs with movies, in-room broadband, in-room data ports, Wi-Fi, sauna, lounge, pub, meeting room, no-smoking rooms* ▤ *AE, DC, MC, V* ⦿ *BP.*

Nightlife & the Arts

The choice of bars and pubs in Karlstad is good for a town of this size. **Harry's** (⊠ Kungsg. 16 ☎ 054/102020) is an American-style bar with a large wooden interior and good beer on tap. English-style pub **Woolpack Inn** (⊠ Järnsvägsg. 1 ☎ 054/158016) is a perennial favorite with the locals.

For late-night dancing try **Plaza Nightclub** (⊠ Västra Torgg. 2 ☎ 054/100200), in the basement of the Radisson SAS Plaza Hotel. This is the place to be seen in Karlstad. Trendies in their mid-20s and beyond dance the night away to the latest club tunes, fueled by lavishly over-the-top cocktails and lots of beer.

Sports & the Outdoors

The Klarälven River runs for 500 km (312 mi). Its rapid waters used since the 18th century for floating logs downstream to sawmills now offer great opportunities for rafting trips. On the way you can swim, fish, and contemplate the beautiful scenery and wildlife (elk, beavers, wolverines, and bears). At night you camp in tents on the water's edge. Two companies, **Sverigeflotten** (☎ 0564/40227 ⊕ www.sverigeflotten. se) and **Vildmark i Värmland** (☎ 0560/14040) operate trips along the river on two-person rafts.

You can canoe or boat on Lake Vänern in the center of the city. **Vänerkajak** (⊠ Östra Rosenlundsv. 54, Hammarö ☎ 054/521627 ⊕ www. vanerkajak.se) rents boats and offers introductory courses.

Shopping

Stores selling clothes, jewelry, furniture, antiques, and crafts are all concentrated on the streets of **Drotninggatan** and **Östra Torggatan.** All the main national retail brands are here, as are individual boutiques.

en route Värmland is, above all, a rural experience. Drive along the **Klarälven,** through the beautiful Fryken Valley, to Ransater, where author Erik Gustaf Geijer was born in 1783 and where Tage Erlander, the former prime minister, also grew up. The rural idyll ends in **Munkfors,** where some of the best-quality steel in Europe is manufactured.

Sunne

② *63 km (39 mi) north of Karlstad, 318 km (198 mi) northeast of Göteborg.*

A small village more than a town, Sunne is mainly known for two things. First, the famed Swedish author Selma Lagerlöf has many connections here. Sunne is also known for the prominent spa that dominates the entrance road to the village. It's a haven for stressed executives from all over Sweden.

In the middle of town, **Sundsbergs Gård** is a beautiful building said to have inspired one of the settings in Selma Lagerlöf's novel, *Gösta Berling*. Sundsberg's Manor House (built in 1780) is now a museum charting the last three centuries of Swedish history. ⊠ *Ekebyv.* ☎ *0565/ 10363* 🎟 *SKr 35* ⊙ *Museum mid-June–mid-Aug., Tues.–Thurs. and weekends noon–4; art exhibition hall and café year-round, Tues.–Thurs. and weekends noon–4.*

A small collection of old buildings makes up **Sunne Hembygdsgård,** a museum showing how life was lived in the 1800s. The well-preserved buildings include a manor house, school, general store, and courthouse. ⊠ *Hembygdsv. 7* ☎ *0565/10120* 🎟 *Free* ⊙ *By appointment.*

> **off the beaten path**

MÅRBACKA – The estate on which Nobel Prize winner Selma Lagerlöf was born in 1858 can be found in this town, 10 km (7 mi) southeast of Sunne. Lagerlöf is considered the best Swedish author of her generation and is known and avidly read by Swedes young and old. The house can be seen by guided tour. Her furnishings, including her study desk and beautiful wood-panel library, have been kept much as she left them at the time of her death in 1940. ⊠ *Östra Ämtervik, 686 26* ☎ *0565/31027* 🎟 *SKr 65* ⊙ *Mid-May–Aug., daily 10–4, tours every hr; July, daily 10–5, tours every ½ hr; Sept., weekends 11–2.*

Ꮯ ROTTNEROS HERRGÅRDS PARK – On the western shore of Fryken Lake, 5 km (3 mi) south of Sunne, is Rottneros Manor, the inspiration for Ekeby, the fictional estate in Lagerlöf's *Gösta Berlings Saga (The Tale of Gösta Berling)*. The house is privately owned, but you can go to the park, with its fine collection of Scandinavian sculpture. Here there are works by Carl Milles, Norwegian artist Gustav Vigeland, and Wäinö Aaltonen of Finland. The entrance fee covers both the sculpture park and the Nils Holgerssons Adventure Park, an elaborate playground for children. ⊠ *Rottneros* ☎ *0565/ 60295* 🎟 *SKr 100* ⊙ *May, weekdays 10–4, weekends 10–5; June, daily 10–5; July, daily 10–6; Aug., daily 10–4.*

Where to Stay & Eat

★ ¢–$ ✕ **Köpmangården.** If you blink, you may miss this tiny bar and restaurant that's on a road of private residences. It looks like a derelict old house from the outside, and the faded carpet, old furniture, and dingy restrooms on the inside aren't much better. But the food is some of the best around. Everything is homemade. The tomato soup with crème fraîche, huge prawn sandwiches, and inch-thick steaks are all delicious. The warm welcome from the little old lady who runs the place is as good as the food. ⊠ *Ekebyv. 40* ☎ *0565/10121* ⊟ *AE, MC, V.*

$$ ✕⌂ **Quality Hotel and Spa Selma Lagerlöf.** This huge complex of a hotel is split onto two sides of the road leading into Sunne. Each side has large rooms furnished in a simple Scandinavian design, public rooms and lobbies, a bar, a restaurant, and a nightclub. The main hotel has a very well-equipped spa and fitness center. Guests can use most of the facilities for free, with a nominal charge for treatments. The restaurants ($$) serve good Swedish classics and French-influenced food. Be sure to try the reindeer if it's available. The extensive grounds of the hotel have many wooded walking and jogging paths. Ask for a room at the front of the hotel, as these have stunning views over the lake. ⊠ *Ekebyv., Lagerlöf, 686 28 Sunne* ☎ *0565/688810* 🖷 *0565/16631* ⊕ *www.selmaspa.se* ⇥ *156 rooms, 10 suites* ⅋ *2 restaurants, room service, in-room data ports, 2 pools, health club, sauna, spa, 2 bars, lounge, 2 nightclubs, convention center* ⊟ *AE, DC, MC, V* ⅋⅋ *BP.*

The Outdoors
You're almost guaranteed to see an elk on an **elk safari** (Gräsmarks turistbyrå; ☎ 0565/40016). Departures are every Wednesday and Friday in July and cost from SKr 150.

Shopping
If you're passing through Sunne and feeling a little ravaged by life, you can pick up some pick-me-ups at the local spa resort. **Quality Hotel and Spa Selma Lagerlöf** (⊠ Sundsberget ☎ 0565/688810) offers all manner of wonderful herb, spice, mud, and clay concoctions.

Filipstad

㉑ *63 km (39 mi) northeast of Karlstad via Rte. 63.*

For hundreds of years Filipstad was the center of the area's mineral mining and metalworking. You can still see many of the ancient mining and stonecutting methods and lifestyles in various working museums and villages such as Nykroppa and Långban. Persberg has the Värmland's only surviving underground mine still producing limestone. Details of mine tours can be obtained from **Filipstad Turistbyrå** (tourist office; ⊠ Stora Torget 3D ☎ 0590/61354). Visitors to **Hornkullens Silver Mine** (⊠ Nykroppa ☎ 070/2841676 Kroppgårdens Vandrarhem) in Nykroppa can pan for gold after the mine tour, although the finds are not likely to finance any Sweden vacations. A hostel takes care of the tour bookings. Guided tours of the limestone mine **Gåsgruvan** (⊠ Persberg ☎ 0590/ 21137), in Persberg, are arranged through Yngens Café.

Långban is interesting not just for its **Långbans Museum** for mining and minerals, but also as the birthplace of inventor John Ericsson. Ericsson left Sweden for England in 1826 at the age of 23, and emigrated from there to America. During the U.S. Civil War the Union asked him to construct an armored ship. His *Monitor* would ultimately defeat the Confederate ship *Merrimack* at Hampton Roads, Virginia. Tours are available in Swedish, English, and German. Groups of five can call ahead to visit during the off-season. ☎ *0590/22181 or 0590/22115* ✉ *SKr 25, with tour SKr 35* ☉ *Early June–late Aug., weekdays 10–5, weekends noon–4. Guided tours at 11, noon, 2, 3, and 4.*

Filipstad's other mainstay is **Wasa** (✉ Konsul Lundströms väg 11 ☎ 0590/18100 ⊕ www.wasa.com), Scandinavia's largest producer of crispbread. The factory runs guided tours, showing the history of the company and how crispbread is produced. Call to arrange a tour.

Where to Stay & Eat

¢ ✕▦ **Hennickehammars Gård.** Big windows, original wooden floors, and antique furniture define the large and airy guest rooms at this old Swedish manor house. The restaurant ($$$) serves traditional Swedish food in a fresh white-and-blue antique dining room with open fire. After you're full from dinner, a stroll around the peaceful grounds is a delight. ✉ *Rte. 64, 6½ km (4 mi) south of Filipstad, Box 52, 682 22* ☎ *0590/608500* 🖷 *0590/608505* ⊕ *www.hennickehammar.se* ↩ *55 rooms, 6 suites* ⚐ *Restaurant, gym, sauna, bar, meeting rooms, free parking* ▤ *AE, DC, MC, V* ⍵ *BP.*

Värmland A to Z

CAR TRAVEL
From Stockholm follow E18 west; from Göteborg take Route 45 north to E18.

TRAIN TRAVEL
There is regular service to Karlstad from Stockholm and Göteborg on SJ. 🚩 **SJ** ✉ Göteborg ☎ 0771/757575.

VISITOR INFORMATION
🚩 **Filipstad** ✉ Stora Torget 3D ☎ 0590/61354 ⊕ www.filipstad.se/main.html. **Karlstad** ✉ Tage Erlanderg. 10 ☎ 054/298400 ⊕ www.karlstad.se. **Sunne** Turistbyrå ✉ Kolsnäsv. 41 ☎ 0565/16400.

The South & the Kingdom of Glass

6

Updated by
Rob Hincks

SOUTHERN SWEDEN IS CONSIDERED, even by many Swedes, to be a world of its own, clearly distinguished from the rest of the country by its geography, culture, and history. Skåne (pronounced *skoh*-neh), the southernmost province, is known as the granary of Sweden. It is a comparatively small province of beautifully fertile plains, sand beaches, thriving farms, bustling historic towns and villages, medieval churches, and summer resorts. These gently rolling hills, extensive forests, and fields are broken every few miles by lovely castles, chronologically and architecturally diverse, that have given this part of Sweden the name Château Country. A significant number of the estates, often surrounded by beautiful grounds and moats, have remained in the hands of the original families, and many are still inhabited.

The two other southern provinces, Blekinge and Halland, are also fertile and rolling and edged by seashores. Historically, these three provinces are distinct from the rest of Sweden: they were the last to be incorporated into the country, having been ruled by Denmark until 1658. They retain the influences of the Continental culture in their architecture, language, and cuisine, viewing the rest of Sweden—especially Stockholm—with some disdain. Skåne even has its own independence movement, and the dialect is so akin to Danish that many Swedes from other regions have trouble understanding it.

Småland, to the north, is larger than the other provinces, with a harsh countryside of stone and woods. A poorer, bleaker way of life here led thousands of peasants to emigrate to the United States in the 19th and 20th centuries. Those who stayed behind developed a reputation for their inventiveness in setting up small industries and are also notorious for being extremely careful with money. The area has many small glassblowing firms, and it is these glassworks, such as the world-renowned Kosta Boda and Orrefors, that have given the area the nickname the Kingdom of Glass.

Perhaps the most significant recent event for the south has been the bridge that opened over the Øresund, linking Malmö to Copenhagen in Denmark. At 8 km (5 mi), the **Øresund Bridge** is the longest in the world that carries both road and rail traffic. It opened on July 1, 2000, amid hopes that it would bring a windfall to the South. As a tourist, your travel alternatives have improved.

Your itinerary should follow a route that sweeps from the western coastal town of Mölle around the southern loop and along the eastern shore, taking a side trip to the Baltic island province of Öland before heading inland to the finish at Växjö. The entire route can be done by train, with the exception of Mölle, Öland, and most of the glassworks in Småland—the Orrefors factory is the only one on the railway line. Continue your journey in any direction from Växjö.

Exploring the South & the Kingdom of Glass

Since it covers a fairly large area of the country, this region is best explored by car. The coastal road is a pleasure to travel on, with scenic views of long, sandy beaches and the welcoming blue sea. Inland, the hills, fertile plains, and thickly wooded forests are interconnected by winding country roads. The southern peninsula around the province of Skåne has the most urban settlements and, thanks to the spectacular Øresund Bridge, fast connections to Denmark and mainland Europe. The rest of the area is more picturesque and slow-paced, inviting you to take your time exploring the pretty fishing villages and ancient castles that dot the landscape.

About the Hotels & Restaurants

The south is Sweden's breadbasket, cashing in on its relatively mild climate to produce top-quality fruit, vegetables, meat, and fish. As in many good food-producing areas, the residents keep the best for themselves. Everything from modern restaurants serving international cuisines to small local eating spots abounds in the region. The emphasis is on high-quality ingredients. There are plenty of good hotels, too, including some very charming old bath hotels on the coast, relics of the days of restorative bathing weekends.

	WHAT IT COSTS In Swedish Kronor				
	$$$$	**$$$**	**$$**	**$**	**¢**
RESTAURANTS	over 420	250–420	150–250	100–150	under 100
HOTELS	over 2,900	2,300–2,900	1,500–2,300	1,000–1,500	under 1,000

Restaurant prices are for a main course at dinner. Hotel prices are for two people in a standard double room in high season.

Timing

The south of Sweden has a relatively mild climate compared to the rest of the country, making it possible to visit any time of year. Like much of Sweden, though, it really comes alive in the summer months, when you will find many more outdoor activities, restaurants, and cafés open than there are in winter. The region's large tracts of agricultural land are at their most spectacular when in full bloom, in July and August. Kivik, Sweden's cider capital on the east coast, is best appreciated in early autumn, when the trees are heavily laden with apples and pears.

July is the best time to visit the classic Skåne markets in the very south of the region; they are reminiscent of old trading days when traveling tinkers used to ply their wares. You'll find everything from horses to handwoven baskets, and from clogs and sweets to ducks and geese.

Mölle

★ ❶ *35 km (21 mi) northwest of Helsingborg, 220 km (132 mi) south of Göteborg, 235 km (141 mi) southwest of Växjö, 95 km (57 mi) northwest of Malmö.*

Mölle, in the far northwest of Skåne, is a small town set in spectacular isolation on the dramatic headland of the Kulla Peninsula. It is an old fishing village with a beautiful harbor that sweeps up to the Kullaberg

Range. You will find beech forests, stupefying views, and rugged shores and beaches, surrounded on three sides by sea.

For those who love nature or want a break from cities and touring, Mölle is perfect. Not only is it a good base from which to explore, but the town itself has a charm that has never been tarnished by an overabundance of tourists or a relentless drive to modernize at all costs.

But Mölle's past isn't all quaintness and tradition. In the late 19th century the town was notorious throughout the country and the rest of Europe as a hotbed of liberal hedonism. This reputation was based on the penchant of locals to enjoy mixed-sex bathing, a scandalous practice at the time. Berliners loved it, and until World War I there was a weekly train that went all the way to Mölle. But as soon as war broke out, the Germans disappeared.

Today it is a relatively wealthy place, as the elaborate residences and the upmarket cars crowding the narrow streets show. Much of this wealth supposedly arrived when the more fortunate men of the sea returned to build mansions. Many of the mansions have local, although perhaps distorted, legends about them.

The **Villa Italienborg** (✉ Harastolsv. 6) was completed in 1910 by a scrap dealer inspired by a trip to the Italian Riviera. The exterior is covered in striking red-and-white tiles that form a checked pattern, which was quite stylish at the time.

The verandas, balconies, and sliding windows all make the two-story **Villa Africa** (✉ N. Brunnsv.) stand out. It was built in a South African colonial style by a local captain to please his South African wife. Legend also has it that while wooing her, he would claim that Mölle's climate was the equal of that of her homeland!

The **Kullaberg nature reserve** is just outside Mölle and covers more than 35 square km (13½ square mi). You can walk, bike, or drive in. This natural playground includes excellent trails through beech forests and along coastal routes. There's a lighthouse here set in stark land that resembles that of the Scottish Highlands—it even has long-haired Highland cattle. The park contains cafés, a restaurant, safe swimming beaches, and a golf course that's one of Sweden's most spectacular. Rock climbers consider the rock structure here to be similar to that of the Himalayas—many climbers planning to travel to that range first train here. ✉ *SKr 30 per car.*

Krapperup Castle was built in 1570 over the ruins of a medieval stronghold dating from the 13th century. The present building was extensively renovated in the late 18th century, although remnants of the stronghold still exist. The garden is among Sweden's best-preserved parks. There's an art gallery and museum inside, and concerts and performance theater are held here in summer. It is 4 km (2½ mi) from Mölle on the main road to Helsingborg. ☎ *042/344190* ✉ *Castle tours for groups of 10 minimum: SKr 75 gallery, museum SKr 35* ☉ *Call to book castle tour for group; gallery and museum May and Sept., weekends 1–6; June–Aug., daily 1–6.*

Just a few kilometers from town, the **Mölle Kapell** is a quaint white church that stands in fields under the Kullaberg. Despite its ancient appearance, the church was built in 1937. Much of the interior—the pulpit, the altar painting, and the pews—was done by local artist Gunnar Wallentin.

The haunting **Nimis and Arx** artworks are built of scrap wood and stone and stand on a rugged beach that can be reached only on foot. The artist Lars Vilks has been working on the weird, highly controversial structures since the 1970s. They are the most visited sight in Kullaberg. Vilks has been under constant legal threat because he didn't apply for permission from the local government, which owns the land. ⊠ *Head 2 km (1 mi) east out of Mölle to a road sign directing you to Himmelstorps Hembygdsgård. Following this sign you will reach a parking lot and an old farmhouse. From here it is a 1-km (½-mi) walk marked by small blue N symbols* ⊕ *www.turism.hoganas.se.*

off the beaten path

ARILD – This beautiful fishing village of bright fishermen's and sailors' cottages has been important since the Middle Ages. It is 6 km (4 mi) east of Mölle. The nicest place to stay is **Hotel Rusthållargården** (⊠ Utsikten 1 ☎ 042/346530), which costs SKr 815 per person, including breakfast. It is one of the original bath hotels of the south coast, and is still an excellent place from which to run down and take to the waters. Also check out the excellent restaurant. If you're looking for a break, continue east from Arild for 2 km (1 mi) to reach the village of **Skäret.** Head for the copper sign shaped like a coffeepot, which marks **Flickorna Lundgren** (⊠ Skäretv. 19 ☎ 042/346044 ☉ Mid-Apr.–mid-Sept.), one of Sweden's most famous cafés. The outstanding gardens look out onto the sea, and the café's regular visitors have included King Gustav IV as well as Gustav V.

Where to Stay & Eat

Most cafés and restaurants in town are in hotels.

$$ ✕ **Gula Boden.** With a local reputation for excellent fish meals and great views of the boat harbor and sunsets, Gula Boden is quite popular. Reservations are essential in July. ⊠ *Vikens Hamn* ☎ *042/238300* ▤ *AE, DC, MC, V* ☉ *Closed Oct.–Apr.*

$–$$ ✕▢ **Grand Hôtel.** The spectacular Grand Hôtel—a turreted building set high up on in town—has an unrivaled setting, great views, and a helpful staff. The best rooms are those with a sea view, but they are all pleasant and decked out with fresh white, blue, and aquamarine prints. For dining you have a choice of two restaurants, the one in the hotel and the attached Captain's Room. The more expensive ($$) and adventurous meals are from the hotel dining room. One hundred years ago people flocked here from Berlin on a weekly train service to enjoy the town's status as Europe's first mixed-sex bathing resort. ⊠ *Bökebolsv. 11, 260 42* ☎ *042/362230* 🖷 *042/362231* ⊕ *www.grand-molle.se* 🛏 *42 rooms* ♿ *2 restaurants, sauna, bar, library, meeting rooms* ▤ *AE, D, MC, V* ⧖ *BP.*

$–$$ ✕⊞ **Turisthotellet.** The rooms at this hotel are well appointed, if a little overly floral, and some have a view of the harbor. The breakfast, included in room rates, is generous and could see you through to dinner. An annex to next-door Hotel Kullaberg, this is nonetheless run as a separate hotel and is a more affordable option. The restaurant ($$),Gran Turismo, serves good Italian food. ⊠ *Kullabergsv. 32, 260 42* ☎ *042/ 347000* 🖶 *042/347100 to Hotel Kullaberg* ⊕ *www.hotelkullaberg.se* 🍴 *14 rooms* ♦ *Restaurant, bar* ▭ *AE, DC, MC, V* ⎟◎⎟ *BP* ☉ *Restaurant closed Sept.–May.*

★ **$$–$$$** ⊞ **Hotel Kullaberg.** At this luxurious hotel all the rooms are plush and decorated in themes. One room suggests *Out of Africa,* and another has a large biplane hanging from the ceiling. You may or may not love it, depending on your feelings about kitsch. But the Kullaberg is lush, with views of the sea and the harbor and ornate reading rooms. ⊠ *Gyllenstiernas Allé 16, 260 42* ☎ *042/347000* 🖶 *042/347100* ⊕ *www.hotelkullaberg.se* 🍴 *18 rooms* ♦ *Library* ▭ *AE, DC, MC, V* ⎟◎⎟ *BP.*

$ ⊞ **Pensionat Solgården.** Run by an artistic woman who spends six months of each year at a bed-and-breakfast in Tonga in the South Pacific, this quaint pension hosts poetry readings outside in summer. ⊠ *Byav. 102 Lerberget* ☎ *042/330430* ☉ *Closed mid-Sept.–mid-Apr.* ⎟◎⎟ *BP.*

Sports
The **Skola Mölle Hamn** (⊠ Special Sports School, Södra Strandv. 6B ☎ 042/347705 or 070/3771210) caters to most outdoor activities. It organizes trips and provides gear and training for mountaineers, scuba divers, and kayakers of all skill levels.

Kullens Hästskjutsar and Turridning (⊠ Himmelstorp 765 ☎ 042/346358) organizes horseback riding.

Mölle Golfklubb (⊠ Kullahalvön ☎ 042/347520 🎫 Greens fees June–Aug. SKr 350, Sept.–May SKr 220), one of the most spectacular 18-hole courses in Sweden, will slake the most fanatic golfers' thirst for their sport.

⎡ **en route** ⎤ Viken and **Lerberget** are two small villages on the way from Mölle to Helsingborg. Viken is a preserved fishing village with narrow stone-walled streets, traditional cottages, and a well-kept example of the old windmills once used in Skåne. If you are here between late spring and fall, you can combine dinner at the Gula Boden seafood restaurant in Viken with a stay at the quaint Pensionat Solgården guesthouse, in nearby Lerberget (a drive of two minutes).

Shopping
In the otherwise unremarkable town of Höganäs (8 km [5 mi] south of Mölle) is a good factory outlet store for ceramics and glassware. **Höganäs Keramik** (⊠ Norreg. 4, Höganäs ☎ 042/361100 🎫 Free guided tours in summer ☉ Sept.–Apr., weekdays 10–6, Sat. 10–4, Sun. 11–4; May, June, and Aug., weekdays 9–6, weekends 10–5; July, weekdays 9–7, weekends 10–5) sells brands such as BodaNova at discounts of up to 40%.

Helsingborg

❷ *221 km (137 mi) south of Göteborg, 186 km (116 mi) southwest of Växjö, 64 km (40 mi) north of Malmö.*

Helsingborg, with a population of 120,000, may seem to the first-time visitor little more than a small town with a modern ferry terminal (there are about 125 daily ferry connections to Denmark and one a day to Norway). The town sees itself differently, claiming titles as Sweden's "gateway to the Continent," and the "pearl of the Øresund" region. Helsingborg was first mentioned in a letter written by Canute, the king of Denmark, in 1085; later it was the site of many battles between the Danes and the Swedes. Together with its twin town, Helsingør (Elsinore in William Shakespeare's *Hamlet*), across the Øresund, it controlled shipping traffic in and out of the Baltic for centuries. Helsingborg was officially incorporated into Sweden in 1658, and totally destroyed in a battle with the Danes in 1710. It was then rebuilt, and Jean-Baptiste Bernadotte, founder of the present Swedish royal dynasty, landed here in 1810.

The **Dunkers Kulturhus** (Henry Dunker Culture Center) includes a theater, the city museum, a music school, a concert hall, an art museum, a cultural center for children and youth, a multimedia center, a bar, and a restaurant. It was designed by Kim Utzon, the son of the controversial architect Jørn Utzon, the Dane who designed the Sydney Opera House. ⊠ *Kungsg. 11* ☎ *042/107400* ⊕ *www.dunkerskultuhus.com* ✉ *SKr 60* ⊗ *Tues. and Wed. 10–5, Thurs. 10–8, Fri.–Sun. 10–5.*

All that remains of Helsingborg's castle is **Kärnan** (the Keep), which was built in the late 14th century. It has walls 15 feet thick. This surviving center tower, built to provide living quarters and defend the medieval castle, is one of the most remarkable relics of its kind in the north. It fell into disuse after the Swedish defeated the Danes in 1658 but was restored in 1893–94. The interior is divided into several floors, which contain a chapel, an exhibition of kitchen implements, old castle fittings, and some weaponry. ⊠ *Slottshagen* ☎ *042/105991* ✉ *SKr 20* ⊗ *Jan.–Mar., Tues.–Sun. 11–3; Apr. and May, Tues.–Fri. 9–4, weekends 11–4; June–Aug., daily 11–7; Sept., Tues.–Fri. 9–4, weekends 11–4; Oct.–Dec., Tues.–Sun. 11–3.*

Maria Kyrkan (St. Mary's), begun in the early 14th century and finished 100 years later, is a fine example of Danish Gothic architecture. St. Mary's has several highlights: the 15th-century reredos, the silver treasure in the sacristy, and a memorial plaque to Dietrich Buxtehude (1637–1707), a prominent German composer as well as the church's organist. ⊠ *Mariatorget, Södra Storg. 20* ☎ *042/372830* ⊗ *Aug.–June, daily 8–4; July, daily 8–6.*

Helsingborg's refurbished harborside area, **Norra Hamnen** (Northern Harbor), has a pleasant marina with a string of architecturally impressive cafés and restaurants.

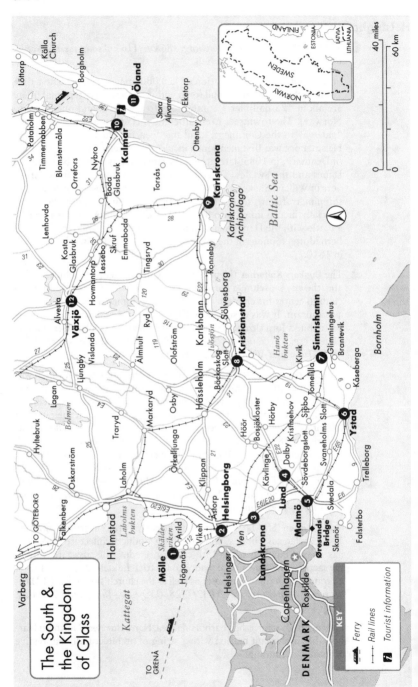

The South & the Kingdom of Glass

Built in 1897, the turreted **Rådhuset** (City Hall) has a richly adorned facade and window paintings by artist Gustav Cederström that depict important dates in Helsingborg's history. Five times a day (at 9 AM, noon,
3, 6, and 9 PM) songs ring from the 216-foot-tall bell tower. ⊠ *Drottningg. 2* ☎ *042/105000.*

Fodor'sChoice In 1865 **Sofiero Slott** (Sofiero Palace) was built in Dutch Renaissance style
★ by Prince Oscar and his wife, Sofia, as a summer home. Half a century
later Oscar II gave the palace to his grandson, Gustav Adolf, and his
wife, Margareta, as a wedding gift. Since the estate is now owned by
the city of Helsingborg, you can gain access to Sofiero's park, a haven
for more than 10,000 samples of 300 kinds of rhododendron, various
statues donated by international artists, and a large English garden; nearby
greenhouses have plant exhibits. A café and fine restaurant are on the
grounds. ⊠ *Sofierov. (on road to Laröd)* ☎ *042/137400* ⊠ *SKr 80*
☉ *Mid-Apr.–Sept., daily 11–5; guided tours only. Park, restaurant, and
café open year-round.*

Where to Eat

$$$ ✕ **Gastro.** A long leather booth divides this dining room into two halves:
one is packed with small tables for groups of two or three, the other
with tables for five or six. Larger parties sit in the more formal back of
the restaurant, but everyone orders from the same menu of Swedish-
based international fare. Fish and seafood are the stars. ⊠ *Södra Storg.
11–13* ☎ *042/243470* ⊟ *AE, DC, MC, V* ☉ *Closed Sun.*

$–$$$ ✕ **Restaurang La Petite.** If you are yearning for the delicacy of French cui-
sine and the genuine look and feel of a French restaurant, then look no
further. La Petite has been here since 1975, suggesting success, and can
also indulge the diner in Spanish and international meals. ⊠ *Bruksg.
19* ☎ *042/219727* ⊟ *AE, DC, MC, V* ☉ *Closed Sun.*

★ $$ ✕ **Pålsjö Krog.** Beside the pier that leads out to the Pålsjö Bath House,
this restaurant offers a beautiful view of the Øresund. The owners have
partially restored the restaurant to its original 1930s style—note the an-
tique sofa in the lounge and the art on the walls. Seafood is the specialty
in summer months, game in winter. Reservations are essential in sum-
mer. ⊠ *Drottningg. 151* ☎ *042/149730* ⊟ *AE, DC, MC, V.*

$$ ✕ **SS Swea.** Those with a nautical bent or nostalgia for past traveling
days will be well served at this restaurant ship modeled after cruise lin-
ers of old. The docked boat specializes in fresh seafood and international
menus. Enjoy the wide-ranging menu but don't forget to disembark—
there are no cabin bunks here. ⊠ *Kungstorget* ☎ *042/131516* ⊟ *AE,
DC, MC, V.*

Where to Stay

$$ ▥ **Elite Hotel Marina Plaza.** This relaxing and stylish modern hotel, with
its enormous central glass atrium, is right next to the Knutpunkten
ferry, rail, and bus terminal. Rooms are spacious and elegantly deco-
rated. ⊠ *Kungstorget 6, 251 10* ☎ *042/192100* 🖶 *042/149616* ⊕ *www.
marinaplaza.elite.se* ➥ *190 rooms* ⚭ *2 restaurants, minibars, in-room
broadband, in-room data ports, sauna, bar, meeting rooms, parking (fee),
no-smoking rooms* ⊟ *AE, DC, MC, V* ⦵ *BP.*

$–$$ 🏨 **Elite Hotel Mollberg.** Only a short walk from the central station, the Mollberg has spacious rooms with hardwood floors and large windows. Corner rooms have balconies that overlook a cobblestone square. The restaurant offers dining at reasonable prices. ⊠ *Stortorget 18, 251 14* ☎ *042/373700* 🖷 *042/373737* 📞 *104 rooms, 7 suites* ⚐ *Restaurant, minibars, room TVs with movies, in-room broadband, sauna, bar, meeting room, parking (fee), no-smoking rooms* ▤ *AE, DC, MC, V* ��ⓞⓛ *BP.*

$–$$
Fodor's Choice
★
🏨 **Radisson SAS Grand Hotel.** One of Sweden's oldest hotels has been completely renovated, maintaining its long-standing reputation for excellence. Public areas here are, as the name suggests, grand, with dark-wood paneling, chandeliers, and a mix of contemporary furniture and antiques. The smell of fresh flowers fills the hotel. Rooms are very well equipped to offer relaxed decadence; floors are rich, dark wood and fabrics, chairs, and cushions are lush brown and soft beige. Sleeping comfortably here is no problem. ⊠ *Stortorget 8–12, 251 11* ☎ *042/380400* 🖷 *042/380404* 📞 *164 rooms, 8 suites* ⚐ *Restaurant, room service, minibars, room TVs with movies, in-room broadband, Wi-Fi, gym, sauna, bar, lounge, meeting rooms, no-smoking rooms* ▤*AE, DC, MC, V* ⓓⓞⓛ*BP.*

¢–$ 🏨 **Villa Thalassa.** This youth hostel 3 km (2 mi) from the city center has fine views over Øresund. In the main building and in bungalow-style buildings, all with private patios, there are 172 bunks in two-, four-, and six-bunk rooms. The SKr 45 breakfast is not included. ⊠ *Dag Hammarskjölds väg, 254 33* ☎ *042/380660* 🖷 *042/128792* 📞 *172 beds in 64 rooms (24 rooms with private shower facilities)* ⚐ *Meeting rooms* ▤ *No credit cards.*

Nightlife & the Arts

The plush culture and art center, **Dunkers Kulturhus** (⊠ Kungsg. 11 ☎ 042/107400), stages an array of events in the fields of music, drama, visual arts, and cultural heritage.

The old-world **Charles Dickens** (⊠ Söderg. 43 ☎ 042/135100) is the oldest pub in town.

Jazz in Helsingborg stages some of its events at a cozy club on Nedre Långvinkelsgatan and some in the culture and arts center Dunkers Kulturhus. If you strike on the right night, you may well find yourself in jazz heaven, since the organizers attract jazz musicians from all over. Admission varies and goes as high as SKr 225. ⊠ *Nedre Långvinkelsg. 22* ☎ *042/184900* ⊠ *Dunkers Kulturhus, Kungsg. 11, Sundstorget* ☎ *042/107400.*

Open weekends only, the **Tivoli** (⊠ Kungsg. 1, Hamntorget ☎ 042/187171 ⊕ www.thetivoli.nu) concentrates on live rock bands, attracting major Swedish and international acts. The moderate-size dance floor has good lighting. If you're looking for a nightclub feel but want to be out of the razzmatazz, check out the vinyl bar. It has a restaurant, too.

Sports & the Outdoors

If your bones are weary, visit **Øresundsmassage.** The professionally trained staff offers various massage services and can deal with problems such as cramping or poor blood circulation. ⊠ *Roskildeg. 4* ☎ *042/127042* ⊕ *www.oresundsmassage.se* 🕐 *20 mins SKr 240; 40 mins SKr 400; 60 mins SKr 500* 🕐 *Mon. and Wed. noon–7, Tues. and Thurs. 10–6.*

Consider taking a relaxing dip in the sound at the late-19th-century **Pålsjöbaden** (Pålsjö Bath House) just north of town. It's a Helsingborg tradition to sweat in a sauna and then jump into the cool waters of the channel—even in winter. After an evening sauna, nearby Pålsjö Krog is a good dinner option. ⊠ *Drottningg. 151* ☎ *042/149730* 🖙 *Single visit SKr 30.*

Ramlösa Brunnspark (☎ 042/105888) is the source of the famous Ramlösa mineral water, which is served in restaurants and cafés throughout the world. Since it opened in 1707, the park has attracted summertime croquet players and those eager to taste the water (an outdoor café also serves beer and wine). Nearby is the **Ramlösa Wärdshus** (☎ 042/296257), which has been serving authentic Swedish cuisine since 1830. To reach the park by bus, take Bus 2 or 8 going south from the central station (Knutpunkten).

Skåne (☎ 042/104350 Helsingborg Tourist Information) is a golfers' delight. There are more than 60 golf courses in the region in total; within an hour's drive of Helsingborg you can find more than 20.

Shopping

Helsingborg has convenient shopping, and it's a good place to run errands. The best place to head is **Kullagatan,** which was the first pedestrians-only street in Sweden. It's a convenient collection of most of the sorts of shops you might need (such as a pharmacy, a photo shop, and a stationery store). If it's cheaper, medium-quality skins, furs, or leathers you want, try the **Skin and Fur Centre** at Kullagatan 7 (☎ 042/124020).

Landskrona

❸ *26 km (16 mi) south of Helsingborg (via E6/E20), 41 km (25 mi) north of Malmö, 204 km (127 mi) southwest of Växjö.*

The 17th-century Dutch-style fortifications of Landskrona are among the best preserved in Europe. Though it appears to be a modern town, Landskrona dates from 1413, when it received its charter.

Landskrona's **Citadellet** (castle) was built under orders of the Danish king Christian III in 1549, and is all that remains of the original town, which was razed in 1747 by decree of the Swedish Parliament to make way for extended fortifications. The new town was built on land reclaimed from the sea. ⊠ *Slottsg.* ☎ *0418/448250* 🖙 *SKr 40* ☉ *Early June–late Aug., Tues.–Sun. noon–4. Guided tours Tues.–Fri. noon, 2, and 4; weekends noon and 2.*

The eclectic **Landskrona Museum** has temporary exhibits as well as permanent coverage of Landskrona history and Swedish contributions to art, medicine, aviation, and architecture. ⊠ *Slottsg.* ☎ *0418/473120* ⊕ *www.landskrona.se/kultur* 🖙 *Free* ☉ *Mon.–Sun. noon–5.*

off the beaten path

TYCHO BRAHE MUSEET – The Danish astronomer Tycho Brahe conducted his pioneering research here from 1576 to 1597. The foundations of his Renaissance castle, **Uranienborg,** can be visited, as can **Stjärneborg,** his reconstructed observatory. The small Tycho Brahe Museet is dedicated to Brahe and his work. ⊠ *Landsv. 182,*

Ven ☎ 0418/72530 ☜ SKr 40 ☺ Apr.–June, daily 10–4; July–mid-Aug., 10–5; mid-Aug.–mid-Sept., 11–4.

From Landskrona Harbor there are regular 25-minute boat trips to the island of **Ven** (SKr 70 round-trip; boats depart every 90 minutes 6 AM–9 PM). It's an ideal place for camping; check with **Landskrona's tourist office** (☎ 0418/473000). There are special paths across Ven for bicycling; rentals are available from Bäckviken, the small harbor.

Sports & the Outdoors

Three kilometers (2 mi) north of Landskrona lies the **Borstahusen** (⌂ 261 61 Landskrona ☎ 0418/10837) recreation area, with long stretches of beach, a marina, and a group of 74 small cabinlike chalets.

Lund

❹ *34 km (21 mi) southeast of Landskrona via E6/E20 and Rte. 16, 25 km (15 mi) northeast of Malmö, 183 km (113 mi) southwest of Växjö.*

One of the oldest towns in Europe, Lund was founded in 990. In 1103 Lund became the religious capital of Scandinavia, and at one time had 27 churches and eight monasteries—until King Christian III of Denmark ordered most of them razed to use their stones for the construction of Malmöhus Castle. Lund lost its importance until 1666, when its university was established—the second-oldest university in Sweden after Uppsala.

FodorsChoice Lund's **Domkyrkan** (Cathedral), consecrated in 1145, is a monumental
★ gray-stone Romanesque cathedral, the oldest in Scandinavia. Since the Reformation it has been Lutheran. Its crypt has 23 finely carved pillars, but its main attraction is an astrological clock, Horologum Mirabile Lundense, dating from 1380 and restored in 1923. The "Miraculous Clock of Lund" depicts an amazing pageant of knights jousting on horseback, trumpets blowing a medieval fanfare, and the Magi walking in procession past the Virgin and Child as the organ plays *In Dulci Jubilo*. The clock plays at noon and at 3 Monday–Saturday and at 1 and 3 on Sunday. The oldest parts of the cathedral are considered the finest Romanesque constructions in Sweden. English and Swedish tours are available, and there are concerts at 10 AM on Sunday. ☎ *046/358700* ☜ *Free* ☺ *Weekdays 8–6, Sat. 9:30–5, Sun. 9:30–6.*

One block east of the cathedral is the **Botaniska Trädgården** (Botanical Garden), which contains more than 7,000 specimens of plants from all over the world, including such exotics as the paper mulberry tree, from the islands of the South Pacific. ⌂ *Östra Vallg. 20* ☎ *046/2227320* ☜ *Free* ☺ *Daily 6 AM–8 PM, greenhouses daily noon–3.*

Historiska museet med Domkyrkomuseet (Cathedral Museum and Museum of History) are just north of the cathedral. The Cathedral Museum has exhibitions and a slide show about the Domkyrkan's history. The Museum of History has Sweden's second-largest collection of treasures from the Stone, Bronze, and Iron ages. It also houses one of the oldest human skeletal finds, dated to 5000 BC. ⌂ *Kraftstorg. 1* ☎ *046/2227944* ☜ *SKr 30* ☺ *Mid-June–mid-Aug., Tues.–Fri. 11–4.*

Right next to the Lund Art Gallery is **Krognoshuset,** Lund's best-preserved medieval residence, and a small but well-presented art gallery. The building itself is worth a look, but most days you will get the added bonus of a contemporary art exhibition showcasing anything from industrial design to video installations. ⊠ *Mårtenstorget 3* ☎ *046/126248* ▧ *Free* ☉ *Daily, year-round 11–5. Call ahead for exhibition details.*

Kulturen (Museum of Cultural History) is both an outdoor and an indoor museum; it includes 20 old cottages, farms, and manor houses from southern Sweden, plus an excellent collection of ceramics, textiles, weapons, and furniture. Kulturen's **gardens** have free admission on summer nights, and on many of those nights there is live music and dancing. Call the museum for further details. ⊠ *Tegnérsplatsen* ☎ *046/350400* ▧ *SKr 50* ☉ *Mid-Apr.–Sept., Thurs.–Tues. 11–5, Wed. 11–9; Oct.–mid-Apr., Tues.–Sun. noon–4.*

The all-brick **Lund Konsthall** (Lund Art Gallery) may have a rather forbidding iron entrance and few windows, but skylights allow ample sunlight into the large exhibit room full of contemporary art by Swedish painters and sculptors, as well as some European artists. ⊠ *Mårtenstorget 3* ☎ *046/355395* ▧ *Free* ☉ *Mon.–Wed. and Fri. noon–5, Thurs. noon–8, Sat. 10–5, Sun. noon–6.*

The Lundagård park separates the Domkyrkan from the oldest parts of **Lund University.** The main building is crisp white and easily spotted among the cobbled streets and traditional cottages. The university was founded in 1666, and today has 30,000 students. Its **History Museum** (☎ 046/350400), part of the **Kulturen** group of museums, exhibits old texts, university regalia, and other items used in the university long ago. ⊠ *Kyrkog.*

need a break?
Just across from the university is a Lund institution—**Conditori Lund** (⊠ Kyrkog. 17), a bakery and coffeehouse. It's easy to imagine the rooms filled with the smoke and loud opinions of intellectuals of the past.

Founded in 1934 in connection with Lund University, **Skissernas Museum** (Sketches Museum) houses more than 20,000 sketches in addition to models and first drafts by major artists. The international collection contains the early ideas of artists such as Henri Matisse, Pablo Picasso, Fernand Léger, and many others. ⊠ *Finng. 2* ☎ *046/2227283* ▧ *SKr 30* ☉ *Tues. and Thurs.–Sun. noon–5, Wed. noon–9.*

Esaias Tegnér, a Swedish poet, lived from 1813 to 1826 in a little house immediately behind the cathedral. The house has since been turned into the **Tegnér Museet,** providing insight into his life and works. ⊠ *Stora Gråbrödersg. 11* ☎ *046/350400* ▧ *SKr 10* ☉ *July and Aug., Sat. noon–3; Sept.–June, 1st weekend of each month noon–3.*

Fodor's Choice ★ The **Heligkorskyrkan i Dalby** (Holy Cross Church of Dalby) was founded in 1060, making it the oldest stone church in Scandinavia. It was for a short time the archbishop's seat until this was moved into town. Among the hidden treasures is a renowned baptismal font, brought here in

1150. The exposed brick within the church is original, and many figures and icons date from medieval times, including a wooden relief at the front of the church of Veronica's Veil, which shows the face of Jesus. The church is on a hill less than 10 km (6 mi) from Lund. ⊠ *Head east on Rte. 16 and follow signs* ☎ *046/208600* ✉ *Free* ⊘ *May–Aug., daily 9–6; Sept.–Apr., daily 9–4.*

off the
beaten
path

ⓒ

BOSJÖKLOSTER – About 30 km (19 mi) northeast of Lund via E22 and Route 23, Bosjökloster is an 11th-century, white Gothic castle with lovely grounds on Ringsjön, the second-largest lake in southern Skåne. The castle's original owner donated the estate to the church, which turned it over to the Benedictine order of nuns. They founded a convent school (no longer in operation) for the daughters of Scandinavian nobility and built the convent church with its tower made of sandstone. The 300-acre castle grounds, with a 1,000-year-old oak tree, also have a network of pathways, a children's park, a rose garden, and an indoor-outdoor restaurant. ⊠ *Höör* ☎ *0413/25048* ⊕ *www.bosjokloster.se* ✉ *SKr 45* ⊘ *Castle grounds Apr.–Sept., daily 8–sunset; restaurant and exhibition halls Apr.–Sept., daily 10–6.*

Where to Eat

★ **$-$$** ✕**Bantorget 9.** The restaurant-bar inside this 18th-century building is true to the past, with restored woodwork and paintings on the ceilings, antique flowerpots and candleholders, and classical statues in the corners of the room. The menu offers traditional Swedish dishes plus some more intriguing entrées such as duck breast with pickled red cabbage in apple honey. Bantorget 9 is a short walk from Lund's central train station. ⊠*Bantorget 9* ☎ *046/320200* ▤ *AE, DC, MC, V* ⊘ *Closed Sun.*

$-$$ ✕**Godset.** Inside an old railroad warehouse right on the tracks near central station, Godset's modern tables and chairs stand on rustic wooden floors between brick walls. On one wall hangs a large 1950s clock taken from Mariakyrkan (Maria Church) in nearby Ystad. The menu is mostly seafood and meat dishes. Try the roasted venison poached in a cream sauce with raspberry vinaigrette. ⊠ *Bang. 3* ☎ *046/121610* ▤ *AE, DC, MC, V* ⊘ *Closed Sun.*

★ **$$** ✕**Restaurang Café Finn.** Connected to the Lund Konsthallen, Café Finn is an excellent option for lunch or dinner. The creamy lobster soup with mussels is perfect if you're not overly hungry, but for a more substantial meal go for the veal fillet with creamy red-onion sauce and grape jelly. The walls have an extensive collection of museum exhibit posters from the '60s, '70s, and '80s. Just outside is the Krognoshuset; built in the 1300s, it is Lund's best-kept medieval residence. ⊠ *Mårtenstorget 3* ☎ *046/130565* ▤ *AE, DC, MC, V.*

¢**-$$** ✕**Dalby Gästgiveri.** This is one of Skåne's oldest inns and a gastronomic delight. The many red-meat dishes on the menu follow a tradition of history and quality, but innovative Swedish fare is served, too. Entrées such as the rich, somewhat gamey deer fillet with mushroom spring rolls and cranberry sauce are not for the faint of heart. Be sure to make reservations in summer. ⊠ *Tengsg. 6* ☎ *046/200006* ▤ *AE, MC, V.*

¢–$ ✕ **Ebbas Skafferi.** Just across the central station, Ebbas Pantry serves a number of excellent sandwiches on bagels, baguettes, or *ciabattas* (a flat Italian bread). ⊠ *Bytareg. 5* ☎ *046/134156* ▭ *MC, V.*

Where to Stay

$$ ⊡ **Concordia.** Formerly a private residence, this elegant city-center property was built in 1890. Rooms have a modern look, but some can be a bit cluttered. ⊠ *Stålbrog. 1, 222 24* ☎ *046/135050* 🖷 *046/137422* ⊕ *www.concordia.se* ↩ *65 rooms* ⚘ *In-room-broadband, Wi-Fi, sauna, meeting room, no-smoking rooms* ▭ *AE, DC, MC, V.*

★ $$ ⊡ **Grand Hotel.** This elegant red-stone hotel is in the heart of the city on a pleasant square close to the railway station. All the rooms are furnished differently, but most have a turn-of-the-20th-century decor and charm in common. The fine restaurant serves an alternative vegetarian menu. ⊠ *Bantorget 1, 221 04* ☎ *046/2806100* 🖷 *046/2806150* ⊕ *www.grandilund.se* ↩ *84 rooms, 1 suite* ⚘ *Restaurant, hot tub, sauna, meeting room, no-smoking rooms* ▭ *AE, DC, MC, V* ⦿ *BP.*

$$ ⊡ **Hotel Lundia.** Only a few hundred feet from the train station, Hotel Lundia is ideal for those who want to be near the city center. Built in 1968, the modern, four-story square building has transparent glass walls on the ground floor. Rooms are decorated in a combination of Scandinavian and Japanese styles. ⊠ *Knut den Stores torg 2, 221 04* ☎ *046/ 2806500* 🖷 *046/2806510* ⊕ *www.lundia.se* ↩ *97 rooms, 1 suite* ⚘ *Restaurant, Wi-Fi, lounge, nightclub, meeting room, no-smoking rooms* ▭ *AE, DC, MC, V* ⦿ *BP.*

$–$$ ⊡ **Oskar.** A charming boutique-style hotel made up of two 19th-century town houses, the hotel offers spacious, modern, and bright rooms with white walls, colorful art, and oiled oak floors. All rooms are individually furnished with designer touches like chairs from Gunilla Allard and lamps by the legendary Arne Jacobsen. Downstairs is a café and a beautiful garden where you can enjoy breakfast in the morning and coffee throughout the day. ⊠ *Bytareg. 3, 222 21* ☎ *046/188085* 🖷 *046/373030* ⊕ *www.hotelloskar.se* ↩ *6 rooms* ⚘ *Café, cable TV, in-room DVD, in-room data ports; no smoking* ▭ *AE, DC, MC, V* ⦿ *BP.*

¢–$$ ⊡ **Djingis Khan.** This rather unattractive Best Western hotel caters to business travelers but is also the place for families or couples seeking a quiet location. The hotel's unusual name comes from a comedy show that has been performed at Lund University since 1954. With squash, tennis, and badminton courts nearby, along with a large swimming pool, it's ideal if you're looking to keep in shape. ⊠ *Margaretav. 7, 222 40* ☎ *046/ 333600* 🖷 *046/333610* ↩ *55 rooms* ⚘ *Wi-Fi, gym, hot tub, sauna, bicycles, meeting room, no-smoking rooms* ▭ *AE, DC, MC, V* ⊙ *Closed July* ⦿ *BP.*

¢–$ ⊡ **STF Vandrarhem Tåget.** So named because of its proximity to the train station and because it's housed inside an old train (*tåget* means "train"), this youth hostel faces a park in central Lund. ⊠ *Bjerredsparken, Vävareg. 22, 222 37* ☎ *046/142820* ↩ *108 beds without bath* ▭ *No credit cards.*

Nightlife & the Arts

★ **Basilika** (⊠ Stora Söderg. 13 ☎ 046/2116660) has a smallish dance floor and also hosts live bands. On Friday and Saturday things don't get going until 11 and rage on until 3. Basilika draws young hipsters and will cost at least SKr 50 to get in.

The **Lundia** (⊠ Knut den Stores torg 2 ☎ 046/2806500) nightclub is in the Hotel Lundia, near the Burger King. Women must be 23 or older to enter, men over 25, and not many attendees are much over 35. It costs SKr 60 to dance to the electronic sounds.

The hot spot in town, **Stortorget** (⊠ Stortorget 1 ☎ 046/139290), has live music as well as a DJ night and is popular with students. You won't get in here unless you are over 22.

Shopping

About 200,000 secondhand books are stacked in crazy piles in **Akarps Antikvariat** (⊠ Klosterg. 11 ☎ 046/2112499), so that the scent of aged literature hits you immediately when you walk inside. The oldest book dates from about 1500, around the time the printing press was developed. Any sort of book can be found, even an airport thriller.

The oldest coins in Europe date from between 500 BC and 600 BC, and the coin shop **Lunds Mynthandel** (⊠ Klosterg. 5 ☎ 046/144369) often has specimens going back that far. Lunds Mynthandel also carries books on numismatics.

The cheese selection at **Bengsons Ost** (⊠ Klosterg. 9) is hard to surpass. The people are friendly, and it's a great spot to fill your picnic hamper. Bring your own wine and have a tasting session. **Saluhallen** (⊠ Corner of Mårtenstorget and Botulfsg.), known as Foodhall, is an adventure in itself, an excellent example of the traditional Swedish food house but also one that stocks delicacies from Italy, Japan, and beyond. Cheese, meats, fresh and pickled fish, and pastries are all in great supply. It is the perfect place to get some food for a picnic in one of Lund's many squares and parks.

Skånekraft (⊠ Östra Mårtensg. 5 ☎ 046/144777) carries a wide range of ceramics, crafts, and designer goods. **Tehuset Java** (⊠ Västra Mårtensg. 8), a well-known tea-and-coffee shop, sells leaves and beans from all over the world. You can also get all the paraphernalia that goes with brewing.

Malmö

❺ *25 km (15 mi) southwest of Lund (via E22), 198 km (123 mi) southwest of Växjö.*

Capital of the province of Skåne, with a population of about 265,000, Malmö is Sweden's third-largest city. It was founded at the end of the 13th century. The remarkable 8-km (5-mi) bridge and tunnel from Malmö to Copenhagen has transformed travel and trade in the area, cutting both time and costs, and replacing the ferries that used to shuttle between the two towns. Eight years in the making, the $3 billion Øre-

SWEET TOOTH

THE SWEDES, LIKE EVERY PEOPLE on earth, have developed an intricate web of storytelling and fairy tales. These are the realms of trolls and elves, of witches and spirits. The myths interweave the good and the bad and reinterpret the experience of life as lived by people with few other ways to explain the apparently inexplicable.

With these thoughts in mind I was on my way to the town of Gränna, on the mystical island Visingsö, which is said to have been created by a giant called Vist. Gränna is home to a great Swedish confectionery tradition: the making of the peppermint stick, which in Swedish is called polkagris and is exported around the world.

I walked into the factory of the oldest stick maker in the land, as the public is welcome to do, to watch the production process. Here the widow Amalia Erikson made the first red-and-white sweets in 1859. As a woman, she had to seek government permission to do so. Behind the glass window the craftsmen ply their trade: brewing, coloring, twisting, and turning something that looked like dough into fluorescent candy sticks. Some 2,000 a day are made in this factory alone. With so much tooth-rotting sugar—about 75% of the product—it made sense of the elfin image: those wicked, toothless grins. Was evil afoot?

Oh, yes. Like the bright-eyed child drawn to Grandma's candy drawer, I marveled at the colors as I watched the candy sticks roll out. It was inevitable that I would take the sugar hit that would take me to Mars. The first bite was pure pleasure, a crunching and splintering of the stick, and then the rush. But it was as if this event was written in the stars, foretold by a wise old troll. There was more crunch than I would have liked and, as if by magic, my tooth bounced onto the floor. The shopkeeper didn't know where to look. This adventure had extracted its price.

I beat an embarrassed retreat, beset with my own toothless grin. It was as if I had known not the facts of the future, but the sense of it. I took the ferry to Visingsö, with its timeless villages, eccentric art history, its rugged coast and people with their own enchanted look. In moments of mindless drift, I cast my eyes toward the woods, the trees, and the toadstools. Would I see one of these underworld creatures? Did they have something to teach?

But the island, as magical as it seemed, proved to be a temporal place. The locals told me the elves mostly come out at night. I, however, saw Visingsö and its origins through the eyes of legend. The giant Vist, returning from a feast with his wife, discovered that, full of food, she could not take Lake Vättern in a step. With great might he lifted a piece of turf and placed it in the lake for her to step on. This is Visingsö's creation story.

As for me? Well, the lesson I had to learn, as I could best understand it, was one of the seven deadly sins, according to the Bible: that of avarice, or greed. From then on Sweden could be seen only in a cautious supernatural light. I never found a troll, but I believe they exist. My dental work is irrefutable and permanent proof.

sund Bridge has proved to be a success, both environmentally and commercially.

The city's castle, **Malmöhus,** completed in 1542, was for many years used as a prison (James Bothwell, husband of Mary, Queen of Scots, was one of its notable inmates). Today Malmöhus houses a variety of **museums,** including the City Museum, the Museum of Natural History, and the Art Museum, which has a collection of Nordic art. Across the street are the Science and Technology Museum, the Maritime Museum, and a toy museum. ⊠ *Malmöhusv.* ☎ *040/344437* ✉ *SKr 40 for all museums* ☉ *June–Aug., daily 10–4; Sept.–May, daily noon–4.*

In the same park as Malmöhus is the **Malmö Stadsbibliotek** (Malmö City Library), designed by the famous Danish architect Henning Larsen. Take a walk through the colossal main room—there's a four-story wall of glass that brings seasonal changes of colors inside. ⊠ *Kung Oscars väg* ☎ *040/6608500.*

☾ On the far side of the castle grounds from Malmöhus, the **Aq-va-kul** water park offers a variety of bathing experiences, from waterslides to bubble baths. ⊠ *Regementsg. 24* ☎ *040/300540* ⊕ *www.aq-va-kul.com* ✉ *SKr 75* ☉ *Weekdays 9–8:30, weekends 9–5:30; Mon. adult sessions 7 PM–9:30 PM.*

The houses and business buildings designed and erected for the 2001 **European Housing Expo** show 58 different types of housing. Wander around the development surrounding the Ribersborgsstranden waterfront, where the expo was held, in order to see the exteriors of more than 500 homes. They were sold as residences after the expo was over. ⊠ *Ribersborgsstranden waterfront.*

A clutch of tiny red-painted shacks called the **Fiskehodderna** (Fish Shacks) is next to a dock where the fishing boats come in every morning to unload their catch. The piers, dock, and huts have been restored and are now a government-protected district. You can buy fresh fish directly from the fishermen Tuesday through Saturday mornings.

★ You can learn about Scandinavian art and design at the **Form/Design Center.** The center is run by SvenskForm, a nonprofit association that promotes top-quality design in Sweden; Swedish and other Scandinavian artworks are on display throughout the center. ⊠ *9 Lilla Torg* ☎ *040/6645150* ⊕ *www.formdesigncenter.com* ✉ *Free admission.* ☉ *Tues.–Fri. 11–5, Thurs. 11–6, weekends 11–4.*

The **Idrottsmuseet** (Museum of Sport) occupies Baltiska Hallen (the Baltic Building), next to Malmö Stadium. It traces the history of sports, including soccer and wrestling, from antiquity to the present. ☎ *040/342688* ✉ *Free* ☉ *Weekdays 8–4.*

Lilla Torg is a cobblestone square with some of the city's oldest buildings, which date from the 17th and 18th centuries. It is clustered with cafés, restaurants, and bars and is a great place to wander or watch the world go by. Walk into the side streets and see the traditional buildings, which were originally used mainly to store grain and produce. Check out the Saluhallen (food hall), which contains **Kryddboden,** one of Sweden's best coffee purveyors.

Founded in 1975, the **Malmö Konsthall** (Malmö Art Gallery) is one of the largest contemporary art museums in Europe, with a huge single room that's more than 20,000 square feet. It arranges about 10 exhibitions a year, from the classics of modern art to present-day experiments. Other activities include theater performances, film presentations, and poetry readings. ⊠ *St. Johannesg. 7* ☎ *040/341286* ⊕ *www.konsthall.malmo. se* ☒ *Free* ⊙ *Mon., Tues., and Thurs.–Sun. 11–5, Wed. 11–9.*

★ The **Øresundbron** (Øresund Bridge) is an engineering miracle. Its train tracks and four car lanes stretch 8 km (5 mi) from the southern coastal suburbs of Malmö to Copenhagen. Designed under the auspices of Øresund Konsortiet, the bridge is a minimalist beauty. ⊠ *Lookout at Øresund Utställningen at the end of Utställningen Rd. Approach on E20 Hwy.* ⊕ *www.oeresundsbron.dk* ☒ *SKr 285 each way for car.*

The **Rådhuset** (Town Hall), dating from 1546, dominates Stortorget, a huge, cobbled market square in Gamla Staden, and makes an impressive spectacle when illuminated at night. In the center of the square stands an equestrian statue of Karl X, the king who united this part of the country with Sweden in 1658. Off the southeast corner of Stortorget is the square Lilla Torg.

Fodor'sChoice
★ One of Sweden's most outstanding art museums, **Rooseum,** is in a turn-of-the-20th-century brick building that was once a power plant. It has exhibitions of contemporary art and a quality selection of Nordic art. ⊠ *Gasverksg. 22* ☎ *040/121716* ⊕ *www.rooseum.se* ☒ *SKr 40* ⊙ *Wed. 2–8, Thurs.–Sun. noon–6. Guided tours in Swedish and English weekends at 2, Thurs. and Fri. at 6:30, Wed. at 6.*

★ In Gamla Staden, the Old Town, look for the **St. Petri Church,** on Kalendegatan; dating from the 14th century, it is an impressive example of the Baltic Gothic style, with distinctive stepped gables. Inside there is a fine Renaissance altar.

off the beaten path
FALSTERBO AND SKANÖR – The idyllic towns of Falsterbo and Skanör are two popular summer resorts on a tiny peninsula, 32 km (20 mi) southwest of Malmö. Falsterbo is popular among ornithologists, who flock there every fall to watch the spectacular migration of hundreds of birds, especially swallows, geese, hawks, and eagles.

TORUPS SLOTT – Built around 1550 near a beautiful beech forest, Torup Castle is a great example of the classic, square fortified stronghold. From Malmö drive 10 km (6 mi) southeast on E65, then head north for another 6 km (4 mi) to Torup. ⊠ *Torup* ☎ *040/ 341853* ☒ *SKr 65* ⊙ *Sun. tours at 1, 2, and 3.*

Where to Eat

★ $$–$$$ ✕ **Årstiderna i Kockska Huset.** Formed by merging two discrete restaurants that were in different locations, the combination is housed in a

16th-century building with beautiful interiors. Several of the dining areas are in an underground cellar. Traditional Swedish dishes, often centered on beef, game, and seafood, are given a contemporary twist. The fried halibut, for example, is served with a crab mousse and a rich shellfish sauce flavored with curry. Like the food, the wine list is excellent. ⊠ *Frans Suellsg. 3* ☎ *040/230910* ▭ *AE, DC, MC, V.*

$$–$$$ ✕ **Johan P.** This extremely popular restaurant specializes in seafood and shellfish prepared in Swedish and Continental styles. White walls and crisp white tablecloths give it an elegant air, which contrasts with the generally casual dress of the customers. An outdoor section is open in summer. ⊠ *Saluhallen, Lilla Torg* ☎ *040/971818* ▭ *AE, DC, MC, V* ☺ *Closed Sun.*

$$ ✕ **Hipp.** Distinguishing this bar-restaurant that dates from 1899 are ornate columns that support a high ceiling painted with flower patterns. Heavy chandeliers hang over the dark-wood bar in the center of the restaurant. Hipp's hearty fare is the perfect cap to a night at the city theater, next door. The finely sliced raw salmon with black roe is a standout, as is the vegetable stir-fry. Dry martinis are the specialty of the bar. ⊠ *Kalendeg. 12* ☎ *040/974030* ▭ *AE, DC, MC, V* ☺ *Closed Sun. and Mon.*

$–$$ ✕ **Anno 1900.** This charming little restaurant sits in a former working-class area of Malmö. It is a popular local luncheon place with a cheerful outdoor garden terrace. Head here for such light dishes as salads and fish, as well as for traditional Swedish lunches built around the potato. The bread is outstanding. ⊠ *Norra Bulltoftav. 7* ☎ *040184747* ⌂ *Reservations essential* ▭ *AE, DC, MC, V.*

$–$$ ✕ **Glorias.** This friendly restaurant and sports bar offers a good value. The food is Tex-Mex, with a few international appetizers thrown in. ⊠ *Södra Förstadsg. 23B* ☎ *040/70200* ▭ *AE, DC, MC, V.*

$–$$ ✕ **Salt & Brygga.** The traditional Swedish kitchen has found some in-
FodorsChoice spiration in the Mediterranean at this quayside restaurant. Endive and
★ Gorgonzola toast, and smoked *saithe* (coalfish) and horseradish *fromage* appetizers are followed by rich shellfish casseroles. The restaurant not only uses only organic produce, but also uses ecologically friendly alternatives for everything from the wall paint to the table linens and the staff's clothes. The restaurant's selection of organic wines and beers is unique for the region. ⊠ *Sundspromenaden 7* ☎ *040/6115940* ▭ *AE, DC, MC, V.*

¢–$ ✕ **B & B.** It stands for *Butik och Bar* (Shop and Bar) and is named as such because of its location in the food hall in central Malmö. There's always good home cooking, with dishes like grilled salmon and beef fillet with potatoes. Sometimes there's even entertainment at the piano. ⊠ *Saluhallen, Lilla Torg* ☎ *040/127120* ▭ *AE, DC, MC, V.*

¢ ✕ **Spot.** Reasonable prices and unpretentious food draw a lively group of regulars to this Italian eatery for lunch. ⊠ *Stora Nyg. 33* ☎ *040/120203* ▭ *AE, DC, MC, V* ☺ *Closed Sun. No dinner.*

Where to Stay

$$ ▦ **Hilton Malmö City.** Ultramodern in steel and glass, the Hilton is one of the city's few skyscrapers—at a modest 20 floors. It provides excellent views all the way to Copenhagen on a clear day. The rooms are plain, modern, and comfortable. ⊠ *Triangeln 2, 200 10* ☎ *040/6934700*

⌂ 040/6934711 ⊕ *www.hilton.com* ⇆ *216 rooms, 6 suites* ◊ *Restaurant, room service, minibars, cable TV, in-room data ports, Wi-Fi, gym, sauna, bar, meeting rooms, no-smoking rooms* ☱ *AE, DC, MC, V* ⦿ *BP.*

★ **$$** ▦ **Mäster Johan Hotel.** The plain exterior of this Best Western hotel disguises a plush and meticulously crafted interior. A top-to-bottom redesign of a 19th-century building, with the focal point an Italianate atrium breakfast room, the Mäster Johan is unusually personal for a chain hotel. The rooms are impressive, with exposed plaster-and-stone walls, recessed lighting, luxurious beds, Bang & Olufsen televisions, marble bathrooms oak floors, Oriental carpets, and French cherrywood furnishings. ✉ *Mäster Johansg. 13, 211 21* ☎ *040/6646400* ⊟ *040/6646401* ⊕ *www.masterjohan.se* ⇆ *69 rooms* ◊ *Room service, room TVs with movies, in-room broadband, in-room data ports, Wi-Fi, sauna, meeting room, no-smoking rooms* ☱ *AE, DC, MC, V* ⦿ *BP.*

$$ ▦ **Radisson SAS Hotel.** Only a five-minute walk from the train station, this modern luxury hotel has rooms decorated in several styles: Asian, maritime, and ecological—the latter being mostly furnished in recycled or biodegradable materials, although you would never know it. There are even special rooms for guests with pets. Service is impeccable. The restaurant serves Scandinavian and Continental cuisine, and there's a cafeteria. ✉ *Österg. 10, 211 25* ☎ *040/6984000* ⊟ *040/6984001* ⊕ *www.radissonsas.com* ⇆ *229 rooms, 4 suites* ◊ *Restaurant, cafeteria, room service, minibars, room TVs with movies, in-room broadband, Wi-Fi, gym, sauna, spa, meeting room, parking (fee), no-smoking rooms* ☱ *AE, DC, MC, V* ⦿ *BP.*

★ **$–$$** ▦ **Baltzar.** This turn-of-the-20th-century house in central Malmö makes a small, comfortable hotel. Rooms have the original hardwood floors and pleasing antique furniture, minichandeliers, and rich swathes of fabric hung at the tall windows. ✉ *Söderg. 20, 211 34* ☎ *040/6655710* ⊟ *040/236375* ⊕ *www.baltzarhotel.se* ⇆ *41 rooms* ◊ *Restaurant, room service, minibars, cable TV, meeting rooms, no-smoking rooms* ☱ *AE, DC, MC, V* ⦿ *BP.*

$ ▦ **Comfort Hotel.** In a rejuvenated part of Malmö Harbor, this low-overhead, minimal-service hotel has small but comfortable rooms equipped with satellite TV, telephone, and radio. The large front entrance and lobby atrium are inventively created out of a narrow strip between two buildings. Though the hotel doesn't add a surcharge to the telephone bill, breakfast does cost extra (SKr 65). ✉ *Carlsg. 10C, 211 20* ☎ *040/330440* ⊟ *040/330450* ⊕ *www.choicehotels.se* ⇆ *109 rooms* ◊ *Cable TV, parking (fee), no-smoking rooms* ☱ *AE, DC, MC, V.*

Nightlife & the Arts

The **Bishop's Arms** (✉ Savoy Hotel, Nora Vallg. 62 ☎ 040/6644888) is a classic and busy English pub. It is in the former grill room of the Savoy Hotel and can hardly fail to impress the pub connoisseur. There's an excellent assortment of old whiskeys.

Étage (✉ Stortorget 6 ☎ 040/232060 ⌐ SKr 50 or more ☉ Mon., Thurs., Fri., and Sat. 11 PM–5 AM) is a centrally located nightclub for hipsters, with two dance floors. It also has a piano bar for relaxing, as well as a restaurant. Dancing begins late under psychedelic lights Thursday, Friday, and Saturday. Karaoke, roulette, and blackjack tables are available.

Five rooms of an old patrician apartment make up **Klubb Plysch** (✉ Lilla Torg 1 ☎ 040/127670 💷 SKr 70 ☉ Sat. 10 PM–3 AM). Lounge about in the superb velvet chairs with champagne and cigars in the early evening, and join the dance floor around 11.

The **Malmö Symfoni Orkester** (☎ 040/343500 ⊕ www.mso.se) is a symphony orchestra that has a reputation across Europe as a class act. Each concert is a finely tuned event. Performances are held at many venues, including outdoors; some are at the impressive Malmö Konserthus.

Wallmans Salonger (✉ Generalsg. 1 ☎ 040/74945 💷 SKr 100–Skr 180) has an artistic, bohemian staff that is part of the entertainment. They may burst into song or start juggling. A dance show with terrific lighting begins at 7, and the nightclub proper begins at 11. There are also a casino and a restaurant.

Sports & the Outdoors

From Ribersborg Beach you can walk on a pier to the **Kallbadhuset Ribersborgsstranden,** which are old baths (the name translates as "cold bathhouses Ribersborg Beach"). Built in 1898, they are a popular place to swim, since a man-made harbor of boulders offers protection from the sea's turbulence. It also hosts cultural events such as poetry readings and has a bar and a café. To get to the beach, follow Citadellsvägen to the west from the central railway station. Walk alongside Øresunds Parken and turn right at the sign for Ribersborg. ✉ *Ribersborg Beach* ☎ *040/ 260366* 💷 *SKr 45* ☉ *Mid-May–mid-Sept., daily 7:30–5.*

Paddle boating on the canals is a great way to see the city. Each boat takes up to four people. Start paddling from Raoul Wallenberg Park, just southeast of Gustav Adolfs Square along Lilla Nygatan. ✉ *Raoul Wallenberg Park* ☎ *0704/710067* 💷 *SKr 100 per hr, SKr 70 for 30 mins* ☉ *June–Sept., daily 11–7.*

Shopping

Malmö has many quality housewares and design stores. An arts-and-crafts shop with a Nordic twist, **Älgamark** (✉ Östra Rönneholmsv. 4 ☎ 040/974960) sells many antiques dating from Viking and medieval times up to the 1600s. The shop also sells gold, silver, and bronze jewelry, much of which is also quite old. **Cervera** (✉ Södra Förstadsg. 24 ☎ 040/971230) carries big-name glassware brands such as Kosta and Orrefors. There's an excellent selection of glass art as well as porcelain and china—and almost everything you might need in housewares. **Duka** (✉ Hansacompagniet Centre, Malmborgsg. 6 ☎ 040/121141) is a high-quality housewares shop specializing in glass, crockery, and glass art. Special tables are set up with Swedish products on display, and hand-carved and hand-painted wood Dala horses are for sale.

Duxiana (✉ Malmborgsg. 6 ☎ 040/232053) sells the world-famous Dux beds, which have elaborate spring systems and are built into wooden frames. Shipping can be arranged. Beds range in price from SKr 25,000 to SKr 57,000. **Formargruppen** (✉ Engelbrektsg. 8 ☎ 040/ 78060) is an arts-and-crafts cooperative owned and operated by its 22 members. It sells high-quality woodwork, including cabinets. Quality ceramics, textiles, metalwork, and jewelry are also for sale. The **Form/ Design Centre** (⊠ Lilla Torg 9 ☎ 040/6645150) sells products related to its changing exhibitions on everything from ceramics to books. Also look here for the very latest in Scandinavian interior design.

At the summer market called **Möllevångstorget,** on the square of the same name, there is usually a wonderful array of flowers, fruit, and vegetables. It is an old working-class area and a nice place to stroll. The market is open Monday–Saturday. **Outside** (⊠ Kyrkog. 3, Stortorget ☎ 040/300910) specializes in high-quality outdoor gear. Everything from sleeping bags, boots, and tents to gas canisters and waterproofing products is stocked here. In addition to such brands as North Face and Patagonia, Outside is the only Scandinavian store to carry products from Mac Pac of New Zealand.

en route One of Skåne's outstanding Renaissance strongholds, **Svaneholms Slott** lies 30 km (19 mi) east of Malmö, on E65. First built in 1530 and rebuilt in 1694, the castle today features a museum occupying four floors with sections depicting the nobility and peasants. On the grounds are **Gästgiveri** (☎ 0411/45040), a notable restaurant, walking paths, and a lake for fishing and rowing. ⊠ Skurup ☎ 0411/45040 ⊠ SKr 25 ☉ May–Aug., weekdays noon–4:30, weekends 1–5; Apr. and Sept., Wed.–Sun. 11–4.

Ystad

❻ 64 km (40 mi) southeast of Malmö (via E65), 205 km (127 mi) southwest of Växjö.

A smuggling center during the Napoleonic Wars, Ystad has preserved its medieval character with winding narrow streets and hundreds of half-timber houses built over a span of five centuries. A good place to begin exploring is the main square, Stortorget.

Charlotte Berlin's Museum is a well-preserved burgher's home from the 19th century. Charlotte Berlin left the home and the contents to the city upon her death in 1916. It has a variety of displays, including one that shows many antique clocks and watches. ⊠ Dammg. 23 ☎ 0411/18866 ⊠ SKr 25 ☉ June–Aug., weekdays noon–5, weekends noon–4.

The Franciscan monastery **Gråbrödraklostret** adjoins St. Peter's church and is one of the best-preserved cloisters in Sweden. The oldest parts date to 1267. Together, the church and monastery are considered the most important historical site in Ystad. ⊠ Sankt Petri Kyrkoplan ☎ 0411/577286 ⊠ SKr 20 ☉ Weekdays noon–5, weekends noon–4.

The principal ancient monument, **St. Maria Kyrka** (St. Mary's Church; ⊠ Lilla Norregatan) was built shortly after 1220 as a basilica in the Romanesque style, though there have been later additions. The watchman's copper horn sounds from the church tower beginning at 9:15 PM and repeating every 15 minutes until 1 AM. It's to proclaim that "all is well."

The church lies behind Stortorget on Lilla Norregatan. The 16th-century Latinskolan (Latin School) is adjacent to the church—it's said to be the oldest schoolhouse in Scandinavia.

Ystads Konstmuseum houses a collection of important Swedish and Danish 20th-century art, as well as a photographic collection that includes a daguerreotype from 1845. ⊠ *St. Knuts torg* ☎ *0411/577285* ⊕ *www. konstmuseet.ystad.se* ⊠ *SKr 30* ☉ *Tues.–Fri. noon–5, weekends noon–4.*

Sweden's best-preserved theater from the late 1800s, **Ystads Teater** (⊠ Sjömansg. 13 ☎ 0411/577199) is a beautiful, ornate building. The dramatic interior adds a great deal to any performance seen here. Outside is a battery of cannons first used in 1712 to defend the harbor from its many marauders, especially the Danes.

off the
beaten
path
★

ALES STENAR – Eighteen kilometers (11 mi) east of Ystad, on the coastal road off Route 9, is the charming fishing village of Kåseberga. On the hill behind it stands the impressive Ales Stones, an intriguing 230-foot-long arrangement of 58 Viking stones in the shape of a ship. Believed to be between 1,000 and 1,500 years old, the stones and their purpose still puzzle anthropologists.

GLIMMINGEHUS – About 10 km (6 mi) east of Ales Stenar and 10 km (6 mi) southwest of Simrishamn just off Route 9 lies Glimminge House, Scandinavia's best-preserved medieval stronghold. Built between 1499 and 1505 to defend the region against invaders, the late-Gothic castle was lived in only briefly. The walls are 8 feet thick at the base, tapering to 6½ feet at the top of the 85-foot-high building. On the grounds are a small museum and a theater. There are concerts and lectures in summer and a medieval festival at the end of August. ⊠ *Hammenhög* ☎ *0414/18620* ⊠ *SKr 50* ☉ *Easter–May, daily 11–4; June–mid-Sept., daily 10–6; mid-Sept.–end of Sept., daily 11–4.*

SÖVDEBORGS SLOTT – Twenty-one kilometers (13 mi) north of Ystad on Route 13 is Sövdeborgs Slott. Built in the 16th century and restored in the mid-1840s, the castle, now a private home, consists of three two-story brick buildings and a four-story-high crenellated corner tower. The main attraction is the Stensal (Stone Hall), with its impressive stuccowork ceiling. It's open for tours if booked in advance for groups of at least 10. Otherwise, the grounds are open. ⊠ *Sjöbo* ☎ *0416/16012* ⊕ *www.sjobo.se.*

Where to Stay & Eat

$–$$ ✕ **Bryggeriet.** A lovely cross-timbered inn, this restaurant brews its own beer—there are two large copper boilers near the bar. It has a pleasant garden, and the brick vaulting of the dimly lighted interior gives it the appearance of an underground cavern. Hearty traditional fare, including reindeer and other game, is Bryggeriet's specialty. ⊠ *Långg. 20* ☎ *0411/69999.*

THE SWEDISH VIKINGS

NOT MUCH IS KNOWN of Scandinavia's ancient warrior race; eyewitness survivors of their foreign sorties were rare, while many of the medieval historians who recorded information about their pillages were priests, who feared not only Viking ferocity but also Viking paganism. Though they left behind a reputation of fierce and lawless behavior, the Vikings were more than just a marauding horde of villains.

Viking society was complex, with a strong hierarchical form. What most people consider a callous race can also be considered a sensitive group, with song, legend, craft, ritual, spirituality, and a fear of the gods at heart.

Perhaps the Viking thirst for foreign conquest was a natural consequence of their greatest talents: the Vikings could build and navigate ships like no one else on earth. Some say they conquered for no other reason than that they could. Perhaps also the harsh, cold lands at home sent them restlessly to the seas.

Viking influence on the manufacture of arms, shipbuilding, and language spread throughout Europe. These master traders and merchants also settled Iceland and helped activate the growth of a new Russian state.

Among the Vikings' most important legacies is the "middle way"—so important that it is still a part of Swedish tradition today. The word lagom, roughly translated as "enough to satisfy your needs, while leaving enough for the next person,"—in short, "moderation"—was a Viking word used in ceremonies to indicate how much mead should be taken from the communal cup. Quite a civilized and enlightened legacy for such an aggressive bunch.

— Rob Hincks

¢–$$ ✕ **Lottas.** In an interesting two-story building on the main square in the heart of town, Lottas offers several lighter fish dishes, including scallops in season. As is typical in Sweden, there are many red-meat options; the steaks are cooked and presented with care. ⊠ *Stortorget 11* ☏ *0411/78800.*

$ ✕▢ **Hotel Continental.** The Continental opened in 1829, and is a truly stunning building, both inside and out. Take a good look at the lobby with its marble stairs, crystal chandelier, stained-glass windows, and marble pillars. No two guest rooms are alike, but are all presented in a style leaning towards Gustavian, with all its requisite carved wood and lace trim. The restaurant ($$) gives each dish its own flair. The meat dishes are served with a selection of root vegetables, including fresh potatoes, carrots, and what the British call *swedes* (rutabagas), when they're in season. ⊠ *Hamng. 13, 271 43* ☏ *0411/13700* ▢ *0411/12570* ⊕ *www. hotelcontinental-ystad.se* ⤳ *52 rooms* ⌂ *Restaurant, meeting rooms, free parking, no-smoking rooms* ☰ *AE, MC, V* ❏◉❏ *BP.*

Fodor's Choice
★

¢–$ ▢ **Anno 1793 Sekelgården Hotell.** Centered around a cobblestone courtyard, this small and comfortable family-owned hotel is in the heart of Ystad, a short walk from St. Maria's Church and the main square. The half-timber buildings that make up the hotel date from the late 18th century, and in the summer breakfast is served in the courtyard. All the rooms are named and all are different. Most have a rural mix of scrubbed, flower-painted desks and chairs, typical of the Dalarna region. ⊠ *Långg. 18 271 23* ☎ *0411/73900* 🖶 *0411/18997* ⊕ *www.sekelgarden.se* 🛏 *18 rooms, 2 suites* ⚭ *Restaurant, sauna, meeting room* ⊟ *AE, DC, MC, V* ⦿ *BP.*

¢–$ 🏨 **Backagården.** This homey, small hotel is centrally located. It dates from the 17th century, has a secluded garden, and serves breakfast. ⊠ *Dammg. 36, 243 91* ☎ *0411/19848* 🖶 *0411/65715* ⊕ *www.backagarden.se* 🛏 *10 rooms* ⊟ *AE, MC, V* ⦿ *BP.*

Shopping

Head to **Sjögrens–Butikerna** (⊠ The Mall, Stora Österg. 6 ☎ 0411/ 17200) for an excellent selection of well-priced design ware, including crystal, jewelry, glassware, china, and pottery. Gifts, souvenirs, clothes, and various household items are sold at **Tidlöst** (⊠ Böckareg. 12 ☎ 0411/ 73029). The wares are a mix of old and new.

Simrishamn

❼   *41 km (25 mi) northeast of Ystad via Rte. 9, 105 km (65 mi) east of Malmö, 190 km (118 mi) southwest of Växjö.*

This fishing village of 20,000 swells to many times that number in summer, though for most, Simrishamn doesn't warrant an overnight stay. Built in the mid-1100s, the town has cobblestone streets lined with tiny brick houses covered with white stucco. The medieval St. Nicolai Kyrka, which was once a landmark for local sailors, dominates the town's skyline.

The **Frasses Musikmuseum** contains an eclectic collection of music oddities, such as self-playing barrel organs, antique accordions, children's gramophones, and what may be the world's most complete collection of Edison phonographs. ⊠ *Peder Mörcks väg 5* ☎ *0414/14520* 🎫 *SKr 20* ☉ *Early June–late June and Aug., Sun. 2–5; July, Mon.–Wed. and Sun. 2–5.*

The construction of **St. Nicolai Kyrka** (St. Nicolai's Church) began around 1161. Inside are models of sailing ships given to the church by sailors as a token of gratitude for their safe return from the Baltic Sea. The two sculptures outside the church are by the famous Swedish sculptor Carl Milles. In July there is a lunchtime concert starting at noon. ⊠ *Stortorget* ☎ *0414/412480* ☉ *Mar.–June 10 and mid-Sept.–Dec., weekdays noon–3, Sat. 10–1, Sun. after service; June 11–mid-Sept., weekdays 10:30–6:30, Sat. 9:30–4, Sun. 11–4.*

> off the
> beaten
> path

BRANTEVIK – Less than 10 km (6 mi) south of Simrishamn on the coastal road is this classic but tiny southern fishing village. It has a marvelous harbor, and the homes are small, brightly colored fishermen's cottages. A hundred years ago only 1,100 people lived here, but the village had Sweden's then-largest sailing fleet with 124 ships. The village hasn't changed much since then. A good place for lunch is **Bronterögen,** a café serving excellent meals right beside the harbor. It will cost between SKr 50 and SKr 140 for an entrée. For something a little more formal or even a night's stay, try the old inn **Brantevik's Bykrog and Hotel** (⊠ Mästergränd 2 ☎ 0414/22069). There are seven rooms here, along with a restaurant.

Fodor's Choice ★
Twenty kilometers (12 mi) west of Simrishamn is the not-to-be-missed hideaway **QVERRESTAD** (⊠ Tomelilla ☎ 0417/32044) – , a nine-room B&B set in a lovingly restored farmhouse. The rooms are ultrastylish, with sisal rugs on stone-tile floors, sumptuous fabrics, and touches of luxury like CD and DVD players in every room. The food is superb, with an optional dinner comprised only of local, seasonal ingredients—offerings such as fresh asparagus with asparagus mousse and a Parmesan wafer sets Qverrestad apart from the usual B&B. Try the sumptuous breakfast of still-warm home-baked bread, homemade orange marmalade, and local sausage. The two owners will go out of their way to make you feel welcome and pampered.

en route
About 20 km (12 mi) north of Simrishamn is the tiny village of **Kivik.** You are now firmly in the heart of Sweden's apple country, a spectacular place to be when the trees are blooming in early to late May. From Kivik follow the signs to the **Äpplets Hus** (House of Apples; ☎ 0414/71900), a museum that tells the history of apple orchards. Alongside is the **cider brewery** and a gift shop full of apple paraphernalia. On the way back from the Äpplets Hus is a small café—and a huge pile of boulders. This is the **Kivik grave,** one of the most remarkable Bronze Age monuments in Sweden. Dating from before 3000 BC, the tomb consists of a cairn nearly 250 feet across. Walk into the tomb and find the cist with eight tombstones engraved with symbols. If you have time, stay a night at **Vitemölle Badhotell** **Fodor's**Choice ★ (⊠ Lejeg. 60 ☎ 0414/70000), a stunning white weatherboard building from the early 1900s, with a glassed-in veranda right on the sand dunes of Kivik. It is the best preserved and best located of the string of original bath hotels that dot this coast. Inside, the rooms have been beautifully decorated in a simple Shaker style. The veranda restaurant offers simple, delicious local food and stunning views of the dunes and the sea beyond.

If you're in the area between June and August, you might want to stop off at **Kronovall Castle** (⊠ Fågeltofta, Tomelilla ☎ 0417/ 19710), about 20 km (12 mi) northwest of Simrishamn. The castle is now a hotel, restaurant, and wine-tasting school, run by restaurateur Petri Pumpa. The staff here are more than glad to give guests a impromptu tour of the castle and grounds, if time allows. The 18th-century castle was given its baroque appearance through a remodeling in 1890 by architect Isak Gustaf Clason, best known for the Nordic Museum in Stockholm. Surrounding the castle is a beautiful park with a magnificent hedge labyrinth.

Kristianstad

❽ *73 km (45 mi) north of Simrishamn via Rtes. 9/19 and E22, 95 km (59 mi) northeast of Malmö (via E22), 126 km (78 mi) southwest of Växjö.*

Kristianstad was founded in 1614 by Danish king Christian IV as a fortified town to keep the Swedes at bay. Today its former ramparts and moats are wide tree-lined boulevards. For most, there isn't much of great interest in the town itself.

About 17 km (11 mi) east of Kristianstad and just north of the E22 highway is **Bäckaskog Slott.** Standing on a strip of land between two lakes, Bäckaskog Castle was originally founded as a monastery by a French religious order in the 13th century. Danish noblemen turned it into a fortified castle during the 16th century. It was later appropriated by the Swedish government and used as a residence for the cavalry. The castle was a favorite of the Swedish royalty until 1900. Today it is a hotel and restaurant. ⊠ *Fjälkinge* ☎ *044/53020* ⊕ *www.backaskogslott.se* ⊡ *Free* ⊙ *Year-round.*

off the beaten path

ÅHUS – Ten kilometers (7 mi) southeast of Kristianstad is this seaside resort. The town has a medieval center and sandy beaches stretching for 60 km (40 mi) down Hanöbukten. The best-known feature of Åhus is the **Absolut Vodka distillery.** Every drop of Absolut Vodka, the world's third-largest vodka brand, consumed in the world is still made in this little town. The distillery gives 1½-hour guided tours, which must be booked ahead by telephone; tickets must be picked up and paid for at the tourist office by 6 PM the day before the tour. ☎ *044/240106 for reservations* ⊡ *SKr 30* ⊙ *Tour mid-June–mid-Aug., Tues. at 12:45.*

en route

Six kilometers (4 mi) east of Kristianstad on E22, take a left turn to Fjälkinge and follow brown signs marked with a white flower. The route, **Humlesingan,** is a scenic drive of 48 km (30 mi) around Skåne's largest lake, Lake Ivösjö. The geology dates from millions of years ago and is rich in minerals. It was a famed hops region until 1959. The old hop houses can still be seen—one is a café. The big mountainous island is Ivö, 440 feet high.

Karlskrona

❾ *111 km (69 mi) east of Kristianstad via E22, 201 km (125 mi) northeast of Malmö, 107 km (66 mi) southeast of Växjö.*

A small city built on the mainland and on 33 nearby islands, Karlskrona achieved great notoriety in 1981, when a Soviet submarine ran aground a short distance from its naval base. The town dates from 1680, when it was laid out in baroque style on the orders of Karl XI. Two churches around the main square, **Trefaldighetskyrkan** and **Frederikskyrkan,** date from this period and were both designed by the architect Nicodemus Tessin the Younger. Because of the excellent state of preservation of the naval museum and other buildings in town, Karlskrona has been designated a World Heritage Site by UNESCO.

Although the archipelago is not as large or as full of dramatic scenery as Stockholm's islands, Karlskrona is still worth the boat trip. One can be arranged through **Skärgårdstrafiken** (☎ 0455/78330).

★ The **Admiralitetskyrkan** (Admiralty Church) is Sweden's oldest wooden church, built in 1685. It is an unusual variant of the Swedish church architecture. Although it was supposed to be temporary, the stone replacement was never built. The wooden statue of constable Matts Rosenborn, who froze to death here one New Year's Eve in the 18th century, stands outside tipping his hat to those who give alms. The church is on Bastionsgatan on the naval island. Walk east a few minutes from Stortorget, the main square to get to the bridge.

★ The **Marinmuseum** (Naval Museum), in a building dating from 1752, is one of the oldest museums in Sweden and has a superb collection perfect for those with a nautical bent. The shed for making rope is ancient (1692) and huge—nearly 1,000 feet long. In the museum are old maps and charts, old navigating equipment, ship designs, and relics from actual ships, as well as weaponry. The museum can also provide you with brochures of the port area, perfect for a pleasant walk. ⊠ *Stumholmen* ☎ *0455/359302* ⊠ *SKr 55* ⊘ *June–Aug., daily 10–6; Sept.–May, daily noon–5.*

Stunning **Kungsholm Fort,** on the island of Kungsholmen, was built in 1680 to defend the town's important naval port. The fortress was on full alert when the Russians blockaded Karlskrona in the 1780s and when the English were cruising the Baltic in 1801. Perhaps the most impressive aspect of the fort is the round harbor, built into the fort itself with only a narrow exit to the sea. The fort is accessible only by a boat booked through the **tourist office** (⊠ Stortorget ☎ 0455/303490) on the main island of Trossö.

The **archipelago** is made up of dozens of islands scattered off the coast of Karlskrona's mainland. They are stunning low-lying islands that make excellent places to walk and picnic. Although some are accessible by road, the best way to take it all in is to go by ferry. The cruises take half a day. Contact **Affärsverken Båttrafik** (⊠ N. Kungsg. 36 ☎ 0455/78300 ⊠ SKr 40–SKr 120), the ferry operators, with offices at the ferry terminal.

Where to Stay & Eat

¢–$$ ✕ **Lisas Sjökrog.** Floating on the sea, this docked ship is a great place to see a sunset and look out over the archipelago. The emphasis here is on seafood, including herring, halibut, and shellfish in season. You can also try well-prepared meat dishes and the popular summer salads. ⊠ *Fisktorget* ☎ *0455/23465* ▤ *AE, MC, V* ⊘ *Closed Sept.–Apr.*

$ ▥ **First Hotel Statt.** The rooms are well appointed, the decor classic, and the style Swedish traditional. Built around 1900, this immaculate hotel with an ornate stairwell and candelabras in the lobby is in the heart of the city and is fully renovated. ⊠ *Ronnebyg. 37–39, 371 33* ☎ *0455/*

55550 🖨 *0455/16909* ⊕ *www.firsthotels.com* 📞 *107 rooms* ♿ *Restaurant, in-room data ports, Wi-Fi, hot tub, sauna, bar, nightclub, meeting rooms, no-smoking rooms* ⊟ *AE, DC, MC, V* ⎢◎⎟ *BP.*

$ ✕ **Lokpalatset.** Formerly an art and design shop with a restaurant inside, the restaurant has taken over completely. The "Lok" part of the name refers to the building's even earlier life as a repair shop for railway locomotives. The restaurant's interior has a creative mix of Scandinavian and Japanese design. The menu is equally creative with Swedish, French, and Italian influences. ⊠ *Bleklingeg. 3, Lokstallarna* 🖀 *0455/333331* ⊟ *AE, DC, MC, V.*

$ 🏨 **Park Inn Karlskrona.** From this seaside hotel the beach is a 10-minute walk. The town center and the naval museum are even closer. The rooms are all decorated with dark-wood floors and headboards and navy fabrics—all appropriately nautical. Many rooms have good views. ⊠ *Skeppsbrokajen, 371 32* 🖀 *0455/361500* 🖨 *0455/361509* ⊕ *www. karlskrona.parkinn.se* 📞 *80 rooms* ♿ *Dining room, in-room data ports, sauna, free parking, no-smoking rooms* ⊟ *AE, MC, V* ⎢◎⎟ *BP.*

¢ 🏨 **Hotel Conrad.** For simple but functional accommodations at a reasonable price, the Hotel Conrad is a good choice. Rooms are colored with very tasteful hues of chocolate brown and beige. It is a short walk from shopping, restaurants, and entertainment. ⊠ *V. Köpmansg. 12, 371 34* 🖀 *0455/363200* 🖨 *0455/363205* ⊕ *www.hotelconrad.se* 📞 *58 rooms* ♿ *Sauna, meeting rooms, free parking, no-smoking rooms* ⊟ *AE, MC, V* ⎢◎⎟ *BP.*

Nightlife & the Arts

In a renovated old theater, **Bio Bar och Matsalar** (⊠ Borgmästareg. 17 🖀 0455/311100) is an ornate setting with crystal chandeliers. The scene varies greatly, but you're more likely to hear Top 40 hits than the latest dance music. Playing on the town's seafaring heritage with its name, **Piraten Nattklubb** (⊠ Ronnebyg. 50 🖀 0455/81853) serves up good cocktails, but amid a decor that suggests the Middle Ages.

The Outdoors

Karlskrona has a reputation for both saltwater and freshwater fishing. The waters of the Karlskrona archipelago are known as the Kingdom of the Pike. **Dragsö Camping** (🖀 0455/15354) offers various fishing packages, which give you a fair chance of catching one of these magnificent fish—or more if you are lucky.

Kalmar

❿ *91 km (57 mi) northeast of Karlskrona via E22, 292 km (181 mi) northeast of Malmö, 109 km (68 mi) southeast of Växjö.*

Kalmar Domkyrkan is a highly impressive building designed by Nicodemus Tessin the Elder in 1660 in the Italian baroque style. Inside, the massive open spaces create stunning light effects. Strangely, the cathedral is the only one in Sweden without a bishop. Music is played at noon during the week. ⊠ *Stortorget* 🖀 *0480/12300* 🎫 *Free* ⊗ *Daily 10–6.*

The **Kalmar Läns Museum** (Kalmar District Museum), with good archaeological and ethnographic collections, contains the remains of the royal ship *Kronan,* which sank in 1676. Cannons, wood sculptures, and old coins were all raised from the seabed in 1980. Another exhibit focuses on Jenny Nystrom, a painter famous for popularizing the *tomte,* a rustic Christmas elf. ⊠ *Skeppsbrog. 51* ☎ *0480/451300* 🎫 *SKr 50* ⊙ *Mid-June–mid-Aug., daily 10–6; mid-Aug.–mid-June, Tues.–Fri. 10–4, weekends 11–4.*

Fodor'sChoice
★

The attractive coastal town of Kalmar, opposite the Baltic island of Öland, is dominated by the imposing **Kalmar Slott,** Sweden's best-preserved Renaissance castle. Part of it dates from the 12th century. The living rooms, chapel, and dungeon can be visited. ⊠ *Slottsv.* ☎ *0480/451490* 🎫 *SKr 80* ⊙ *Apr., May, and Sept., daily 10–4; June and Aug., daily 10–5; July, daily 10–6; Oct.–Mar., 2nd weekend of every month 11–3:30.*

off the beaten path

PATAHOLM AND TIMMERNABBEN – Numerous seaside towns dot the coastline along E22, opposite Öland. **Pataholm** has a cobblestone main square, and **Timmernabben** is famous for its caramel factory. Miles of clean, attractive, and easily accessible—if windy—beaches line this coastal strip.

Where to Stay & Eat

$$ ✕ **Källaren Kronan.** Given the quality of the eclectic international dishes here, the meals are surprisingly cheap. Try the pheasant breast with Calvados sauce or the fillet of venison with black currant sauce. The building dates from the 1660s and has been preserved as a cultural heritage site. ⊠ *Ölandsg. 7* ☎ *0480/411400* ⊟ *AE, DC, MC, V.*

★ $–$$ ✕ **Byttan.** In fine weather this restaurant's large outdoor eating area and beautiful gardens are the perfect place for a leisurely meal. Served with a vast range of freshly baked breads, the summer salads, especially the chicken salad with limes, are terrific. You can also choose a heartier entrée of traditional herring with mashed potatoes. ⊠ *Slottsallén* ☎ *0480/ 16360* ⊟ *MC, V* ⊙ *Closed Oct.–Apr.*

¢–$$ ✕ **Ernesto Salonger.** This outdoor Italian restaurant serves everything from pizza to pasta. On Friday and Saturday nights a nightclub and casino are in action. ⊠ *Larmtorget 4* ☎ *0480/20050* ⊟ *AE, DC, MC, V.*

$$ 🏨 **Calmar Stadshotell.** In the city center, Stadshotellet is a fairly large hotel with modern, fresh interiors. The main building, dating from 1907, is a beautiful art-nouveau centerpiece for the town. Guest rooms are simply decorated in cream, white, and wood, with touches of moss-green and light brown; all have hair dryers and radios, among other amenities. There's also a fine restaurant. ⊠ *Stortorget 14, 392 32* ☎ *0480/ 496900* 🖷 *0480/496910* ⊕ *www.profilhotels.se* 🛏 *126 rooms* ♿ *Restaurant, cable TV, hot tub, sauna, bar, meeting room, no-smoking rooms* ⊟ *AE, DC, MC, V.*

$$ 🏨 **Slottshotellet.** On a quiet street, this gracious old house faces a waterfront park that's a few minutes' walk from both the train station and Kalmar Castle. Guest rooms are charmingly individual, with carved-wood bedsteads, old-fashioned chandeliers, pretty wallpaper, wooden floors, and antique furniture. The bathrooms are spotlessly clean. Breakfast is served year-round, and full restaurant service is available in summer.

✉ *Slottsv. 7, 392 33* ✆ *0480/88260* ⌂ *0480/88266* ◈ *www.slottshotellet. se* ➙ *44 rooms* ♪ *Restaurant, sauna, meeting room, no-smoking rooms* = *AE, DC, V* ❯◎❮ *BP.*

¢–$ ☐ **Frimurare.** Set inside a spacious park, the attractive Frimurare radiates calm and peacefulness. Both the rooms and the hotel itself have old-time touches. It's a short walk from here to the castle. ✉ *Larmtorget 2 393 32* ✆ *0480/15230* ⌂ *0480/85887* ◈ *www.frimurarehotellet.gs2. com* ➙ *34 rooms, 31 with bath* ♪ *Meeting rooms* = *MC, V.*

Öland

★ ④ *8 km (5 mi) east of Kalmar via the Ölandsbron (Öland Bridge).*

The island of Öland is a magical and ancient place—and the smallest province in Sweden. The area was first settled some 4,000 years ago and is fringed with fine sandy beaches and dotted with old windmills, churches, and archaeological remains. In the 16th century King Gustav Vasa used land he had confiscated from the church to establish farms around the country. These farms were meant to foster the country's agricultural development and supply the court and the army with grain, meat, butter, and wool. The king founded five farms on Öland: Borgholm, Halltorp, Horn, Gärdslösa, and Ottenby. Of these, Ottenby, Borgholm, and Horn are still operating farms.

The island also has spectacular bird life—swallows, cranes, geese, and birds of prey. Many migrate to Öland from Siberia. The southern part of the island, known as **Stora Alvaret,** is a UNESCO World Heritage Site due partly to its stark beauty and unique flora and fauna. Private car travel is prohibited, so let the public bus shuttle you around the island.

To get to Öland, take the 6-km (4-mi) bridge from Kalmar. Be sure to pick up a tourist information map (follow the signs as soon as you get on the island). Most of the scattered sights have no address. Close to the bridge is the popular **Historium,** where slide shows, wax figures, and constructed dioramas illustrate what Öland was like 10,000 years ago.

Head clockwise around the island. **Borgholms Slott,** the largest castle ruin in northern Europe, is just outside the island's principal town, Borgholm (25 km [15 mi] north of the bridge). Nearby is the royal family's summer home at **Solliden.** If you get hungry, try Pappa Blå, a restaurant on Borgholm's pleasant square. It serves a variety of food, from pizzas to sandwiches to steaks, which run about SKr 60–SKr 160. From Borgholm follow the signs north to **Knisa Mosse,** a marshland area that's home to many bird species.

Heading farther north brings you to Löttorp. From here, drive west to **Horns Kungsgård,** a nature preserve on a lake that has a bird-watching tower and walking trails. Horns Kungsgård is also a royal estate, meaning "king's farm" or "king's estate." The government maintains it to look as it did in 1900.

Some 5 km (3 mi) north along the coast from Horns Kungsgård is **Byrum,** a nature preserve with striking, wind-carved limestone cliffs. The botanist Linnaeus (Carl von Linné) discussed this area in his writings.

Just a few more kilometers on is **Skäftekärr,** which has a culture museum, a café, an Iron Age farm with an arboretum, and walking trails. At the northernmost tip is the Långe Erik lighthouse.

Turning back you will find one of the island's three nature centers, **Troll-skogen.** On its trails are some majestic old oaks, prehistoric barrow graves, and pines. A little to the south is northern Europe's longest beach, a great swimming spot with sparkling white sand.

Pass back through **Löttorp,** heading south. Keep an eye out for the signs leading east off the main road for the intriguing **Källa** church ruins, some of the best on the island. Return to the main road and head south to **Kappelludden,** one of the island's best year-round bird sites. A medieval chapel's ruins and a lighthouse make this coastal spot very scenic.

Gärdslösa, to the southwest of Kappelludden, has an excellently preserved medieval church. Look for the Viking inscriptions on its wall.

Continuing south, turn right at Långlöt for the **Himmelsberga Museum** (☎ 0485/561022 ⊠ SKr 50 ⊙ May–Aug., daily 10–6), a farm museum dating from the end of the 18th century. The buildings and furnishings include horse buggies and horse sleds. The old stables were home to the small, swift Öland horses, which were extinct by the beginning of the 19th century. Old documents claim that they could dance to horns and drums and jump through hoops.

Gråborg, a 6th-century fortress with massive stone walls 625 feet in diameter, is a must-see. To get here, retrace your steps back to Långlöt, head south, and turn right at Norra Möckleby.

Return to Norra Möckleby and head south. About 2 km (1 mi) north of Seby are some strings of **rune stones:** engraved gravestones dating from 500 BC to AD 1050, stone circles, and cists and cairns. Continue south to come to the southeastern edge of Stora Alvaret. This bleak and eerie area has been farmed for 1,000 years.

Just before you reach the 5th-century fortified village of **Eketorp,** you'll reach a turnoff for the **Gräsgård,** an important fishing village. Eketorp's castle is partially renovated; the area includes small tenants' fields from the Iron and Middle ages. Admission to the castle and its grounds is SKr 50.

Ottenby is the southernmost tip of Öland and was a hunting area as long as 5,000 years ago. It's now a popular site for bird-watching. The entrance fee to the burial fields is SKr 50 per car or SKr 10 per person arriving by bus.

Now drive north up the west coastal road. Shortly after **Södra Möckleby** you'll come across the impressive burial grounds of **Gettlinge.** More than 200 graves lie across a distance of 2 km (1 mi). The site was in use from the time of Christ into the Viking era, which lasted until 1050. Beginning in late spring, the land north of here blooms with many different wild orchids.

Farther on is **Mysinge Tunukus,** a Bronze Age site. A group of rune stones here is placed in a shape resembling a ship: it's beautiful at sunset. From here, continue on back the remaining 20 km (12 mi) to the bridge and mainland Sweden.

Where to Stay & Eat

$ ⊡ **Halltorps Gästgiveri.** This 17th-century manor house has modernized duplex rooms decorated in Swedish landscape tones and an excellent restaurant. Driving north from Ölandsbron, it's on the left side of the road. ⊠ *387 92 Borgholm* ☎ *0485/85000* 🖷 *0485/85001* ⊕ *www. halltorpsgastgiveri.se* ↩ *36 rooms* ⌂ *Restaurant, 2 saunas, meeting room, free parking, no-smoking rooms* ▭ *AE, DC, MC, V.*

¢ ⊡ **Eksgården Värdshus.** The red cottages at this hotel resemble farmhouses. The pleasant dining room often hosts cultural performances. There's even a museum with farm and domestic implements and footwear, and an arts-and-crafts shop. ⊠ *Gårdby, 386 93 Färjestaden* ☎ *0485/33450* 🖷 *0485/33435* ↩ *13 rooms* ⌂ *Dining room, shop* ⊙ *Closed Sept.–Jan.*

¢ ✕⊡ **Guntorps Herrgård.** Spacious parkland surrounds this manor house, which is 2,500 feet from the center of Borgholm. Outside, there's a heated pool. The restaurant has hardwood floors, a grandfather clock on one wall, and copper pots hanging on another. ⊠ *387 36 Borgholm* ☎ *0485/ 13000* 🖷 *0485/13319* ⊕ *www.guntorpsherrgard.se* ↩ *32 rooms* ⌂ *Restaurant, sauna, no-smoking rooms* ▭ *AE, DC, MC, V.*

¢ ⊡ **Värdshuset Briggen Tre Liljor.** Large trees stand alongside this lovely, old stone-clad hotel, which is 25 km (15 mi) north of Borgholm. The rooms are spacious and old-fashioned, making you feel as if you've stepped into the past. The restaurant serves good traditional food. ⊠ *Lofta, 387 91 Borgholm* ☎ *0485/26400* 🖷 *0485/26420* ⊕ *www.briggentreliljor. com* ↩ *20 rooms* ⌂ *Restaurant, meeting room* ▭ *AE, MC, V.*

The Kingdom of Glass

Stretching roughly 109 km (68 mi) between Kalmar and Växjö.

Småland is home to the world-famous Swedish glass industry. Scattered among the rocky woodlands of Småland province are isolated villages whose names are synonymous with high-quality crystal glassware. This spectacular creative art was at its height in the late 19th century. The conditions were perfect: large quantities of wood to fuel the furnaces and plenty of water from the streams and rivers. At the time, demand was such that the furnaces burned 24 hours a day.

The region is still home to 16 major glassworks, many of them created through the merging of the smaller firms. You can still see glass being blown and crystal being etched by craftspeople. You may also be interested in attending a *Hyttsill* evening, a revival of an old tradition in which Baltic herring (*sill*) is cooked in the glass furnaces of the *hytt* (literally "hut," but meaning "the works"). Most glassworks also have shops selling quality firsts and not-so-perfect seconds at a discount.

Though the glass factories generally prospered before and during the 1900s, this wealth didn't filter down to many of their workers or to Småland's other inhabitants. Poverty became so widespread that the area lost vast numbers of people to the United States from the late 19th through the 20th century. If you're an American with Swedish roots, chances are your ancestors are from this area. The Utvandrarnas Hus (Emigrants' House) in Växjö tells the story of this exodus.

The Kingdom of Glass's oldest works is **Kosta Glasbruk**. Dating from 1742, it was named for the two former generals who founded it, Anders Koskull and Georg Bogislaus Stael von Holstein. Faced with a dearth of local talent, they initially imported glassblowers from Bohemia. The Kosta works pioneered the production of crystal (to qualify for that label, glass must contain at least 24% lead oxide). You can see glassblowing off-season (mid-August–early June) between 9 and 3. To get to the village of Kosta from Kalmar, drive 49 km (30 mi) west on Route 25, then 14 km (9 mi) north on Route 28. ⊠ *Kosta* ☎ *0478/34529* ⊕ *www.kostaboda.se* ⊙ *May, June, and Aug–mid-Sept., weekdays 9–10 and 11–3, Sat. 10–3; July, daily 10–4; mid-Sept–Apr., weekdays 9–10 and 11–3.*

Orrefors is one of the best-known glass companies in Sweden. Orrefors arrived on the scene late—in 1898—but set particularly high artistic standards. The skilled workers in Orrefors dance a slow, delicate minuet as they carry the pieces of red-hot glass back and forth, passing them on rods from hand to hand, blowing and shaping them. The basic procedures and tools are ancient, and the finished product is the result of unusual teamwork, from designer to craftsman to finisher. One of Orrefors's special attractions is a magnificent display of pieces made during the 19th century; you can appease bored children in the cafeteria and playground. From early June to mid-August you can watch glass being blown. ⊠ *On Rte. 31, about 18 km (11 mi) east of Kosta Glasbruk* ☎ *0481/34000* ⊕ *www.orrefors.se* ⊙ *July, weekdays and Sat. 10–4, Sun. noon–4; Aug.–June, weekdays 9–3.*

Mystical animal reliefs and female figures play a big role in the work at **Målerås,** which was founded in 1890. The glassworkers are great to watch; they use classic techniques with names such as "the grail." Overlooking the factory is a pleasant restaurant with panoramic views. ⊠ *12 km (7 mi) north of Orrefors* ☎ *0481/31400* ⊙ *June–Aug., weekdays 9–6, Sat. 10–5, Sun. 11–5; Sept.–May, weekdays 10–6, Sat. 10–4, Sun. 11–4.*

Boda Glasbruk, part of the Kosta Boda Company, is the second-oldest glassworks, founded in 1864. The work here has an ethereal theme, with the designers drawing on cosmic bodies such as the sun and the moon. Much of the work has veils of violet and blue suspended in the crystal. ⊠ *Just off Rte. 25, 42 km (26 mi) west of Kalmar* ☎ *0481/42410* ⊙ *July–mid-Aug., weekdays 9–6, Sat. 10–5, Sun. 11–5; mid-Aug.–June, weekdays 9–6, Sat. 10–4, Sun. noon–4.*

Continue west from Boda Glasbruk for 20 km (12 mi) to the town of Lessebo. From mid-June to mid-August you can visit the 300-year-old **Lessebo Handpappersbruk,** which is the only handmade-paper factory in Sweden. Since the 18th century the craftsmen have been using much the same techniques to produce fine paper, which is available from the shop. Guided tours take place on weekdays. ⊠ *Storg., Lessebo* ☎ *0478/*

47691 ⊕ www.lessebo.se ☒ Tours free ☉ Weekdays 7–4; June–Aug., guided tours at 9:30, 10:30, 1, and 2:15.

Skruf Glasbruk began in 1896. Today it's a purveyor to the king of Sweden. The royal family, the ministry of foreign affairs, and the parliament have all commissioned work from Skruf. Local farmers encouraged the development of the glassworks because they wanted a market for their wood. The museum takes you through the historic eras of fine glass craft in Småland. The factory specializes in lead-free crystal, which has a unique iridescence and form. ☒ *10 km (6 mi) south of Lessebo. Turn left at Åkerby* ☎ *0478/20133* ⊕ *www.skruf-bergdala. se* ☉ *Weekdays 9–6, weekends 10–4. Glassblowing demonstrations weekdays 7–4.*

★ ⚲ Founded in 1889, **Bergadala Glasbruk** is one of the most traditional glassworks. Alongside the main road are the former workers' homes, now used mainly as long-term rentals. Note the impressive circular furnace that stands in the middle of the wooden floor. Bergadala is often called the blue glassworks, since many of its pieces have a rich cobalt hue. A stone's throw from the smelter is a children's playground and a glass-painting workshop that will keep them occupied for hours. From here you are 10 km (6 mi) from Växjö. ☒ *About 15 km (9 mi) northwest of Lessebo, toward Växjö* ☎ *0478/31650* ☉ *Weekdays 9–6, weekends 10–4. Glassblowing demonstrations weekdays 7–4.*

Where to Stay

¢ ▦ **Hotell Björkäng.** Set in a park that will give you plenty of opportunity to take evening strolls, the Björkäng has well-kept rooms. They have some rustic decorations, such as traditional ornaments, wood carved by nature, and glass pieces. You also have the opportunity to spend an evening in the glassblowing room. The dining room offers a range of good traditional Swedish food. ☒ *Stora Vägen 2, Kosta* ☎ *0478/50000* 🖶 *0478/ 50437* ⤸ *24 double and 2 single rooms* ♨ *Dining room, sauna, billiards, meeting rooms, free parking* ▤ *MC, V* ⦿⦿ *BP.*

¢ ▦ **Orrefors.** Simplicity and affordability are this small hotel's selling points. Set in a gray-color house from the 1930s, just a three-minute walk from the old Orrefors factory, rooms here are straightforward and very pleasant, with minimal furnishings. The staff is extremely friendly, the atmosphere is cozy, and the hotel is set in the authentic center of the Kingdom of Glass. The restaurant and bar are both pleasant. ☒ *Kantav. 29, Orrefors* ☎ *0481/30035* 🖶 *0481/30035* ⤸ *10 rooms* ♨ *Restaurant, bar, meeting room, no smoking* ▤ *MC, V* ⦿⦿ *BP.*

Växjö

⓬ *109 km (68 mi) northwest of Kalmar via Rte. 25, 198 km (123 mi) northeast of Malmö, 228 km (142 mi) southeast of Göteborg, 446 km (277 mi) southwest of Stockholm.*

Some 10,000 Americans visit this town every year, for it was from this area that their Swedish ancestors departed in the 19th century. A large proportion of those emigrants went to Minnesota, attracted by the affordable farmland and a geography reminiscent of parts of Sweden. On the second Sunday of every August, Växjö celebrates Minnesota Day: Swedes and Swedish-Americans come together to commemorate their common heritage with American-style square dancing and other festivities. Beyond this, the city is really just a stopover.

★ The **Smålands Museum** is famous for its presentation of the development of glass and has the largest glass collection in northern Europe. Its excellent display puts the area's unique industry into perspective and explains the different styles of the various glass companies. ⊠ *Södra Järnvägsg. 2* ☎ *0470/704200* ⊕ *www.smalandsmuseum.se* ☒ *SKr 40* ⊙ *June–Aug., weekdays 10–5, weekends 11–5; Sept.–May, Tues.–Fri. 10–5, weekends 11–5.*

The **Utvandrarnas Hus** (Emigrants' House), in the town center, tells the story of the migration, when more than a million Swedes—one quarter of the population—departed for the United States. The museum exhibits provide a vivid sense of the rigorous journey, and an archive room and a research center allow Americans with Swedish blood to trace their ancestry. The archives are open for genealogy research on weekdays. ⊠ *Vilhelm Mobergsg. 4* ☎ *0470/20120* ⊕ *www.swemi.se* ☒ *SKr 40* ⊙ *May–Aug., weekdays 9–5, Sat. 11–4; Sept.–Apr., weekdays 9–4, weekends 11–4.*

off the beaten path

KRONOBERGS SLOTTSRUIN – About 5 km (3 mi) north of Växjö, this 14th-century castle ruin lies on the edge of the Helgasjön (Holy Lake). The Småland freedom fighter Nils Dacke used the castle as a base for his attacks against the Danish occupiers during the mid-1500s; now it's an idyllic getaway. In summer you can eat waffles in the shade of birch trees by the café, or take a dinner or sightseeing cruise around the lake on the small, toylike *Thor,* Sweden's oldest steamboat. ☎ *0470/63000 Café Ryttmästargården, 0470/704200 boat tours* ☒ *Castle ruins SKr 10; dinner cruise SKr 400; 2½-hr canal trip to Årby and back SKr 125; 1-hr lake trip SKr 100 (includes coffee)* ⊙ *Castle tours offered late June–late Aug.; dinner cruise Sun.*

Where to Stay

$–$$ 🏨 **Hotel Statt.** Now a Best Western hotel, the Statt is popular with tourist groups. It has a convenient, central location. The building dates from 1853, but the rooms are up to modern standards. The hotel has a cozy pub, bistro, and café. ⊠ *Kungsg. 6, 351 04* ☎ *0470/13400* 🖷 *0470/44837* 🛏 *124 rooms* ⚍ *Restaurant, café, gym, sauna, pub, meeting room, no-smoking rooms* ⊟ *AE, DC, MC, V.*

¢–$ 🏨 **Esplanad.** In the town center, the Esplanad is a small family-run hotel with basic amenities. The rooms are sparse, to say the least, with brown plastic flooring and more brown furnishings besides. But the location and the friendly welcome from the owner make it worthwhile. ⊠ *Norra Esplanaden 21A, 352 31* ☎ *0470/22580* 🖷 *0470/26226* ⊕ *www.hotell-esplanad.com* 🛏 *23 rooms* ⚍ *Free parking, no-smoking rooms* ⊟ *MC, V* ⍩ *BP.*

The South & the Kingdom of Glass A to Z

AIR TRAVEL

CARRIERS   Four airlines serve the Malmö airport (Sturup).

🛪 **Direktflyg** ☎ 0243/444700. **Malmö Aviation** ☎ 0771/550010. **RyanAir** ☎ 0900/ 2020240 in Sweden ⊕ www.ryanair.com; use Web when booking from abroad. **SAS** ☎ 0770-727727.

AIRPORTS

Malmö's airport, Sturup (MMX), is approximately 30 km (19 mi) from Malmö and 25 km (15 mi) from Lund. Buses for Malmö and Lund meet all flights at Sturup Airport. The price of the trip is SKr 90 to either destination. A taxi from the airport to Malmö or Lund costs about SKr 470.

🛪 **Bus Information** ☎ 040/6696290. **Sturup** ☎ 040/6131100. **Taxi and Limousine Service** ☎ 040/70000.

BOAT & FERRY TRAVEL

Since the inauguration of the Øresund Bridge between Malmö and Copenhagen, it is no longer possible to travel by ferry between the two cities, but there is still regular ferry service between Helsingborg in Sweden and Helsingør in Denmark (by Scandlines, HH-Ferries, and Sundsbussarna). From Ystad there is ferry service to Swinoujscie in Poland (by Polferries), and from Trelleborg ferries run to Sassnitz and Rostock in Germany (by Scandlines). Stena Line ferries run between Karlskrona and Gdynia in Poland.

🛪 **HH-Ferries** ☎ 042/198000 ⊕ www.hhferries.se. **Polferries** ☎ 040121700 ⊕ www. polferries.se. **Scandlines** ☎ 0410/65000 ⊕ www.scandlines.se. **Stena Line** ✉ Danmarksterminalen, Masthuggskajen, Göteborg ☎ 031-7040000 in Göteborg, 0455366300 in Karlskrona ⊕ www.stenaline.se. **Sundsbussarna** ☎ 042/385880 ⊕ www. sundsbussarna.se.

CUTTING COSTS   The Malmökortet (Malmö Card) entitles the holder to, among other benefits, free travel on the city buses; free parking; discounts on tours; free admission or discounts to most museums, concert halls, nightclubs, and theaters; the Royal Cab company; and many shops and restaurants. A one-day card costs SKr 130, a two-day card SKr 160, and a three-day card SKr 190. Cards are available from the tourist office in Malmö.

CAR RENTAL

If you are coming from Denmark and want to rent a car as soon as you arrive, several rental companies have locations at Malmö Harbor, including Avis, Hertz, and Europcar. Hertz car rentals are available for less than SKr 600 a day on weekends (less in summer) if you book an SAS flight.

🛪 **Avis** ☎ 040/77830. **Europcar** ☎ 040/71640. **Hertz** ☎ 040/330770.

CAR TRAVEL

Copenhagen and Malmö are connected by the Øresund Bridge. It costs SKR 285 one-way.

Malmö is 620 km (386 mi) from Stockholm. Take the E4 Highway to Helsingborg, then the E6/E20 to Malmö and Lund. From Göteborg take the E6/E20.

Roads are well marked and well maintained. Traveling around the coast counterclockwise from Helsingborg, you take the E6/E20 to Landskrona, Malmö, and Lund, then the E6/E22 to Trelleborg; Route 9 goes along the south coast from there all the way to Simrishamn and then heads north until just before Kristianstad. It's there that you can pick up E22 all the way through Karlshamn, Ronneby, Karlskrona, and on across the east coast to Kalmar. From Kalmar, Route 25 goes almost directly west through Växjö to Halmstad, on the west coast between Helsingborg and Göteborg.

EMERGENCIES
As elsewhere in Sweden, call 112 for emergencies.

TRAIN TRAVEL
The major towns of the south are all connected by rail.

There is regular service from Stockholm to Helsingborg, Lund, and Malmö. Each trip takes about 6½ hours, and about 4½ hours by high-speed (X2000) train. All three railway stations are centrally located in their respective towns.

Trains between Malmö and Copenhagen take 35 minutes and run three times an hour during the day and once an hour at night. A one-way ticket is SKr 90.
🄵 **SJ** ☎ 0771/757575 ⊕ www.sj.se.

TRANSPORTATION AROUND THE SOUTH
A special 48-hour Øresund Runt (Around Øresund) pass is available from the Malmö Tourist Office or any train station in Skåne. Costing between SKr 199 and SKr 249, depending on where you start your trip, the ticket covers a train ticket from the Skåne province to Malmö, a train from Malmö to Helsingborg, a ferry to Helsingør, a train to Copenhagen, and a ferry back to Malmö (or if you so prefer, the same trip clockwise).

VISITOR INFORMATION
🄵 **Helsingborg** ⊠ Södra Storg. 1 ☎ 042/104350 ⊕ www.helsingborgsguiden.com. **Jönköping** ⊠ Järnvägsstationen [central train station] ☎ 036/105050. **Kalmar** ⊠ Ölandskajen 9 ☎ 0480/417700 ⊕ www.kalmar.se/turism/index2.html. **Karlskrona** ⊠ Stortorget 2 ☎ 0455/303490. **Kristianstad** ⊠ Stora torg ☎ 044/135335 ⊕ www.kristianstad. se. **Landskrona** ⊠ Storg. 36 ☎ 0418/473000 ⊕ www.tourism.landskrona.se. **Lund** ⊠ Kyrkog. 11 ☎ 046/355040 ⊕ www.lund.se. **Malmö** ⊠ Centralstationen [central train station]) ☎ 040/341200 ⊕ www.malmo.se. **Öland** ⊠ Träffpunkt Öland, Färjestaden ☎ 0485/560600. **Ronneby** ⊠ Västra Torgg. 1 ☎ 0457/18090. **Simrishamn** ⊠ Tullhusg. 2 ☎ 0414/819800. **Växjö** ⊠ Stationen, Norra Järnvägsg. 3 ☎ 0470/41410. **Ystad** ⊠ St. Knuts Torg ☎ 0411/577681 ⊕ www.visitystad.com.

Dalarna: The Folklore District

7

Updated by
Rob Hincks

A PLACE OF FORESTS, MOUNTAINS, AND RED-PAINTED wooden farm-houses and cottages by pristine, sun-dappled lakes, Dalarna is considered the most traditional of all the country's 24 provinces. It is the favorite center for celebrations on Midsummer Day, when Swedes don folk costumes and dance to fiddle and accordion music around maypoles covered with wildflower garlands.

Dalarna played a key role in the history of the nation. It was from here that Gustav Vasa recruited the army that freed the country from Danish domination during the 16th century. The region is also important artistically, both for its tradition of naive religious decoration and for producing two of the nation's best-loved painters, Anders Zorn (1860–1920) and Carl Larsson (1853–1915), and one of its favorite poets, the melancholy, mystical Dan Andersson (1888–1920). He sought inspiration in the remote forest camps of the old charcoal burners, who spent their days slowly burning wood to make the charcoal for factory furnaces.

Visitors to the Dalarna—many from elsewhere in Scandinavia or from Germany—make use either of the region's many well-equipped campsites or of *stugbyar* (small villages of log cabins, with cooking facilities), usually set near lakesides or in forest clearings.

Our itinerary circles Siljan, the largest of the 6,000 lakes in the province and the center of Dalarna's folklore. The main points can all be reached by train, except for the southern side of Lake Siljan.

Exploring Dalarna

Dalarna is a gloriously compact region, mostly consisting of a single road that rings Lake Siljan, the area's main attraction. A drive round the lake will take in most of the highlights, leaving you only to decide whether to travel clockwise or counterclockwise. The lake itself provides a focal point for the region, providing fish to eat, and swimming and boating to entertain. The tiny villages and towns strung around the lake each have their own particular attraction to offer, making Dalarna a well-ordered, neat little package of a region to explore.

About the Hotels & Restaurants

The shores of Lake Siljan has some delightful hotels, some dating back hundreds of years. Many are painted in classic Swedish red, and all are rustic and welcoming. It's difficult to find a region in Sweden where it is easier to relax than in Dalarna.

WHAT IT COSTS In Swedish Kronor				
$$$$	$$$	$$	$	¢
RESTAURANTS over 420	250–420	150–250	100–150	under 100
HOTELS over 2,900	2,300–2,900	1,500–2,300	1,000–1,500	under 1,000

Restaurant prices are for a main course at dinner. Hotel prices are for two people in a standard double room in high season.

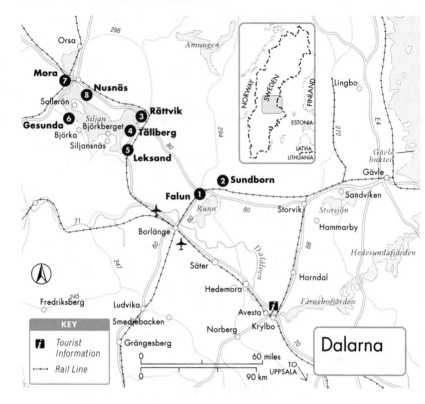

Timing

Dalarna is truly a region for all seasons. In June and July it is where every Swede wants to be, an idyllic reflection of everything that is good about Swedish summer. In the winter months, Dalarna offers some very fine skiing, skating, and winter sports. And spring and autumn bring changing colors and fine fishing in Lake Siljan.

Falun

❶ *230 km (143 mi) northwest of Stockholm via E18 and Rte. 70.*

Falun is the traditional capital of Dalarna, though the adjacent nondescript railway town of Borlänge has grown in importance as a business center. Falun's history has always been very much bound to its copper mine, worked since 1230 by Stora Kopparbergs Bergslags AB (today just Stora), which claims to be the oldest limited company in the world. During its great period of prosperity in the 17th century, it financed Sweden's "Age of Greatness," when the country became the dominant Baltic power. In 1650 Stora produced a record amount of copper; probably as a result of such rapid extraction, 37 years later its mine shafts caved in. The collapse was on Midsummer Day, when most miners were off duty, and as a result no one was killed. The mine eventually closed in 1992.

Today the major part of the mine is an enormous hole in the ground that,

★ in combination with the adjoining **Stora Museum,** has become Falun's principal tourist attraction. The one-hour tour through a network of old shafts and tunnels begins with a hair-raising 150-foot descent in an old elevator. Wear old shoes and warm clothing, since the copper-tinged mud can stain footwear and it's cold down there. The Stora Museum puts into perspective the lives of the men who worked the mines and has eye-opening displays on just how bad working conditions were below ground. ☎023/ 782030 ⊕ www.kopparberget.com ⊠ Mine SKr 90, museum free with mine tour ⊙ Mine May–Aug., daily 10–5; Sept.–mid-Nov., Mar., and Apr., weekdays 11–5, weekends 11–4. Museum May–Aug., daily 10–5; Sept.–Apr., weekdays 11–5, weekends 11–4.

The folk art, folklore, clothing, and music of the area are all well covered at **Dalarnasmuseet** (Dalarna Museum). There is also a grand reconstruction of the study in which Selma Lagerlöf (1858–1940), the celebrated Swedish author, worked after she moved to Falun in 1897. ⊠ Stigareg. 2–4 ☎ 023/765500 ⊠ SKr 40 ⊙ Weekdays 10–5, weekends noon–5.

Where to Stay & Eat

$$ ✕ **MS Slussbruden.** This restaurant on a boat offers "prawn cruises." For a set price you can feast on as many prawns as you can shell during the 3½-hour cruise. If you're not inclined to eat seafood, you can preorder either a chicken or a Greek salad. Live music acts serenade you all the while. Limitless bread and butter, cheese, fruits, and coffee are included. Wine and drinks are extra, and the choice is a little limited but good nonetheless. Combined with the beautiful scenery, the dinner cruise is a great hit. The cruise departs at 7 PM. ⊠ Strandv. ☎ 070/6385005 ⚑ Reservations essential ☰ AE, DC, MC, V ⊙ Closed Nov.–Apr.

$–$$ ✕ **Blå Apelsinen.** The Blue Orange serves up Swedish food with a French twist. Simple, pork, beef, and fish dishes are all offered in a dining room decked out in the white, blue, and terra-cotta shades of the Mediterranean. The rather strange moniker is taken from a restaurant chain of the same name in the Mediterranean, which is one of the owner's favorites. ⊠ Bergskolegränd 8A ☎ 023/29111 ☰ AE, MC, V.

$$ ▦ **Scandic.** Outside Falun, the ultramodern Scandic was built for the 1993 World Skiing Championships that took place in the Lungnet sports and recreation center. The building itself looks like a giant ski jump made of Legos. The comfortable rooms have good views of the giant ski jump that's still used for competitions. ⊠ Svärdsjög. 51, 791 31 Falun ☎ 023/ 6692200 ▦ 023/669211 ⊕ www.scandic-hotels.se ⚑ 153 rooms ⚑ Restaurant, room TV with movies, in-room broadband, Wi-Fi, indoor pool, sauna, pub, meeting room, no-smoking rooms ☰ AE, DC, MC, V.

$ ▦ **First Grand Hotel.** Part of the First Hotel chain, this conventional modern hotel is close to the town center. The bright rooms are decorated with Chippendale-style furniture. ⊠ Trotzg. 9–11, 791 71 ☎ 023/ 794880 ▦ 023/14143 ⊕ www.firsthotels.se ⚑ 151 rooms 1 suite ⚑ Restaurant, in-room data ports, indoor pool, gym, sauna, bar, convention center, no-smoking rooms ☰ AE, DC, MC, V.

$ ⊞ **Park Inn Bermästaren.** This small, cozy hotel in the town center is built in rustic Dalarna style, but decorated in a modern way, with primary colors, wooden floors, simple desks, and asymmetric chairs in the rooms. There is a pleasant relaxation area where the hot tub and sauna will let you unwind from the day's stresses. ⊠ *Bergskolegränd 7, 791 12* ☎ *023/701700* 🖷 *023/701709* ⊕ *www.falun.parkinn.se* 📞 *88 rooms, 84 with bath* ⌂ *Restaurant, in-room data ports, Wi-Fi, hot tub, sauna, meeting room, no-smoking rooms* ⊟ *AE, DC, MC, V.*

$ ⊞ **Hotel Falun.** Margaretha Eriksson runs this small, friendly, but bland-looking hotel just 1,300 feet from the railway station. The five rooms that share baths are offered at a lower rate. The front desk closes at 9 PM. ⊠ *Centrumhuset, Trotzg. 16, 791 30* ☎ *023/29180* 🖷 *023/13006* 📞 *22 rooms, 17 with bath* ⌂ *No-smoking rooms* ⊟ *AE, DC, MC, V.*

¢ ⊞ **Birgittagården.** The Dalarna Sisters of Birgitta religious order runs this small hotel, 8 km (5 mi) outside town. It's smoke- and alcohol-free and set in a fine park. ⊠ *Uddnäsv. 58, 791 46* ☎ *023/32147* 🖷 *023/32471* 📞 *20 rooms* ⌂ *Meeting room; no room phones, no room TVs, no smoking* ⊟ *No credit cards.*

Sports & the Outdoors

A 25-minute walk from the center of Falun, east on Svärdsjögatan, takes you to **Lungnet** (☎ 023/83500), Falun's sports complex and national ski stadium. Horseback riding, swimming, bowling, an indoor sports center, and running tracks are all available. The ski stadium is home to the 260-foot ski jump (used only in competitions). In winter you can watch the daredevil jumpers fly through the air, and in summer, when the snow has gone, you can go to the top yourself and admire the view across Falun and beyond.

SKIING At the **Bjursås Ski Center** (☎ 023/774177 ⊕ www.bjursas-ski.se), 25 km (15 mi) northwest of Falun on Route 80, you can make use of the resort's seven lift systems and 18 varied pistes. It's open between December and April and has numerous hotels, restaurants, and cafés.

Sundborn

❷ *10 km (6 mi) northeast of Falun off Rte. 80.*

★ In this small village you can visit **Carl Larsson Gården,** the lakeside home of the Swedish artist (1853–1915). Larsson was an excellent textile designer and draftsman who painted scenes from his family's busy domestic life. The house itself was creatively painted and decorated by Larsson's wife, Karin, also trained as an artist. Their home's turn-of-the-20th-century fittings and furnishings have been carefully preserved; their great-grandchildren still use the house on occasion. Waits for guided tours in summer can take two hours. You'll receive a timed ticket and can visit the café or stroll around the garden or lake while you wait. ☎ 023/60053 ⊕ *www.clg.se* ✉ *Guided tours only, SKr 90* ⊙ *May–Sept., daily 10–5; Jan.–Apr., 1 guided tour daily, weekdays at 11 in English.*

SAUNA CULTURE

T IS AUTUMN on the Stockholm archipelago island of Finnhamn today, but you could be forgiven for thinking it is winter, as an arctic wind scythes bitterly across the landscape. To the north, clouds that are surely laden with snow creep south and the people shiver. You need heat, and lots of it.

There is a solution, one forged in defense against the cold for eons of time by the people who have populated these frozen lands. And it is as traditionally Swedish as Absolut vodka and just as warming. The bastu (sauna) has been the answer to frozen Nordic bones since long before medieval times, although its true date of origin has not been determined.

The bastu takes many different shapes and forms, but the classic model is little more than a small wooden shed, parked beside a freezing lake or the sea. The one on Finnhamn looks like something from the fairy-tale writings of Hans Christian Anderson (admittedly Danish). It is painted a traditional rust red and is no more than 16 feet long. It sits on a creaky wooden pier under bleak, leafless trees, plumb against the sea.

This evening it is a welcome sight, and there is no alternative but to take the plunge into a dry heat that will soar to 80°C–90°C (176°F–194°F). The snow clouds have arrived, and snowflakes the size of golf balls are swirling and drifting. The sea is churning and the wind is coaxing the trees into an eerie dance. Through a small glass window you can see the storm.

Taking a sauna has reached a fine art in Sweden. It is often a social event. Some men do business here (a last bastion of gender exclusion), and there is a definite ritual. The practice is about heat and cleansing. In fact, the bastu has historically been the primary cleansing place in times when running water was scarce. Nordic people came here for their weekly (or less-often) bathing routine. It was also used as the place for medical treatment, due to its hygienic setting. Babies were born here. Corpses were brought to lie here. The sauna was once a sacred place.

A visit begins with showering off the wrath of the day. Completely dry yourself, allowing the heat to properly open your pores for a clean sweat. Take a seat, buck naked, on a towel—a must for hygienic protocol.

Now the work begins. And it is work, although it may not feel like it at first. It will take a while, but the sweat will trickle, then flood. Put some water on the coals to wet the air. When you reach near-fission, the next and most daring step awaits: the big freeze. On Finnhamn I stepped unadorned out into the snow, down the frozen steel ladder. Sha-la-la! By the powers, it was cold, head-splitting cold.

Back on terra firma within microseconds, your skin begins to tingle and your head spins in dizziness and shock. Absolute elation. Make haste to the bastu. The next rule is to dry off in the warming room. This is one full cycle. Keep going until you can take no more. At the end an ocean of warmth and exhaustion will engulf you.

The Swedish believe in the practice of sauna as an elixir, and proclaim it aids good health, vigor, and long life. But do beware: some of those with a heart condition or who are otherwise in ill health have come to grief in the bastu. Everything in moderation, the saying goes.

Rättvik

❸ *48 km (30 mi) northwest of Falun via Rte. 80.*

On the eastern tip of Lake Siljan, Rättvik is a pleasant town of timbered houses surrounded by wooded slopes. A center for local folklore, the town has several shops that sell handmade articles and local produce.

Every year in June, dozens of people wearing traditional costumes arrive in longboats to attend midsummer services at the town's 13th-century church, **Rättviks Kyrka**, which stands on a promontory stretching into the lake. Its interior contains some fine examples of local religious art. Next to the church are 90 stables, the oldest from the 1400s, where churchgoers once rested their horses.

The open-air museum **Rättviks Gammelgård,** a 20-minute walk along the banks of the lake north of Rättvik, reconstructs peasant life of bygone days. More than 3,500 pieces of art, clothing, ceramics, tools, and furniture are on display in the old buildings. Tours in English can be arranged through the Rättvik tourist office. ☎ *0248/797210 🖾 Free; guided tour SKr 20 ⊘ Mid-June–mid-Aug., daily 11–6; tours at 1 and 2:30.*

Just to the west of Rättvik in the forest is **Vidablick.** The top of this tall wooden tower, more than 100 years old, will give you some of the most stunning views across Lake Siljan that you can find.

★ Once a lucrative open chalk mine, the huge multitier quarry left at **Dalhalla** (7 km [4½] mi north of Rättvik) has become one of the world's most beautiful outdoor stages. One side is banked with seats, and the stage, surrounded by water and supported on pillars, appears to float on the cobalt-blue lake at the quarry's bottom. Opera, rock concerts, and amazing light shows are all presented here, where the sound is enhanced by the quarry's incredible acoustics. There is also an exhibition covering the meteor crash that formed Lake Siljan 360 million years ago, the chalk mining that still takes place, and the history of mining. Guided tours of the more remote parts of the quarry can be booked year-round. ⊠ *Stationshuset, Rättvik* ☎ *0248/797950 🖾 SKr 50 for exhibition and tour ⊘ Exhibition mid-May–Sept., daily 11–3; July, daily 10–6.*

Where to Stay & Eat

¢–$ ✕ **Strandrestaurangen.** A family-style restaurant with a huge outdoor seating area by the lake, Strandrestaurangen serves such standard Swedish fare as meatballs, sausages, and pork chops. It's all well prepared and filling. Kids enjoy the beach, miniature golf, ice-cream bar, and swimming pool. For adults, there's a pub attached, which has live music in the evening. ⊠ *Rättvik* ☎ *0248/13400 🖃 AE, MC, V ⊘ Mid-June–mid-Aug.*

¢ 🏨 **Hotell Vidablick.** Set on its own grounds, with a pleasant view of the lake from the veranda, this small hotel makes a welcome, relaxing stop. Rooms are modern and sparsely furnished, and there's a small private beach where you can take to the water, if it's warm enough. ⊠ *Hantverksbyn, 795 36* ☎ *0248/30250 🖨 0248/30660 ⊕ www.hantverksbyn.se ➔ 37 rooms ♣ Beach, bar 🖃 AE, DC, MC, V 🍽 BP.*

Tällberg

❹ *9 km (5½ mi) south of Rättvik via Rte. 70, 57 km (35 mi) northwest of Falun via Rte. 80.*

Tällberg is considered by many to be the real Dalarna. It was a sleepy town that few knew about, but an 1850 visit from Hans Christian Andersen put an end to all that. He extolled its virtues—tiny flower-strewn cottages, sweet-smelling grass meadows, stunning lake views—to such an extent that Tällberg quickly became a major tourist stop. This tiny village, one of the smallest in the region with only about 200 permanent residents, is packed with crowds in summer.

The farm buildings that make up **Klockargården** have become a living museum of handicrafts and local industry. Artists and craftsmen work in the old buildings, performing such skills as blacksmithing, baking flat bread, making lace, and weaving textiles. ⊠ *Tällberg* ☎ *0247/50265* ⬚ *Free* ☾ *June–Aug., daily 10–7.*

Where to Stay & Eat

★ $ ✕⬚ **Åkerblads.** A sprawling, low-built hotel, with parts dating from the 1400s, Åkerblads is known primarily for its gourmet achievements. The restaurant ($$) serves an interesting blend of Swedish and French cuisine, including such dishes as pork roasted with eggplants and blueberries, and salmon with asparagus, truffle, and burgundy wine sauce. On Sunday and during the low season, the restaurant often carries a limited, but equally delicious menu. The hotel rooms are comfortable, and most have very good views of Lake Siljan. ⊠ *Sjögattu 2, 793 70* ☎ *0247/50800* 🖷 *0247/50652* ⊕ *www.akerblads-tallberg.se* ⇗ *69 rooms, 3 suites* ⭗ *Restaurant, in-room data ports, pool, sauna, spa, bar, free parking* ⊟ *AE, DC, MC, V* ❚◉❚ *BP.*

Fodor'sChoice ★ ¢ ✕⬚ **Hotel Dalecarlia.** There's a homey feel to this first-class hotel, which has exacting standards and good lake views. The lobby's comfy sofas and darkened corners are welcoming spots to sink into. Rooms are large and done in soft colors, and there is a spa and fitness center with pool, sauna, and beauty treatments. The restaurant ($$) is candlelighted and reminiscent of a farmhouse. It has oak beams, crisp white linen, and a large open fireplace perfect for an after-dinner brandy. The food is well presented and emphasizes local and regional specialties. The game is especially good. ⊠ *793 70 Tällberg* ☎ *0247/89100* 🖷 *0247/50240* ⊕ *www.dalecarlia.se* ⇗ *80 rooms, 5 suites* ⭗ *Restaurant, in-room data ports, Wi-Fi, pool, gym, sauna, spa, bar, convention center, free parking* ⊟ *AE, DC, MC, V* ❚◉❚ *BP.*

$ ⬚ **Tällbergsgården.** A classic Dalarna red-wood building, this one claiming to be the oldest in the village, is home to a small hotel with stunning lake views. The guest rooms are light and airy, with neutral shades and wooden floors. ⊠ *Holgattu 1, 793 70* ☎ *0247/50850* 🖷 *0247/50200* ⊕ *www.tallbergsgarden.se* ⇗ *38 rooms, 6 suites* ⭗ *Restaurant, in-room data ports, sauna, bar, meeting rooms, free parking* ⊟ *AE, DC, MC, V* ❚◉❚ *BP.*

Leksand

❺ *9 km (5½ mi) south of Tällberg via Rte. 70, 66 km (41 mi) northwest of Falun via Rättvik.*

Thousands of tourists converge on Leksand every June for the midsummer celebrations; they also come in July for *Himlaspelet* (*The Play of the Way that Leads to Heaven*), a traditional musical with a local cast that is staged outdoors near the town's church. It is easy to get seats; ask the local tourist office for details.

Leksand is also an excellent vantage point from which to watch the "church-boat" races on Siljan. These vessels are supposedly the successors to the Viking longboats. They were used in the 13th and 14th centuries to take peasants from outlying regions to church on Sunday. On midsummer eve the longboats, crewed by people in folk costumes, skim the lake once more.

In the hills around Leksand and elsewhere near Siljan are many *fäbodar*, small settlements in the forest where cattle were taken to graze in summer. Less-idyllic memories of bygone days are conjured up by **Käringberget**, a 720-foot-high mountain north of town where alleged witches were burned to death during the 17th century.

Fodor'sChoice
★
The oldest parts of **Leksands Kyrka** date from the 13th century, and the current exterior dates from 1715. The Leksand Church's interior contains some interesting touches: a German font from the 1500s, a crucifix from 1400, and Dalarna's oldest organ. But what makes this church really shine is its location, perhaps one of the prettiest in the country. The peaceful tree-lined churchyard and the view across the entire lake are both breathtaking. ⊠ *Kyrkudden* ☎ *0247/80700.*

At the **Leksands Hembygdsgårdar,** the site of the oldest farm buildings in Dalarna, you can learn more about the famous red structures that dot the region's landscape. Other displays look at building techniques that arose in the Middle Ages as well as the history of country living in Dalarna. ⊠ *Kyrkallén* ☎ *0247/80245* ⌦ *SKr 20* ☉ *June–Aug., daily noon–4.*

Famous local doctor and author Axel Munthe (1857–1949) built **Munthes Hildasholm** as a present for his English wife in 1910. The house and gardens, filled with exquisite antiques, paintings, and furniture from across Europe, can now be visited and seen exactly as they were left. You can have coffee and cake in the café, set in beautifully manicured gardens and lawns. ⊠ *Klockareg. 5, Kyrkudden* ☎ *0247/10062* ⊕ *www.hildasholm.org* ⌦ *SKr 70* ☉ *June–Sept., Mon.–Sat. 11–6, Sun. 1–6.*

Where to Stay & Eat

¢–$$ ✕ **Bosporen Restaurang.** The large terrace outside this restaurant is a great place to dine in summer. The menu is long and interesting, with some great Swedish classics. The best bet is the selection of pizzas, which make use of such ingredients as arugula, pine nuts, Gorgonzola, and pears. Wine by the glass is of good quality, and the beers are wide-ranging and cheap. ⊠ *Stortorget 1* ☎ *0247/13280* ⊟ *AE, MC, V.*

¢ ⌂ **Hotell Korstäppan.** The beautiful rooms, many with traditional tile fire-places and all with wooden floors, are the main attraction at this large, yellow-wood hotel. All the rooms are spacious and simply furnished with stylish antiques and beautiful old rugs. ⊠ *Hjortnäsv. 33, 793 31* ☎ *0247/ 12310* 🖷 *0247/14178* ⊕ *www.korstappan.se* ⇨ *30 rooms* ♨ *Restaurant, in-room data ports, meeting rooms, free parking* ▤ *AE, MC, V* ⦿⦿ *BP.*

★ ¢ ⌂ **Leksands Gästhem.** Simplicity bordering on minimalism is the theme at this converted old school near a farmyard just outside Leksand. The bedrooms have plain, scrubbed wooden floors, large windows, and pale-blue chairs. Each bathroom is shared by several rooms. In the hall-way—where you can still see the low coat hooks for the schoolchildren—is a sweeping wood staircase that leads to a TV and lounge area. Wonderful breakfasts are included in the rate; nearly everything is home-made. ⊠ *Krökbacken 5, 793 90* ☎ *0247/13700* 🖷 *0247/13737* ⊕ *www. leksandsguesth.nu* ⇨ *13 rooms* ♨ *Lounge* ▤ *AE, DC, MC, V* ⦿⦿ *BP.*

Sports & the Outdoors

Leksand is the perfect base for a bike ride around Lake Siljan. There are many paths and tracks to choose from, and maps and rental bikes are available from the **tourist office** (☎ 0247/796130).

Gesunda

6 *38 km (24 mi) northwest of Leksand.*

A chairlift from Gesunda, a pleasant little village, will take you to the top of a mountain for unbeatable views over the lake. The large island of **Sollerön** is connected to the mainland by a bridge at Gesunda. The island has fine views of the mountains surrounding Siljan. Several ex-cellent beaches and an interesting Viking grave site are also here. The church dates from 1775.

Ⓒ **Tomteland** (Santa World), on Gesundaberget, claims to be the home of Santa Claus, or Father Christmas. Toys are for sale at Santa's workshop and at kiosks. There are rides in horse-drawn carriages in summer and sleighs in winter. ⊠ *Gesundaberget, Sollerön* ☎ *0250/21200* ⊕ *www. santaworld.se* 🖾 *SKr 125* ⊙ *Mid-June–mid-Aug., daily 10–4; late Nov.–early Jan., daily 10–4.*

Mora

7 *50 km (31 mi) northwest of Leksand, 40 km (25 mi) northwest of Rättvik via Rte. 70.*

To get to this relaxed lakeside town of 20,000, you can follow the northern shore of Lake Siljan (there is a bridge at Färnäs), or follow the lake's southern shore through Leksand and Gesunda to get a good sense of Dalarna.

Mora is best known as the finishing point for the world's longest cross-country ski race, the Vasalopp, which begins in March 90 km (56 mi) away at Sälen, a ski resort close to the Norwegian border. The race com-memorates a fundamental piece of Swedish history: the successful at-tempt by Gustav Vasa in 1521 to rally local peasants to the cause of ridding Sweden of Danish occupation. Vasa, only 21 years old, had fled the capital and described to the Mora locals in graphic detail a massacre of Swedish noblemen ordered by Danish king Christian in Stockholm's Stortorget. Unfortunately, no one believed him, and the dispirited Vasa was forced to abandon his attempts at insurrection and take off on either skis or snowshoes for Norway, where he hoped to evade King Christian and go into exile.

Just after he left, confirmation of the Stockholm bloodbath reached Mora, and the peasants, already discontent with Danish rule, sent two skiers after Vasa to tell him they would join his cause. The two men caught up with the young nobleman at Sälen. They returned with him to Mora, where an army was recruited. Vasa marched south, defeated the Danes, and became king and the founder of modern Sweden.

The commemorative race, held on the first Sunday in March, attracts thousands of competitors from all over the world, including the Swedish king. There is a spectacular mass start at Sälen before the field thins out. The finish is eagerly awaited in Mora, though since the start of live television broadcasts, the number of spectators has fallen.

You can get a comfortable glimpse of the Vasalopp's history in the **Vasaloppets Hus,** which contains a collection of the ski gear and photos of competitors, news clippings, and a short film detailing some of the race's finer moments. ⊠ *Vasag.* ☎ *0250/39225* 🖼 *SKr 30* 🕑 *Mid-June–mid-Aug., daily 10–5; mid-Aug.–mid-June, weekdays 10–5.*

Mora is also known as the home of Anders Zorn (1860–1920), Sweden's leading impressionist painter, who lived in Stockholm and Paris before returning to his roots here and painting the local scenes for which he is now known. His former private residence—**Zorngården**— a large, sumptuous house designed with great originality and taste by the painter himself, has retained the same exquisite furnishings, paintings, and decor it had when he lived there with his wife. Next door, the ★ **Zorn Museet** (Zorn Museum), built 19 years after the painter's death, contains many of his best works. ⊠ *Vasag. 36* ☎ *0250/592310* ⊕ *www. zorn.se* 🖼 *Museum SKr 40, home SKr 50* 🕑 *Museum mid-May–mid-Sept., Mon.–Sat. 9–5, Sun. 11–5; mid-Sept.–mid-May, Mon.–Sat. noon–5, Sun. 1–5. Home (guided tours only) mid-May–mid-Sept., Mon.–Sat. 10–4, Sun. 11–4; mid-Sept.–mid-May, Mon.–Sat. noon–4, Sun. 1–4.*

On the south side of town is **Zorns Gammelgård,** a fine collection of old wooden houses from local farms, brought here and donated to Mora by Anders Zorn. One of them holds the **Textilkammare** (Textile Chamber), a collection of textiles and period clothing. ⊠ *Yvradsv.* ☎ *0250/ 16560 (June–Aug. only)* 🖼 *SKr 30* 🕑 *June–Aug., daily noon–5.*

off the beaten path

ORSA – Fifteen kilometers (9 mi) north of Mora on Route 45 is a small sleepy town that becomes a big chaotic symphony every Wednesday in July. It's then that the **Orsa Spelmän,** groups of traditional folklore music players, take part in what's called the Orsayran (Orsa Rush). The musicians take over the streets of the town, wandering and playing their instruments. This soon becomes a free-for-all in which all the people in town, whether accomplished or not, bring out their instruments and play. It's great fun.

ORSA GRÖNKLITTS BJÖRNPARK – Just outside Orsa is the wildlife reserve inhabited by Sweden's native brown bears and other animals, including wolves. There's a limited chance of spotting one of these shy creatures, but if you do, it is an unforgettable sight. Start at the shop (plenty of cuddly bears for the kids) and visitor center, then wind your way up a steep, hillside path to a viewing platform at the top. There are chances all the way up to see the magnificent creatures, but they are always behind fences, so it's perfectly safe.

SILJANSFORS SKOGSMUSEUM (Siljansfors Forest Museum) – Partly because there's always been a lot of wood available for firing furnaces, the area around Mora is well known for its metalworking. This outdoor museum shows the smithies' many connections to local forestry, in particular with the art of charcoal burning. A track through the forest will take you to smithies, ironworks, woodcutting sheds, and charcoal-burning towers. The walks are all linked together at the information center near the entrance. ⊠ *20 km (12 mi) southwest of Mora on Rte. 45* ☎ *0250/20331.*

Where to Stay & Eat

$$ ✕ **Lilla Krogen.** In one of Mora's oldest industrial buildings (1879), Lilla Krogen serves high-quality, classic Swedish home cooking and international dishes. The tables are bare antique oak, the wooden chairs are of a traditional Leksand style, and the linen napkins are woven locally. In the bar area, furnished in birch and stainless steel, the large windows allow for great views over the lake. ⊠ *Strandg. 6* ☎ *0250/15020* ⊟ *AE, DC, MC, V.*

$ ▦ **First Hotel Mora.** Part of the First Hotel group, this pleasant little hotel is in the town center, 5 km (3 mi) from the airport. Its comfortable rooms are brightly decorated. ⊠ *Strandg. 12, 792 30* ☎ *0250/592650* 🖷 *0250/18981* ⊕ *www.firsthotels.se* ⇌ *141 rooms* ⚭ *Restaurant, in-room data ports, indoor pool, sauna, spa, bar, meeting room, free parking, no-smoking rooms* ⊟ *AE, DC, MC, V* ⍩ *BP.*

$ ▦ **Kung Gösta.** A modern, reasonably sized hotel, the Kung Gösta is 2 km (1 mi) from the town center and only 330 feet from the Mora train station. The small rooms are brightly furnished, with wood floors and large windows. ⊠ *Kristinebergsg. 1, 792 32* ☎ *0250/15070* 🖷 *0250/17078* ⊕ *www.trehotell.nu* ⇌ *47 rooms* ⚭ *Restaurant, indoor pool, sauna, meeting room, free parking, no-smoking rooms* ⊟ *AE, DC, MC, V* ⍩ *BP.*

$ ▦ **Mora Parken.** Rooms are small and simply furnished with pastel fabrics and plain wood furniture at this modern hotel. It's in a park by the bank of the Dala River, not far from the town center. ⊠ *Parkg. 1, 792 37* ☎ *0250/27600* 🖷 *0250/27615* ⊕ *www.moraparken.se* ⇌ *75 rooms* ⚭ *Restaurant, sauna, convention center, free parking, no-smoking rooms* ⊟ *AE, DC, MC, V* ⍩ *BP.*

$ ▦ **Siljan.** Aside from the uninterrupted views over the lake, there's nothing to write home about here (unless the idea of having a radio is worthy of a postcard), but the small, modern hotel's central location is unbeatable. There is an excellent and lively pub, as well as a restaurant specializing in game. ⊠ *Morag. 6, 792 22* ☎ *0250/13000* 🖷 *0250/13098* ⊕ *www.swedenhotels.se* 🖘 *44 rooms* ♨ *Restaurant, room service, Wi-Fi, sauna, bar, meeting room, free parking, no-smoking floor* ⊟ *AE, DC, MC, V* †○┤ *BP.*

Sports & the Outdoors

SKIING   Dalarna's principal ski resort is **Sälen**, starting point for the Vasalopp, about 90 km (56 mi) west of Mora. Snow here is pretty much guaranteed from November to May, and there are more than 100 pistes to choose from, from simple slopes for the beginner to challenging black runs that weave through tightly forested slopes. For more information contact any of the tourist offices in Dalarna.

WALKING   For the energetic traveler it's possible to walk the 90-km (56-mi) **track from Sälen to Mora** that's used for the Vasalopp ski race in March. Along the way you may very well see some elk wandering through the forest. Day shelters, basic night shelters, fireplaces, tables, signposts, and restrooms are set up along the trail. Facilities are free, but a donation of SKr 25 is suggested for the night shelters. Maps and other details can be obtained from the **Mora tourist office** (⊠ Stationsv. ☎ 0250/592020).

Nusnäs

❽ *6 km (4 mi) southeast of Mora via Rte. 70, 28 km (17 mi) northwest of Falun.*

The lakeside village of Nusnäs is where the small, bright red–painted, wooden Dala horses are made. These were originally carved by the peasants of Dalarna as toys for their children, but their popularity rapidly spread in the 20th century. Mass production of the little horses started at Nusnäs in 1928. In 1939 they achieved international popularity after being shown at the New York World's Fair, and since then they have become a Swedish symbol (although today some of the smaller versions available in Stockholm's tourists shops are actually made in East Asia). At Nusnäs you can watch the genuine article being made, now with the aid of modern machinery but still painted by hand.

Shopping

Shops in the area are generally open every day except Sunday. The best place to buy painted horses is **Nils Olsson** (⊠ Edåkersv. 17 ☎ 0250/37200).

Dalarna A to Z

AIRPORTS

There are six flights daily from Stockholm to Dala Airport, which is 8 km (5 mi) south of Borlänge. Flights also arrive from Göteborg and Malmö. Bus 601 runs every half hour from Dala Airport to Borlänge; the trip costs SKr 15. From Borlänge there are connecting buses to Falun and other parts of the region. Mora Airport has three Skyways flights daily from Stockholm on weekdays, fewer on weekends. The airport is 6 km (4 mi) from Mora; no buses serve the airport.

A taxi from Dala Airport to Borlänge costs around SKr 125, to Falun approximately SKr 275. A taxi into Mora from Mora Airport costs SKr 100. Order taxis in advance through your travel agent or when you make an airline reservation. Book a cab by calling the Borlänge taxi service.

🚖 **Dala Airport** ☎ 0243/64500 ⊕ www.dalaairport.se. **Borlänge Taxi** ☎ 0243/13100. **Mora Airport** ☎ 0250/30175.

BUS TRAVEL

Swebus runs tour buses to the area from Stockholm on weekends. The trip takes about four hours one-way.

🚖 **Swebus Express** ☎ 0200/218218 ⊕ www.swebusexpress.se.

CAR RENTAL

Avis has offices in Borlänge and Mora. Europcar has an office in Borlänge. Hertz has an office in Falun, and independent company Bilkompaniet, formerly a part of Hertz, rents cars in Mora.

🚖 **Avis** ⊠ Borlänge ☎ 0243/87080 ⊠ Mora ☎ 0250/16711. **Bilkompaniet** ⊠ Mora ☎ 0250/28800. **Europcar** ⊠ Borlänge ☎ 0243/19050. **Hertz** ⊠ Falun ☎ 023/58872.

CAR TRAVEL

From Stockholm take E18 to Enköping and follow Route 70 northwest. From Göteborg take E20 to Örebro and Route 60 north from there. Villages are well signposted.

EMERGENCIES

For emergencies dial 112. There are no late-night pharmacies in the area. Vasen Pharmacy, in Falun, is open 9–7 weekdays and 9–noon on Saturday.

🚖 **Falun Hospital** ☎ 023/492000. **Mora Hospital** ☎ 0250/493000. **24-hour medical advisory service** ☎ 023/492900. **Vasen Pharmacy** ⊠ Åsg. 25, Falun ☎ 0771/450450.

TOURS

Call the Falun tourist office for English-speaking guides to Falun and the region around Lake Siljan; guides cost about SKr 900 per day.

BOAT TOURS Just next to the Mora train station, on the quay in the center of town, is the MS *Gustaf Wasa*, a beautiful old steamship that's used for sightseeing tours of Lake Siljan. Trips can take from two to four hours and range in price from SKr 80 to SKr 120. It's a good way to see the stunning countryside from another perspective.

🚖 **MS *Gustaf Wasa*** ☎ 070/5421025.

TRAIN TRAVEL

There is regular daily train service from Stockholm to both Mora and Falun.

🚖 **SJ** ⊕ www.sj.se.

VISITOR INFORMATION

On the approach to the area from the south via Route 70, a 43-foot, bright orange-red Dala horse marks a rest stop just south of Avesta. It has a spacious cafeteria and a helpful tourist information center.

🚖 Tourist Information **Falun** ⊠ Trotzg. 10-12 ☎ 023/83050 ⊕ www.visitfalun.se. **Leksand** ⊠ Stationsg. 14 ☎ 0247/796130. **Ludvika** ⊠ Fredsg. 10 ☎ 0240/86050. **Mora** ⊠ Stationsv. ☎ 0250/592020 ⊕ www.siljan.se. **Rättvik** ⊠ Riksv. 40 ☎ 0248/797210. **Sälen** ⊠ Sälen Centrum ☎ 0280/18700.

Norrland & Norrbotten

8

WORD OF MOUTH

"At the Ice Hotel, remember you could sleep in the igloo for one night then spend the other nights in a snug log cabin."

—Kate

"Our tour guide raved about ice-swimming, and in a moment of holiday-induced craziness, we agreed to do it. We went to a hut that contained a sauna and the naked guy in charge of the operation. There's a hole cut in the ice, and next to it is a hot tub. You warm up in the hot tub, jump in the hole, and then scream loudly and get out as fast as you can. Still can't believe I did it."

—Cushla

Updated by
Rob Hincks

THE NORTH OF SWEDEN, Norrland, is a place of wide-open spaces where the silence is almost audible. Golden eagles soar above snowcapped crags; huge salmon fight their way up wild, tumbling rivers; rare orchids bloom in arctic heathland; and wild rhododendrons splash the land with color.

In summer the sun shines at midnight above the Arctic Circle. In winter it hardly shines at all. The weather can change with bewildering speed: a June day can dawn sunny and bright; then the skies may darken and the temperature may drop to around zero as a snow squall blows in. Just as suddenly, the sun comes out again and the temperature starts to rise.

Here live the once-nomadic Lapps, or Sámi, as they prefer to be known. They carefully guard what remains of their identity while doing their best to inform the public of their culture. Many of the 17,000 Sámi who live in Sweden still earn their living herding reindeer, but as open space shrinks the younger generation is turning in greater numbers toward the allure of the cities. As the modern world makes its incursions, the Sámi often exhibit a sad resignation to the gradual disappearance of their way of life. A Sámi folk poem says it best: "Our memory, the memory of us vanishes/We forget and we are forgotten."

Yet there is a growing struggle, especially among some younger Sámi, to maintain their identity, and, thanks to their traditional closeness to nature they are now finding allies in Sweden's Green movement. They refer to the north of Scandinavia as Sapmi, their spiritual and physical home, making no allowance for the different countries that now rule it.

Nearly all Swedish Sámi now live in ordinary houses, having abandoned the *kåta* (Lapp wigwam), and some even herd their reindeer with helicopters. Efforts are now being made to protect and preserve their language, which is totally unlike Swedish and bears a far greater resemblance to Finnish. The language reflects their closeness to nature. The word *goadnil,* for example, means "a quiet part of the river, free of current, near the bank or beside a rock."

Nowadays many Sámi depend on the tourist industry for their living, selling their crafts, such as expertly carved bone-handle knives, wooden cups and bowls, bark bags, silver jewelry, and leather straps embroidered with pewter thread.

The land that the Sámi inhabit is vast. Norrland stretches 1,000 km (625 mi) from south to north, making up more than half of Sweden; it's roughly the same size as Great Britain. In the west there are mountain ranges, to the east a wild and rocky coastline, and in between boundless forests and moorland. Its towns are often little more than a group of houses along a street, built around a local industry such as a mine, a lumber company, or a hydroelectric facility. Thanks to Sweden's excellent transportation infrastructure, however, Norrland and the northernmost region of Norrbotten are no longer inaccessible. Even travelers with limited time can get at least a taste of the area. Its wild spaces are ideal for open-air vacations. Hiking, climbing, canoeing, river rafting, and fishing are all popular in summer; skiing, ice-skating, and dogsledding are winter activities.

A word of warning: in summer mosquitoes are a constant nuisance, even worse than in other parts of Sweden, so be sure to bring plenty of repellent (you won't find anything effective in Sweden). Fall is perhaps the best season to visit Norrland. Roads are well maintained, but be careful of *gupp* (holes) following thaws. Highways are generally traffic free, but keep an eye out for the occasional reindeer.

Dining and lodging are on the primitive side in this region. Standards of cuisine and service are not nearly as high as prices—but hotels are usually exceptionally clean and staff scrupulously honest. Accommodations are limited, but the various local tourist offices can supply details of bed-and-breakfasts and holiday villages equipped with housekeeping cabins. The area is also rich in campsites—but with the highly unpredictable climate, this may appeal only to the very hardy.

Norrbotten is best discovered from a base in Kiruna, in the center of the alpine region that has been described as Europe's last wilderness. You can tour south and west to the mountains and national parks, east and south to Sámi villages, and farther south still to Baltic coastal settlements.

Exploring Norrland & Norrbotten

Exploring the vast wilderness of Norrland and Norrbotten can be extremely rewarding, but it must be done with care. The harsh plains and rugged mountains of this region are best entered with caution, with someone who has experience in these matters. Having said that, by using one of the larger towns as your base, it is perfectly possible to explore the extreme beauties that the region has to offer without having to make any additional arrangements for your overnight accommodations.

About the Hotels & Restaurants

Adventurous eaters should prepare themselves for a lot of fun in Norrland and Norrbotten. The harsh living conditions have historically driven the locals to resort to some unusual ingredients and combinations. On menus in this region you might see, among other things, whale meat, seal, and coffee with cheese.

WHAT IT COSTS In Swedish Kronor				
	$$$$	$$$	$$	$	¢
RESTAURANTS	over 420	250–420	150–250	100–150	under 100
HOTELS	over 2,900	2,300–2,900	1,500–2,300	1,000–1,500	under 1,000

Restaurant prices are for a main course at dinner. Hotel prices are for two people in a standard double room in high season.

Timing

Unless you are interested in winter sports and extreme weather conditions, summer is probably the best time to visit Norrland and Norrbotten. Days are long, sometimes never-ending, and there are many more restaurants and shops open. But winter has its advantages up here too. If you can stand the cold, there are skiing and sledding, reindeer sleigh rides,

THE FAR NORTH'S
DARKNESS & LIGHT

N A WORLD GONE CRAZY with 24-hour services that are always on hand, it is novel and refreshing to experience the vast spaces and uninhabited landscape of the north of Sweden. You can drive for hours in Norrland and Norrbotten and find nothing to do except marvel at the dramatic beauty surrounding you. Summer brings the midnight sun to the north of Sweden, bathing the country in sunlight around the clock. For a period of about three weeks (it can last as long as 50 days) it doesn't get dark at all. It's an amazing thing to see the sun shining all the time, even if it does do strange things to your body clock—drinking beer and fishing at 4 AM has never seemed so natural. If you can stand the cold, winter in the north also holds distinctive pleasures. From November to March, instead of days of light, you can immerse yourself in

darkness—not pitch black, but rather a kind of twilight during the day. If you're visiting around the winter solstice in December, you really will be in darkness all the time. And if it's a dark and clear night sky, look out for the northern lights—there's a good chance you'll see them.

and the wonderful northern lights. And if you want to visit the world-famous Icehotel in Jukkasjärvi, you have to go in winter—between December and April to be precise.

Kiruna

❶ *1,352 km (840 mi) north of Stockholm.*

About 250 km (155 mi) north of the Arctic Circle, and 1,804 feet above sea level, Kiruna is Sweden's northernmost municipality. Although its inhabitants number only around 26,000, Kiruna is Sweden's largest city geographically—it spreads over the equivalent of half the area of Switzerland. Until an Australian community took the claim, Kiruna was often called "the world's biggest city." With 20,000 square km (7,722 square mi) within the municipal limits, Kiruna boasts that it could accommodate the entire world population with 43 square feet of space per person.

Kiruna lies at the eastern end of Lake Luossajärvi, spread over a wide area between two mountains, Luossavaara and Kirunavaara, that are largely composed of iron ore—Kiruna's raison d'être. Here is the world's

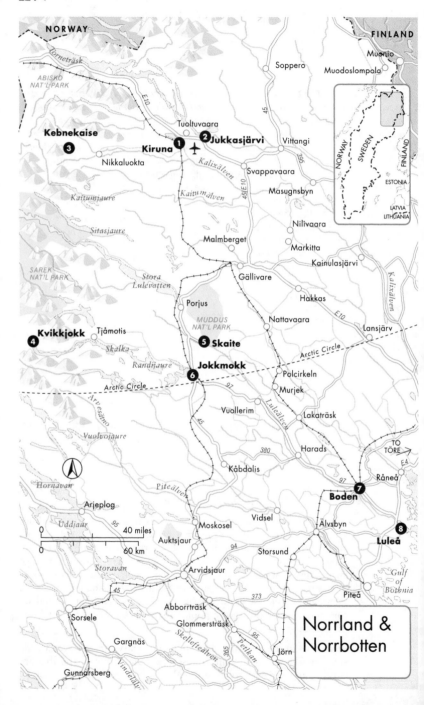

Norrland & Norrbotten

largest underground iron mine, with reserves estimated at 420 million tons. Automated mining technology has largely replaced the traditional miner in the Kirunavaara mine, which is some 500 km (280 mi) long and has an underground network of 400 km (249 mi) trafficable roads. Of the city's inhabitants, an estimated fifth are Finnish immigrants who came to work in the mine in the 1950s.

The city was established in 1900 as a mining town, but true prosperity came only with the building of the railway to the Baltic port of Luleå and the northern Norwegian port of Narvik in 1902.

Like most of Norrland, Kiruna is full of remarkable contrasts, from the seemingly pitch-black, months-long winter to summer, when the sun never sets and it is actually possible to play golf round-the-clock for 50 days at a stretch. Here, too, the ancient Sámi culture persists side by side with the high-tech culture of cutting-edge satellite research. Since the 1960s the city has supported the Esrange Space Range, about 40 km (24 mi) east, which sends sounding rockets and strato-spheric balloons to probe the upper reaches of earth's atmosphere, and the Swedish Institute of Space Physics, which has pioneered the in-vestigation of the phenomenon of **the northern lights.** The city received a boost in 1984 with the opening of Nordkalottvägen, a 170-km-long (106-mi-long) road to Narvik.

One of Kiruna's few buildings of interest is **Kiruna Kyrka** (Kiruna Church; ⊠ Gruvv.), near the center of the city. It was built in 1921, its inspira-tion a blending of a Sámi kåta with a Swedish stave church. The altar-piece is by Prince Eugen (1863–1947), Sweden's painter prince.

Where to Stay & Eat

$ ✕⬜ **Kebne och Kaisa.** These twin modern hotels—named after the local mountain, Kebnekaise—are close to the railway station and the airport bus stop. Rooms are bland but modern and comfortable. The restau-rant is one of the best in Kiruna; it's open for breakfast and dinner and serves excellent local and national specialties, particularly, when in sea-son, very good elk. ⊠ *Konduktörsg. 3, 981 34* ☎ *0980/12380* 🖨 *0980/ 68181* ⊕ *www.hotellkebne.com* 🛏 *54 rooms* ♨ *Restaurant, 2 saunas, no-smoking rooms* ▤ *AE, DC, MC, V.*

$$ ⬜ **Ferrum.** Part of the Scandic Hotels chain, this late-1960s-vintage hotel is near the railway station. Rooms have wood floors and standard modern furniture. The hotel's best feature are its three saunas, located on the sixth floor, from which you have magnificent views across the mountains while you sweat away. ⊠ *Lars Janssonsg. 15, 981 31* ☎ *0980/ 398600* 🖨 *0980/398600* ⊕ *www.scandic-hotels.com* 🛏 *171 rooms* ♨ *3 restaurants, in-room data ports, gym, saunas, 2 bars, dance club, meeting room, no-smoking rooms* ▤ *AE, DC, MC, V.*

¢ ⬜ **Järnvägshotellet.** Dating from 1903, this small hotel has the advan-tage of being close to the railway station. The entire building was re-furbished in 2002, and the previously tired rooms received a much-needed update. Still, at these prices, don't expect luxury. ⊠ *Bangårdsv. 7, 981 34* ☎ *0980/84444* ⊕ *www.jarnvagshotellet.com* 🛏 *20 rooms* ♨ *Restau-rant, sauna, meeting room, no-smoking rooms* ▤ *MC, V* ⑩ *BP.*

Jukkasjärvi

❷ *16 km (10 mi) east of Kiruna.*

The history of Jukkasjärvi, a Sámi village by the shores of the fast-flowing Torneälven (Torne River), goes back to the early 16th century, when there was already a market here. It has a wooden church from the 17th century and a small open-air museum that evokes a sense of Sámi life in times gone by.

If you are gastronomically adventuresome, you may want to sample one of the most unusual of all Sámi delicacies: a cup of thick black coffee with *kaffeost,* small lumps of goat cheese. After the cheese sits in the coffee for a bit, you fish it out with a spoon and eat it, then drink the coffee.

Where to Stay & Eat

★ ¢ ✕🏨 **Icehotel Restaurang.** The restaurant specializes in Norrland cuisine—featuring reindeer, wild berries, mushrooms, dried and smoked meats, salted fish, fermented herring, and rich sauces using thick creams—and is the life's work of its manager, Yngve Bergqvist, who is still here, even after the place was taken over by the adjacent Icehotel. There are 45 cabins around the main building, 30 with bathroom, kitchen, and two bedrooms with bunk beds. Breakfast is not included. River-rafting and canoeing trips can be arranged. ✉ *Marknadsv. 63, 981 91* 🕾 *0980/66800* 🖷 *0980/66890* ⊕ *www.icehotel.com* 🛏 *45 cabins* △ *Restaurant, sauna, meeting room* ▤ *AE, DC, MC, V.*

$$$ 🏨 **Icehotel.** At the peak of winter, tourists are drawn by the annual con-
Fodor'sChoice struction of the world's largest igloo, which opens for business as a hotel
★ in mid-December through April, after which it melts away, until being revised and built again nine months later. Made of snow, ice, and sheet metal, the Icehotel offers rooms for 40 guests, who spend the night in specially insulated sleeping bags on top of layers of reindeer skins and spruce boughs. At the Absolut Icebar, colored electric lights liven up the solid-ice walls. Breakfast is served in the sauna, with a view of the (nonelectric) northern lights. Staying here is an amazing experience, and one not to be missed, even if the prices do seem a little steep for such discomfort. ✉ *Marknadsv. 63, 981 91* 🕾 *0980/66800* 🖷 *0980/66800* ⊕ *www.icehotel.com* 🛏 *120 beds without bath, 18 suites* △ *Restaurant, sauna, cross-country skiing, snowmobiling, bar, meeting room; no smoking* ▤ *AE, DC, MC, V* ☺ *Closed May–Nov.*

Sports & the Outdoors

A challenging local activity is riding the rapids of the Torne River in an inflatable boat. In winter Jukkasjärvi also offers dogsled rides and snowmobile safaris. For more information call the **Icehotel** (🕾 *0980/66800*) or the Kiruna Lappland Tourist Office.

Kebnekaise

❸ *85 km (53 mi) west of Kiruna.*

At 7,000 feet above sea level, Kebnekaise is Sweden's highest mountain, but you'll need to be in good physical shape just to get to it. From Kiruna you travel about 66 km (41 mi) west to the Sámi village of Nikkalu-okta (there are two buses a day from Kiruna in summer). From Nikkalu-okta it is a hike of 19 km (12 mi) to the Kebnekaise Fjällstation (mountain station), at the foot of Kebnekaise, though you can take a boat 5 km (3 mi) across Lake Ladtjojaure. Kebnekaise itself is relatively easy to climb, provided there's good weather and you're in shape; extensive mountaineering equipment is not necessary. If you feel up to more walking, the track continues past the Kebnekaise Fjällstation to become part of what is known as **Kungsleden** (the Royal Trail), a 500-km (280-mi) trail through the mountains from Abisko National Park, in the north, to Hemavan, in southern Lappland.

Where to Stay

¢–$ Kebnekaise Fjällstation. This rustic, wooden mountain station consists of six buildings. Choose between the main building, with its heavy wood beams, wood floors, and wood bunk beds—five per room—and the newer annexes, where more modern rooms each contain two or four beds. All guests share the use of a service house, with toilets, showers, and sauna. Though the main lodge is closed in fall and winter, one annex stays open year-round. The facility is 19 km (12 mi) from Nikkaluokta and can be reached by footpath, a combination of boat and hiking, or helicopter. Guided mountain tours are available. ⊠ 981 29 Kiruna ☎ 0980/55000, 0980/40200 off-season contact (Abisko tourist office) ⇥ 196 beds without bath ⌂ Restaurant, sauna, bar ☰ AE, V ⊗ Closed mid-Aug.–mid-Mar.

Sports & the Outdoors

All the regional tourist offices can supply details of skiing holidays, but never forget the extreme temperatures and weather conditions. For the really adventuresome, the **Kebnekaise mountain station** (☎ 0980/55000) offers combined skiing and climbing weeks at around SKr 9,000, including lodging and all meals. It also offers weeklong combined dogsledding, skiing, and climbing holidays in the mountains. Because of the extreme cold and the danger involved, be sure to have proper equipment. Consult the mountain station well in advance for advice.

Kvikkjokk & Sarek National Park

❹ 310 km (193 mi) southwest of Kiruna via Rte. 45.

Sarek is Sweden's largest high-mountain area and was molded by the last ice age. The mountains have been sculpted by glaciers, of which there are about 100 in the park. The mountain area totals 487,000 acres, a small portion of which is forest, bogs, and waterways. The remainder is bare mountain that is either totally barren or covered by low-growing alpine vegetation. The park has 90 peaks some 6,000 feet above sea level.

The Rapaätno River, which drains the park, runs through the lovely, desolate Rapadalen (Rapa Valley). The area is marked by a surprising variety of landscapes—luxuriant green meadows contrast with the snowy peaks of the mountains. Moose, bears, wolverines, lynx, ermines, hares, arctic foxes, red foxes, and mountain lemmings inhabit the terrain. Bird life includes ptarmigans, willow grouse, teals, wigeons, tufted ducks, bluethroats, and warblers. Golden eagles, rough-legged buzzards, and merlins have also been spotted here.

Visiting Sarek demands a good knowledge of mountains and a familiarity with the outdoors. The park can be dangerous in winter because of avalanches and snowstorms. In summer, however, despite its unpredictable, often inhospitable climate, it attracts large numbers of experienced hikers. At Kvikkjokk, a major overnight base for visitors, hikers can choose between a trail through the Tarradalen (Tarra Valley), which divides the Sarek from Padjelanta National Park to the west, or part of the Kungsleden Trail, which crosses about 15 km (9 mi) of Sarek's southeastern corner.

Skaite & Muddus National Park

❺ *225 km (140 mi) south of Kiruna via E10 and Rte. 45.*

Established in 1942, Muddus National Park is less mountainous and spectacular than Sarek. Its 121,770 acres are mainly taken up by virgin coniferous forest, some of whose trees may be as much as 600 years old. The park's 3,680 acres of water are composed primarily of two huge lakes at the center of the park and the Muddusjåkkå River, which tumbles spectacularly through a gorge with 330-foot-high sheer rock walls and includes a waterfall crashing 140 feet down. The highest point of Muddus is Sör-Stubba Mountain, 2,158 feet above sea level. From Skaite, where you enter the park, a series of well-marked trails begins. There are four well-equipped, overnight communal rest huts and two tourist cabins. The park is home to bears, lynx, wolverines, moose, ermines, weasels, otters, and many bird species. A popular pastime is picking cloudberries (a member of the raspberry family) in autumn.

Jokkmokk

❻ *225 km (140 mi) south of Kiruna via E10 and Rte. 45.*

Jokkmokk is an important center of Sámi culture. Every February it is the scene of the region's largest market, where everything from frozen reindeer meat to Sámi handcrafted wooden utensils is sold. If you're an outdoor enthusiast, Jokkmokk may be the best base in Norrland for you. The village has good campsites and is surrounded by wilderness. The local tourist office sells fishing permits, which cost SKr 50 for 24 hours, SKr 100 for three days, SKr 175 for one week, and SKr 350 for the entire year. The office can also supply lists of camping and housekeeping cabins.

Where to Stay

$ 🏨 **Hotel Jokkmokk.** A modern hotel this luxurious seems incongruous
FodorśChoice   in this remote region, but is welcome nevertheless. The hotel is in the
★   town center, but the staff can arrange dogsled rides and helicopter trips to the Sarek and Muddus national parks; there is excellent fishing nearby. ✉ *Solg. 45, 962 23* ☎ *0971/77700* 🖨 *0971/77790* ⊕ *www. hoteljokkmokk.se* ❧ *75 rooms* ⚒ *Restaurant, sauna, meeting room, no-smoking rooms* ▤ *AE, DC, MC, V.*

¢ 🏠 **Gästis.** This small hotel in central Jokkmokk opened in 1915. Rooms are standard, with television, shower, and either carpeted or vinyl floors. ✉ *Herrev. 1, 962 31* ☎ *0971/10012* 🖷 *0971/10044* 🛏 *30 rooms* ⚐ *Restaurant, sauna, meeting room, no-smoking rooms* ▤ *MC, V.*

¢ 🏠 **Jokkmokks Turistcenter.** This complex is in a pleasant forest area near Luleälven, 3 km (2 mi) from the railway station. ✉ *Nortudden, Box 75, 962 22* ☎*0971/12370* 🖷*0971/12476* 🛏*59 cabins* ⚐*4 pools, sauna, meeting room* ▤ *MC, V.*

Boden

❼ *290 km (180 mi) southeast of Kiruna, 130 km (81 mi) southeast of Jokkmokk on Rte. 97.*

Boden, the nation's largest garrison town, dates from 1809, when Sweden lost Finland to Russia and feared an invasion of its own territory. The **Garnisonsmuseet** (Garrison Museum) contains exhibits from Swedish military history, with an extensive collection of weapons and uniforms. ✉ *Sveav. 10* ☎ *0921/68399* 🎟 *Free* ☉ *Mid-June–late Aug., Mon.–Sat. 11–4, Sun. noon–4.*

Luleå

❽ *340 km (211 mi) southeast of Kiruna via E10 and E4.*

The northernmost major town in Sweden, Luleå is an important port at the top of the Gulf of Bothnia, at the mouth of the Luleälv (Lule River). The town was some 10 km (6 mi) farther inland when it was first granted its charter in 1621, but by 1649 trade had grown so much that it was moved closer to the sea. **Gammelstad Church Town,** at the site of the original city, is now protected by the UNESCO World Heritage list. The development of Kiruna and the iron trade is linked, literally, by a railway, with the fortunes of Luleå, where a steelworks was set up in the 1940s. Like its fellow port towns farther south—Piteå, Skellefteå, Umeå, and Sundsvall—Luleå is a very modern and nondescript city, but it has some reasonable hotels. A beautiful archipelago of hundreds of islands hugs the coastline. Many of these islands can be reached by car in the wintertime through a 250-km (166-mi) network of roads on the frozen sea. Wintertime visitors with kids shouldn't miss the ice slide in the city park: each year it's in the shape of a different indigenous animal.

The **Norrbottens Museum** was established in 1870 to gather and record information on the social development of this vast area of Sweden. Today their collection consists of more than 1 million photographs, collections of tools, period clothes, models of housing, and other documents and displays relating to the ways of life of local people spanning several generations. The museum has one of the best collections of Sámi ethnography in the world. ✉ *Hermelinsparken 2* ☎ *0920/243502* 🎟 *Free* ☉ *Weekdays 10–4, weekends noon–4.*

Where to Stay & Eat

★ **$–$$** ✕🏠 **Arctic.** The imposing redbrick building that houses this hotel may at first seem a little oppressive. Step inside, though, and you are struck by the family-run feeling. There is always a small snack buffet in the reception, with coffee, cookies, sandwiches, and fruit—not to mention everready smiles from the staff. Rooms are light and simple, with white walls, plump blue sofas and chairs, and burgundy curtains. The restaurant is perfect for those wanting to sample the excellent local ingredients, such as salmon and game. All in all, for the price, this is a magical place. ⊠ *Sandviksg. 80, 972 34* ☎ *0920/10980* 🖷 *0920/60787* ⊕ *www. arctichotel.se* ⇒ *94 rooms* ⚹ *Restaurant, hot tub, sauna, meeting room, no-smoking rooms* ▤ *AE, DC, MC, V.*

$$$ 🏨 **Elite Stadshotellet.** This large, central hotel has nightly—sometimes boisterous—dancing. Rooms in the building dating from 1903 are spacious and carpeted, with turn-of-the-20th-century furnishings. ⊠ *Storg. 15, 97128* ☎ *0920/274000* 🖷 *0920/67092* ⊕ *www.elite.se* ⇒ *135 rooms, 3 suites* ⚹ *Restaurant, café, minibars, sauna, lounge, dance club, meeting room, no-smoking rooms* ▤ *AE, DC, MC, V* � *BP.*

$$ 🏨 **Scandic.** This hotel on a small tarn has an extremely pleasant setting and is 2 km (1 mi) from the railway station. The three-story, redbrick building won't be winning any prizes for architecture, but rooms are of the standard you would expect from this national chain. The color scheme of burgundy and mustard-yellow is a little alarming, but with wood floors, a comfortable chair, and a good-size bathroom, there is a lot of bang for your buck. The restaurant and bar are a welcome alternative if you seek some human contact. ⊠ *Banv. 3, 973 46* ☎ *0920/276400* 🖷 *0920/276411* ⊕ *www.scandic-hotels.com* ⇒ *160 rooms* ⚹*Restaurant, indoor pool, gym, sauna, meeting room, no-smoking rooms* ▤ *AE, DC, MC, V.*

$ 🏨 **Aveny.** Certainly the welcome and the service here are as friendly as you could wish. As for charm, you need look no further than the randomly furnished rooms, seemingly made up of a collection of furniture picked up over many years in many places. It's Aveny's location that is the real seller, right across from the main railway station. ⊠ *Hermelinsg. 10, 973 46* ☎ *0920/221820* 🖷 *0920/220122* ⊕ *www.hotellaveny.com* ⇒ *24 rooms* ⚹ *No-smoking rooms* ▤ *AE, DC, MC, V.*

Norrland & Norrbotten A to Z

AIR TRAVEL

CARRIERS
There are two nonstop SAS flights a day from Stockholm to Kiruna Airport and two additional flights via Umeå. Check SAS for specific times.
🚩 **SAS** ☎ 0770/727727, 8/7972688 from outside Sweden.

AIRPORTS

In summer, buses connect Kiruna Airport, which is 5 km (3 mi) from Kiruna, to the city center; the fare is about SKr 50. A taxi from the airport to the center of Kiruna costs SKr 200 and up; book through the airline or call the taxi directly.
🚩 **Kiruna Airport** ☎ 0980/68001 ⊕ www.lfv.se. **Taxi Kiruna** ☎ 020/979797.

CAR RENTAL

🚩 Major Agencies **Avis** ⊠ Kiruna Airport, Kiruna ☎ 0980/13080. **Europcar** ⊠ Forv. 33, Kiruna ☎ 0980/80759. **Hertz** ⊠ Industriv. 5, Kiruna ☎ 0980/19000.

CAR TRAVEL

Since public transportation is nonexistent in this part of the country, having a car is essential. The few roads are well built and maintained, although spring thaws can present potholes. Keep in mind that habitations are few and far between in this wilderness region.

EMERGENCIES

For emergencies dial 112. A medical advisory service in Luleå is available 24 hours a day.

There are no late-night pharmacies in Norrbotten. The pharmacy at the Gallerian shopping center in Kiruna is open weekdays 9:30–6 and Saturday 9:30–1.

🚩 **Gallerian Pharmacy** ✉ Föreningsg. 6, Kiruna ☎ 0771/450450. **Jokkmokk Health Center** ✉ Lappstav. 9, Jokkmokk ☎ 0971/44455. **Kiruna Hospital** ✉ Thuleg. 29, Kiruna ☎ 0980/73000. **Sunderby Hospital Luleå** ✉ Luleå ☎ 0920/282000.

TOURS

Local tourist offices have information on guided tours involving dogsledding, snowmobiling, and ice fishing. Samelands Resor arranges tours to points of interest. Call the Swedish Sámi Association for Sámi tours.

🚩 **Samelands Resor** ✉ Hermelinsg. 20, 962 33 Jokkmokk ☎ 0971/10606 ⊕ www.samelandsresor.com. **Swedish Sámi Association** ✉ Brog. 5, 903 25 Umeå ☎ 090/141180.

TRAIN TRAVEL

The best and cheapest way to get to Kiruna is to take the evening sleeper from Stockholm. There are two trains a day, seven days per week. Fares range from SKr 800 per person for simple bunks to SKr 1000 per person for beds. You'll arrive at around lunchtime the next day. To book a train, call Connex, the rail company that handles this route.

🚩 **Connex** ☎ 0771/260000 ⊕ www.connex.se.

VISITOR INFORMATION

Norrbottens Turistråd is the regional tourist office. Local tourist offices are listed below by town.

🚩 **Abisko** ☎ 0980/40200. **Gällivare** ✉ Centralplan 3 ☎ 0970/16660. **Jokkmokk** ✉ Stortorget 4 ☎ 0971/22250. **Kiruna** ✉ Folkets Hus ☎ 0980/18880. **Luleå** ✉ Storg. 43B ☎ 0920/293500. **Norrbottens Turistråd** ☎ 0920/94070.

UNDERSTANDING
SWEDEN

SWEDEN AT A GLANCE

Fast Facts

Name in local language: Sverige
Capital: Stockholm
National anthem: *Du gamla, Du fria*
(*Thou old, thou free*), old folk song
with lyrics by Richard Dybeck (1844)
Type of government: Constitutional
monarchy, parliamentary democracy
Administrative divisions: 21 counties
Independence: June 6, 1523 (Gustav
Vasa elected king)
Constitution: January 1, 1975
Suffrage: 18 years of age; universal
Legislature: Unicameral parliament
(*Riksdag* in Swedish) with 349 seats;
members are elected by popular vote on
a proportional representation basis to
serve four-year terms.
Population: 9 million
Population density: 50 people per square mi
Median age: Male 39.49; Female 41.75
Life expectancy: Male 78; Female 82
Infant mortality rate: 2.77 deaths per
1,000 live births
Literacy: 99%
Language: Swedish (official); recognized
minority languages include Sámi (Lapp),
Finnish, and Meänkieli (Tornedalen
Finnish)
Ethnic groups: Swedish, Finnish, and Sámi
minorities (indigenous populations) and
foreign-born or first-generation
immigrants
Religion: 87% of the population belongs
to the Evangelical Lutheran Church of
Sweden. Religious minorities include
Roman Catholic, Orthodox, Baptist,
Muslim, Jewish, and Buddhist
Discoveries & Inventions: Centigrade
(1742), the propeller (1836), dynamite
(1867), the ball bearing (1907), the
zipper (1913), the turbo engine
(1976)

*If I have a thousand ideas and only
one turns out to be good, I am
satisfied.*
— Alfred Nobel (1833–96), Swedish
chemist and engineer who created
the Nobel Prize with his fortune

*Only he deserves power who every
day justifies it.*
— Dag Hammarskjöld (1905–61),
Swedish statesman and United
Nations Secretary General

*Fools are more to be feared than the
wicked.*
— Queen Christina of
Sweden (1626–89)

Geography & Environment

Land area: 410,934 square km (158,662
square mi), slightly larger than California
Coastline: 3,218 km (2,000 mi) along
the Gulf of Bothnia and the Baltic Sea
to the east and Kattegat and Skagerrak
to the west
Terrain: Mostly flat or slightly hilly; there
are mountains in the west (highest point
is Kebnekaise, 7,000 feet above sea level)
Islands: Öland and Gotland in the Baltic
Sea; the Stockholm archipelago has
some 25,000 islands

Natural resources: Iron ore, lead, zinc,
gold, copper, silver, tungsten, uranium,
arsenic, timber, hydropower
Natural hazards: Ice floes, especially in
the Gulf of Bothnia, at times interfere
with boat traffic
Environmental issues: Acid-rain damage;
pollution of the Baltic Sea and the
North Sea

Economy

Currency: Swedish krona
Exchange rate: 7.9 kronor = $1
GDP: $255.4 billion
Per capita income: $28,400
Inflation: 0.7%
Unemployment: 5.6%
Workforce: 4.46 million
Debt: $143 million
Economic aid donor: ODA, $1.7 billion
Major industries: Wood pulp and paper products, motor vehicles, iron, steel, processed foods, telephone parts
Agricultural products: Barley, sugar beets, meat, wheat, milk
Exports: $121.7 billion
Major export products: Paper products, pulp and wood, machinery, motor vehicles, iron and steel products, chemicals
Export partners: United States 10.7%, Germany 10.3%, United Kingdom 7.2%, Denmark 6.6%, Norway 6.2%, Finland 5.9%, Belgium 5.1%, Netherlands 4.8%, France 4.7%, Other 38.5%
Imports: $97.97 billion
Major import products: Machinery, motor vehicles, petroleum and petroleum products, chemicals, iron and steel, clothing
Import partners: Germany 20.2%, Denmark 8.2%, United Kingdom 7.9%, Netherlands 7.2%, Finland 7%, France 6.1%, Norway 5.9%, Belgium 4.5%

Did You Know?

• Sweden's far north has 100 days per year of midnight sun.

• More than one-third of the moose in Europe roam Sweden's green spaces.

• Swedish King Gustav III (1746–92) was assassinated at a masquerade ball. Giuseppe Verdi based his 1859 opera *Un Ballo in Maschera* on the assassination.

• Sweden is the third-largest music-exporting nation in the world, after the United States and Great Britain.

• Every Swedish citizen can request to read the entire electronic correspondence of politicians and public officials, thanks to Sweden's "principle of publicity."

• In the Sámi language, *sámi* means "human being." *Sapmi* refers both to the land of the Sámi and the people who live in it. The Sámi also call themselves "the people of the sun and the wind."

• Crown Princess Victoria (born 1977) is Europe's only female heir to a throne.

• Sweden holds the world records in a few snow and ice categories. The world's longest Nordic ski race is the annual Vasalopp in Sweden, which covers a distance of 90 km (56 mi), while the Icehotel in northern Sweden was the world's largest in 2002, with a total floor area of 54,000 square feet, accommodating 60 double rooms, 25 suites, an ice bar, and an ice church.

• Sweden has the greatest representation of women in parliament. Following the general election in 2002, approximately 45% of the members of the Swedish parliament are women.

CHRONOLOGY

ca. 12000 BC The first migrations into Sweden take place.

ca. 2000 Tribes from southern Europe, mostly Germanic peoples, migrate toward Denmark.

ca. 770 The Viking Age begins. For the next 250 years Scandinavians make frequent expeditions from the Baltic to the Irish seas, and even to the Mediterranean as far as Constantinople and to North America, employing superior ships and weapons and efficient military organization.

ca. 800– ca. 1000 Swedes control river trade routes between the Baltic and Black seas; they establish Novgorod, Kiev, and other cities.

830 Frankish monk Ansgar makes one of the first attempts to Christianize Sweden and builds the first church in Slesvig, Denmark. Sweden is not successfully Christianized until the end of the 11th century, when the temple at Uppsala, a center for pagan resistance, is destroyed.

1000 King Olof Skötkonung becomes the first Swedish king to be baptized and becomes the country's first Christian king.

1100 Christianity is spread throughout Sweden by German missionaries in the 800s and English missionaries in the 1000s.

1248 Erik Eriksson puts Birger Jarl in charge of military affairs and expeditions abroad.

1250 Stockholm is officially founded.

1319 Sweden and Norway form a union that lasts until 1335.

1370 The Treaty of Stralsund gives the North German trading centers of the Hanseatic League free passage through Danish waters and full control of Danish herring fisheries for 15 years. German power increases throughout Scandinavia.

1397 The Kalmar Union is formed as a result of the dynastic ties between Sweden, Denmark, and Norway, the geographical position of the Scandinavian states, and the growing influence of Germans in the Baltic. Erik of Pomerania is crowned king of the Kalmar Union.

1477 University of Uppsala, Sweden's oldest university, is founded.

1520 Christian II, ruler of the Kalmar Union, executes 82 people who oppose the Scandinavian union, an event known as the Stockholm Bloodbath. Sweden secedes from the union three years later. Norway remains tied to Denmark and becomes a Danish province in 1536.

1523 Gustav Ericsson founds Swedish Vasa dynasty as King Gustav I Vasa.

1527 A Swedish national church is created by parliamentary decree at the Swedish Riksdag in Västerås.

1534 Count Christoffer of Oldenburg and his army demand the restoration of Christian II as king of Denmark, initiating a civil war between supporters of Christian II and supporters of Prince Christian (later King Christian III).

1541   The Bible is published in Swedish.

1593   The Lutheran Church is adopted as the national church of Sweden.

1611–16   The Kalmar War: Denmark wages war against Sweden in hopes of restoring the Kalmar Union.

1611–60   This crucial era is initiated by the actions of Gustav II Adolphus, the great warrior king (he dies in 1632). During this time Sweden defeats Denmark in the Thirty Years' War and becomes the greatest power in Scandinavia as well as in northern and central Europe.

1632–54   Queen Christina reigns. In 1654 she abdicates the throne, converts to Catholicism, leaves for Rome, and is accepted by the pope.

1660   The Peace of Copenhagen establishes the modern boundaries of Denmark, Sweden, and Norway.

1666   Lund University, Scandinavia's largest university, is founded in Lund, Sweden.

1668   The Bank of Sweden, now the world's oldest central bank, is founded.

1700–21   In the Great Northern War, Sweden, led by Karl XII, broadens its position, then loses it to Russia, to which it is forced to cede southeastern Finland and three Baltic provinces.

1773   Gustavo III creates the Swedish Opera Institution, which is still functioning today.

1782   The Royal Opera House in Stockholm, designed by architect C. F. Adelcrantz, is inaugurated.

1801–14   The Napoleonic Wars are catastrophic for Denmark economically and politically. Sweden, after Napoléon's defeat at the Battle of Leipzig, attacks Denmark and forces the Danish surrender of Norway. The Treaty of Kiel, in 1814, calls for a union between Norway and Sweden.

1807   During the Napoleonic Wars, Swedish king Gustav III joins the coalition against France.

1809   Sweden surrenders the Åland Islands and Finland to Russia; Finland becomes a grand duchy of the Russian Empire. The Instrument of Government, Sweden's constitution, is adopted.

1818   Sweden takes a Frenchman as king, Karl XIV Johann, who establishes the Bernadotte dynasty.

ca. 1850   The building of railroads begins in Scandinavia.

1889   The Swedish Social Democratic Party is founded.

1896   The first moving picture film is shown in Sweden.

1901 Alfred Nobel, the Swedish millionaire chemist and industrialist, initiates the Nobel prizes.

1905 Norway's union with Sweden is dissolved.

1911–1960 Jussi Björling lives to become Sweden's most renowned tenor singer and is said to be the world's second best in history, after Caruso.

1914 At the outbreak of World War I Sweden declares neutrality but is effectively blockaded.

1918 Swedish women gain the right to vote, with some restrictions.

1918 Birgit Nilsson, Sweden's best-known and most acclaimed woman opera singer, is born. In 1958 she became the first non-Italian to open the season at famed La Scala opera house in Milan.

1920 The Scandinavian countries join the League of Nations.

1921 Restrictions on women's suffrage are lifted.

1932 The Social Democrat Party wins the parliamentary elections and Per Albin Hansson becomes prime minister. The Social Democrats hold power for the next 44 years.

1939 Sweden declares its neutrality in World War II.

1945 Swedish diplomat Raoul Wallenberg disappears into the Soviet gulag. Two years later Soviet officials report that Wallenberg has died in captivity, but evidence remains inconclusive.

1946 Sweden joins the United Nations.

1949 Sweden declines membership in NATO.

1952 The Nordic Council, which promotes cooperation among the Nordic parliaments, is founded.

1957 A Swedish referendum votes yes to a compulsory state pension for people age 67 and over.

1972 Sweden, on the basis of its neutral foreign policy, declines membership in the European Union (EU).

1974 The pop group ABBA wins the European song contest in Brighton, England, with the song *Waterloo*.

1975 Sweden's Instrument of Government of 1809 is revised and replaced with a new Instrument of Government. This constitution makes the voting age 18 and removes many of the king's powers.

1976 At only 20 years old, Björn Borg wins the first of five Wimbledon titles. King Carl XIV Gustaf marries Silvia Sommerlath of Germany. A right-wing coalition wrings power from Sweden's Social Democrats, ending the latter's uninterrupted 44-year reign.

1980 Fifty-eight percent of Sweden's voters advocate minimizing the use of nuclear reactors at Sweden's four power plants.

1980 Björn Borg wins his fifth consecutive Wimbledon tennis title.

1981 Björn Borg wins the French Tennis Open for the sixth time.

1982 Swedish actress Ingrid Bergman, the winner of three Oscar awards, dies at the age of 67. She was best known for the films *Casablanca* and *Spellbound*.

1986 Sweden's prime minister, Olof Palme, is assassinated for unknown reasons. Ingvar Carlsson succeeds him.

1986 Sweden is the first country to detect nuclear fallout from the Soviet power plant in Chernobyl, unknown to the West at the time.

1987 The Swedish national ice hockey team, Tre Kronor, wins the world ice hockey championship in Vienna for the first time in 25 years.

1991 The Social Democrats are voted out of office, and the new government launches a privatization policy.

1992 Sweden's Riksbank (National Bank) overnight raises interest rates to a world record of 500% in an effort to defend the Swedish krona against speculation.

1994 The ferry *Estonia,* en route from Tallinn to Stockholm, sinks in the worst maritime disaster in Europe since World War II. The right-wing coalition government loses the parliamentary elections to the Social Democrats, and Ingvar Carlsson steps up as prime minister.

1995 Finland and Sweden join the EU in January.

1998 Stockholm is named the 1998 Cultural Capital of Europe. The Social Democrats, led by Göran Persson, win the parliamentary elections.

2000 The Øresund road/rail bridge linking Sweden with Denmark is opened.

2001 Sweden holds the presidency of the EU for six months.

2002 As most of Europe adopts the euro currency, Sweden, Denmark and Britain opt to keep their respective currencies. Prime Minister Göran Persson wins a second term in the parliamentary elections.

2003 Sweden's foreign minister, Anna Lindh, is assassinated in Stockholm. The Swedish people again reject adopting the euro as their national currency in a referendum in September.

2004 Swedish–Yugoslavian Mijailo Mijailovic confesses to the murder of Anna Lindh and is sentenced to 20 years in Swedish prison.

Swedes unite in grief over the Southeast Asian tsunami, as Sweden suffers the most total casualties of any country outside the region.

2005 Constitutional change sees June 6, formerly Day of the Swedish Flag, become the inaugural Swedish National Day and a national holiday.

In an effort to encourage more people to attend Sweden's state-owned museums, the government abolishes all entrance charges.

SWEDISH SPECTACULAR

SWEDEN REQUIRES THE VISITOR TO TRAVEL FAR, in both distance and attitude. Approximately the size of California, Sweden reaches as far north as the arctic fringes of Europe, where glacier-top mountains and thousands of acres of pine, spruce, and birch forests are broken here and there by wild rivers, countless pristine lakes, and desolate moorland. In the more populous south, roads meander through mile after mile of softly undulating countryside, skirting lakes and passing small villages with sharp-pointed church spires. Here the lush forests that dominate Sweden's northern landscape have largely fallen to the plow.

Once the dominant power of the region, Sweden has traditionally looked inward to find its own Nordic solutions. During the cold war it tried with considerable success to steer its famous "middle way" between the two superpowers, both economically and politically. Its citizens were in effect subjected to a giant social experiment aimed at creating a perfectly just society, one that adopted the best aspects of both socialism and capitalism.

In the late 1980s, as it slipped into the worst economic recession since the 1930s, Sweden made adjustments that lessened the role of its all-embracing welfare state in the lives of its citizens. The long-incumbent Social Democrats were voted out in favor of a conservative coalition in 1991, but further cuts saw the Social Democrats voted back in in 1994, by a public hoping to recapture the party's policy of cradle-to-grave protection. The world economy didn't exactly cooperate; although Sweden appeared to be crawling toward stability in the mid-1990s, the struggle to balance the budget intensified again by the end of the decade. The Social Democrats won a further victory in 2002, but the social safety net once so heavily relied upon by the Swedes remains

somewhat incomplete; a reflection perhaps of modern economics rather than any temporary budgetary hiccup.

Sweden took off with the rest of the globe with the explosion of the Internet and new technology and watched with it as the bubble burst at the start of the new millennium. It continues to be one of the world's dominant players in the information-based economy. Although many startup companies (and well-established giants such as Ericsson) have taken their share of economic bumps and bruises, as a whole there remains a lively entrepreneurial spirit and an intense interest in the business possibilities of the Internet and wireless communications. During the past few years Sweden has received substantial international press coverage for its innovative technological solutions, new management philosophies, and unique Web design.

On the social front, an influx of immigrants, particularly from countries outside Europe, is reshaping what was once a homogeneous society. Sweden continues to face political and social difficulties in the areas of immigration and integration, although the tension appears to be fading slightly as more and more artists, musicians, actors, directors, and writers with immigrant backgrounds are receiving national recognition for their work. As considerable public debate about these issues sweeps the country, a society known for its blue-eyed blondes is considering what it means to be a Swede.

Another sign that Swedes seem more willing than ever to refashion their image was Sweden's decision to join the European Union (EU) in January 1995, a move that represented a radical break with its traditional independent stance on international issues. Thus far, the domestic benefits of membership are still debated heavily, but the country's exporting industries have made considerable gains. During its relatively short membership Sweden has held the presidency of the union and hosted the first-ever visit by a sitting U.S. president, when George W. Bush visited Göteborg for a meeting with EU member states. Despite these landmark moments and perhaps partly because of the lack of concrete results in being part of the EU, the first years of the millennium have seen citizens undecided about the value of membership and politicians struggling to demonstrate its importance.

The country possesses stunning natural assets. In the forests, moose, deer, bears, and lynx roam, coexisting with the whine of power saws and the rumble of automatic logging machines. Logging remains the country's economic backbone. Environmental awareness, however, is high. Fish abound in sparkling lakes and tumbling rivers, and sea eagles and ospreys soar over myriad pine-clad islands in the archipelagoes off the east and west coasts.

The country is Europe's fourth largest, 410,934 square km (158,662 square mi) in area, and its population of 9 million is thinly spread. If, like Greta Garbo—one of Sweden's most famous exports—you enjoy being alone, you've come to the right place. A law called Allemansrätt guarantees public access to the countryside; NO TRESPASSING signs are seldom seen.

Sweden stretches 1,563 km (977 mi) from the barren arctic north to the fertile plains of the south. Contrasts abound, but they are neatly tied together by a superbly efficient infrastructure, embracing air, road, and rail. You can catch salmon in the far north and, thanks to the excellent domestic air network, have it cooked by the chef of your luxury hotel in Stockholm later the same day.

The seasons contrast savagely: Sweden is usually warm and exceedingly light in summer, then cold and dark in winter, when the sea may freeze and northern iron railway lines may snap. Spring and fall tend to make brief appearances, if any.

Sweden is also an arresting mixture of ancient and modern. The countryside is dotted with runic stones recalling its Viking past: trade beginning in the 8th century went as far east as Kiev and as far south as Constantinople and the Mediterranean, expanded to the British Isles in the 9th through 11th centuries, and settled in Normandy in the 10th century. Small timbered farmhouses and maypoles—around which villagers still dance at midsummer in their traditional costumes—evoke both their pagan early history and more recent agrarian culture.

Many of the country's cities are sci-fi modern, their shop windows filled with the latest in consumer goods and fashions, but Swedes are reluctant urbanites: their hearts and souls are in the forests and the archipelagoes, and there is where they faithfully retreat in summer and on weekends to enjoy their holidays, pick berries, or just listen to the silence. The skills of the wood-carver, the weaver, the leather worker, and the glassblower are highly prized. Similarly, Swedish humor is earthy and slapstick. Despite the praise lavished abroad on introspective dramatic artists such as August Strindberg and Ingmar Bergman, it is the simple trouser-dropping farce that will fill Stockholm's theaters, the scatological joke that will get the most laughs.

Sweden's cultural tenor incorporates a host of global trends. Most radio stations play a mix of Swedish, American, and British hits, and a number of Swedish television programs track international music, art, and culture. Films from all over the world can be seen at the box office, although it's Hollywood that dominates. And when it comes to fashion and design, Stockholm is certainly among the trendiest cities in the world. Glossy magazines like *Wallpaper* seem to be in constant discussion about "cool Stockholm" and the like.

Despite the much-publicized sexual liberation of Swedes, the joys of hearth and home are most prized in what remains in many ways a conservative society. Conformity, not liberty, is the real key to the Swedish character. Swedes remain devoted royalists and patriots, avidly following the fortunes of King Carl XVI Gustaf, Queen Silvia, and their children in the media and raising the blue-and-yellow national flag each morning on the flagpoles of their country cottages.

It is sometimes difficult in cities such as Stockholm, Göteborg, or Malmö to realize that you are in an urban area. Right in the center of Stockholm you can fish for salmon or go for a swim. In Göteborg's busy harbor you can sit aboard a ship bound for the archipelago and watch fish jump out of the water; in Malmö hares hop around in the downtown parks. It is this pristine quality of life that can make a visit to Sweden a step out of time, a relaxing break from the modern world.

— Updated by Rob Hincks

REFLECTIONS OF STOCKHOLM

A T A RECEPTION FOR VISITING DIGNI-TARIES, the mayor of Stockholm surprised his guests by serving them glasses of a clear liquid that turned out to be water. It came, he explained, from the water surrounding this island city, and the purpose of the tongue-in-cheek gesture was to demonstrate that modern cities can afford clean environments. In fact, Stockholm has won the European Sustainable City Award in competition with 90-odd other cities, and a large swathe of Stockholm, including the vast royal domains, has been declared a national park for the benefit and enjoyment of the populace.

There were sound, practical reasons for building Stockholm on the 14 islands that command access from the Baltic Sea to Lake Mälaren. Back in the 13th century, after the Vikings had retired from plunder and discovery, Estonian pirates had taken to pillaging the shores of the lake, which extends deep into the Swedish heartland. Birger Jarl, the ruler who founded Sweden's first dynasty, put a stop to all that by stockading the islands the pirates had to pass. His effigy lies in gilded splendor at the foot of the city hall tower.

Stockholm without water would be unthinkable. It's the water that gives it beauty, character, life. The north shore and the south are, to be truthful, rather Germanic in character, not too different from, say, Zürich or Berlin. But watch them from across a busy waterway, mirrored in the blue lake, and they become invested with a lively charm.

The pearl in the oyster, however, is the small island known as Gamla Stan, or Old Town, dominated by the tawny-color, massive Royal Palace, designed by Nicodemus Tessin in the 17th century and completed in the 18th. In the Middle Ages so many German merchants settled here that a law was passed to limit their number on the city council to fewer than half the members. The winding streets are lined with old houses in yellow, ocher, and the occasional oxblood red. Some of the city's most attractive small hotels, gourmet restaurants, and lively jazz clubs are here. To many people, the greatest treasure, dating to 1489, is found inside Storkyrkan, the Stockholm cathedral, next door to the palace: a larger-than-life, polychrome wooden statue of St. George slaying the dragon.

Skeppsholmen, a smaller island east of Gamla Stan and once the nation's principal navy base, is an idyllic place for a stroll and great for art-lovers. The Museum of Modern Art by the Spanish architect Rafael Moneo opened in 1998 and is one of the great contemporary museums. It blends in well with other structures, such as the "old" modern museum, a former armory and a trendsetter since its opening in 1958; it is now the Museum of Architecture. Also on Skeppsholmen is the exquisite Museum of Far Eastern Antiquities, another Tessin creation, which houses one of the world's finest collections of Chinese art.

After you cross the bridge from Skeppsholmen on your way back to the city center, you'll walk past the Nationalmuseum. You'll do well to stop there—not just for its Rembrandts and Swedish masters of centuries past, but also for its new atrium restaurant, one of the city's best, in the piazzalike inner courtyard.

The piers of Stockholm's islands are lined with so many vessels of every category, from cruise ships and seagoing roll-on/roll-off vessels to island-hopping steamboats and pocket-size ferries, that it would seem impossible to squeeze in another motorboat, sailboat, or sloop. There were more than 100,000 of them at last count, and still the number keeps growing. The waterborne traffic jam when they return on a Sunday night in summer after a weekend at sea is something to behold.

Most Stockholm sailors travel no farther than one of the 25,000 islands and skerries that make up the Stockholm archipelago, extending 73 km (45 mi) east into the Baltic Sea. A red-timber cottage on one of these islands in the Baltic is most Swedes' idea of ultimate bliss, and there they seek to re-create the simple life as they imagine their forefathers to have lived it.

A fair approximation of archipelago life is just a 25-minute ferry ride from the city center. This is Fjäderholmarna, or Feather Island, an islet that not long ago was a navy munitions dump. The rock is worn smooth by retreating Ice Age glaciers, there's a clump of yellow reeds at the water's edge, and on the rock is the inevitable red cottage, windows and corners trimmed with white, against a backdrop of dark green foliage. There's a restaurant serving excellent Swedish specialties and a small colony of craftsmen making high-quality souvenirs.

Take a boat trip west from the city, and you're in a different world, verdant and tranquil. An hour away and you're at Drottningholm Palace, also designed by Nicodemus Tessin and now the residence of the royal family. The palace and its formal French garden are impressive and the little Chinese Pavilion enchanting, but the real gem is the 200-year-old and perfectly intact Drottningholm Court Theater, where period performances of operas by Mozart, Gluck, and other 18th-century composers are presented every summer. The orchestra wears wigs, the singers appear in original costumes, and the ingenious old stage machinery produces thunder and storms.

As you wander through the reception areas and dressing rooms, you'll be struck by the sparse, cool elegance of the decor and furnishings, a style borrowed from Louis XV but stripped down to the bare essentials. It may strike you, too, that this is not very different from modern Swedish interiors and design. Then you will have discovered a well-hidden truth: the Swedes, who take such pride in being modern, rational, and efficient, are secretly in love with the 18th century.

— Eric Sjogren

Eric Sjogren, a Swedish travel writer based in Brussels, is a frequent contributor to the New York Times *and other publications.*

ASTRID LINDGREN

APPROPRIATELY, the career of Astrid Lindgren, Sweden's best-known children's writer, author of the *Pippi Longstocking* books and many others, has a fairy-tale beginning. Once upon a time, Lindgren's seven-year-old daughter, Karin, ill in bed with pneumonia, begged her, "Tell me a story . . . tell me the story of Pippi Longstocking."

"Neither she nor I know where on earth she got that name from," says Lindgren. "That was the first time I ever heard it. I made up the character right there and then, told her a story, and only wrote it down much later."

Thus was born one of the most memorable characters in children's fiction, her adventures translated from Lindgren's native Swedish into more than 50 languages.

Pippi continues to strike a responsive chord: a little girl of indeterminate age, she has a gap-toothed smile, a freckled face, and a wild mop of ginger hair from which a braid juts lopsidedly out over each ear.

Phenomenally strong, irrepressibly cheeky, Pippi lives independently of adults, with a horse and monkey in a tumbledown house, supporting herself from a hoard of gold coins. She has no table manners and doesn't go to school. She does just what she likes when she feels like doing it.

It would be well-nigh impossible to find a Swede who has not heard of Lindgren. She is remembered as *Tant Astrid,* Aunty Astrid, a gray-haired, nearsighted little old lady who is a symbol of hearth and home, of faith in traditional values and of love of rural Sweden, with its deep, dark pine forests, wide blue lakes, and meadows dotted with red-painted wooden houses.

The independent spirit that created such an unconventional character as Pippi Longstocking remained until the end of Lindgren's life and, using her awesome popularity, Lindgren was partly responsible for the fall of one Swedish government and for forcing a second one in 1989 to draft radical new legislation protecting the rights of pets and farm animals, about which she had a bee in her bonnet.

To look to Lindgren's beginnings, one can look to the stories of the Bullerby children—stories that Lindgren claimed most closely approximated her own childhood. These feature the adventures of children from three families in a little village somewhere in Sweden and eulogize rural life set against a fondly painted picture of seasonal contrast. The Bullerby children are Lindgren's *nicest* characters: playful but, unlike Pippi, unwilling to overstep the line.

Bullerby is based on the little village of Sevedstorp, set amid the dense pine-and-spruce forests that cover the southern Swedish province of Småland, the province where Lindgren was born.

Home was a simple clapboard house, painted red and with a glassed-in porch, surrounded by well-tended flower beds, daisy-strewn lawns, and apple trees. The family was reasonably well off, though there was rarely money left over for luxuries. Lindgren's father, Samuel, was an excellent storyteller, and many of the anecdotes he told his children surfaced later in Lindgren's books.

She enjoyed a warm relationship with Samuel, a fact that is reflected time and again in her books, peopled in the main with warm, understanding, though often gruff fathers. She described her mother, on the other hand, as a rather distant person, recalling that she hugged Lindgren only once when she was a child. It was from her that Lindgren inherited her willpower, energy, and stubbornness, she says.

At school she was a conscientious pupil, remembered by classmate Ann-Marie Fries (who was the inspiration for Madicken, another of Lindgren's characters) as "unbelievably nimble. I remember her in the gym; she could climb from floor to ceiling like a monkey."

Astrid also began to show evidence of literary talents. Her essays were frequently read to the rest of the class, and when she was 13, one of them was even published in *Wimmerby Tidning*, Vimmerby's local newspaper. This one was titled "Life in Our Backyard," and described two small girls and the games they played. "They joked and called me Vimmerby's answer to Selma Lagerlöf, and I decided that if there was one thing I would never be it was an author."

She left school at 16 and was given a job at *Wimmerby Tidning* reading proofs, and was even allowed to do some reporting when she was assigned to cover some local events such as weddings and funerals.

In 1926 Astrid's blissful childhood came to a very definite end when, at the age of 18, she had an affair and became pregnant. In recent years Sweden has developed a reputation for liberality in such matters, but in those days, pregnant and unmarried, she created a huge scandal in Vimmerby, a small town steeped in traditional Lutheran values.

Astrid left home and traveled to the capital, Stockholm, where she gave birth to a son, Lars, whom she handed over to foster parents in Copenhagen. She returned to Stockholm to study shorthand and typing and to land a job at a local firm working for the father of Viveca Lindfors, the Swedish-born actress.

However, her luck seemed to have turned. Astrid found an editorial job with KAK, the Swedish automobile association. There she met Sture Lindgren, whom she married in the spring of 1931. Her son returned to live with them, and in 1934 she gave birth to her daughter, Karin.

* * *

T WAS IN THE WINTER OF 1941 that Karin asked her to tell the story of Pippi Longstocking. "Much later I was out walking in the park when I slipped and sprained my ankle," she recalled. "I was forced to lie in bed, so I began to write down the stories I had told to Karin."

Then in 1945 Lindgren revised her Pippi Longstocking manuscript and entered it in a contest for books aimed at children ages 6–10, along with a new effort, *All About the Bullerby Children*, in which she lovingly re-created her childhood in Vimmerby. *Pippi Longstocking* won first prize. *All About the Bullerby Children* failed to take an award but was bought for publication. The first Pippi Longstocking book was well received by both critics and public and soon sold out. However, a year later, the follow-up, *Pippi Goes Abroad*, caused a furor, with Lindgren accused of undermining the authority of parents and teachers.

The third and last Pippi Longstocking book, *Pippi in the South Seas*, was published in 1948. In this one Pippi sails away to a Pacific island for a reunion with her father, returning to Sweden for Christmas, which she spends alone. It could be an allegory on the fate of nonconformists in Sweden, a country where the good of the collective has traditionally been prized above that of the individual.

* * *

ALTHOUGH SHE NEVER ATTEMPTED a "serious" adult novel ("I never really wanted to; I'm not sure I'd be any good at it"), Astrid Lindgren was never shy about exploring themes considered improper for children. In 1973 controversy raged once more, this time over *The Brothers Lionheart*, in which a dying child dreams of meeting, in another world, the brother he idealizes who has died heroically in a fire. The two boys ride off to fight the forces of evil.

Shortly after this, in 1976, Lindgren, a lifelong voter for the Social Democrats, caused a still greater fuss when she became embroiled in a row with Sweden's Socialist government.

It all started with a demand from the tax authorities, which would, she calculated, exceed her actual income. She wrote a fairy story for *Expressen*, the Stockholm newspaper. Its main character, Pomperipossa, has always loved her country and respected its rulers. Now she turns against them: " 'O you, the pure and fiery social democracy of my youth, what have they done to you?' thought Pomperipossa, 'How long shall your name be abused to protect a dictatorial, bureaucratic, unjust, authoritarian society?' "

In that year's general election the Social Democrats lost power, after more than 40 years in office. An analysis of the result by the influential Sifo public-opinion research institute named the controversy over Lindgren's story as a major contributory factor.

Throughout her life, Lindgren was the recipient of countless awards, including in 1989 the Albert Schweitzer Award, given for her work on behalf of animal rights. At a time in life when most people would be content to wind down, she joined forces with veterinarian Kristina Forslund in a campaign to persuade Sweden to introduce more stringent rules on animal husbandry.

A string of articles and open letters soon brought the government to its knees. Prime Minister Carlsson announced new legislation that he dubbed "Lex Astrid" and called on Lindgren personally to tell her about it.

Astrid Lindgren died peacefully, at home in Stockholm, on January 28, 2002. She was 94 years old. Her death sparked a national mourning, the likes of which have rarely been seen in Sweden. In her life she published more than 100 books, which sold tens of millions of copies and inspired many television and screen adaptations.

— Chris Mosey

BOOKS & MOVIES

Books

Relatively few Swedish writers have been translated into English, and the ones who have generally fall into the classic category, leaving the contemporary genre sadly underrepresented.

The classics include 1909 Nobel Prize laureate Selma Lagerlöf, whose *The Wonderful Journey of Nils Holgersson,* written on request as a geography textbook for schoolchildren, takes the reader on an adventure through the entire country with a little boy called Nils Holgersson.

The plays of Swedish writer August Strindberg greatly influenced modern European and American drama. Perhaps the most enduringly fascinating of these is *Miss Julie* (1888), which mixes the explosive elements of sex and class to stunning effect.

Vilhelm Moberg's series of novels about a poor Swedish family that immigrated to America, *The Emigrants* (1949), *Unto a Good Land* (1956), and *The Last Letter Home* (1956–59) give insight into what life was like in the second half of the 19th century, when Sweden was one of the most backward agrarian countries in Europe and one-quarter of its population left for North America.

Proletarian writer Moa Martinson rose from illegitimacy and poverty to become an acclaimed novelist. Two of her novels, her debut, *Women and Appletrees* (1933), and the novel often regarded as her best, *My Mother Gets Married* (1936), have been translated into English. Both novels tell of the struggles of working-class women in a time when women had little say in the decisions affecting their lives. In *Women and Appletrees,* three generations of women struggle to overcome poverty, hardship, and loneliness.

My Mother Gets Married is the first of Martinsson's autobiographical trilogy. It is a wrenching portrait of poverty; brutal, boozing men; and the stigma of illegitimacy. Mia is six years old when her mother gets married for the first time. The book follows her into young adulthood with a language that draws heavily on oral tradition.

Eyvind Johnson's autobiographical four-volume epic about Olof (1934–37), a logger in the Swedish north and, like Johnson himself, alone from an early age, blends fairy tale and realism. The series was the basis for the author's 1974 Nobel Prize award (*The Year was 1914, Here is Your Life!, Don't Look Back!,* and *Postlude to Youth*).

Pär Lagerkvist, 1951 Nobel Prize laureate, wrote novels best described as refined and timeless. *Barabbas* (1950) is about man's desire to believe, told through the story of the man whose place Jesus took on Golgata. Staying close to the biblical story, Lagerkvist still manages to subtly question every truth.

Evil is the theme of Lagerkvist's *The Dwarf.* Written in 1944, it is Lagerkvist's protest of war and warning of what can happen when evil is unleashed. The dwarf, a servant at a medieval court and a heartless, Machiavellian, scheming character, takes no responsibility for the deeds he carries out on the behalf of his master, the Prince. Despite the medieval setting, *The Dwarf*'s theme still resonates today.

Lagerkvist's mythical *The Sibyl* (1956) struggles with good and bad, the divine and the human. A man is cursed and believes in the curse. He seeks the help of an oracle who shows him that God is both love and hate and that the two are not contradictory.

Only one of poet and novelist Karin Boye's novels, the masterly futuristic *Kallocain* (1940), has been translated into English. Often compared to George Orwell's *1984, Kallocain* is a depiction of a world under totalitarian rule seen through the eyes of idealistic scientist Leo Kall. Convinced he is furthering the common good, Kall perfects the truth drug Kallocain. Where Orwell is purely political, Boye's take on totalitarianism is much more existential.

Göran Tunström's *The Christmas Oratorio* (1983) spans three generations of the Nordensson family. Incredible journeys, doomed love, and freak accidents fill this story, which, like most of Tunström's novels, starts out in the province of Värmland. With his amazing prose, fluctuating from poetic to fantastic to realistic, Tunström has secured his place in Swedish literature.

Since his poetry was first published in 1954, the writer and poet Tomas Tranströmer's work has been much admired in Sweden. Unfortunately, only his more obscure titles have been translated into English, including the collection titled *For the Living and the Dead.*

Captain Nemo's Library (1991), by Per Olov Enquist, is a fine family drama set in the 1940s on the northern coast of Sweden.

Hugely popular in Sweden and exported abroad are the TV dramatizations of the police thrillers about police chief Martin Beck written by the husband-and-wife team of Maj Sjövall–Per Wahlöö from 1965 until Wahlöö's death in 1975. One of Sjövall-Wahlöö's thrillers, *The Terrorists,* was even prophetic with a scene in which a Swedish prime minister is shot, a precursor to the assassination of Olof Palme in 1986. All of this team's books (*The Laughing Policeman, Roseanna, The Locked Room, The Man on the Balcony, The Man Who Went Up in Smoke,* and *The Terrorists*) have been translated into English.

Perhaps the most successful of Sweden's thriller writers though is Henning Mankell, whose books about lackluster police chief Kurt Wallender have been translated into more than seven languages, including English, and have sold more than 20 million copies (in Germany, Kurt Wallender is more popular than Harry

Potter). The entire Wallender series (*Faceless Killers, The Dogs of Riga, The White Lioness, The Man Who Smiled, Sidetracked, The Fifth Woman, One Step Behind,* and *Firewall,*) have been translated into English, as well as two books (*Before the Frost* and *Return of the Dancing Master*) from outside the series.

Other Swedish writers in the thriller genre whose works have been translated into English are Jan Guillou (*Enemy's Enemy,* from 1989, and *Vendetta: Coq Rouge VI,* from 1991) and Kerstin Ekman (*Black Water,* 1996, set in the secluded landscape of northern Sweden).

Mikael Niemi's *Popular Music from Vittula* (2001) is a raw, amusing, and sometimes surreal account of the author's childhood in Tornedalen, in the north, close to the Finnish border. The area around Vittula is no place for the weak. If they want any respect at all, it seems, real men need to learn how to work, fight, and hold down their alcohol.

Acclaimed author Per Olov Enquist broke a 10-year word drought in 2002 with the publication of the novel *The Royal Physician's Visit,* a tale of the doctor to the Danish King in 1768. The book traces themes of power, corruption, love, and tragedy as, aided by the king's mental illness, the physician uses his position to issue 632 decrees in the name of the king.

For historical background, try *A History of the Vikings* (Oxford University Press, 1984). The book recounts the history of the seafaring traders and plunderers whose journeys stretched as far from Scandinavia as Constantinople and North America. Gwyn Jones's lively account makes learning the history enjoyable.

Myth and Religion of the North, by E. O. G. Turbille-Petre, explains the history and the evolution of the diverse mythological tales and pagan religions of Sweden.

One of the most exhaustive and comprehensive studies of Sweden published in

English in recent years is *Sweden: The Nation's History,* by Franklin D. Scott (University of Minnesota Press). Chris Mosey's *Cruel Awakening: Sweden and the Killing of Olof Palme* (C. Hurst, London, 1991) gives an overview of the country's recent history with a focus on the events surrounding the assassination of Palme and the farcical hunt for his killer.

Movies

Mention Swedish film, and most people automatically think of Ingmar Bergman. A mainstay of the Swedish cultural scene for 50 years, Bergman shaped Swedish filmmaking like no other director. From his first triumph in Cannes in 1956 with *Smiles of a Summer Night,* Bergman continued to please his critics. Three of his movies won the Oscar award for best foreign film over the years: *The Virgin Spring* in 1960; *Through a Glass, Darkly* in 1961; and *Fanny and Alexander* in 1983.

Bergman's movies were always daring and different. *The Summer with Monika* caused a big scandal upon its release in 1952 because of an exposed breast. The most memorable of all of Bergman's films, however, might be *The Seventh Seal,* a medieval tale where the main character, a noble knight just back from a crusade, buys more time from Death by challenging him to a chess game. The crusader's resistance of the inevitable and the separation he feels from God are rather enduring themes.

Fanny and Alexander was the first in a trilogy about Bergman's parents. The second part, *Best Intentions,* came in 1992, and the conclusion, *Private Confessions,* in 1996. *Private Confessions* was directed by Bergman's friend and onetime lover, Liv Ullmann, a star of many of his movies and herself an acclaimed director.

If Bergman gave Swedish directors a reputation for seriousness, some might say gloom, the younger generation is altering that image. Beirut-born Swedish director Josef Fares's *Jalla Jalla,,* from 2000, is a hilarious low-budget production about the arranged engagement between a young immigrant park worker, Roro, and the girl his father has picked out for him. The sudden engagement causes some friction, to say the least, between Roro and his Swedish girlfriend, and Roro and his best friend have only days to set things straight. Only 25 when he made *Jalla Jalla,* Fares has been dubbed the wonder child of Swedish film.

Equally funny is Måns Herngren and Hannes Holm's 1997 *Adam and Eve.* Four years into their relationship, Adam and Eve find out that eternity is a very long time, and sometimes a bit boring. They both realize change is needed, but classical gender differences lead them to seek change in very different ways.

Sometimes the best perspective is offered at a distance. British-born director Colin Nutley has amazed Swedish moviegoers with his discerning depictions of Swedish society. His big breakthrough came in 1993 with *House of Angels,* in which a cabaret singer and her gay best friend show up at a funeral in a small Swedish village. The man in the casket, the villagers find out, was the singer's grandfather, and as the sole relative she moves into his house. The pair's perceived decadence causes unease in the community, and they are told straight-out to leave. Avoiding the usual stereotypical pitfalls, Nutley explores bias and fears without becoming preachy or overbearing.

Nutley made headlines overseas in 2000, when his *Under the Sun* was nominated for an Oscar for best foreign film. There is nothing new about this sweet and subtle love story, set against a 1950s countryside backdrop, and this is on purpose. The movie borrows its title from Ecclesiastes: "What was will be again; what has been done will be done again; and there is nothing new under the sun."

Another Swedish director to win recognition abroad is Lasse Hallström. Although *My Life as a Dog* (1985) failed to win an Oscar, it got the New York Film Critics Circle award for best foreign-language film in 1987. Hallström's big break in the United States came with *What's Eating Gilbert Grape,* starring Johnny Depp and Leonardo DiCaprio. His other movies include *Cider House Rules* (1999), *Chocolat* (2000), and *The Shipping News* (2001).

Human despair has been the theme of Lukas Moodysson's two latest movies, *Lilya 4-Ever* (2002) and *A Hole in My Heart* (2004), both of which were shot in an in-your-face documentary style. The former tells the story of Lilya, a teenage girl who, trying to escape hardship in the former Soviet Union, finds herself forced into prostitution and trafficked to Sweden. The latter deals unemotionally with the issues of morality and friendship, centered on the shooting of an amateur pornographic movie in a decrepit apartment. Both movies are moving, emotional pieces.

Moodysson's 1998 debut of *Show Me Love* was called "a young master's first masterpiece" by none other than Ingmar Bergman. Shot with a grainy, home-movie-like quality, *Show Me Love* is a love story between two teenage girls in a small Swedish town where nothing ever seems to happen. Themes of suburban alienation, teen angst, and the disconnect between well-meaning parents and their children avoids becoming clichéd through Moodysson's subtle storytelling.

His 2001 follow-up to *Show Me Love,* the charming *Together,* solidified Moodysson's reputation as one of Sweden's brightest new filmmakers. In that film the leader of a mid-'70s commune tries to keep the place together after his sister and her children move in, introducing into the collective such evils as toy guns, television, and Pippi Longstocking.

Perhaps Sweden is better known abroad for its stars than for its directors.

The greatest of them all was Greta Garbo, a silent film star in Sweden before immigrating to Hollywood in the 1920s. With movies such as *Anna Karenina* (silent in 1927 and with sound in 1935), *A Woman of Affairs* (1929), *Queen Christina* (1934), *Camille* (1937), and *Ninotchka* (1939), Garbo became the epitome of a Hollywood star.

The next Swedish-born actress to conquer Hollywood was Ingrid Bergman in an American 1939 remake of her Swedish breakthrough *Intermezzo.* She went on to star with such Hollywood big names as Humphrey Bogart (*Casablanca*), Gary Cooper (*For Whom the Bell Tolls*), Bing Crosby (*The Bells of St. Mary*), and Gregory Peck (*Spellbound*).

Other Swedish actresses to light up movie screens worldwide over the years have been Anita Ekberg (*La Dolce Vita*), Lena Olin (*The Unbearable Lightness of Being, Chocolat, The Ninth Gate*), and Pernilla August (*Star Wars, Episode II*).

For the sake of equality, a few male Swedish actors deserve a mention. Stellan Skarsgård (*Breaking the Waves, Good Will Hunting, Dogville*), Max von Sydow (whose long list of movie credits is as disparate as *The Exorcist* and *Snow Falling on Cedars*), and Peter Stormare (*Fargo, Dancer in the Dark, Armageddon*) have proved the most enduring in the Hollywood competition.

James Bond has always been fond of Swedish costars. Maud Adams (*The Man with the Golden Gun, Octopussy*), Britt Ekland (*The Man with the Golden Gun*), Mary Stavin (*A View to a Kill*), Kristina Wayborn (*Octopussy*), and Isabella Scorupco (*Goldeneye*) have all starred with the British agent.

VOCABULARY

	English	Swedish	Pronunciation
Basics			
	Yes/no	Ja/nej	yah/nay
	Please	Var snäll; Var vänlig	vahr snehll vahr vehn-leeg
	Thank you very much.	Tack så **mee**-keh	tahk soh mycket.
	You're welcome.	Var så god.	vahr shoh **goo**
	Excuse me. (to get by someone)	Ursäkta.	oor-**shehk**-tah
	(to apologize)	Förlåt.	fur-**loht**
	Hello/Hi	God dag/Hej	goo **dahg**/hey
	Goodbye	Adjö	ah-**yoo**
	Good luck!	Lycka till!	licka teel
	How are you?	Hur mår du?	hoor moh doo
	Fine	Bra	bra
	Just fine, thanks.	Bara bra, tack.	**bah**-ra bra,tahk
	Today	I dag	ee **dahg**
	Tomorrow	I morgon	ee **mor**-ron
	Yesterday	I går	ee **gohr**
	Morning	Morgon	**mohr**-on
	Afternoon	Eftermiddag	**ehf**-ter-meed-dahg
	Night	Natt	naht
Numbers			
	1	ett	eht
	2	två	tvoh
	3	tre	tree
	4	fyra	fee-rah
	5	fem	fem
	6	sex	sex
	7	sju	shoo
	8	åtta	oht-tah
	9	nio	nee
	10	tio	tee
Days of the Week			
	Monday	måndag	mohn-dahg
	Tuesday	tisdag	tees-dahg
	Wednesday	onsdag	ohns-dahg

Thursday	torsdag	tohrs-dahg
Friday	fredag	freh-dahg
Saturday	lördag	luhr-dahg
Sunday	söndag	sohn-dahg

Months

January	januari	ya-nuh-**ah**-ree
February	februari	feb-ruh-**ah**-ree
March	mars	mah-sh
April	april	apreel
May	maj	mahy
June	juni	**yoo**-nee
July	juli	**yoo**-lee
August	augusti	ah-**gus**-tee
September	september	sep-**tem**-ber
October	oktober	ok-**too**-ber
November	november	noh-**vem**-ber
December	december	deh-**sem**-ber

Useful Phrases

Do you speak English?	Talar ni engelska?	tah-lahr nee ehng-ehl-skah
I don't speak . . .	Jag talar inte svenska . . .	yah tah-lahr **een**-teh **sven**-skah
I don't understand.	Jag förstår inte.	yah fuhr-**stohr** **een**-teh
I don't know.	Jag vet inte.	yah **veht een**-teh
I am American/ British.	Jag är amerikan/ engelsman.	yah ay ah-mehr-ee-**kahn**/ **ehng**-ehls-mahn
I am sick.	Jag är sjuk.	yah ay **shyook**
Please call a doctor.	Jag vill skicka efter en läkare.	yah veel **shee**-kah **ehf**-tehr ehn **lay**-kah-reh
How much does it cost?	Vad kostar det?/ Hur mycket kostar det?	vah **kohs**-tahr deh/hor **mee**-keh **kohs**-tahr deh
It's too expensive.	Den är för dyr.	dehn ay foor **deer**
Beautiful	Vacker	**vah**-kehr
Help!	Hjälp	yehlp
Stop!	Stopp, stanna	stop, **stahn**-nah

How do I get to . . .	Kan Ni visa mig vägen till . . .	kahn nee **vee**-sah may **vay**-gehn teel
the train station?	stationen	stah-**shoh**-nehn
the post office?	posten	**pohs**-tehn
the tourist office?	en resebyrå	ehn-**reh**-seh-**bee**-roh
the hospital?	sjukhuset	**shyook**-hoo-seht
Does this bus go to . . . ?	Går den här bussen till . . . ?	gohr dehn hehr **boo**-sehn teel
Where is the W.C.?	Var är toilett/ toaletten	vahr ay twah-**leht** twah-**leht**-en
On the left	Till vänster	teel **vehn**-stur
On the right	Till höger	teel **huh**-gur
Straight ahead	Rakt fram	rahkt **frahm**

Dining Out

Please bring me . . .	Var snäll och hämta åt mig	vahr snehl oh hehm-tah oht may
menu	matsedeln	maht-seh-dehln
fork	en gaffel	ehn gahf-fehl
knife	en kniv	ehn kneev
spoon	en sked	ehn shehd
napkin	en servett	ehn sehr-veht
bread	bröd	bruh(d)
butter	smör	smuhr
milk	mjölk	myoolk
pepper	peppar	pehp-pahr
salt	salt	sahlt
sugar	socker	soh-kehr
water	vatten	vaht-n
wine	vin	veen
beer	öl	ool
fish	fisk	fisk
meat	kött	schoott
dessert	efterrätt	ehf-**tahr**-aht
coffee	kaffe	**ka**-ffe
Enjoy your meal!	Smaklig måltid!	**smahk**-lee **mool**-teed
Cheers!	Skäl!	skohl
I'm a vegetarian.	Jag år vegetarian.	yah ay ve-gee-ta-ri-**an**
Is this dish spicy?	Är den här rätten kryddstark?	ay dehn hahr **ree**-ten kreed-stark
The check, please.	Får jag be om notan?	fohr yah beh ohm **noh**-tahn

Accommodation

Do you have a vacant room?	Har Ni något rum ledigt?	hahr nee noh-goht **room leh**-deekt
I'd like a different room.	Jag vill byta till ett annat rum.	yah veel **bee**-ta til eht **ahn**-at ruhm
I'd like a single/ double room.	Jag skulle vilja ha ett enkel/dubbel rum.	yah **sko**-leh **veel**-ya hah eht **ehn**-kel/ **duh**-bel ruhm
I'd like a room with a shower.	Jag skulle vilja ha ett rum med dusch.	yah **sko**-leh **veel**-ya hah eht ruhm med douche

Shopping

shirt	tröja	**troh**-ya
pants	byxor	**bik**-sor
skirt	kjol	shool
shorts	shorts	schohrts
jacket	jacka	**ya**-ka
socks	strumpor	**strom**-pur
sale	rea	**reh**-ah
shop	affär/butik	ah-**fayr**/bou-tiq
craft store	hantverksaffär	**hahnt**-veerks-ah-**fayr**
art gallery	konstgalleri	kohnst-galleh-**ree**
department store	varuhus	**vah**-roo-hoos
grocery store	mataffär	maht-ah-**fayr**
liquor store	Systembolaget	sees-**tem**-boo-**lah**-get

INDEX

PHOTO CREDITS

Cover Photo: (Medieval festival, Gotland): *SIME s.a.s./eStock Photo.* F7, *Chad Ehlers/age fotostock.* F10, *Peter Lilja/age fotostock.* F12, *Walter Bibikow/viestiphoto. com.* F14, *Bjorn Svensson/age fotostock.* F15, *Joe Viesti/viestiphoto.com.* F16, *Walter Bibikow/viestiphoto.com.* F17 (left), *Nils-Johan Norenlind/age fotostock.* F17 (right), *Joe Viesti/viestiphoto.com.* F18, *Nils-Johan Norenlind/age fotostock.* F21, *Ken Ross/ viestiphoto.com.* F22, *Joe Viesti/viestiphoto.com.*

NOTES

NOTES

NOTES

NOTES

NOTES

NOTES

NOTES

NOTES

NOTES

ABOUT OUR WRITERS

British journalist Rob Hincks primarily writes and edits for food and travel magazines in Sweden and England. Rob has lived in Stockholm since 2000, but through his Swedish wife, Mikaela, his associations with the country go back much farther. Since the birth of his two daughters, Annie and Jessie, Rob has focused his energies on getting to know Sweden even better, in an effort to impress his girls when homework time comes around.

Growing up in the north of Sweden, Karin Palmquist used to dread summer vacations when her parents would pack the camper with kids and pets and slowly make their way down to her grandparent's house in the south, stopping at every church and archaeological site on the way. Yet, somehow, those road trips awoke in her a lifelong love for travel. Now a freelance writer for newspapers including the *Washington Times* and *Washington Post,* Karin roams the globe for six months a year. She spends the rest of her time in Washington, D.C., her adopted home.